The Writer's Palette

The Writer's Palette: Developing Paragraphs and Essays

E. B. Buchanan

Green River Community College

THOMSON

HEINLE

Australia   Canada   Mexico   Singapore   Spain   United Kingdom   United States

The Writer's Palette: Developing Paragraphs and Essays
E. B. Buchanan

Publisher: *Michael Rosenberg*
Acquisitions Editor: *Stephen Dalphin*
Development Editor: *Charles King*
Production Editor: *Lianne Ames*
Executive Marketing Manager: *Ken Kasee*
Manufacturing Coordinator: *Mary Beth Hennebury*

Compositor: *Carlisle Communications*
Project Manager: *Emily Bush*
Photo Manager: *Sheri Blaney*
Cover Designer: *Lianne Ames*
Text Designer: *Seventeenth Street Studios*
Printer: *Phoenix Color Corporation*

Cover Image: © *David Shopper/Index Stock Imagery*

Printed in the United States of America.
1 2 3 4 5 6 7 8 9 10   06 05 04 03 02

For more information contact Heinle, 25 Thomson Place,
Boston, Massachusetts 02210 USA, or you can visit our
Internet site at http://www.heinle.com

For permission to use material from this text or
product contact us:
Tel   1-800-730-2214
Fax   1-800-730-2215
Web   www.thomsonrights.com

ISBN: 0-15-506891-1

Library of Congress Cataloging-in-Publication Data
Buchanan, Esther
   The writer's palette: developing paragraphs and
essays/Esther Buchanan
     p. cm.
   ISBN 0-15-506891-1
   1. English language—Paragraphs—Problems,
exercises, etc. 2. English language—Rhetoric—
Problems, exercises, etc.
   3. Report writing—Problems, exercises, etc. I. Title
PE1439.B76 2002
808/.042—dc 21   2002038753

To
Ronald Lloyd Bohuslov
and
John Anthony Wyatt and Ruth Elizabeth Pearson

Preface

The Writer's Palette: Developing Paragraphs and Essays, a rhetoric with readings, will help students think critically, read actively, and write effectively and persuasively. The emphasis on the writing process and the thorough review of grammar, mechanics, usage, and sentence skills will enable students to become strong writers who can write unified, coherent paragraphs and essays.

Key Features of the Book

- *The elements of effective writing are key to this text.* Part 1 emphasizes writing as a process—planning, prewriting, writing, revising, editing, and proofreading. Part 2 stresses the importance of unity, coherence, and support. The traditional essay is emphasized. Effective introductory paragraphs, body paragraphs that support the thesis in the introduction, and strong concluding paragraphs are emphasized, with models that show how to build each type of paragraph. Suggestions and models for testing unity and coherence are included. Parts 3 and 4 emphasize the importance of writing varied, correct, strong sentences.

- *The book contains numerous exercises, writing suggestions, and discussion questions.* In Part 2 there are over fifteen sets of writing suggestions and over ten sets of discussion questions. Part 7 contains eighteen sets each of writing suggestions and discussion questions. The entire book contains almost three hundred activities.

- *Connected discourse (a group of related sentences that develop one topic) in the exercises lets students learn about their culture while they are learning to become stronger writers.* The exercises—drawn from history, religion, music, philosophy, mythology, science, and technology—spark interest and broaden the students' sphere of knowledge.

- *Numerous student and professional paragraphs and essays are included.* In Part 2 there are twelve student paragraphs, twelve student essays, and twelve professional paragraphs. In Part 7 there are eighteen professional selections.

- *The eighteen reading selections reflect the thinking of professional writers about current social issues and conditions.* In Part 7 the selections are arranged thematically:

  - Language and Writing
  - Everyday World
  - A Sense of Beauty
  - History and Culture
  - Media and Behavior
  - Men and Women

Each reading selection contains a list of related readings, definitions, vocabulary in context, discussion questions, and writing suggestions.

- *The book is versatile and full.* This versatility and fullness lets instructors choose the concepts and skills that they want to emphasize at a particular time, thus adapting the book to the needs of their students and to their own teaching style.

- *The differences between spoken language and written language are vigorously addressed.* In Part 5 spelling and usage problems are explored, concentrating on causes and corrections rather than on lists of errors.

- *ESL notes and explanations are given in problem areas for students whose first language is not English.* Appendix D contains information on the use of prepositions, idioms, and common irregular verbs.

- *Resource material is available.* It includes readability levels (Fry and Dale-Chall), the answers to review exercises in the book, alternative tests for each chapter, and alternative cumulative tests for each major part of the book. The following teaching aids—often included in supplementary material—are included in the book so that they are readily available to the students.

  - Checklists for sentences, paragraphs, essays
  - Checklists for grammar, mechanics, and usage
  - Peer response evaluation sheets
  - Suggestions for summarizing and paraphrasing

Acknowledgments

First, I thank the reviewers who contributed to this book through their careful and concise readings of the manuscript in progress and their helpful suggestions and comments. They include:

Gail C. Caylor
Mesa Community College, Mesa, AZ

Donna Lenhorn
Butte Community College, Oroville, CA

Ted Walkup
Clayton College & State University, Morrow, GA

Michael M. Dinielli
Chaffey College, Rancho Cucamonga, CA

Ted Wadley
Georgia Perimeter College, Decatur, GA

Virginia Brackett
Triton College, River Grove, IL

Patricia Colella
Bunker Hill Community College, Boston, MA

Jane Long
Southwestern Oklahoma State University, Weatherford, OK

Edward Fryzel
Henry Ford Community College, Dearborn, MI

Elizabeth Semtner
Rose State College, Midwest City, OK

Patricia Krech
Memphis State University, Memphis, TN

Dennis Kriewald
Laredo Community College, Laredo, TX

Next, I thank my students in Washington; Sao Paulo, Brazil; Mexico City; and California for their contributions to this book and to my growth as a teacher.

Finally, I want to thank my family, friends, and colleagues who have given me encouragement, support, advice, and inspiration. They include Sam, Morgan, and Mark Pearson; Dan, Tim, and Suzy Wyatt; Trena Lee Bristol; Jim and Jean Buchanan; Charlie and Blanche Buchanan; Ruth Whitney; Mary Campbell; Mike and Henrietta Fisher; Mary Kay Henderson; Peggy Knight; Jeanette and Don Weber; Oreva Grey; Bob and Dallas Chase; Laverne Travis; Carolyn Harrison; Trudy Richmond; André Ouelette; Ken Kloepfer; Hank Galmish; Sylvia Mantilla; Larry

Galloway; Julie Moore; Marcie Sims; Wayne Luckman; Liz Peterson; Brad Johnson; Eric Nelson; Walter Lowe, and Doug Johnson. I want to give special thanks to Jeannette Casenave—always my faithful friend, reader, and critic—and to Fred Brune, who has diligently and carefully read every draft of this book and made countless suggestions for its improvement.

E. B. Buchanan

Literary Credits

Brief Contents

Contents

Part 7 Reading, Thinking, and Writing Critically 373

Understanding the Writing Process

True ease in writing comes from art, not chance.

As those move easiest who have learned to dance.

'Tis not enough no harshness gives offense,

The sound must seem an echo to the sense.

—ALEXANDER POPE (1688-1744)
An Essay on Criticism

Writing is a skill, and, like other skills, is acquired through training and practice. The process of writing is somewhat akin to eating a whole loaf of bread. You cannot eat it without breaking it into bite-sized pieces. Writing, like eating a loaf of bread, can best be done by breaking it into bite-sized pieces. It is not a one-unit task. It is a cyclic process that involves five separate but overlapping steps. Although these steps may appear to be linear, they are not. Good writing comes from continual thinking, rethinking, arranging, rearranging, adding, and deleting during the writing process.

The Writing Process

Planning	Focusing—Choosing a topic and an idea about it
	Considering purpose, audience, and tone
Prewriting	Generating ideas and information about the topic
Writing	Presenting an idea about the subject and fully supporting it
	Organizing and connecting the material according to a plan
Revising	Making major revisions in the whole paper and minor revisions in sentences
Editing, Formatting, and Proofreading	Making corrections in punctuation, mechanics, spelling and usage; using a standard format; and proofreading for typographical errors

Planning—Thinking Before Writing

The first step in the writing process is planning. *Planning* is the thinking you do before you begin writing. You write because you have something to say about yourself, other people, things, conditions, or situations. Select a subject and tentatively decide what you want to say about it, how you want to say it, and what you want to accomplish. Then, think about your audience and the tone you are going to use.

Focusing—Choosing a Subject and a Tentative Main Idea

First, look at broad topics such as the following ones and ask yourself if you know something about any of them or have an interest in any of them:

gardening   music   jobs   vehicles   hobbies   relationships   schools politicians   parenting   sports   welfare   religion   vacations   restaurants cooking   computers

Unless you intend to fill part of a library, write a multivolume series, or at least write a book, these topics are too broad at this stage. After you choose a broad topic that interests you, choose only one aspect of it. After you choose one aspect of a broad topic, begin *narrowing the topic.* Where you stop the narrowing process will depend on the extent of the writing task. Are you going to write an essay, a paragraph, or just a few sentences? As you practice writing, you will become more skilled at narrowing a topic. Right now, your main concern is to get a thorough understanding of the first step in the writing process—planning.

EXERCISE 1

Choose two categories from the preceding list and reduce them to a topic that you think you can fully develop in a paragraph of about 150 words.

sports   > noncontact sport > golfing   > grip   > putting

1. __________ > __________ > __________ > __________ > __________

2. __________ > __________ > __________ > __________ > __________

Choose two other categories from the preceding list and reduce them to a topic that you think you can fully develop in an essay of about 500 words.

Olympic Games > track and field   > track events   > racing   > walking races

1. __________ > __________ > __________ > __________ > __________

2. __________ > __________ > __________ > __________ > __________

Deciding on Purpose

After you have a manageable topic for a specific writing task, clarify your purpose. Writing is a way of sending a purposeful message to a particular audience. The *purpose* is what you want to accomplish. It is your major reason for writing. Most good writing will have one of the following as its major purpose: **to entertain, to write for oneself, to explain,** or **to persuade.**

▶ **Entertaining**   If your purpose is to entertain, how are you going to use your ideas to entertain other people? Are you going to write a humorous letter to a friend or relative, a story for adults or for children, an article for a magazine, or an amusing paragraph or essay in response to a writing assignment?

▶ **Expressing Yourself**   If your purpose is to write for yourself, you will probably make journal entries in a notebook or in your computer. You may use these entries to record your ideas and keep them as a personal record of your life and thinking process. At a later time you may draw upon them to write for an audience other than yourself.

▶ **Explaining**   Writing to explain something is called *expository* writing. In college and in the world of work, you will use a variety of developmental patterns to explain your ideas—*examples, process, cause and effect, comparison and contrast, definition,* and *division and classification.* When your purpose is to explain, you need to decide if you already have enough information to clearly and accurately explain your ideas about your topic or if you need to get additional information from other sources.

▶ **Persuading**   When your purpose is to convince or persuade, you need to think about the outcome you want to achieve. Do you want to get your readers to agree with your opinion about an issue that can be argued more than one way? Do you want them to look at an issue in a different light? Do you want them to do something? Do you want them to take an action that you recommend?

Analyzing the Audience

After you have identified your purpose, think about your audience. Your *audience* is your readers. Your audience affects what you say and the way you say it. To accomplish your purpose, you need to tailor your writing to your audience. As you think about your audience, think about *perceptual reality*—the way people perceive new information and experiences. Consider people's age, gender, education, social and economic status, values (religious, political, or cultural), ethnic background, and past experiences (training and job responsibilities).

When you analyze an audience, you may find the following questions helpful, but remember that these questions are only guides. Do not fall into the trap of common stereotypes. Not all young people are liberal, and not all older people are conservative. Often one element of perceptual reality will cancel or contradict another element.

Audience Analysis Questions

1. Who are the members of your audience?

2. Does your audience know a great deal about your subject?

3. Is your audience interested in your subject?

4. Does your audience know little about your subject?

5. Does your audience have different interests and different levels of information about the subject?

6. How much do you need to tell the members of your audience?

7. Do you need to define any words or terms that may not be familiar to them?

8. Are any of their characteristics (age, sex, education, politics, personal assumptions, biases, socioeconomic status, residency, religion, hobbies, value system, ethnicity, occupation, and so on) relevant to your subject and purpose?

9. Are there any potentially offensive or insensitive ideas or words that you need to avoid?

10. What is your relationship with the members of your audience? Are you one of them? Do they trust you? Do they respect your opinions? Do you have to win them over?

EXERCISE 2

To better understand the influence the audience has on your writing, write different letters to two different audiences—a high school friend and your grandmother—describing a recent date you had or a party you attended. What is your purpose in each letter? Did any of the audience analysis questions affect what you said and how you said it?

Choosing the Tone

With purpose and audience clearly fixed in your mind, you are ready to work with tone. *Tone* is your attitude toward your material and your audience. It affects the response of the audience. Tone comes from the type of words, sentence structure, and ideas that you use. If you are striving for a serious and thoughtful tone, use more formal words and sentence structures. If you want a lighter tone, use a conversational style, less formal words, and more casual sentence structures. Think of tone as being similar to your tone of voice when you speak. Tone reflects a wide range of emotions, including *anger, sadness, irritability, sarcasm, happiness, excitement, seriousness, thoughtfulness, detachment, condescension,* and so on. The tone of the following speech is one of sadness. Chief Santanta gave this speech when he and other chiefs of Plains tribes accepted a treaty limiting where they could live and hunt.

> I love the land and the buffalo and will not part with it. I want you to understand well what I say. . . . I hear a great deal of good talk from the gentlemen whom the Great Father sends us, but they never do what they say. I don't want any of the medicine lodges [schools and churches like those of the white settlers] within the country. I want the children raised as I was . . . I have heard that you intend to settle us on a reservation near the mountains. I don't want to settle. I love to roam over the prairies. There I feel free and happy, but when we settle down we grow pale and die. . . . A long time ago this land belonged to our fathers; but when I go up the river I see camps of soldiers on its banks. These soldiers cut down my timber; they kill my buffalo; and when I see that, my heart feels like bursting; I feel sorry. I have spoken.
>
> —Chief Santanta, "My Heart Feels Like Bursting"

EXERCISE 3

To get a better understanding of the relationship of tone and audience, relate an experience you had using a hair product that turned your hair green. Write a letter of complaint to the manufacturer of the product and one to a friend who had a similar experience. Have you used a different tone in the letters? What is the tone of each one? Are the tones appropriate for your purpose and audience?

Prewriting–Generating Ideas and Information

In the first step of the writing process, you learned to plan your project. Now, you are ready to prewrite. When you prewrite, you put ideas on paper. They are just that—ideas. Prewriting not only lets you put ideas on paper, it moves you past that time of staring at a blank piece of paper and wondering what you are going to write about. This condition is known as *writer's block*. By following a writing process, you can usually avoid writer's block because you are more relaxed. When you are relaxed, you can more readily come up with ideas because you know that you do not have to write a first-draft masterpiece. You have certain things to do at each step. Only when you have completed all the steps are you responsible for the entire piece. Think of prewriting as the process of generating raw material. Some of the ideas may be useful, and some may not be. Following are some frequently used prewriting techniques.

Freewriting

Think about your subject, and then write for ten minutes without stopping. Choose a quiet place where you will not be interrupted and set a timer for ten minutes. Do not worry about spelling, grammar, or punctuation. Do not be concerned if some of the ideas that pour into your mind and leak out onto the paper seem irrelevant to your topic. You may discard them later. After you have written for ten minutes, look at what you have written, highlight the ideas that seem to be the most important ones, and use them for *focused writing*. After you have let your ideas and fingers rest for a time, again write for ten minutes, focusing on the ideas you highlighted.

The following student example was in response to this prompt: "Write a brief paper about a recent decision you made."

This is a nobrainer. The biggest decision Ive made was which college to choose. Mom and dad wanted me to go to a four year college cause both of them went to the university but I just didn't feel like I wanted to go or leave home right now. Actually that is not the whole truth I just didnt want to leave my girlfriend who is still in high school. We been dating for two years and I feel she is real special and that our relationship is to important to take a chance on loosing it. She's only got two more year of high school and then she wants to go to the U and major in art. I think I want to be an engineer, but Im not sure yet. I'll have plenty of time to make up my mind after I take a few more college course. I didn't tell mom and Dad—I know better than that because they would probly just say its puppy love and I shouldnt let it interfere with a decision that will affect my life for years to come. Man I was sweating bullets. I had to think of something and in a hurry. had to have some excuse or reason. Needed to convince them that I would be better off going to a community college for two years and then transferring to a fouryear college. Now my parents aren't stingy but they know the value of a buck so I decided that i would play the $ angle. I checked the cost of tuition at the university and the cost of dorms and all that stuff and then checked the cost of attending a local community college—what a hassle. Took me a while to get all the dope together. They could have been more cooperative in giving me the info. I finally got one person who was really helpful—even gave me some advice. I got all the figures together and laid them out and showed my parents how much money they could save if I went to the nearby college. And then I cinched the deal by telling them that I wasn't ready for those big classes and that I needed more individual attention than I would get at the U. I felt pretty good when I convinced them that it was a good idea, and me and Leslie went out and celebrated when I told her that I was not going to have to leave her.

EXERCISE 4

Choose one of the following topics and freewrite about it for ten minutes.

1. The six most important words in the English language: I admit I made a mistake.

2. The five most important words in the English language: You did a good job.

3. The four most important words in the English language: What is your opinion?

4. The three most important words in the English language: If you please.

5. The two most important words in the English language: Thank you.

6. The one least important word in the English language: I.

7. A public event that changed your private life.

8. Bearing a grudge.

9. Leaving home.

10. Starting a new job.

EXERCISE 5

Highlight the most promising ideas in your freewriting, and, again, write for ten minutes, focusing on these ideas.

Clumping

This particular type of prewriting goes by a variety of names. Some writers call it *clustering;* some call it *bubbling;* others call it *mapping* or *webbing*. The name is not particularly important, but the concept is. This technique calls for some type of visual representation to connect words that represent ideas. Begin with one key word in your topic, and write down words that come to your mind as you think about the key word or about some of the other words. Many writers circle the words and use double lines to connect first-level words to the topic word, single lines for second-level words, and broken lines for third-level words. The following student example was in response to this prompt: "Write a brief essay about the most exciting vacation you have ever taken."

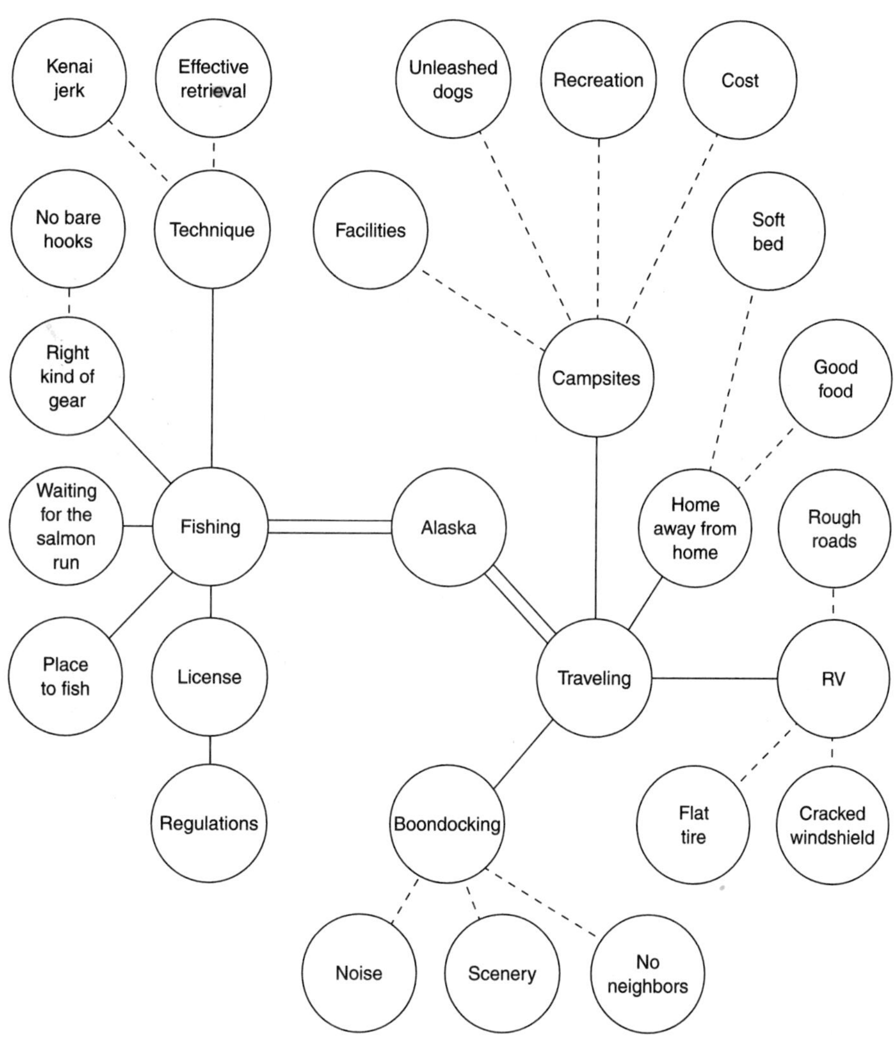

EXERCISE 6

Use the clumping method of prewriting and generate material for one of the following prompts.

1. A family get-together (Christmas, Thanksgiving, or other special event such as a wedding)

2. A favorite (or least favorite) pet

3. The way you deal with telemarketers

4. An incident in your childhood that you still have not revealed to your parents

5. A skill that you have

Listing and Grouping

The listing and grouping technique, like clumping, goes by a variety of names. It may be called *making a scratch outline, making an informal outline,* or some other name. This technique calls for making a catalog list of everything that comes to your mind when you think about your topic. After you have finished the list, go over it and group similar items. Discard items that do not fit into any group. After you have grouped like items, give each group a heading. If you intend to write a paragraph, choose only one group. If you intend to write an essay, choose a group for each body paragraph. The following student example was in response to this prompt: "Write a short paper in which you tell about your return to a place you once knew well but have not seen for some time—a school, a house, a vacation spot, a restaurant, a town, and so on."

INITIAL LIST		GROUPED LISTS		
		House and Yard	**Family**	**Friends and Neighbors**
white house	friends	big tree	Dad	Betty Sue
big tree	Brother	lava rocks	Mom	the Smiths
yard	neighbors	herbs	Brother	fussy old lady
family	yard	flowers		
Dad	lava rocks	white house		
Mom	herbs			
flowers	the Smiths			
Betty Sue	fussy old lady			

EXERCISE 7

Generate material for one of the following prompts using listing and grouping.

1. A memorable high school experience—social or academic

2. Your first day in college

3. A chain of events in your life that led to a major decision

4. Buying your first car

5. Your best vacation

Asking Journalistic Questions

Journalists answer the five Ws and one H questions when they are working on a story.

> **Journalistic Questions**
>
> Who?   Where?
>
> What?   When?
>
> Why?   How?

You can use these questions to generate raw material for any type of assignment. You may answer each question with a word or phrase and then later turn those words or phrases into sentences. The following student example was in response to this prompt: "Write about the one event in your life that you would like to re-live. You may choose an event that you just want to relive or one that you want to relive and change."

Who? *My high school sweetheart, me, and the baby we made.*

What? *My boyfriend and I decided to abort the baby I was carrying.*

When? *We were in our second year of college.*

(continued)

Where? *The college was in a city in another state.*

Why? *We were confused, alone, ambitious, scared, and selfish.*

How? *We had decided to go to the same college so that we would not be separated. Being away from family and friends and familiar surroundings, we felt that we had each other and were capable of making our own decisions even if they were in conflict with the moral values instilled in us by our parents.*

EXERCISE 8

Respond to the five journalistic questions to generate material for one of the following prompts.

1. Choosing your college

2. Your life's goal

3. An expensive error in judgment

4. Something that you once valued but no longer do

5. A valuable lesson you learned

Brainstorming

Brainstorming includes elements of freewriting, clumping, listing and grouping, and asking journalistic questions. This type of prewriting comes from group brainstorming—a form of problem solving in which all members of the group spontaneously contribute ideas. When you use brainstorming, list ideas as they come to mind; ask questions; use symbols, words, phrases, or even sentences. As in other types of prewriting, do not be concerned about relevancy of ideas, grammar, or spelling. Later you can discard irrelevant ideas and correct spelling and grammatical flaws.

Brainstorming can be used effectively in collaboration with others. You may brainstorm with one person or with people in a small group. Collaborative brainstorming involves discussing, arguing, and recording. Although there is no set format for this type of prewriting, you may find it helpful to have a leader to lead the discussion, a recorder to quickly write down ideas as they come up, and a clarifier to help clarify ambiguous ideas.

EXERCISE 9

1. Choose a prompt from one of the previous exercises and brainstorm for about ten minutes, making notes as ideas come to mind.

2. Choose one or more prompts from previous exercises and brainstorm with a friend or with a small group of people. If you are brainstorming with a group, you may want to have one person use a large marker board to record ideas as they come up. This shared information usually enlivens the discussion as participants use others' ideas as springboards for their own thinking.

Outlining

You may use outlining in the prewriting process. Take the material you generated using another technique and put it in outline form. When you know a great deal about the subject, you may be able to put your ideas in outline form without doing any other prewriting. A formal outline uses a system that divides and ranks items according to their importance. Many writers use the following system that includes Roman numerals, capital letters, Arabic numerals, and lowercase letters.

I.

   A.

      1.

         a.

Note: You cannot have a single designation in an outline. If you have a **I**, you must have a **II**. If you have an **A**, you must have a **B.** If you have a **1**, you must have a **2.** If you have an **a**, you must have a **b.**

An outline may be put in *topic form* (a word or short phrase for each entry) or in *sentence form* (a complete sentence for each entry). Either one is acceptable. Just remember to be consistent. Do not mix the two types. Some writers like to write a topic outline first and then convert it into a sentence outline. The following student outline is in response to this prompt: "Write an essay detailing the geography and early people of the New World."

Topic Outline	**Sentence Outline**

Topic Outline

I. New World Continents

  A. Mountain Chain

    1. South America Peaks

    2. North America Peaks

  B. Bodies of Water

    1. Arctic Ocean

    2. Pacific Ocean

    3. Atlantic Ocean

    4. Gulf of Mexico

II. Origins of Earliest American

  A. Migrants from Siberia

  B. Reasons for Migration

    1. Displacement

    2. Better Living Conditions

Sentence Outline

I. The New World is made up of two large continents.

  A. A mountain chain links North America and South America.

    1. The Andes are the highest peaks in South America.

    2. The Rocky Mountains are the highest peaks in North America.

  B. Great bodies of water are on all sides of the two continents.

    1. The Arctic Ocean is to the far north.

    2. The Pacific Ocean is to the west.

    3. The Atlantic Ocean is to the east.

    4. The Gulf of Mexico runs along the shores of the United States and Mexico.

II. Scholars have several theories about the origins of the earliest Americans.

  A. Evidence suggest that most of the early migrants crossed the Bering Strait from Siberia to Alaska.

  B. The reasons for the migration are not known.

    1. The migrants may have been displaced by others.

    2. The migrants may have been searching for better living conditions.

EXERCISE 10

Choose a subject with which you are very familiar and outline it. You might consider historical or sporting events, a trend in music or fashion, or another trend in society.

Generally, you can use any of these prewriting techniques (*freewriting, clumping, listing and grouping, asking questions, brainstorming,* or *outlining*) to easily and quickly generate material for any writing assignment. Two other techniques—keeping a journal and doing research—take more time, but they are the ones that produce the best results for longer and more complex assignments.

Keeping a Journal

Keeping a journal allows you to record your observations of people and situations and, in general, keep track of the world as you perceive it. Journal writing is an integral part of many instructors' writing programs, and the part it plays in the writing process varies from instructor to instructor. If you are not required to keep a journal, you might try keeping one. Set your own rules. Write as often and as much as you feel represents your thinking or observations on the topic you have chosen. After you have kept your journal for a time, review it and decide if keeping a journal is of value to you. Have you been able to draw upon your private journal entries for your public writing—class assignments and so on? When you reread journal entries, do they help you clarify your ideas on a given point? Do they help you keep track of the growth process of your thinking?

Researching

You will need to research a subject when you need more information than your own knowledge. To fully research a topic, you must

- do the research

- examine and evaluate the results of the research

- write a paper based on your understanding of the results of your research

EXERCISE 11

Choose three prompts and use a different type of prewriting to generate ideas and information about each one. Save your prewriting. You may use it later to develop a paragraph or an essay.

1. The electronic revolution of the past ten years.

2. Sportsmanship is only a word.

3. Grades do (or do not) encourage learning.

4. Recall an event that gave you an increased awareness of yourself and explain how the effects of the experience have made a difference in your perception of yourself and of others.

5. Struggling to juggle school, work, and play.

6. The fine art of lying.

7. A truly obnoxious person.

8. Special family traditions.

Writing—Composing and Organizing

In the first step of the writing process, you learned to plan; in the second step, you learned to generate raw material; and in this step you will take the material that you generated and begin the composing process. The literal meaning of the word *compose* is "to form by putting together." When you compose a paragraph or an essay, you are putting material together in an organized manner. To clearly communicate your ideas, your compositions must be

- **unified**—focused on one main point about the subject

- **coherent**—organized according to a specific plan with material smoothly connected

- **adequate**—fully developed

Achieving Unity

A composition is unified when one idea is dominant throughout, and all other ideas are subordinate to it. Achieve unity in a paragraph by discussing only one idea—the one stated in the topic sentence. Achieve unity in an essay by designing an effective introduction and conclusion, developing coherent body paragraphs and discussing only one idea—the one in the thesis statement. *See* Part 2: Achieving Unity (pp. 34–35).

Achieving Coherence

Coherence is the glue that holds a composition together. It is that quality of writing that comes from careful ordering of sentences in paragraphs and paragraphs in essays. It allows readers to follow step-by-step the development of ideas. One idea grows out of another or is linked to another in such a way that the relationship is clear. The most common and natural way to achieve coherence in writing is to carefully follow an organizational pattern: *time, place or space,* or *logical.* Transitions add to coherence because they help connect one thought with another. *See* Part 2: Achieving Coherence (p. 48).

ESL Notes: The symbol is used to flag areas that are often problematic for students whose first language is not English.

The concept of an English paragraph may be new to you. Writing an English paragraph may seem like writing in your native language, but is not. Words, phrases, and ideas of one language do not fit together in the same way as they do in another language. Each culture has its own special way of thinking, and the way people think affects the way they write. The development of an English paragraph generally follows a straight line of thinking. The paragraph usually opens with a statement of the central idea (*topic sentence*) and all the following facts, examples, and reasons used to develop that idea must be relevant to it. In following this straight line of thinking, the English paragraph differs from paragraphs of other languages. For example, Asian writers tend to follow a circular line of development, circling around the topic rather than addressing it directly. French and Spanish writers often include rather complex digressions. Arabic writers tend to develop an idea by a variety of parallel constructions.

Revising—Overhauling the Whole Composition

The word *revision* simply means "re-seeing," so in this step you are looking at what you have written and rewriting or rearranging it to make it more effective.

Working with Other People

After you have written the first draft of a paragraph or an essay, take a break from it. Do not reread it immediately. Wait a few hours, or a day if you can afford the time. This break will allow you to be more objective when you read what you have written. At this time you may want to get responses from other people—friends, family members, or classmates. Many instructors will ask you to turn in your first draft to them so that they and/or your classmates can make comments on the content. The first purpose of getting early responses is to find the strengths in the content of the paper, and the second is to get suggestions for improvements in content. After you reflect on the responses and suggestions for the improvement of the content and begin the process of revising the paper, you may want to get another round of responses in which people make suggestions for revisions. (*See* Appendix B: Evaluating Essays, p. 513.)

Making Comprehensive Revisions

In the revising process, first make comprehensive revisions. Do not worry about polishing sentences and cleaning up mechanical flaws. You will make these revisions and corrections later. At this time, concentrate on the big issues: *focus, purpose, audience, tone, content,* and *organization.* There is no right order for making revisions. Study your draft, and when you find a big issue that is inadequate, make a note of possible ways to rewrite or rearrange this material to make it more effective.

▶ **Tighten the Focus**   In the first step of the writing process, you chose a broad topic and then focused on one main idea. Now that you have a draft of your composition, you need to reexamine your main idea.

> Reword a thesis or topic sentence when it is awkward or not clear.

> Reword a thesis or topic sentence that contains more than one idea.

> Cut out material that does not support your thesis or topic sentence.

▶ **Clarify the Purpose**   Your purpose must be clear. If you are getting feedback from other people, ask them if they readily recognize what you want to accomplish. If they are not sure of your purpose, then you need to revise the text to clearly show that your purpose is to entertain, to explain, or to persuade. You may have a combination of these purposes, but one purpose should be dominant.

▶ **Reconsider the Audience and the Tone**   As you wrote the first draft, you may have gotten insights into the audience and tone that you did not have when you began the process. You may want to reconsider the amount of evidence you present and/or the tone that you use. Make sure that you have let your readers know why they are reading your material.

▶ **Strengthen and Balance the Content**   When you revise the *content,* be sure that the composition is neither too thick nor too thin. Use enough facts, examples, details, and reasons to be convincing, but do not pad the composition with irrelevant or redundant material. Make sure the parts are balanced. If you supplied excessive support in one part—usually the first part—and then skimped on other parts, prune the excess and add more support to the thinner parts.

▶ **Improve the Organization**   Clearly identify the *organizational pattern (time, place or space,* or *logical)* that you used. *See* Part 2: Achieving Coherence (p. 48). Make a note of it on the draft. If you have strayed from your original plan, reorganize the material so that it is presented in a consistent manner. If the original pattern you chose does not work well, try a different one. Highlight linking words and transitional expressions. If you do not have enough of these expressions to help move your readers smoothly from one sentence to the next or from one paragraph to the next, revise. Add more transitions and/or rewrite the sentences that are jarring.

▶ **Use Revision Checklists**   Using revision checklists makes the task of rewriting and rearranging material much easier. It allows you to systematically revise one part at a time. If you do not receive checklists from your instructor, use the ones in Appendix A Revising Sentences, Paragraphs, and Essays.

▶ **Making Sentence Revisions**   After you have made the major revisions, turn your attention to the structure of the sentences. If your instructor does not give you a sentence revision checklist, use the one in Appendix A to help you correct, clarify, and improve sentences.

Editing, Formatting, and Proofreading

After you have made the revisions in your composition, read it aloud, or better yet, have someone read it aloud to you. Good writing usually sounds good. Does your composition sound good? Does it flow? Does it sound natural? Does it sound like you? Generally, you can more easily identify rough spots when you read the work aloud. If your ear tells you that something is awkward or cumbersome, look at that passage, revise it, and read it aloud again to see if you have made it smoother.

Editing

To help you make corrections in punctuation, mechanics, usage, and spelling, use the editing checklist in Appendix A. Keep a list of your editing problems. Many writers tend to make the same errors over and over. Update your list. Check off editing skills that no longer cause you difficulty. Study the ones that you continue to make.

Formatting

If your instructor does not tell you that he or she prefers a particular format, use the form in Appendix A: Formatting College Papers (p. 499).

Proofreading

After you have made all the revisions and have properly formatted your work, read it carefully and correct any typographical errors. Some writers find it helpful to proofread the material backward—word-by-word. After you have finished reading it to yourself, read it aloud or have a friend read it aloud; often the ears can hear what the eyes did not see.

Building Sentences, Paragraphs, and Essays

Work on good prose has three steps: a musical stage when it is composed, an architectonic one when it is built, and a textile one when it is woven.

—WALTER BENJAMIN, ONE-WAY STREET,
"Caution: Steps"

A paragraph is a series of sentences developing one topic. An *essay*, no matter how long it is, consists of a series of paragraphs. Each paragraph helps to develop the essay, and, at the same time, develops its own topic. A sentence is a miniature paragraph. It is the expression of one complete thought. Sometimes you can say what you have to say in a sentence. At other times you will need to write a paragraph to express an idea. When you cannot express an idea in a paragraph, you will need to write a series of paragraphs—an essay.

Building Sentences

Classified according to structure, there are four kinds of sentences: *simple, compound, complex,* and *compound-complex.* Use these patterns to vary your writing and make it more effective. Monotonous repetition of patterns often causes readers to lose interest in what you are saying.

Building Simple Sentences

A *simple sentence* has one independent clause and no dependent clauses. An *independent clause* has a subject part and a verb part and expresses a complete thought. The *subject* is that part about which something is being said. The *verb* is that part that says something about the *subject.*

The simple sentence is key to the other sentence structures. The other sentences are built by connecting simple sentences in certain ways to show the relationship of ideas. Do not confuse a short sentence with a simple sentence. Length has nothing to do with the type of structure of a sentence. Sentences of any type may be long or short. The subject and verb parts are separated with a slash in the following sentences.

The unhappy baby/cried loudly.   He/had lost his favorite stuffed animal.

EXERCISE 1

Complete the following simple sentences by adding the missing subject or verb part.

1. _______________________________/ went fishing.

2. We/ _______________________________.

3. My father and I/ ____.

4. ____/were late for the party.

5. The best quarterback in our league/ _______________________________________.

6. ____ /collapsed at my feet.

7. ____ /is the best movie I have ever seen.

8. John Wayne/ ____.

9. ____/included reserved and an all-you-can-eat buffet.

10. ____/may go with me.

Building Compound Sentences

A *compound sentence* has two or more independent clauses and no dependent clause. When you have two equally important ideas about the same subject, you may put each idea into an independent clause and join the clauses to form a *compound sentence.* Independent clauses may be joined with a comma and a connecting word (*coordinating conjunction*) or with a semicolon. You can easily remember the connecting words by using a memory trick: Use the first letter of each connecting word (*for, and, nor, but, or, yet, so*) to form the word—FANBOYS.

▶ **Commas and Connecting Words**   Join independent clauses with a comma and a connecting word.

> The second Sunday in May is Mother's Day. The third Sunday in June is Father's Day.

> The second Sunday in May is Mothers' Day, **and** the third Sunday in June is Father's Day.

> Pink flowers honor living mothers. White flowers honor deceased mothers.

> Pink flowers honor living mothers, **but** white flowers honor deceased mothers.

Note: *While, then,* and *also* are not coordinating conjunctions.

 To join independent clauses with a comma and a connecting word, you need to know not only the connecting words but what they mean.

CONNECTING WORDS	PURPOSES OF CONNECTIONS
For	Cause (reason, object, aim, or purpose of an action or activity)
And	Addition (together or along with, in addition to, as well as)
Nor	Negation (not the case, not either, and not, or not)
But	Contrast (on the contrary, contrary to expectation, exception)
Or	Choice (an alternative, uncertainty, indefiniteness)
Yet	Difference (emphasize or show difference, despite, nevertheless)
So	Effect (result, consequence, in order that)

EXERCISE 2

Combine the paired simple sentences to form a compound sentence, using a comma and a logical connecting word. Remember, the comma goes *before* the connecting word—not after it.

1. Each state has jurisdiction over its holidays.

   Technically, the United States observes no national holidays.

2. The president and Congress can legally designate holidays only for the District of Columbia and for federal employees.

   Most states observe the federal legal public holidays.

3. Easter is the oldest festival in the Christian world.

   It commemorates the resurrection of Jesus after his crucifixion.

4. In the West it falls on a Sunday between March 22 and April 25.

   The date of Easter is calculated differently in the Orthodox Eastern Church.

5. Our Easter bunny and Easter eggs probably came to us from Germany.

   According to legend, many years ago in Germany a white hare hid eggs in the garden the night before Easter.

6. The early Christians wanted to change the focus of February 14, which was the date of a fertility festival in ancient Rome.

   They Christianized it in memory of the martyr St. Valentine.

7. According to legend, St. Patrick used the shamrock to explain the Trinity.

   This plant, with leaves composed of three leaflets, became the emblem of Ireland.

8. St. Patrick was probably not named Patrick.

   He was probably not born in Ireland on March 17.

9. December 25 was called Midwinter Feast.

   In the ninth century it was renamed Christmas.

10. On April Fools' Day people play practical jokes on others.

    They want to make them look like fools.

▶ **Semicolons and Transitional Expressions**   Join independent clauses with a semicolon or with a semicolon and a transitional expression.

> Labor Day began in New York.

> Labor unions wanted recognition for their services to the world.

> Labor Day began in New York; labor unions wanted recognition for their services to the world.

> Memorial Day was instituted in 1868 to honor the Civil War dead.

> It now commemorates all war dead.

> Memorial Day was instituted in 1868 to honor the Civil War dead; **however,** it now commemorates all war dead.

Caution   Transitions cannot be used alone to join two independent clauses; they must have a semicolon in front of them and usually a comma after them.

No   Egyptians began their year at the autumn equinox—September 21 **however** the ancient Greeks began their new year at the winter solstice—December 21.

Yes   Early Christians began their new year on March 25**; however,** in the 1700s, Germany, Denmark, and Sweden moved their New Year's Day from March 25 to January 1.

Yes   England changed its New Year's Day to January 1 in 1752**; subsequently,** the colonies changed their New Year's Day to January 1.

 ### Commonly Used Transitions, the Relationships They Express, and Their Meanings

When you join two independent clauses with a transitional expression, the transitional expression shows the relationship of the two clauses. To show the appropriate relationships, you need to know some of these expressions and the relationships they express.

Time, Place, Space Relationships

finally/at the end

next/afterward

then/next in time, at that time

meanwhile/in the intervening time

subsequently/following in time or order

Result, Reason, Summary, Consequence Relationships

accordingly/so, since

hence/for this reason, from now

therefore/on account of, as a result

consequently/as a result

then/next in time, at that time

thus/in this way, as a result

Addition Relationships

also/in addition

furthermore/in addition

besides/in addition, also

moreover/in addition, more, plus

Difference, Contrast Relationships

conversely/contrarily, on the contrary, if or when reversed

however/in spite of, by contrast   *instead*/as a substitute

nevertheless/in spite of   *nonetheless*/nevertheless, however

otherwise/under other circumstances

Emphasis Relationships

indeed/in fact   *certainly*/sure, inescapable

Similarity Relationships

likewise/in the same way, similarly   *similarly*/as, like, as if

EXERCISE 3

Combine the following pairs of simple sentences, forming compound sentences by adding appropriate transitional expressions, semicolons, and commas.

1. Halloween is an old, old holiday. It is older than the Christian religion.

2. The ancient druids (priests of the Celts) celebrated this time of year.

   They lighted bonfires and believed that on this night the god of death summoned to him the souls of all the wicked who had died during the previous year.

3. The ancient Romans observed this same date.

   To honor the goddess of fruits and gardens, they used nuts and apples in their ceremonies.

4. The night before All Saints' Day is rich in superstitions.

   It is thought to be a time when ghosts and witches have one last fling before the holy day.

5. Remnants of past Halloweens linger in today's celebrations. Bonfires are lit in pumpkins.

6. Ghosts and goblins bob for apples.

   Spirits in the form of peel-and-paste cats and witches sail across mirrors and windows.

7. Armistice Day, November 11, is observed in the United States.

   It commemorates the armistice that ended World War I.

8. In 1954 it was renamed Veterans Day.

   It was given the added significance of honoring all veterans of the armed services.

9. It was the medieval Germans who gave us our Christmas tree.

   It was the Dutch who gave us Santa Claus (St. Nicholas).

10. Holly and mistletoe were sacred to the druids. They used these plants in their rituals.

EXERCISE 4

Write five compound sentences joined with a semicolon and five different transitions.

Building Complex Sentences

A *complex sentence* has one independent clause and one or more *dependent clauses*. A *dependent clause* has a subject and a verb but does not make a complete statement by itself. It depends on an independent clause to make its statement complete. These clauses begin with words that make them dependent. Attach the dependent word to the least important idea in the sentence. Generally, put a comma after a dependent clause when it is the first part of the sentence. To get a better understanding of dependent words, study the following common dependent words and the relationships they express.

Dependent Words and the Relationships They Express

RELATIONSHIP	WORDS
Cause	as, because, inasmuch as, now that, since, why
Choice	rather than, than, whether
Qualification	as much as, as though, even though, if, in order that, inasmuch as, provided, unless, how, what, whatever, which, who, whoever

Difference	although, even if, even though, in spite of, though, whereas
Place	where, wherever
Result	in order that, so, so that, that
Time	after, afterward, before, ever since, now that, once, since, until, when, whenever, while

In the following examples, independent clauses are underlined, and dependent clauses are double underlined. When the dependent clause comes before the independent clause, it is usually followed by a comma.

Because Secretary of State Seward paid the Russians $7, 200,000 for the whole of Alaska, many Americans laughed at him. They called the land "Seward's icebox" because they thought it was a useless piece of land. While the people blamed Seward for spending the money, it turned out to be an excellent bargain because the gold alone taken from the Yukon valley since 1897 has paid for Alaska many times over.

EXERCISE 5

Combine the pairs of simple sentences to form complex sentences, using a dependent word that best expresses the relationship between them.

1. Gold was discovered in the Klondike in the late 1890s.

   It set off one of the world's biggest gold rushes.

2. News of the discovery reached the outside world. Thousands of people went to the Klondike.

3. The Klondike was located in the Yukon Territory of Canada.

   Most people went through Alaska to reach the gold fields.

4. Boomtowns sprang up overnight.

   Over thirty thousand people passed through Alaska on their way to the Yukon Territory.

5. It was one of the greatest gold rushes in history.

   People came from all over the world, hoping to get rich in the Klondike.

6. Shiploads of people from Vancouver, Seattle, and San Francisco headed for the gold fields.

   Most of them landed at Skagway.

7. The gold fever reached its peak. Gold was discovered in Nome, Alaska.

8. Over 100 million dollars in gold was mined in about ten years.

   Many of the prospectors returned home poorer than when they went to the gold fields.

9. The gold rush was over. Ten thousand of the newcomers left Alaska.

10. Today, people travel through Alaska.

    They can see remnants of towns that were once thriving boomtowns.

Building Compound-Complex Sentences

A *compound-complex sentence* contains at least two independent clauses and at least one dependent clause.

> Although the purchase of Alaska was a bargain, it brought difficulties at first, for there were serious disputes between the United States and other countries. The Americans contended that they should be the only ones who could hunt seals in the Bering Sea because it belonged to them, but other countries wanted part of that lucrative trade. Because military rule did not work out well, the laws of Oregon were extended to Alaska, and a civilian government was set up. Gold had been discovered in Alaska before the purchase, but it did not affect the development of Alaska because it was not a significant find.

EXERCISE 6

Combine each group of sentences, turning them into one compound-complex sentence. You will need to add necessary commas, connecting words, and the dependent words that best express the relationship between two independent clauses.

1. William H. Seward, the secretary of state, negotiated Alaska's purchase from Russia.

   He was allowed to name it. He chose an Aleut word that means "great country."

2. In 1741 Captain Vitus Bering and his men were exploring the Aleutian Islands.

   They ventured onto the mainland. They were the first white men to visit the land now known as Alaska.

3. Captain Bering died on the way home. His men returned to Russia across Siberia.

   They claimed the land for their czar.

4. The explorers returned to Russia. Many traders and trappers went to Alaska.

   They established a few trading posts.

5. The Russians claimed much of the land. By the late 1700s English explorers claimed the coast of south Alaska. The British Hudson's Bay Company set up trading posts there.

6. An American trading company had established posts in Alaska by 1788. It eventually merged with a Russian company. The new company had problems. The owners signed treaties thereby averting war.

7. A white settlement was established on Kodiak Island. It was a sad day for the indigenous people. The newcomers oppressed them. They were no better than slaves.

8. The settlers on Kodiak Island had depleted the nearby hunting grounds of game.

   They moved to Sitka. They resumed their lucrative business.

9. The Civil War interfered with the American government's plan to buy Alaska from the Russians. An agreement was not reached until 1867. It was at this time that Seward made his famous deal.

10. U. S. Secretary of State Seward got his treaty through the Senate. The vast territory that had belonged to Russia now belonged to the United States. "Seward's Folly" increased the lands of the United States by an area more than twice the size of Texas.

Review   In this section you have learned to combine simple sentences using a

- comma and a connecting word to form a *compound sentence*

- semicolon to form a *compound sentence*

- semicolon and a transitional expression to form a *compound sentence*

- dependent clause and an independent clause to form a *complex sentence*

- dependent clause and two independent clauses to form a *compound-complex sentence*

Following is a review chart of these sentence combinations.

COMPOUND SENTENCES

Independent clause	+	, FANBOYS	+ independent clause
Independent clause	+	;	+ independent clause
Independent clause	+	; transitional expression,	+ independent clause

COMPLEX SENTENCES

Independent clause			+ dependent clause
Dependent clause	+	,	+ independent clause

COMPOUND-COMPLEX SENTENCES

Independent clause	+	, FANBOYS + independent clause	+ dependent clause
Dependent clause	+	, independent clause + , FANBOYS	+ independent clause

Review Exercises

Combine each group of sentences, turning them into a compound sentence, a complex sentence, or a compound-complex sentence. You will need to add necessary commas, connecting words, semicolons, and dependent words.

REVIEW EXERCISE 7

1. Courtship in the animal kingdom is an interesting and often risky business.

   Instead of finding a mate, the male may often find an untimely end.

2. The praying mantis is a predatory insect.

   It is so named because when it rests, it folds its front legs as if in prayer.

3. The praying mantis male is greatly at risk.

   His intended lady love will eat anything that moves, including him.

4. The wily male approaches the female from behind. She can only see things that move.

5. He bides his time. His intended is distracted by another insect. Mating takes place.

6.He mates with this rapacious female. His chance of escape is still slim to none.

She will try to grab him as he moves away from her.

7.A male bumblebee fares better than the praying mantis. He still dies shortly after mating.

8.He has no stinger, produces no honey, and does no work. The drone in the honeybee world has one important job—mating with the queen bee.

9.The male mole cricket is a music aficionado. He wants to attract a female. He rubs his wings together to make a chirping song.

10.The female of a New World spider is infamous for her toxic venom. She is better known for devouring her mate. That is how she earned her name—the black widow.

REVIEW EXERCISE 8

1.The female moth is a masterful perfume maker.

She exudes a scent that can be detected by a male as far as six miles away.

2.Courtship in the world of mammals and birds is less dangerous.

It is often gentle and considerate in nature.

3.Elephants court. They often spend weeks together in gentle play. They will stand for hours playfully entwining their trunks.

4.The Australian satin bowerbird has brilliant plumage. He uses his skill as an architect and interior decorator to attract a prospective mate, not his good looks.

5.The mating season arrives. The bowerbird begins his yearly project of building an elaborate home, or bower.

6.He uses twigs and sticks as his basic building material. He uses sticks to construct two twelve-inch parallel walls that are two inches thick.

7.The bower is complete. He decorates it with colorful objects.

8. He uses flowers, scraps of foil, parrot feathers, and bits of glass. Then he waits for a female to fly by and inspect his beak work.

9. A female appears. He flashes his beautiful plumage. He regales her with a croaking sound.

10. The pair mate. The female flies away from the beautiful bower that was constructed for only one purpose—courtship.

Building Paragraphs and Essays

A *paragraph*—a complete composition on a small scale—and an *essay*—a series of paragraphs—deal with one subject that is introduced, developed, and concluded. A paragraph requires a sentence that contains a topic and an idea about it that determines the sentences that will be included in the paragraph. The structure of an essay may be regarded as an expansion of a single paragraph. Generally, an essay contains an introductory paragraph, body paragraphs, and a concluding paragraph. An essay requires a sentence that contains a topic and an idea about it that determines the paragraphs that will be included in the essay. To clearly communicate your ideas, your compositions must be

- unified—focused on a main point about the subject

- coherent—organized according to a specific plan with material smoothly connected

- complete—adequately developed

Achieving Unity

▶ **Paragraphs**   A *paragraph* is a group of related sentences developing one topic. To achieve unity in a paragraph, clearly state your idea in a *topic sentence* and develop the paragraph by supplying detailed information that supports that idea. Although the topic sentence may appear in different places (*See* Appendix C: Placement of the Topic Sentences), for the time being, make the topic sentence the first sentence.

Writing Topic Sentences   A *topic sentence* is the sentence that expresses the main idea of a paragraph. It contains a topic and an idea about that topic that clearly states the purpose of that paragraph. The idea is commonly called the *controlling idea*. The controlling idea is the word, phrase, or clause that clearly states the idea that is to be developed in the paragraph. In the following topic sentences, the topics are underlined, and the controlling ideas are italicized.

Smoking *should be banned in restaurants that have fewer than six tables.*

Diners in small restaurants *are unfairly forced to breathe second-hand smoke.*

Do not make the topic sentence *too narrow.* If it does not have a controlling idea, it is not a viable topic sentence because it does not focus on an idea.

Too narrow   A kite is a toy.

Focused   Kites have often been used as more than playthings.

Do not make the topic sentence *too broad.* A sentence that is too broad may contain a controlling idea, but that idea is too broad to be developed in a paragraph of average length (about 150 words).

Too broad   _Body positions_ *will affect your golf game.*

Narrowed   _The way you stand_ *will affect your golf swing.*

Narrowed   _The way you hold your club_ *will affect your golf swing.*

EXERCISE 9

Practice identifying topic sentences by labeling the following sentences. Use **TS** for topic sentences, **TN** for sentences that are too narrow, and **TB** for sentences that are too broad.

1. Working in a fast food restaurant has given me valuable experience. ______

2. The cafeteria needs to be improved. ______

3. The tongue is a remarkable muscle. ______

4. In many sports, skill is more important than strength. ______

5. I am a tall person. ______

6. The cafeteria is operated by the Mediocre Meals Company. ______

7. The breakfast selections in the cafeteria are not sufficient. ______

8. He is a well-groomed young man. ______

9. He is a first-year student in college. ______

10. My height is my greatest asset. ______

EXERCISE 10

Each of the following topics can be developed into a paragraph. Choose three and write a topic sentence for each one.

1. Road rage
2. Immature behavior
3. Attitude of a jock or jocks
4. A ridiculous person (slang: geek)
5. Atmosphere in one of your classes

6. Your favorite beverage
7. An unsafe driving practice
8. An attribute of your pet
9. Family arguments
10. Your best or worst trait

Writing Support Sentences   First, write a topic sentence (TS) that is focused on one idea and can be developed in about 150 words. After you have written the topic sentence, write sentences that contain details that directly support the controlling idea in the topic sentence. These sentences are called *major support* sentences (MA). To determine if a sentence supports the controlling idea, read the topic sentence, think *because* or *for example* and read the support sentence. If it makes sense, it supplies major support.

Topic Sentence: During the last year, <u>digital photography</u> has *zoomed in popularity.*

because: It has become more affordable. (Yes, it has become more popular because it has become less expensive.)

because: The software for it has become more powerful and user-friendly. (Yes, it has become more popular because the software has been improved.)

because: It captures pictures electronically rather than on film. (No, this sentence does not explain why it has become popular.

Note: The words *because* or *for example* are used as convenient terms to keep you close to your topic sentence. In certain paragraphs, they may seem awkward or inappropriate. Just keep in mind the purpose of the words and the way they are intended to be used, and you should be able to use them to find the sentences that directly support the topic sentence.

<u>Responsible citizens</u> have certain *legal obligations.* (TS)

for example: They must pay taxes. (MA)

for example: They must obey just laws. (MA)

for example: They must serve jury duty, if called. (MA)

for example: They must serve in the military services or their equivalent, if called. (MA)

Paragraphs are not limited to major support sentences because other sentences are often needed to give additional information. These sentences are called *minor support sentences* (MI) because they supply support for the major support sentences.

<u>Citizens</u> have rights and privileges that aliens do not have. (TS)

for example: They are able to vote and to serve on juries. (MA)

for example: They may decide which candidate gets elected and which accused person gets acquitted or punished. (MI)

because: They can run for public office or hold certain federal government jobs. (MA)

because: Aliens cannot run for public office or hold some federal jobs. (MI)

because: They may obtain licenses that aliens cannot obtain. (MA)

because: When they travel abroad, they are protected by the U. S. government. (MA)

because: Only U. S. citizens have this protection. (MI)

After you have written a paragraph, chart it. Read the topic sentence, think *because* or *for example,* and then read each support sentence. Instead of using the labels TS, MA, and MI to chart a paragraph, you may find it easier to use a **1** for the topic sentence, **2s** for major support sentences, and **3s** for minor support sentences.

1. <u>Kites</u> have often been used as *more than playthings.*

   2. *for example:*   In 1749, a scientist in Scotland sent up thermometers in a kite to find out the temperature of the upper air.

   2. *for example:*   Three years later Benjamin Franklin made a great discovery by flying a kite in Philadelphia.

     3. *for example:*   He sent it into a thunderstorm, let lightning strike it, and proved that lightning is the same thing as electricity.

   2. *for example:*   Until the airplane was invented, kites were used to find out about conditions high in the air.

     3. *for example:*   The U. S. Weather Bureau sent up box kites, flying them in groups and putting scientific instruments in them.

     3. *for example:*   Some kites were flown with as much as ten miles of fine wire and climbed as high as five miles.

EXERCISE 11

Chart the sentences in the following paragraph. A **1** has been assigned to the topic sentence, which is the first sentence. Assign **2s** to major support sentences and **3s** to minor support sentences. Assign **NS** to sentences that do not support the topic sentence.

a. State governments protect their citizens in many ways._**1**_

b. Laws are passed to protect the health of the people. ______

c. They try to find, prevent, and control contagious diseases. ______

d. Sick people may be isolated to prevent the spread of disease. ______

e. They protect the safety of their citizens. ______

f. Speed limits and licensing drivers and cars provide road protection. ______

g. State laws identify what actions are crimes and penalize people who break the law. ______

h. The state government provides for the general welfare of its citizens. ______

i. Many laws provide for the general welfare of children. ______

j. Child labor is prohibited. ______

k. Children are required to attend school. ______

l. Job safety and working hours and conditions are concerns of the state. ______

m. The state's attempts to legislate the morals of the citizens are often controversial. ______

EXERCISE 12

1. Write two topic sentences with a definite controlling idea, or take two of the topic sentences in Exercises 9 and 10 and write three *because* or *for example* sentences supporting each one.

2. Write a topic sentence and four major sentences that support the controlling idea; then, write one minor support sentence for each of the four major sentences.

3. Write a topic sentence with a definite controlling idea and write several major support sentences and several minor support sentences.

Review Exercises

REVIEW EXERCISE 13

Label the following sentences, using **TS** for topic sentences, **TN** for sentences that are too narrow to be topic sentences, and **TB** for sentences that are too broad to be topic sentences.

1. Parrots are famous for their ability to reproduce human speech. _______

2. Parrots and mynah birds can reproduce human speech. _______

3. My neighbor has a large collection of bonsai plants. _______

4. Growing dwarfed trees is a challenging craft. _______

5. To be thoroughly enjoyed, walking tours should be taken alone. _______

6. Abraham Lincoln was a great president. _______

7. Napoleon was one of the greatest generals in history. _______

8. As a general, Napoleon was one of the greatest strategists in history. _______

9. Tikal is a ruined Mayan city of northern Guatamala. _______

10. Slum districts foster many social ills. _______

Chart the sentences in Exercises 14 and 15, using a **1** for the topic sentence, **2s** for major support sentences, **3s** for minor support sentences, and **NS** for nonsupport sentences.

REVIEW EXERCISE 14

Chart the following sentences, using **1** for the topic sentence, **2s** for major support sentences, **3s** for minor support sentences, and **NS** for nonsupport sentences.

a. Gettysburg is a *historic shrine.* _______

b. Gettysburg is a town in southern Pennsylvania. _______

c. It was the site of a major Union victory in the Civil War. _______

d. The Union checked Robert E. Lee's invasion of the North. _____

e. Many unknown soldiers are buried here. _____

f. Gettysburg is a popular tourist destination. _____

g. Several states have erected monuments. _____

h. Guides take tourists over the battlefields and explain the history of the battles. _____

i. Lincoln gave his "Gettysburg Address" here at the dedication of the Civil War cemetery. _____

j. He eloquently stated his grief for the soldiers and the principles for which they died. _____

k. This brief address is probably the most often quoted speech of all time. _____

REVIEW EXERCISE 15

a. People say that the ghosts of famous dead people often return to their favorite places. _____

b. King Arthur returns each spring to Tintagel Castle. _____

c. It was here that he ruled over the Knights of the Round Table. _____

d. On calm summer nights, the people of Stratford-upon-Avon say they have seen young William Shakespeare strolling toward a certain cottage. _____

e. The cottage belonged to Ann Hathaway, his future wife. _____

f. After three hundred years, the bard still visits this well-maintained cottage. _____

g. Late night travelers on the east shore of the Hudson report that they have seen Ichabod Crane riding wildly down a road. _____

h. This road is probably not Ichabod's favorite place, but he may return to it because it is the source of his fame. _____

i. He was in love with Katrina Van Tassel, but so was Brom Bones, the "headless horseman" who chased poor Ich down that dark road. _____

▶ **Essays**   Just as a paragraph must be unified, an essay must be unified. Essay unity is the combination or arrangement of paragraphs into a satisfying whole. To achieve unity in an essay, clearly state your intent in a sentence called a *thesis statement*. Develop the essay by writing paragraphs that supply detailed information in support of the thesis statement.

Writing Viable Thesis Statements   A *thesis statement* is the statement that expresses the main idea of an essay. It contains both the topic and the writer's idea about the topic. Writing a thesis statement is akin to writing a topic sentence. A topic sentence gives direction to a paragraph, and a thesis statement gives direction to an essay. Each of them contains a *controlling idea*. In the following thesis statements, the topics are underlined, and the controlling ideas are italicized.

> The <u>powwow</u> is *the most important event for preserving Native American culture.*

> The <u>potlatch</u> was an *important, lavish ceremonial feast* among Northwest indigenous people.

> The <u>Old House</u> is *my favorite restaurant.*

> <u>Marijuana</u> *should be legalized.* <u>Marijuana</u> *should not be legalized.*

After you write a thesis statement, check it for viability. To be viable, it must not

- be too narrow

- be too broad

- be an announcement

- contain more than one idea

A statement is *too narrow* if it does not contain an idea or point. A *broad statement* may contain an idea or point, but it is not viable if it needs more support than can be developed in an essay of average length (about 500 words). An *announcement* does not contain a point about the topic. It just announces it. A statement that contains *more than one idea* is confusing because it is not focused. It must focus on one idea; otherwise, readers will not know which idea is going to be developed. A *thesis statement* focuses on only one idea and is neither too narrow nor too broad to be developed in an essay of about 500 words.

> **Too narrow**   I play college football.
>
> **Too broad**   Our college football team has prospects for the coming season.

Announcement	This paper will be about our college football team.
Two ideas	Our college football team has good prospects for the coming season, but it has many problems.
Thesis	I am optimistic about our college football team's prospects for the coming season.
Too narrow	Mr. Gomez was my first college math teacher.
Too broad	Mr. Gomez affected my life.
Announcement	I am going to tell you about an influential instructor.
Two ideas	Mr. Gomez changed the way I thought about myself, and more instructors should encourage young women to take more math classes and learn to deal with test anxiety.
Thesis	Mr. Gomez helped me overcome my math anxiety.
Too narrow	The American Revolutionary War was between Great Britain and the American colonies.
Too broad	The colonists were struggling among themselves for control of their local government.
Announcement	In this essay, I am going to discuss some causes of the American Revolution.
Two ideas	The colonists protested against the laws that Parliament passed restricting colonial navigation and trade.
Thesis	Most of the friction between England and the colonists arose over trade.

EXERCISE 16

Practice identifying thesis statements by labeling the following sentences. Use **THS** for thesis statements, **TN** for sentences that are too narrow, and **TB** for sentences that are too broad.

1. Dr. Martin Luther King, Jr., was a Baptist minister. ______

2. Dr. Martin Luther King, Jr., advocated passive resistance to segregation. ______

3. Dr. King delivered his "I Have a Dream" speech during a March on Washington.______

4. Dr. King was a moving orator. _______

5. Mahatma Gandhi was a great spiritual leader. _______

6. Mahatma Gandhi forced Great Britain to grant independence to India. _______

7. Gandhi used passive resistance to force Great Britain to grant independence to India. _______

8. Henry David Thoreau objected to paying a poll tax to finance the Mexican War. _______

9. The Mexican War, 1846–1848, was an armed conflict between the United States and Mexico. _______

10. Although there were other factors involved, the principal cause of the Mexican War was the desire of the United States to acquire California. _______

EXERCISE 17

Label the following sentences. Use **THS** for thesis statements, **A** for announcements, and **2** for sentences with two or more ideas.

1. As early as 1651, the British government began to pass acts restricting American trade. _______

2. The colonists vehemently denounced the Stamp Act of 1765, which required all new printed matter to be stamped and required all legal documents to be drawn up on stamped paper, the cost varying from a penny to several pounds. _______

3. This essay will discuss the steps England took to more strictly control the American colonies. _______

4. The new acts of Parliament united the colonists from North to South. _______

5. The laboring classes were particularly violent in their demonstrations. _______

6. Sons of Liberty clubs resisted the Stamp Act, and a Stamp Act Congress convened at New York with delegates from nine colonies to protest taxation without representation. _______

7. I am going to tell you about the Townshend Acts. _______

8. The colonists vigorously objected to the Townshend Acts that placed duties on imported items. _______

9. This essay will explain the "Boston Massacre" and the "Boston Tea Party."______

10. The colonists objected to paying a tax on each pound of tea brought into America and to the fact that a British tea company could sell its tea at a price lower than colonial tea importers could.______

EXERCISE 18

Write a thesis statement for five of the following topics. Put one line under the topic and two lines under the idea about it.

1. On being an only child, or the oldest child, or the youngest child.

   ____

2. A famous person in recent news.

   ____

3. Your favorite artist (singer, poet, novelist, and so on).

   ____

4. An important decision you made or will have to make in the near future.

   ____

5. A trait that gets you into trouble.

   ____

6. A great sports figure.

   ____

7. A vacation.

   ____

8. Your pet or your vehicle.

   ____

9. A concert that you attended.

____

10. A part-time job.

____

Writing Support Paragraphs   After you have written a thesis statement that is focused on one idea and can be developed in an essay of about 500 words, then write a topic sentence for each body paragraph. In a unified paragraph, the topic sentences in the body paragraphs support the idea presented in the thesis statement. In the following examples, the topics are underlined, and the ideas are italicized.

Thesis statement   The <u>Civil war</u> has often been called the "Second American Revolution" because it so thoroughly *upset the old ways of doing things.*

Topic sentence 1   The <u>Civil War</u> *brought about political change.*

Topic sentence 2   <u>It</u> *brought about an economic change.*

Topic sentence 3   The *most spectacular change* was in <u>the frontier.</u>

To check supporting topic sentences

- read the thesis statement

- think "because" or "for example"

- read each topic sentence

If the connection makes sense, then the topic sentence probably supports the thesis statement.

Thesis: The <u>industrial revolution</u> *brought about many changes.* Think *because* or *for example.*

for example: Hours of labor were sharply reduced.

for example: The standard of living was greatly improved.

for example: Length of life was dramatically increased.

Review Exercises

REVIEW EXERCISE 19

Check the following thesis statements and the supporting topic sentences. Use an **S** to show that a topic sentence does support the thesis, and use **NS** to show that a topic sentence does not support the thesis. The thesis statements are italicized.

1. *Arizona has an amazing array of natural marvels.*

   Nature used part of northern Arizona as a canvas for the spectacular Painted Desert. _____

   The Petrified Forest is like no other forest ever seen._____

   The Grand Canyon is one of nature's masterpieces. _____

2. *Many TV commercials are offensive.*

   Some TV commercials are irritating._____

   Although irritating commercials are offensive, they are not as offensive as insulting commercials._____

   The dangerous commercials are the worst TV commercials._____ .

3. *Children use a variety of forms to send secret messages to their friends.*

   One of the most common forms of children's secret writing involves the use of invisible ink. _____

   The word *cryptography* (krip-**TOG**-ruh-fee) comes from two Greek words that mean "to conceal" and "to write." _____

   Using a special made-up code is another popular form of children's secret writing. _____

4. *Recently several different kinds of Western hand-crafted cheeses have enjoyed a renaissance.*

   Young cheeses, such as fresh mozzarella and ricotta, are popular cheeses that have the delicate flavor of fresh milk. _____

   Soft-ripened cheeses, such as camellia and teleme, are favorites of people who like cheeses with edible rinds. _____

The semifirm cheeses that include gouda and crumbly blues sell well. _______

The hard cheeses, such as dry jack and parmesan, are popular grating cheeses. _______

5. *If you drive through Miles City, Montana, you will see why it is called the Cow Capital of the West.*

   The local radio station is KATL-AM._______

   Main Street is lined with bars with colorful names such as Range Riders Bar._______

   One bar sports longhorn steer heads and other turn-of-the-century bovine touches. _______

   They hold an annual bucking horse sale there. _______

6. *Barr Trail is a classic hiker's route up 14,110-foot Pikes Peak.*

   It is a long, rigorous climb._______

   The trail switchbacks through foothill, montane, and subalpine life zones. _______

   Pikes Peak is located in Manitou Springs, Colorado._______

7. *Being parents should be an Olympic event.*

   Running is one of their strong points._______

   They are masters of endurance. _______

   They are totally dedicated to their sport._______

8. *To have an enjoyable hike, always follow the Boy Scout motto, "Be Prepared."*

   Wearing shoes and clothes that are appropriate for the terrain and the climate is essential. _______

   Taking an adequate amount of water and appropriate food is part of being prepared. _______

   Encountering trail pests such as ticks and poison oak can spoil a hike._______

   Carrying maps, compass, knife, flashlight, and first aid kit is important. _______

9. *Two recent studies suggest that folate may be an element in preventing or treating certain illnesses.*

   The results of one study indicate that folate may reduce the risk of heart attack. _______

   One suggests possible links between folate and decreased risks of colon cancer._______

   Another study suggests possible links between folate and certain types of memory loss. _______

   Folate and folic acid are forms of the same B vitamin, but they are not exactly the same. _______

10. *Captain James Cook was one of England's great explorers.*

He explored the islands and coastlines of the Pacific._____

He discovered the Hawaiian Islands. _____

These islands were once called the Sandwich Islands._____

Cook claimed Australia and New Zealand for England._____

EXERCISE 20

Choose a viable thesis statement from a previous exercise and write three topic sentences that support it. Use the "because" or "for example" method to test each topic sentence.

Achieving Coherence

Just as careful writers strive for unity in paragraphs and essays, they strive for coherence too. *Coherence* is the logical ordering of the material. It is the glue that holds the composition together. The sentences in paragraphs and the paragraphs in essays need to be logically connected so that the result is consistent and satisfying. A composition is coherent when it follows a clear pattern and is tightly organized. To achieve coherence

- arrange sentences and paragraphs in a definite order

- use pronouns

- repeat key words

- use transitional words and expressions

- make structures parallel

▶ **Using Organizational Patterns**   Arrange the details according to a definite pattern (*time, place* or *space,* or *logical* relationship). Material presented in an organized form holds together and helps readers follow the development of the ideas.

Patterns of Development

Time	Ideas presented in the order in which they happen.
Place/Space	Ideas presented in relationship to the space they occupy.
Logical	Ideas presented in such a way that they grow out of each other.
General-to-Specific	General statement supported with specific details, examples, or reasons.
Specific-to-General	Series of details build to a general concluding statement.
Order of Importance	Least important idea to the most important idea. Most important idea to least important idea.
Familiar-to-Unfamiliar	Familiar concepts followed by less familiar concepts.
Problem-to-Solution	Problem followed by solution.
Question-to-Answer	Question in topic followed by answer.

Time Pattern   Time (also called *chronological*) order emphasizes the time sequence of events such as explaining how to do something, how something works, or a series of events that led to an event or condition. Use *time* order to relate the events in the order in which they happen or in the order in which they are revealed to you or in explanatory paragraphs where you are explaining the steps in a process. Use transitional words such as *at first, in the beginning, next, later,* and so on to more clearly establish the sequence of events.

Time Pattern Paragraph

The oldest of the important Southern cities was Richmond, the capital of Virginia. The site of Richmond was discovered by Captain John Smith and Captain Newport as they explored along the James River in 1607. The first permanent settlement made there was on land bought from the Indian chief Powhatan in 1609. Originally called "Nonesuch," it was later abandoned. In about 1645, Fort Charles was erected on the site. The fort was built for defense against the Indians. The city did not flourish until after 1733 when Colonel Byrd founded the town called Richmond. From that time until 1860, Richmond was the center of much of the charming plantation life of Old Virginia.

Space Pattern   Space (also called *spatial)* order helps readers form a picture in their minds such as a description of a scene, a work of art, or a person. Use *space* order in descriptive writing and in writing that deals with ideas about geography, layouts, designs, astronomy, and so on. Strive for a clear word picture that sticks together by showing exactly where the various items in the picture or scene are located. Use expressions such as *in the foreground, to the right, next to,* and so on. Clearly show how the parts of the picture are related spatially.

Space Pattern Paragraph

Hard by the farmhouse was a vast barn that might have served for a church, every window and crevice of which seemed bursting forth with the treasures of the farm: [my italics] The flail was busily resounding within it from morning to night; swallows and martins skimmed twittering about the eaves; the rows of pigeons. . . . were enjoying the sunshine on the roof. Sleek, unwieldy porkers were grunting in the repose and abundance of their pens. . . . A stately squadron of snowy geese were riding in an adjoining pond, convoying whole fleets of ducks. . . . Before the barn door strutted the gallant cock. . . . sometimes tearing up the earth with his feet, and then generously calling his ever-hungry family of wives and children to enjoy the rich morsel which he had discovered. —Washington Irving

Logical Patterns   These patterns include *general-to-specific, specific-to-general, importance, familiar-to-unfamiliar, problem-to-solution,* and *question-to-answer* orders.

General-to-Specific Patterns   These patterns are useful in comparison and contrast and cause and effect compositions. This presentation moves from the most general information to the most specific. It is a common way of organizing material.

General-to-Specific Paragraph

Initiative 695 protects taxpayers by requiring voter approval for any tax increase. [my italics] Most states limit excessive taxation, but Washington does not. With I-695, politicians must look at other options first: using existing revenues, utilizing tax surpluses, prioritizing programs. I-695 limits excessive taxation and offers the first meaningful tax relief to the little guy since the voters eliminated the sales tax on food 20 years ago. —Washington State Voters Pamphlet, 1999

Specific-to-General Plan   The specific-to-general order is less common. In this pattern, the details that support the topic sentence or thesis statement are presented first. This pattern is particularly useful in persuasive and argumentative writing.

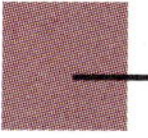 ### Specific-to-General Paragraph

In the first half of the nineteenth century, several million people moved into the Southern wilderness and transformed it into an important agricultural section. These Southerners adopted very different ways of working and living from their Northern countrymen. The Northern people were living more and more by manufacturing and trade; the Southerners were living almost entirely by farming. What was the reason for the difference between the two sections? In the South, the climate was favorable, and the land was level and fertile. There were nearly 400,000 square miles of land suitable for growing cotton. *It was the geography of the South that gave rise to the great cotton kingdom that so greatly affected the lives of the people.*

Order of Importance Pattern   The order of importance (also called *climactic*) pattern is a common way of presenting information. You may begin with the least important idea and move to the most important idea, or you may begin with the most important idea and move to the least important idea. Generally, in college writing, begin with the least important idea and save the most important idea for the end because, generally, you can expect your college audience to read the material in its entirety—not just scan it. On the other hand, if you are doing journalistic or business writing, you cannot be sure that your audience will not just scan the material. For these audiences, it is often a good idea to begin with the most important material and save the least important for the end, even if the result is a weak ending. In the following example, all the ideas are important, but the last one is clearly the most important.

 ### Order of Importance Pattern Paragraph

Several factors, mostly geographic, helped to turn the states north of the Ohio and east of the Mississippi into an industrial section. Power is essential for industrial growth, and the industrial section grew up in the Northeastern states largely because of water power in the hilly and mountainous country and coal and oil power in Pennsylvania, Ohio, Indiana, Illinois, and nearby regions. Just as power was necessary for manufacturing, it also required huge supplies of raw materials, particularly iron. The United States had great quantities of iron, and most of it was in the Northeastern states. In addition to the sources of power and the abundance of iron, the people of the Northeastern states had money to invest in manufacturing. The shipping business was declining, and ship owners and merchants who had made fortunes from the sea were willing to invest their capital in the new factories. Capital was necessary to turn natural resources into industry.

Familiar-to-Unfamiliar Pattern   Sometimes you may want to use the familiar-to-unfamiliar plan when you are explaining a process—how to do something or how something works. By beginning with something that is familiar to the audience, you can develop the process by showing the similarities and/or differences between what members of the audience know and what you want them to learn.

Familiar-to-Unfamiliar Pattern Paragraph

In criminal cases in the United States, accused people are entitled to their day in court. Both the accused and the government are represented by lawyers. Each lawyer presents his or her case, and a judge says what kinds of evidence and testimony are allowable. The jury decides whether the accused is guilty or innocent, and the judge sets the punishment if the jury finds the accused guilty. Civil cases are quite different. They are divided into two classes: breach of contract and tort. A contract is a legal agreement between two parties. If either party breaks that agreement, that party is guilty of breach of contract. A tort is any civil wrong that does not involve a breach of contract. The civil case begins when an accuser files a legal complaint against the accused. These cases are often not heard before a jury. Frequently, the judge hears the case and makes a decision as to who is guilty and then orders the guilty party to pay for any damages the injured party sustained.

Problem-to-Solution Pattern   This is an effective way of solving a problem or answering a question, but you must still choose the order in which you want to present the elements of the problem or question and the steps in the solution or answer. In this pattern, the problem is presented in the topic sentence or thesis statement, and the solution is offered in the supporting material.

Problem-to-Solution Pattern Paragraph

Initiative 695 goes too far. It does nothing to control government spending. We'd all like to pay lower taxes, but I-695 means that money for essential services must come from other sources. Most states with license tab fees as low as [those proposed by] I-695. . .make up the difference with an income tax. Is that what the voters of Washington State want? —Washington State Voters Pamphlet, 1999

Question-to-Answer Pattern   Ask a question in the topic sentence and answer it in the supporting material.

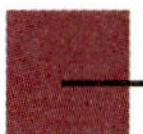 **Question-to-Answer Pattern Paragraph**

Do citizens have *rights and privileges that aliens do not have?* Yes, they do. They are able to vote and to serve on juries. They may decide which candidate gets elected and which accused person gets acquitted or punished. They can run for public office or hold certain federal government jobs. Aliens cannot run for public office or hold some federal jobs. Citizens may obtain licenses that aliens cannot obtain. When they travel abroad, they are protected by the U. S. government. Only U. S. citizens have this protection.

EXERCISE 21

Choose one of the following topics and write a paragraph of about 150 words. Begin with a topic sentence, and then develop it with supporting details. To make sure that the details will follow one another logically and smoothly, arrange them according to the plan that you think is the most appropriate for the topic.

1. A novel, an article, or short story that you have read recently.

2. The way your parent(s) taught you one virtue.

3. A high school's emphasis (too much or too little) on a sport.

4. Every college student should or should not engage in some extracurricular activity.

5. The major difficulty in learning a second language.

6. The difference between older buildings in the South and older buildings in the North.

7. Your favorite escape reading.

8. The role luck plays in a particular sport or event.

9. Wasting time.

10. The major advantage or disadvantage of working part-time while you are in school.

▶ **Strengthening Coherence** Strengthen coherence by using *pronouns; repeating key words; using transitional words, phrases,* or *clauses;* and *making structures parallel* to link or connect ideas. These structures help readers move smoothly from one idea to the next.

Pronouns   Use pronouns to link ideas together by referring to words or ideas in previous sentences. A *pronoun* is a word used in place of a noun or a noun substitute. Commonly used pronoun links are *he, she, they, this, that, these, those, them, it.* Sometimes the words *this, that, these,* and *those* are used as adjectives, but they still serve as linking words just as they do when they are used as pronouns. In the following passage, pronouns are italicized:

> Rene Descartes (day-**KART**) is often spoken of as "the father of modern philosophy." Descartes liked to stay in bed late every morning. *He* was not being lazy. *He* was thinking. *He* got into this habit when *he* was a boy because *he* was a weak child. Because Jesuit fathers were concerned about *his* health, *they* granted *him* special privileges. Even as a boy, *he* did so much thinking for *himself* that *he* would take nothing for granted that *these* priests taught *him*.

Key Words   Repeat key words to link ideas, but use them sparingly because writing becomes dull when they are overused. To avoid overuse of key words, use different forms of them and use synonyms. In the following introduction to Eli Whitney's letter to his father and excerpts from the letter, the key word *invention* is repeated and is referred to by a variety of other words which are italicized:

> In 1792 Eli Whitney, a young schoolteacher, had a *brilliant idea* which was to change the agricultural produce of the South and to a considerable extent the textile industry of New England. After being graduated from Yale, he accepted a teaching position in a small town in the South. On his way there, he changed his plans and gave up teaching altogether. He wrote his father the following letter in which he tells him about his change of plans and about his *invention:*

> Dear Parent—

> . . .During this time I heard much said of the extreme difficulty of ginning cotton, that is, separating it from its seeds. There were a number of very respectable gentlemen at Mrs. Greene's who all agreed that if a *machine* would be invented which would clean cotton with expedition, *it* would be a great *thing* both to the country and to the inventor. I involuntarily happened to be thinking on the *subject* and struck out a plan of a *machine* in my mind, which I communicated to Miller; he was pleased with the *plan* and if *it* would answer, he would be at the whole expense. . . . In about ten days I made a little *model,* for which I was offered, if I would give up all right and title to *it,* a hundred guineas. I concluded to relinquish my school and turn my attention to perfecting the *machine.* I made *one* before I came away which required the labor of one man to turn *it.* . . . One man and a horse will do more than fifty men with the old machines. *It* makes the labor fifty times less, without throwing any class of people out of the business.

Transitional Words and Expressions   Use transitional words and expressions to connect preceding material with material that is to follow. They serve as bridges between what has been said and what follows and keep the ideas flowing. The following list groups transitional expressions according to their relationships. They show time, place, and logical relationships.

Transitional Words and Expressions and the Relationships They Express

RELATIONSHIP	WORDS AND EXPRESSIONS
Time	*afterwards, again, as soon as, at first, at last, at length, at the same time, before, currently, earlier, eventually, finally, first, immediately, later, meanwhile, next, now, second, soon, subsequently, third, then, until*
Place	*above, across, adjacent, below, beside, beyond, here, in the front, in the back, in the background, nearby, next to, there*
Logical	
Addition	*also, and, besides, equally important, finally, furthermore, in addition, moreover, too, then*
Consequence	*accordingly, as a result, because, consequently, since, so, then, therefore*
Difference	*although, but, despite, even though, however, in contrast, instead, meanwhile, nevertheless, nonetheless, on the contrary, on the other hand, still, whereas, yet*
Concession	*admittedly, certainly, granted, indeed, of course, to be sure*
Example	*for example, for instance, namely, specifically, thus*
Result	*accordingly, as a result, so, therefore, thus*
Similarity	*also, by the same token, in comparison, likewise, similarly*
Summary	*finally, hence, in brief, in conclusion, in short, in summary*
Result	*accordingly, as a result, so, therefore, thus*
Similarity	*also, by the same token, in comparison, likewise, similarly*
Summary	*finally, hence, in brief, in conclusion, in short, in summary*

In the following passage the **transitional words and expressions** are italicized.

In 1709 there were few power-driven machines in America. In England, *however,* textile machines were coming into use, and the steam engine was a commercial success. *Consequently,* the English were producing more goods with less labor. These new time-saving, money-making machines were not unknown to the colonists, for newly arrived emigrants from Europe and colonists who had visited England and returned brought word of them. England, *however,* did not want other countries to have these machines; *therefore,* the English passed a law to prevent not only the machines from leaving the country, but the plans and drawings of the machines as well. *Admittedly,* the English prevented the machines and plans from leaving the country, but they could not prevent mechanics from memorizing the plans of the machinery. When Samuel Slater, an English weaver and an excellent mechanic, came to the United States, he brought with him considerable knowledge of weaving. *More importantly, however,* he brought within his head the plans for the machines. *Soon,* he built machines that carded and spun, and *before* a year had passed, his mill was running successfully. The establishment of Slater's cotton mill marked an important point in the development of the industrial revolution in America.

EXERCISE 22

Underline the pronouns, repeated key words, and transitional expressions in the following sentences. [sentence numbers have been added.]

1. What is the worth of liberty? 2. Within the limits of this inquiry all that I propose to say on the present occasion will be confined. 3. Of course, I refer mainly to civil liberty, although I do not exclude all reference to liberty in its most spiritual relations. 4. I do not attempt to define liberty either civil or moral. 5. What civil liberty is we all practically comprehend; and if we do not, defining it would not enable us. 6. I will simply mention the following as a few of the attributes that belong to it: supremacy of the law; equality of all before the law; the representation of all in the enactment or changes of the law. 7. To these we may add the provisions which wisdom and experience suggest by which such conditions can be most thoroughly attained and most inviolately preserved. —Henry Giles "On the Worth of Liberty"

Parallel Structures To strengthen coherence, put all items in a series and list in parallel form. Such parallelism makes the material easier to read, smoother, and more effective. Items are parallel when they are consistent in form. To make elements parallel, put nouns with nouns, adjectives with adjectives, prepositional phrases with prepositional phrases, *to + a verb* phrases with *to + a verb* phrases, *-ing* words with *-ing* words, and so on. Do not mix the forms. The following mixed forms are from student papers.

Mixed   Basketball is a game of skill that requires *good conditioning, basic skills,* and *to know the rules.*

Parallel   Basketball is a game of skill that requires *being in good condition, having the basic skills,* and *knowing the rules of the game.*

Mixed   *Taking responsibility* for my own actions, *the Golden Rule,* and *not lying* are values that have shaped my life.

Parallel   *Taking responsibility* for my own actions, *practicing the Golden Rule,* and *not lying* are values that have shaped my life.

Mixed   To successfully make this dish, you must *have the necessary ingredients, preparation,* and *correct cooking instructions.*

Parallel   To successfully make this dish, you must *assemble the necessary ingredients, prepare them properly,* and *cook them according to the instructions.*

In the following quotation from Dr. Martin Luther King's speech "I Have a Dream," the *parallel phrases* are italicized:

I have a dream that one day *every valley shall be exalted, every hill and mountain shall be made low, the rough places shall be made plain,* and *the crooked places shall be made straight* and the glory of the Lord will be revealed and all flesh shall see it together.

Note: For a more complete discussion of parallelism, see Part 4: Using Parallelism (p. 220).

EXERCISE 23

In the following sentences, change the mixed forms to parallel forms.

1. Within our minds we arrange our perceptions and thoughts into what we call concepts. The ideas of justice, courage, and practicing self-restraint are concepts.

2. Many of our ideas depend on what we have been taught by those around us; and what they teach us depends on when we are born, where we are born, and the status of our parents.

3. Our ideas change with time. Once people thought men had a right to have more than one wife and that it was all right for parents to sacrifice their children to the gods.

4. Years ago a person could be imprisoned, tortured, and being put to death for stealing.

5. Plato said, "No real evil can ever happen to a good man, and it is worse to do an act of injustice than being treated unjustly."

6. Plato knew that good people may suffer pain, losing their property, and being treated unjustly.

7. He did not consider these things to be real evils. He felt that the only real evil was thinking an unjust or unkind thought or to do an unjust or unkind act.

8. Aristotle was the son of the court physician at King Philip of Macedon's court, was Plato's most brilliant student, and tutored the young prince who became Alexander the Great.

9. After Alexander became king, Aristotle returned to Athens, establishing a school there and teaching his students as they walked with him.

10. Socrates wanted to make the world better by leading his students to think truer and higher thoughts, and Plato wanted to do the same by planning a better form of government; however, Aristotle's plan to improve the world included widening the sum of knowledge.

▶ **Linking Paragraphs Together in an Essay**   Your paragraphs need to be linked together to prevent awkward gaps between them as you move from one idea to the next. To prevent this gap and move smoothly from one idea to the next, always include a reference in one paragraph that will be the topic of the next paragraph. One way of doing this is to introduce a point in the last sentence of one paragraph and then expand on it in the first sentence of the next paragraph. The expanded sentence is often called a *transitional sentence*. It may function purely as a transition, or it may also function as a transition and as the topic sentence of the new paragraph. Sometimes the transitional sentence may be delayed, but it still links the two paragraphs. In the following sentences, the linking words or phrases in the two paragraphs are italicized.

Transition Only

Last sentence in a paragraph: That's mainly what happens in Miller commercials: Burly American men go around, drenched in perspiration, *shaking each other's hands* in a violent and patriotic fashion.

First sentence in next paragraph: You never find out exactly why these men spend so much time *shaking hands*. —Dave Barry, from "Red, White, and Beer"

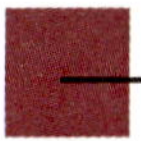

Transition and Topic Sentence

Last sentence in a paragraph: *Democracies,* with no models of high breeding before them, *at least escape the necessity of daily looking at bad copies thereof.*

First sentence in next paragraph: *Democracies manners are never so refined as among aristocracies,* but they are also never so coarse. —Alexis de Tocqueville, from "Some Reflections on American Manners"

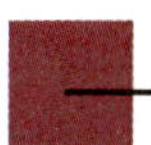

Delayed Transition

Last sentence in a paragraph: When we saw a movie in class, everybody won: teachers didn't have to teach, and pupils didn't have to learn. I suspect that *classroom computers are popular today for the same reasons.*

First sentence in next paragraph: Most important, educators should learn what parents and most teachers already know: you cannot teach a child anything unless you look him in the face. *We should not forget what computers are.* —David Gelernter, from "Unplugged: The Myth of Computers in the Classroom"

▶ **Checking Coherence**   After you have written a paragraph or an essay, check it for coherence. Do you have a viable topic sentence in a paragraph and a viable thesis statement in an essay? What pattern of development did you use? If you used one of the logical patterns, which one was it? Have you followed that pattern throughout the paper? Have you used pronouns, repeated key words, and used transitional expressions to help your readers move smoothly through the paper? If you have any lists, items in a series, or compound structures, check them. Are they parallel? Have you balanced nouns with nouns, prepositional phrases with prepositional phrases, main clauses with main clauses, and so on? When you are checking an essay, make sure that the paragraphs are smoothly linked together.

EXERCISE 24

The following essay was written by an ESL student who was taking her first mainstream English course in college. She was responding to the following prompt: "Write a five-paragraph essay (about 500 words) explaining how to do something. Be sure that you give your readers a rationale for their needing this information." Is the essay coherent? Can you identify the pattern that she uses to present the material? Does she repeat words and use pronouns and transitional words, expressions, and sentences? Can you identify them? Do the transitional sentences serve only as transitions, or do they also serve as topic sentences?

Secrets of a Successful Camping Trip

Imagine the discomfort, frustration, disappointment, and anger that you might experience on a camping trip. After looking forward to it for weeks, or even months, it could be completely ruined because you did not have a plan or were not sufficiently prepared for it. Forgetting small, but important things, can lead to problems if something unexpected happens. The vacation place may turn out to be a complete disappointment if you know nothing about it. Planning for a successful trip is important because your enjoyment depends on it. The three things that you should keep in mind when getting ready for a camping trip are scheduling, picking a suitable place, and packing.

Setting up a schedule is important because it will help you manage your time wisely. Choose the days for your vacation. After you make that decision, pick the time and day you are going to leave and the approximate day you need to return. Remember that every hour counts. Plan your trip with care. Let your family know where you are going to be at certain times so that they can find you in case of an emergency.

After you have prepared your schedule, you need to find out as much information as you can about the place you want to visit. What is the climate there? What kind of activities can you do while there? Are there any wild animals you should know about? Is water available? Are bathrooms available? Getting the answers to these questions will help you be more prepared. Choosing the place and finding out information about it is important because it is the main reason you are taking time off to go there.

When the schedule and all information about your vacation place are complete, you are ready to pack. Depending on the time of year you are going on the camping trip and on the characteristics of the place you are planning to visit, you will select what to take with you. Make sure you do not leave anything behind. All those small things such as a flashlight, matches, pocket knife, hat, extra clothes, blankets, and first aid kit will help make your trip more enjoyable and will be most useful in case of an emergency.

Trying to schedule a trip, deciding on the destination, and packing your gear on the morning of your departure is not a good idea. You will be stressed about the scheduling and the destination, and more than likely you will forget some essential gear. To prevent almost certain disaster, set up a schedule for the trip several weeks in advance. Get all the information that you can about the destination in advance. Pack several days before you plan to leave home. Remember, the success of your camping trip depends on the way you plan and prepare for it.

—Svetlana Scherbinskaya, Student

Adequately Developing Paragraphs and Essays

▶ **A Fully Developed Paragraph**   A paragraph is the development of the controlling idea in the topic sentence. Although there is no absolute rule about the length of a paragraph, generally you can adequately develop a viable topic sentence in about 150 words. If your one-paragraph composition contains fewer than 100 words, it may not contain enough material to be convincing, or the topic sentence may not be viable because it is too narrow. If your paragraph contains more than 200 or 250 words, it may contain material that does not support the topic sentence, or the topic sentence may not be viable because it is either too broad or contains more than one idea. To be adequately developed, a paragraph must contain enough information to make the controlling idea in the topic sentence clear and convincing.

▶ **A Fully Developed Essay**   As in a paragraph, there is no absolute rule about the length of an essay. Generally, for most college work, a viable thesis sentence can be fully developed in about 500 words. If an essay contains fewer than 400 words, it may not have enough information to be convincing, or the thesis may be too narrow. If an essay contains 600 or 700 words, it may contain irrelevant material that does not support the thesis, or the thesis may be too broad, or it may contain more than one idea. Essays may be made up of a few paragraphs or several. One of the most common essays is the five-paragraph essay that uses three points to develop the thesis sentence. It contains an introductory paragraph, three body paragraphs, and an ending paragraph. (*See* Appendix A: Shaping a Five-Paragraph Essay, p. 501.)

▶ **Titles**   A title is important because it is the first thing your readers see. Choose a title carefully. You want to arouse your readers' interest, but not overburden them with information. Look for an appropriate title in the composition. Often the topic sentence or thesis statement contains words that may be used in the title. A common mistake college students make is using their topic for a title. Topics used as titles are generally boring, do not arouse interest, and give away too much information.

Topic How to Have a Successful Date   **Title** Date Rating

Topic Comparing and Contrasting Two Neighbors   **Title** Drumming Dan and Warring Wes

Topic The Importance of Taking Class Notes   **Title** Getting Your "A" Out of a Class

In addition to looking in your own writing for a title, the Bible, Greek tragedies, and the works of Shakespeare are excellent title sources. Often you can use titles that allude to some well known piece of writing to give your readers additional information or to create certain expectations.

"Female Athletes: They've Come a Long Way, Baby"—P. S. Wood

This quote alludes to the Virginia Slims advertisement, "You've Come a Long Way, Baby."

Note: Instructor preference varies when it comes to titling paragraphs. Check with your instructor before titling a paragraph. For correct title form, see Appendix A: Formatting College Papers (p. 499).

Writing Introductory Paragraphs

An introductory paragraph contains *a lead-in, background information, a thesis sentence,* and *a plan of development.* The lead-in gets the readers' attention. The background gives them the information they need to understand why the essay is being written. The thesis statement gives direction to the entire essay. The plan of development lets the readers know how and in what order the essay is going to be developed.

▶ **Lead-Ins**   A lead-in is important because it gets the readers' attention, and unless you get their attention right away, they may not read the essay. In college, your instructors and peers read your material, even if it is not interesting. In real life, most people will not read material that is not interesting. To make a lead-in interesting, think about your purpose and your audience, and use a lead-in that will further your purpose and appeal to your audience. Following is a list of frequently used lead-ins with definitions and examples.

Frequently Used Lead-Ins

Allusion   *An indirect reference to a person or thing that is probably familiar to the audience.* It's the worst of times; it's the best of times. That's how we feel as we navigate from a paternal society, now discredited, to a society in which impulse is given its way. —Robert Bly, "A World of Half-Adults" (The reference is to the opening lines of *A Tale of Two Cities* by Charles Dickens: "It was the best of times, it was the worst of times. . . .")

Analogy   *A comparison suggesting similarities between things that are otherwise dissimilar.* A colony of ants is like an army.

Description   *Usually words that appeal to the senses used to intensify a mood or impression.* A black father, a black mother, and a black child tramped through muddy fields, leading a tired cow by a thin bit of rope. —Richard Wright

A list of related examples   *A list of examples that are connected to the topic.* When I was a boy, there was but one permanent ambition among my comrades in our village on the west bank of the Mississippi River. That was, to be a steamboatman. We had transient ambitions of other sorts, but they were only transient. When a circus came and went, it left us all burning to become clowns; the first Negro minstrel show that ever came to our section left us all suffering to try that kind of life; now and then we had a hope that, if we lived and were good, God would permit us to be pirates. These ambitions faded out, each in its turn; but the ambition to be a steamboatman always remained. —Mark Twain, "The Cub-Pilot"

Personal experience   *A short story or anecdote taken from the life of the writer.* There were moments in that jail when the confinement and heat nearly drove me mad. At those times, I desperately needed to take my thoughts beyond the concrete and steel. When I felt restless tension rising, I'd try anything to calm it. I'd slap-box with other inmates until I got exhausted, or play chess until my mind shut down. When all else failed, I'd pace the cellblock perimeter like a caged lion. Sometimes, other inmates fighting the temptation to give in to madness joined me, and we'd pace together, round and round, and talk for hours about anything that got our minds off our misery. —Nathan McCall, "Makes Me Wanna Holler"

Question   *A question that causes readers to think or reflect on the topic.* So? Are you just back? Or are you, perhaps, staying on there for the extra week? By "there" I mean, of course, one of the few spots left where the machine has not yet gained the upper hand. . . . —Brigid Brophy, "The Menace of Nature"

Quotation   *The words of another person that shed light on the topic or support the writer's point.* When I was a child, I spake as a child, I understood as a child, I thought as a child; but when I became a man, I put away childish things. —Corinthians 13:11

Startling statement or statistic   *A statement that shocks or forcefully calls the readers' attention to a topic.* In Moulmein, in Lower Burma, I was hated by large numbers of people—the only time in my life that I have been important enough for this to happen to me. —George Orwell, "Shooting an Elephant"

Statement of a problem or a common misconception   *A brief description of a problem or an explanation of something that is often misunderstood.* The name Wyoming comes from an Indian word meaning "at the great plains," but the plains are really valleys, great arid valleys, 1600 square miles, with the horizon bending up on all sides into mountain ranges. This gives the vastness a sheltering look. —Gretel Ehrlich, "Wyoming: The Solace of Open Spaces"

Statement of common interests   *A statement that connects the readers to the topic through a common experience.* My son has never met a sport he did not like. I have met a few that left an ugly tingle—boxing and rodeo and pistol shooting, among others—but then, I have been meeting them for forty-four years, Jesse only for twelve. Our ages are relevant to the discussion, because, on the hill of the sporting life, Jesse is midway up the slope and climbing rapidly, while I am over the crest and digging in my heels as I slip down. — Scott Russsell Sanders, "Reasons of the Body" (This lead-in would probably be of interest to athletes, young boys, or middle-aged fathers.)

Statement of fact or opinion   *A clear statement of something that is true or a statement of the writer's opinion.* I am not sure where to classify the mind of my cat Jeoffry. He is a small Abyssinian cat, a creature of elegance, grace, and poise, a piece of moving sculpture, and a total mystery. —Lewis Thomas, "Crickets, Bats, Cats, & Chaos"

Story or joke   *A brief narrative account of an incident, personal or otherwise, that is directly related to the topic.* For the ultimate in food as pageantry, you must go to the Ahwahnee Hotel in Yosemite National Park for their annual Christmas Bracebridge Dinner. Getting here, though, is a matter of chance. There's an elaborate lottery system through which the lucky (one in ten) participants are chosen. Originally (in 1927, to be exact), a special dinner— "to enhance and dignify the Christmas season for Yosemite guests"—was planned. The following year, a drama director from San Francisco was brought in to produce the first Bracebridge Dinner, a Christmas festival based on Old Christmas: From the Sketch Book of Washington Irving. —Alice M. Geffen & Carole Berglie, *Food Festival The Guidebook to America's Best Regional Food Celebrations*

▶ **Background**   You will probably want to give a brief overview of the subject and a summary of basic facts. Keep the background information as short as possible. The amount of information will vary. Let the makeup of the audience determine the extent of the information you supply. If the audience knows a great deal about the topic, then you will only need to give limited information. If the members of the audience are unfamiliar with the topic, then you will have to supply them with enough information so that they can understand the subject and your purpose.

> What we are just beginning to realize is the false implication of the word disposable. Matter is indestructible, not disposable. . . . and it will remain so for practical purposes until some method is discovered for applying the magic formula to a garbage dump. . . . What we manufacture we are not even in practical terms disposing of. We are merely moving it somewhere else or turning it into something different but still not disposable.

> —Joseph W. Krutch, "Our Values Hurt the Environment"

▶ **Thesis Statement and Plan of Development**   After you have written the lead-in and the appropriate background, write the *thesis statement* and the *plan of development* (POD). The plan of development lists the main points that support the thesis statement. It may be a separate sentence, or it may be included in the thesis statement. Some instructors want students to write separate sentences. Others want them to combine the thesis and plan, and some have no preference. Check with your instructor before you begin writing an introductory paragraph to determine his or her preference.

Separate thesis	<u>The industrial revolution in America</u> *brought about many changes in most people's lives.*
Separate POD	*The hours of labor, the standard of living, and the length of life were among the many changes.* (least important to most important pattern)
Combined thesis and POD	<u>The industrial revolution in America</u> *brought about many changes in most people's lives, including the number of hours people had to work, their standard of living, and the length of their lives.*

When you write a POD, use as many points as you intend to develop to support your thesis. Use a three-point POD to develop a five-paragraph essay; use a two-point POD to develop a four-paragraph essay, and so on. Always list the points in the order that you intend to develop them.

Three-point POD	<u>South Dakota</u> is *famous* for *The Badlands, Crazy Horse Memorial,* and *Mt. Rushmore National Memorial.*
Two-point POD	<u>South Dakota</u> is *famous* for its two great memorials: *Mt. Rushmore* and *Crazy Horse.*
Combined thesis and two-point POD	The <u>colonists</u> were *concerned about two important political issues:* the method *of choosing the governor* and the *way the governing power should be divided between the governor and the assembly.*

EXERCISE 25

1. Choose a viable thesis statement in a previous exercise; choose an appropriate pattern of development, and write a one-sentence three-point plan.

2. Which plan did you choose and why?

3. Write a topic sentence for each of the three points in your POD.

4. Use the think "because" or "for example" method to test the topic sentences for unity.

Writing Unified, Coherent Body Paragraphs

To fully develop a thesis sentence, write a body paragraph for each point in your plan of development. A body paragraph is a one-paragraph composition that supports the thesis statement by developing one point in the plan of development. Keep the body paragraphs balanced. Do not give too many details in one body paragraph—usually the first one—and skimp on the details in the other paragraphs. A body paragraph is unified when all the sentences in it fully and logically support the controlling idea in the topic sentence. In a coherent body paragraph, the sentences in it are logically and smoothly related to the topic sentence.

Writing Concluding Paragraphs

Avoid writing weak endings by introducing new material or including expressions such as *I am not an expert, but in my opinion, this essay proves, I think, I believe,* and so on. Strive for a well-balanced ending. The ending paragraph should reinforce the ideas developed in the essay. The following techniques are commonly used by successful writers—sometimes separately and sometimes combined.

1. Restate the thesis and summarize the major points.

   This all sounds angry; it is. After a lifetime spent with winds of sexual change buffeting me this way and that, it still makes me angry to read the same dumb quotes with the same dumb stereotypes that I was reading when I was 18. It makes me angry to realize that after so much change, very little is different. It makes me angry to think that these two female sanitation workers will spend their days doing a job most of their co-workers think they can't handle, and then they will go home and do another job most of their co-workers don't want. —Anna Quindlen, "It's Not That I Don't Like Men."

2. Explain the importance of the subject.

   It is hard to imagine anything worse than being murdered while neighbors do nothing. But something worse exists. When those same neighbors shrink back from justly punishing the murderer, the victim dies twice. —Edward I. Koch, "Death and Justice: How Capital Punishment Affirms Life"

3. Make a prediction or give a warning.

   Perhaps no-parole life sentences for certain sex crimes would be a more straightforward answer. In any event, such laws offer our only hope against an epidemic of sexual violence that threatens to pollute our society beyond the possibility of its own rehabilitation. —Andrews Vachss, "Sex Predators Can't Be Saved"

4. Call for action.

   By linking homelessness to poverty, advocates obscure the real root of the problem. If we really wanted to help the homeless, we would pay far more attention to their mental health and substance abuse problems. —Joseph Perkins, "Homeless: Expose the Myths"

5. Summarize the broad implications of the subject.

   Perhaps the reason American education has declined so markedly is because America has raised a generation of part-time students. And perhaps our economy will continue to decline as full-time students from Japan and Europe continue to out-perform our part-time students. —Walter S. Minot, "Students who Push Burgers"

6. End with a question or questions that will make readers think about what you have said.

   When I am through with school and have a job, I want my wife to quit working and remain at home so that my wife can more fully and completely take care of a wife's duties.

   My God, who wouldn't want a wife? —Judy Syfers, "I Want a Wife"

7. Illustrate the thesis by using an anecdote, joke, or quotation.

> And while both substances have been implicated in auto accidents, Frank Chaloupka, an economist at the Chicago campus of the University of Illinois, believes that substitution of marijuana is, on balance, a life saver. In a statistical analysis. . . . he found that states without criminal sanctions against marijuana possession suffered fewer auto fatalities.
>
> "If the choice is more marijuana use or more dead teen-agers," Mrs. Reuter concludes, "the choice is easy."
>
> —Peter Passell, "Less Marijuana, More Alcohol?"

Note: As the first sentence in the introductory paragraph is key, the last sentence in the concluding paragraph is key. Since it is the last thing the readers see, always try to make it memorable. Sometimes writers even separate the final sentence from the rest of the ending paragraph (items 6 and 7 in preceding list) to emphasize it.

Developing Different Kinds of Paragraphs and Essays

All writing may be divided into the four following modes (*manners of development*):

Exposition	Explaining
Argumentation	Attempting to convince or persuade
Narration	Telling a story
Description	Painting a mental picture with words—exploration through the senses

Often you will use a combination of modes to express your ideas; however, generally, one type will be dominate. Your reason for writing and what you write go hand in hand. The reason determines the kinds of material you use and the way you organize it. You may use definitions, explanations, details that appeal to the emotions, details that appeal to the intellect, statistics, facts, opinions of experts, and so on.

Exposition

Expository writing—also called *informative* writing—includes compositions developed by

■ **Example**	Supporting the thesis with examples—illustrating ideas
■ **Process Analysis**	Explaining how to do something or how something works
■ **Comparison and Contrast**	Showing the similarities or differences of two or more subjects
■ **Cause and Effect**	Connecting reasons and results
■ **Definition**	Explaining what a word or expression means
■ **Division and Classification**	Breaking an item into parts and separating parts according to likeness

▶ **Example**   The use of examples to support or illustrate a given point is one of the most common methods of development. Often when we make a point, either in writing or in speech, we support that point with examples.

Paragraph Developed by Example   Illustrations or examples are used to support the topic sentence by showing, proving, or explaining it. When you develop a topic sentence into an example paragraph, you may use one example or several. To develop an effective paragraph, always use well-detailed, concrete examples to support and clarify your point. In the following paragraph, several examples support and clarify the author's point: The English language contains words and phrases that cause difficulty for non-native speakers of the language because these expressions are used to express totally different concepts.

Professional Example Paragraph

To be fair, English is full of booby traps for the unwary foreigner. Any language where the unassuming word *fly* signifies an annoying insect, a means of travel, and a critical part of a gentleman's apparel is clearly asking to be mangled. Imagine being a foreigner and having to learn that in English one tells *a* lie but [one tells] *the* truth, that a person who says "I could care less" means the same thing as someone who says, "I couldn't care less," that a sign in a store saying ALL ITEMS NOT ON SALE doesn't mean literally what it says (that every item is *not* on sale) but rather that only some of the items are on sale, that when a person says to you, "How do you do?" he will be taken aback if you reply, with impeccable logic, "How do I do what?"

—Bill Bryson, *Mother Tongue*

Writing Suggestions

Use one of the following topics and write an example paragraph.

1. The advantages or disadvantages of body piercing

2. A lesson learned from an unlikely source

3. Hair style makes the person

4. Following fads pays big dividends

5. The feature that you find most attractive in the opposite sex

Essay Developed by Example   When you develop an essay by examples, introduce the thesis statement—a general statement or a question—and develop it by giving specific examples in the body paragraphs to illustrate it. The following essay was written by a Head Start student in response to prompt 5 in the following writing suggestions. In this essay, he illustrates the point that he came to know and respect his deceased grandfather through reliving his childhood memories and listening to family stories. The three body paragraphs support the thesis by illustrating the way the writer learned about his grandfather's personality, his hardships, and his capacity for love.

Student Example Essay

The Best Man I Never Knew

I was too young to know my grandfather on a man-to-man basis. I was only seven when he died. My memories are a few things I have left of him—memories of his waking me early in the morning and taking me to the garden to pick raspberries for the breakfast my grandmother was already cooking. I never picked the raspberries. I just kicked the puffy seeds of spent dandelions while Grandfather found the reddest, juiciest berries. Occasionally, he would stop and give me a handful of the choice pick. Reliving my childhood memories and hearing family stories about Grandfather have enabled me to get to know him better even though he is gone. From the memories and stories, I have learned about his personality, his hardships, and his capacity for love.

My grandfather had an ambivalent personality. He was a tight-wad, a penny pincher, and a bullheaded man; yet he was a most generous man. Every time my grandfather bought something he haggled over the price with the salesperson. However, if I or any of the other grandchildren needed new clothes, we got them—from Grandfather. I remember opening up a large package and finding a new winter jacket with the pockets stuffed with candy bars. I called to tell him how much I liked it, and he replied that the postage was too high. I once heard him haggling over a bag of potatoes, trying to save ten cents. However, when my uncle needed a loan for a new house my grandfather handed him a blank check and told him to find a place with a yard so the kids would have a place to play.

Perhaps Grandfather was both stingy and generous because of his rough childhood. Perhaps he had lost so much that he wanted to save as much as he could, yet he was generous to his family because he never knew how long his family was going to be there. When he was only seventeen, his mother, a brother, and two sisters died from spinal meningitis. They died within two weeks of each other. My grandfather was left with his dad and brother to manage a large farm in North Dakota. The farm rarely produced an adequate crop, so often they were cold and hungry during the winter months. With half a family and no money, he worked his way through seminary by cutting hair—not exactly the easy way to become a minister.

The stories I hear most often are about his love for his church, his God, and his family. In his later years, as a Lutheran minister, his mission in life was to promote and raise funds for the Tacoma Lutheran Home and Retirement Community. He devoted countless hours working on this project. It was a testament to his faith and his love for God. However, he also worked tirelessly on the retirement home for my grandmother because he felt sure that she would outlive him, and he wanted to take care of her after he was gone. The home was built, and my grandmother has lived there for the past five years.

The last time I saw Grandfather was at Tacoma General Hospital. He had cancer. The whole family was there—in a cramped little room. The door opened, and Grandfather was wheeled in. Pale, thin, and with tubes coming out of his nose, he asked his grandchildren to sing a song to him. We sang "Jesus Loves the Little Children," and his eyes filled with tears. Afterwards, he gave each of us a Tootsie-pop—mine was raspberry. He died shortly thereafter. I feel closer to him and feel I know him better when I remember him and think of the stories about his ambivalent personality, indescribable hardships, and his extraordinary love for his family. I never knew Grandfather on a man-to-man basis, but I wish I had.

—Philip J. Wilson

Thinking and Discussing

1. Is the title effective?

2. What kind of lead-in does the writer use?

3. Can you clearly identify the elements in the introductory paragraph (lead-in, background, thesis, and plan of development)?

4. Does each body paragraph have a topic sentence? If so, are all topic sentences fully supported?

5. Is the last sentence memorable?

6. What conclusions can you draw about the writer's values?

Writing Suggestions

Choose one of the following prompts and write a five-paragraph example essay using illustrations to support your thesis statement.

1. People are often judged by the company they keep.

2. From my experience, the old saying "You can't judge a book by its cover" is true (or it is not true).

3. I have learned more from my failures than from my successes.

4. Through hard work and perseverance, I have turned my dreams (or a dream) into reality.

5. Choose a person you admire—living or dead—and write an essay explaining why you admire that person.

6. The perfect mate for you.

7. The advantages or disadvantages of owning a particular pet.

8. Explain the basis for your enjoyment of your favorite sport.

9. Absence does or does not make the heart grow fonder.

10. Frustrations of being in a new environment such as city, state, country, school, or neighborhood.

▶ **Process Analysis**   Generally, use a time order plan to develop a process analysis paper. Use this type of development to show how something works, how something happened, or how to perform a process.

Paragraph Developed by Process Analysis   A process paragraph explains how something is done (directional) or how something happens (informational). It often involves both narration and description. When you develop a process paragraph, give the directions or explanations step-by-step in the appropriate order. In the following directional paragraph, the writer, a skilled bass fisherman—who thought he had nothing to write about until the instructor asked him what he did in his leisure time—introduces the topic of fishing, and then makes the point that he is going to teach the reader how to fish successfully.

Student Directional Process Paragraph

Have you ever gone bass fishing and got skunked? Well, here are three ways to prevent getting skunked. First, you must find the fish. You can do this by using high tech sonar equipment or by casting and retrieving a series of lures at a series of depths. Usually, bass will be near the bank. On a sunny day, they will be close to cover because the sun hurts their sensitive eyes. On a cloudy day, they will be in more open water searching for food. Cloudy days are usually the best days for catching bass. Second, you need to determine the type of bait that is attractive to them. Most of the time bass will bite any big hunk of meaty-looking food that swims by; however, at other times they can be very picky and will bite only the most realistic lures. By means of trial and error, find out what the bass want, and give it to them. Finally, you have to know how to use the lure you have selected. You must find out how deep to use the lure, the speed to use, and finally the appropriate presentation technique. Once you have mastered these steps, you should be a successful angler. Remember, always catch and release.

—Dan Caffrey

In the following informational process paragraph, the first sentence of the paragraph lets the readers know that they are going to be told how our numbering system came into being. Then, the writer chronologically traces its evolution. Although he was a reluctant English student—taking the course because it was required—he found this assignment enjoyable because he could talk about his interest in numbers.

Student Informational Process Paragraph

Two Plus Two Equals Four

The road to developing the number system that we use today was a long and arduous one. The development of a counting system arose in response to practical needs. People needed some way of keeping track of things: Early people used their fingers for counting, just as children often do today. At first they made plain marks such as // for two, //// for four, and so on. These plain marks did not allow them to write large numbers. Eventually, some ancient people—probably the Egyptians—invented a special mark that looked liked an upside down U that they used to represent ten. They could add the plain marks to the upside down U and write larger numbers such as ////U (14) or ////UUU (34). With this system, they could count by the hundreds. The Babylonians used wedge-shaped marks on soft clay tablets (and counted by sixties in the same way that we count minutes and seconds today) to keep track of the goods in the temple storehouses. Throughout history, different peoples have used other ways of counting—some by twos, some by fives, and some by twenties. Most Europeans, however, like the Egyptians, have always counted by tens because of the ten fingers on two hands. The Romans, who learned from the Egyptians and Phoenicians, made up a new system that was easier than the other European systems. Eventually, the Arabs gave Europe the Arabic numerals that we use today. Actually, the Arabs did not invent the numerals. They came from the Hindus in India who taught them to the Arabs, and the Arabs gave them to the world.

—Bill Lloyd

Writing Suggestions

Choose one of the following topics and write a process paragraph.

1. How to bathe a hermit crab or some other unusual pet

2. How to effectively deal with a rude person or one who asks impolite questions

3. How a particular play in some sport is executed

4. How a piece of equipment works

5. How to do some common task

Essay Developed by Process Analysis   See "Secrets of a Successful Camping Trip," (p. 60). In this essay the student explains the process of planning a successful camping trip. She uses a time order pattern and focuses on three aspects of planning: scheduling, choosing a destination, and packing.

Writing Suggestions

Choose one of the following prompts and write a five-paragraph process essay. Your instructor may ask you to write either an instructional or informational essay or both.

1. How to make something: ice cream, a latte, an impromptu speech, or a good impression

2. How to build something: a compost pile, a doll house, a planter box, or a bird cage

3. How to perform something: care for roses, sail a boat, navigate a mall, repair an appliance, administer a life-saving technique, eat with chopsticks, shoot a basket, or put on makeup

4. How to make something happen: arrange an "accidental" meeting with a person of interest, succeed in a particular sport, lose weight permanently, or become more attractive

5. How something works: a pump, a combustion engine, a small business, or a bicycle

6. How to establish or manage something: a business, a team, a club, or a study group

7. How something is produced: an appliance, a product, or a movement

8. How to promote someone or something: a candidate, an issue, a group, or a song

▶ **Comparison and Contrast**   Comparison shows the similarities or likeness of two or more people or things, and contrast shows the differences. These methods of development may be used together or separately. You may use facts, examples, and argumentation or persuasion to show how *like* or *unlike* two or more things may be. When you are comparing or contrasting two people or things, you are doing so for a reason. Simply comparing them to show how they are alike and how they are different has no value.

Paragraph Developed by Comparison and Contrast   State your point—your judgment—in the topic sentence, and then use comparison and contrast to support it. The support for comparison and contrast essays may be arranged in two ways: **subject-by-subject** or **point-by-point.** If the topics are broad and not too complex or detailed, you may want to arrange the support in a subject-by-subject pattern in which you fully discuss subject A and then go on to discuss subject B. If the topics are complex or contain many details, you may want to arrange the support in a point-by-point pattern in which you compare and contrast the subjects on point one, then on point two, then on point three, and so on. In the following paragraph, the writer arranges the details in a point-by-point pattern. She introduces the two subjects and her reasons for comparing and contrasting them. She then makes her judgment statement, which is her topic sentence.

SUBJECT-BY-SUBJECT	POINT-BY-POINT
Merrells	**Shape**
Shape	Merrells
Comfort	Adidas
Durability	**Comfort**
Adidas	Merrells
Shape	Adidas
Comfort	**Durability**
Durability	Merrells
	Adidas

Student Paragraph

Walking Boots

When I bought a new pair of hiking boots this week, I considered two top brands: Merrells and Adidas. Although the Adidas have many features that I liked, they did not measure up to the Merrells in shape, comfort, and durability. The Merrells have a curved toe, which is comfortable and attractive, and they are quite flexible. This flexibility is important to me because I hike on rough trails. The Adidas did not have the curved toe, nor were they as flexible as the Merrells. When I put the Merrells on and walked around, I could feel the cushion under my feet, which I couldn't feel when I put on the other boots. The last thing I considered was the quality of the material of the boots. The Merrells are made of a smooth leather that can withstand the punishment of even the roughest terrain. The Adidas, on the other hand, are made of a soft suede-like fabric that would not be good for hiking on rough trails. At least once a week, my new Merrells and I comfortably and safely explore the rugged hiking trails of Eastern Washington.

—Keri Miller

Writing Suggestions

1. Using the subject-by-subject arrangement, write a paragraph comparing and contrasting two methods of accomplishing similar tasks: washing dishes, making coffee, building a fire, setting up a tent, performing a particular sport activity such as a chip shot in golf, cleansing a fresh minor wound, or taking a walk.

2. Using the point-by-point arrangement, write a paragraph comparing and contrasting two people, places, or things: pets, aunts, houses, trips to the beach, or shopping malls.

Essay Developed by Comparison and Contrast   The point of a comparison and contrast essay is to arrive at a judgment based on the likeness (comparison) or the unlikeness (contrast) of two or more people or things. The comparisons and contrasts are made to support a judgment—not to simply show how two things are alike or different. To write an effective comparison and contrast essay,

- pick the subjects you are going to compare and contrast

- use common elements for comparing and contrasting

- organize the points—subject-by-subject or point-by-point

In the following essay, the student writer compares and contrasts two vacations he has taken: One to San Francisco and one to Hawaii. This student said he always felt that he had good ideas but had no idea how to arrange them. He liked the idea of having clear instructions and models he could emulate. In the following essay he arranges the material in a point-by-point pattern:

SUBJECT-BY-SUBJECT	POINT-BY-POINT
I. Hawaii	I. Setting
A. Setting	A. Hawaii
B. Activities	B. San Francisco
C. Food	

<table>
<tr><td>II. San Francisco</td><td>II. Activities</td></tr>
<tr><td>A. Setting</td><td>A. Hawaii</td></tr>
<tr><td>B. Activities</td><td>B. San Francisco</td></tr>
<tr><td>C. Food</td><td>III. Food</td></tr>
<tr><td></td><td>A. Hawaii</td></tr>
<tr><td></td><td>B. San Francisco</td></tr>
</table>

He then identifies three categories that the two vacation destinations have in common—settings, attractions, and food. He then contrasts the elements of these three categories to support his judgment statement that he prefers to vacation in Hawaii.

Student Comparison and Contrast Essay

Surfing versus Riding Cable Cars

I have taken many vacations, but two of the most enjoyable ones were to Hawaii and to San Francisco. Not only were they the two best vacations I have ever had, I went to both places the same summer. Both are wonderful vacation destinations and offer different and exciting experiences. After comparing the settings, the activities, and the cuisine, Hawaii won the title "My Best Vacation."

Although both destinations are set in fascinating places, Hawaii's luscious location and balmy weather make it my favorite. Hawaii is a series of tropical islands nestled in the South Pacific. They are covered with lush rain forests, beautiful palm trees, flowering plants and trees beyond compare, soft sandy beaches, and are surrounded by warm, crystal-clear water. On the other hand, San Francisco is the second largest city on the West Coast. It is located in Northern California on the south side of San Francisco Bay. The city is a concrete jungle with towering skyscrapers and fascinating shops. The weather is far from being balmy. The average high temperature in the summer is around sixty-four degrees, and the lows are in the upper forties.

Although Hawaii was clearly the winner in the setting category, the activities each destination offers was a close call, but, again Hawaii was the winner. During the day, hiking, surfing, or just lying on the beautiful beaches are pure "heaven on earth" experiences. At night, the nightclubs of the cities light up and feature local performers, and discos are still to be found in Hawaii. The daytime activities in San Francisco differ greatly from the laid-back activities in Hawaii. In the City by the Bay, tourists ride cable cars down crooked streets, tour museums, shop in fascinating stores, tour historic China Town, and take a boat ride over to The Rock—the former famous prison, Alcatraz. By night, the pace is no less hectic. Big name bands, world-class theater, and strange and bizarre titillating sights and sounds are all part of San Francisco after dark.

In the cuisine category, San Francisco was clearly the winner. Hawaii's food is great, but it simply cannot compare with the variety and elegance of the food in San Francisco. Hawaii features the ever-popular luau where tourists can eat whole roasted pig and sample many ethnic Hawaiian dishes, such as poi, a gooey substance made from cooked, pounded, and fermented taro corm (a short, thick, solid food-storing underground stem). Restaurants—both fast-food and elegant ones—abound and offer a great variety of ethnic foods, including Hawaiian, Polynesian, Chinese, Japanese, and others. San Francisco offers all this and more. Some of the best chefs in the country ply their trade in the city that was once called Bagdad by the Bay. Tourists can enjoy *dim sum* in China Town, feast on crab and sourdough bread at one of the many crab shacks along Fishermen's Wharf, partake of fine homemade Italian food in Little Italy, or dine elegantly at any of the many famous restaurants.

My vacations in Hawaii and San Francisco were both satisfying and enjoyable. Both places are beautifully located, offer a great variety of activities, and feature outstanding food, but I prefer Hawaii because it has the qualities that are important to me. I would rather hear the pounding of the surf than the clang of trolley cars. I like swimming and surfing more than going to museums. Although San Francisco's dining scene is unparalleled, I can be happy with the food in Hawaii as I enjoy its other pleasures.

—Jacob Canini

Thinking and Discussing

1. Is the title effective? What alternative title would you suggest?

2. How could the introductory paragraph be improved?

3. Is the essay convincing?

4. What do you like most about the essay?

5. How can it be improved?

Writing Suggestions

Choose one of the topics and write a five-paragraph comparison and contrast essay. You may arrange the material in a subject-by-subject pattern or a point-by-point pattern, which ever you think is most appropriate for the topic and your ideas about it. Remember: You must have a judgment statement.

1. Two vehicles

2. Two styles of parenting

3. Your childhood and that of one of your parents

4. Two places you have lived

5. Your religious beliefs now and those of your youth

6. Two sports

7. Two kinds of dates

8. High school and college

9. Two leadership styles

10. Two types of shopping

▶ **Cause and Effect** Cause and effect reasoning is a common, everyday way of thinking. In this type of reasoning, the reasons and results are connected.

Paragraph Developed by Cause and Effect You may begin a cause and effect paragraph with the effect and then explore its cause or causes, or you may begin with the cause and explore its effects or possible effects. Either way you develop the paragraph, you are tracing a process. When you move from cause to effect, you are tracing forward. When you move from effect to cause, you are tracing backward. In the following paragraph, the writer states the effect in the topic sentence and then traces the causes backwards that led to the effect.

Student Cause and Effect Paragraph

Brotherly Error

When Napoleon gained control of Spain in 1808 and replaced the Spanish king with his brother, Joseph, he made one of his greatest errors. The people refused to accept a French king and rebelled. The British came to the aid of the Spaniards, and with their help the Spanish drove the French out in 1812. Subsequently, Napoleon went to war with England. When Russia did not honor its promise to join Napoleon in the fight against the British and began trading with them, Napoleon invaded Russia and was defeated, not by the Russians, but by the weather. Returning to France, he had to raise a new army because only twenty thousand of his soldiers returned from Russia. Meanwhile England and several other countries had formed an alliance and agreed to declare war on France. The armies of these allies defeated Napoleon. He abdicated his throne and was exiled to Elba, an island off the Italian coast, but he escaped a year later and returned to France. Again he declared himself emperor, but his reign was short-lived. English and Prussian armies defeated him on a battlefield near the Belgian village of Waterloo. This time he was exiled to St. Helena, an island off the west coast of Africa, where he remained until he died in 1821.

—Elizabeth Ruse

Thinking and Discussing

1. Is the title effective? If not, write a title that you think is more appropriate.

2. Do all the sentences directly or indirectly support the topic sentence?

3. Could the paragraph be improved by writing a different topic sentence? If so, write a topic sentence that you think is more appropriate.

Writing Suggestions

Use one of the following topics and write a cause and effect paragraph.

1. A quarrel with a friend

2. A recent decision

3. An incident that changed our way of thinking about something or someone

4. Baseball hats worn backwards or some other type of dress adopted by a group of people

5. A recent policy change in your school

Essay Developed by Cause and Effect   When you develop a cause and effect essay, you want to show that one situation is the cause—or effect—of another situation. A cause and effect essay attempts to show a relationship between two situations. You may develop the essay by examining a cause or causes and then discussing the effect or effects or making predictions, or you may develop the essay by examining the effect or effects, and then discussing the contributing cause or causes. In the following essay, the student writer—a recent emigrant in the United States—identifies the media, lack of parental supervision, and social cliques as being the causes of school violence in America.

Student Cause and Effect Essay

Suburban Warfare

Last April in suburban Littleton, Colorado, two boys went to Columbine High School and opened fire on their fellow students, killing fifteen and wounding others. In Jonesboro, Arkansas, a fifth grader and a third grader went to school and shot their fellow classmates and teachers with their grandfather's guns. Are these incidents isolated? Are they just a fluke, or is there more to the story? There have also been other incidents in places like Springfield, Oregon; Paducah, Kentucky; and Moses Lake, Washington. School violence was, at one time, solely an inner city phenomenon. What has caused this teenage violence in America's suburbs? The three main causes of school violence in America's suburbs are the media, the lack of parental supervision, and social cliques.

The media has always been a scapegoat for many people who wish to blame someone or something for society's problems. The media, however, has never come under as much scrutiny and criticism as it has over the past few years. There is increasingly more and more violence on TV and in music than there has ever been. The successful media tycoons realize what sells. Sex and violence get high TV ratings and successful record sales. If ratings are down on a TV show, an increase in violence and sex is always a quick fix. With the amount of violence shown on television and the ability of the entertainment industry to make it look realistic, the average person has become desensitized to many forms of violence, and teenagers are "home alone" watching television and seeing countless acts of violence.

Teenagers and children are at home watching violent programs because they are unsupervised. The American economy and the prevalent attitudes towards status and achievement have made it almost mandatory for both parents to work outside the home. American parents have been supplanted by video games and television. They are not there when their children are doing things that they should not be doing. For instance, in the Jonesboro tragedy, the children stole the guns from one of their grandfathers. In Colorado, the teenagers were building pipe bombs in the family garage. With a parent at home these acts may have been prevented, or, at least, they might have been detected.

Social cliques are also a contributing factor to teenage violence. A teenager's appearance, intelligence, wealth, and education are all judged by their social group. High school life is cruel if a student is not in the good graces of the other students. Supposedly, the two students in Littleton wanted revenge. They wanted to retaliate against the people they perceived had caused their discontent. Perhaps the cliques in suburbia are not the Crips and the Bloods, but they are just as deadly.

In conclusion, the three main reasons for teenage violence are the media's lack of conscience, today's economic and social atmosphere that forces parents to leave their children unsupervised, and the social structure of America's high schools. To stem this tide of suburban violence, television must be more responsible, parents must reassess their priorities, and school officials must find ways to de-emphasize and defuse high school cliques.

—Andrew Mackend

Thinking and Discussing

1. Do you agree or disagree with Mackend's ideas about TV violence?

2. Is family breakdown a contributing factor to school violence?

3. What are the strongest points of this essay?

4. What are the weakest ones?

5. What has been your experience with high school cliques?

6. Do high school cliques have a deleterious effect on students and on the school?

7. What do you think are the three major contributors to school violence?

Writing Suggestions

Choose one of the following prompts and write a five-paragraph cause and effect essay.

1. The relationship of an influence or influences on your life and the person you are today

2. A current social issue that you are concerned about

3. Your being a college student

4. Requiring welfare recipients to work

5. Legalizing same-sex marriages

7. Making all records available to adoptees

8. Mandatory licensing of handguns

9. Abolishing affirmative action

10. High school cliques

▶ **Definition**   Definition is the expansion of a word or term's meaning. When a word may be interpreted in several different ways, you must define the word so that your readers will know what you have in mind when you use the word. You may define words by giving another word that means about the same as the word you are defining. You may give a formal or dictionary definition, or you may give an extended definition. When you are using an abstract word that may be interpreted differently by different people, then you need to give an extended definition.

Paragraph Developed by Definition   When a one-sentence definition is not adequate to clearly express what you mean by a word or expression, you will need to write a definition paragraph. Paragraphs developed by definition often involve explanations, descriptions, and examples. A definition paragraph explains what something is, what it includes, and what it excludes. Give a general definition in the topic sentence and develop the paragraph by adding sentences that contain details that clarify and extend the general definition. This student claimed that he had nothing to write about, but in a brainstorming session with other students, he realized that he knew a great deal about detective stories—his favorite reading. In the following paragraph, he gives a general definition of a detective story, says what it is not, adds a more specific illustrated definition, gives examples of it, and explains what it does.

Student Definition Paragraph

Who Did It?

A detective story or novel is a narrative in which a detective solves a mystery by gathering and interpreting clues. It is not a serious form of fiction. It is a form of light entertainment and generally includes details about a would-be-perfect crime, the bumbling of the official investigator (usually the police), the extraordinary brilliance of the detective and his or her dogged determination, and a surprise ending. Edgar Allan Poe established this form of writing in 1841 in *The Murders in the Rue Morgue* and other similar tales. A well-crafted detective story cannot withhold or give misleading information to the reader. The clues from which a solution can be found must be given to the reader at the same time and in the same form as the detective receives them. Part of the appeal of detective stories is the pitting of wits of the reader and the detective. A detective story aficionado tries to solve the mystery before the detective presents the solution. The works of Poe and of Sir Arthur Conan Doyle (the Sherlock Holmes stories) are some of the finest works of this type.

—Gordon Bush

Thinking and Discussing

1. Chart the sentences in this paragraph, using 1 for the topic sentence, 2s for major support sentences, 3s for minor support sentences, and NS for nonsupport sentences (if any).

2. If you like mysteries, who is your favorite mystery writer?

3. What sets his or her work apart from other writers?

4. How do you go about outwitting the detective in the story?

Writing Suggestions

1. Write a paragraph in which you define a word that has more than one meaning, depending on one's point of view (such as *beauty, love, success,* or *liberal*).

2. Lack of agreement on the definition of words often complicates discussion of current social issues. Choose one of these words (such as *drunk, pornography, death,* or *censorship*) and define it in one paragraph.

3. Choose one of the following words and define it in one paragraph by telling what it *is not* as well as what *it is: fun, friend, sportsmanship, style, taste,* or *leader.*

Essay Developed by Definition   Through an extended definition you can use examples, description, or comparison and contrast to let readers know what you mean when you use a particular word. Abstract words such as *love, hatred, happiness, freedom, pornography* must be defined. In the following essay, the student presents an extended definition of the word *procrastinator* through an analysis of his experiences as a procrastinator. He uses his lack of focus, lack of interest, and lack of motivation to explain the meaning of the word. Prior to completing this essay, he had never turned in a well-written essay on time.

Student Definition Essay

I'll Write this Later

I'm a born procrastinator. I've done countless assignments and projects at the last minute. But exactly what is a procrastinator? The dictionary's definition of a procrastinator is "one who procrastinates, or defers the performance of anything; someone who postpones work, especially out of laziness or habitual carelessness." This is not necessarily true. I am neither lazy (well, maybe a little) nor careless. From my experience, there are three main characteristics that define a procrastinator. These characteristics are lack of focus, lack of interest, and lack of motivation.

A lack of focus is a good start for any procrastinator. All it takes is a good imagination. I have successfully used lack of focus on several occasions. I've used this method often, mainly, because it is fun. It involves allowing the mind to wander, start up a nice daydream, and presto! Welcome to Procrastinators' Anonymous. Lack of focus, however, is the weakest procrastinator characteristic. Without substantial help from its counterparts, it can easily be robbed of victory.

A lack of interest is stronger than a lack of focus. This is because not only is it effective single-handedly, the lack of interest can facilitate or even create a lack of focus. The absence of interest is a characteristic familiar to most people. Take math class, for example. Who really cares what time the fast train will pass the slow train, traveling twice as fast, in the opposite direction? I always prefer drawing choo-choos on a collision course with happy little "woo-woo" noises floating about.

Just as lack of focus is weaker than lack of interest, lack of interest is no match for lack of motivation. Lack of motivation doesn't care about focus or interest. It will ably prevent any progress a procrastinator is in danger of making, with or without help. This is the characteristic of choice of well-seasoned, serious procrastinators. I've had several assignments that—heaven forbid—I was interested in or focused on. Thankfully, my lack of motivation stepped in, and I successfully procrastinated. Unfortunately, lack of motivation is the toughest trait to bring out. The easiest way that I have found is to convince myself that the project has no urgency and that there will be plenty of time later. Although lack of motivation is less common than lack of focus and lack of interest, the impressive rate of success more than makes up for its rarity.

Lack of focus, lack of interest, and lack of motivation are the key defining elements of any true procrastinator. A person simply postponing work is not a true procrastinator. The three key characteristics must come together to form a delicate balance between the delay and the completion of projects and assignments. Laziness and carelessness strive not for balance, but merely to defer and ultimately avoid any work at all. Procrastination requires skill and finesse. So, what really is a procrastinator? A procrastinator is an artist.

—Christopher M. Lamm

Thinking and Discussing

1. Are you a procrastinator?

2. If you are a procrastinator, what conditions contribute to your "I'll do it later" syndrome?

3. Label the thesis statement with a TS. Check the topic sentences in each body paragraph. Does each topic sentence directly support the thesis statement?

4. Is the concluding paragraph strong?

5. Is the last sentence memorable? Why or why not?

Writing Suggestions

Choose one of the following expressions and write a five-paragraph definition essay.

1. Pornography
2. Sexual harassment
3. A good education
4. A decent wage
5. Alcoholism

6. Style
7. Trafficking
8. Drugs
9. Ethnic minority
10. Attention deficit disorder

▶ **Division and Classification**   To develop division and classification paragraphs and essays, take one large unit and break it into smaller subunits and categorize them according to their relationships. Division involves dividing a subject into its component parts. Use division to split large or complicated subjects into manageable parts. Classification involves dividing a subject into categories—according to some consistent principle—and then grouping the elements of the categories according to their relationships, always moving from larger to smaller categories.

Paragraph Developed by Division and Classification   In the following excerpt the writer divides Americans into three groups—smokers, nonsmokers, and reformed smokers. Based on their attitudes toward smoking, he classifies the reformed smokers as zealots, evangelists, the elect, and the serene.

Professional Division and Classification Paragraph

from Confessions of an Ex-Smoker

Americans can be divided into three groups—smokers, nonsmokers and that expanding pack of us who have quit. . . .For almost all of us ex-smokers, smoking continues to play an important part in our lives. . . .I have observed four [groups] of them; and in the interest of science I have classified them as those of the zealot, the evangelist, the elect and the serene. . . .

One explanation for the zealot's fervor in seeking to outlaw tobacco consumption is his own tenuous hold on abstaining from smoking. . . .The evangelist does not condemn smokers. . . . [He] spends an enormous amount of time seeking and preaching to the unconverted. . . . [The] elect think they are different from friends and relatives who continue to smoke. They feel superior. . . .The serene ex-smoker accepts himself and also accepts those around him who continue to smoke. . . .

—Franklin Zimring

In the following excerpt the writer divides the first aid rules for serious emergencies into four categories: breathing, bleeding, shock, moving.

Professional Division Paragraph

from First Aid for Your Family

First aid is *first*—what to do before the doctor comes. It is never a substitute for medical help. First aid is the means by which an informed layman can take lifesaving measures in emergencies and avoid doing harm. . . . If a patient has stopped breathing, give immediate mouth to mouth resuscitation. . . .If bleeding is serious, apply pressure directly over the wound until bleeding stops. . . . [To] prevent shock, cover patient, keep him comfortably warm, not hot or sweaty. . . . Never move patient from scene of accident while waiting for medical help unless absolutely necessary. . . .

—Donald G. Cooley

In the following paragraph, philosopher Mortimer Adler uses the guiding principle of the relationship of books and their owners to classify three kinds of book owners.

Professional Paragraph of Classification

from How to Mark a Book

There are three kinds of book owners. The first has all the standard sets and best-sellers—unread, untouched. (This deluded individual owns woodpulp and ink, not books.) The second has a great many books—a few of them read through, most of them dipped into, but all of them as clean and shiny as the day they were bought. (This person would probably like to make books his own, but is restrained by a false respect for their physical appearance.) The third has a few books or many—each one of them dog-eared and dilapidated, shaken and loosened by continual use, marked, and scribbled in from front to back. (This man owns books).

—Mortimer J. Adler

Thinking and Discussing

1. Chart the sentences in the preceding paragraphs, using TS for topic sentences, MS for major support sentences, and MI for minor support sentences.

2. Do you mark your books? Why or why not?

3. If you make notes in a textbook, do you find those notes helpful in clarifying your thinking about the material?

4. Do you find highlighting and using symbols helpful?

Writing Suggestions

1. Use one of the following topics and write a division paragraph: friends, trucks, snow sports, areas of a shopping mall, sections of a medical facility. Be sure to establish a reason for the division.

2. Use one of the following topics and write a classification paragraph: race, age, appearance, or occupation. You may want to discuss the fallacy of such classifications.

3. Use one of the following topics and write a division and classification paragraph: certain groups of people and their attitudes towards a particular activity such as diet, exercise, reasons for going to college, recreational activities, and so on.

Essay Developed by Division and Classification　　In this essay the writer divides adult fairy tale females into three groups—good mothers, bad mothers, and witches—and classifies them according to their attitudes toward the young heroines. Good mothers who are present help the young heroines achieve wealth and happiness; absent mothers are replaced by bad mothers—wicked stepmothers—who try to deprive the young heroines of status or their life; good witches protect the young heroines, and bad witches try to destroy them.

Adult Fairy Tale Females

The old woman sighed sympathetically. "My pretty dear," she said, "you must be cheerful and stop worrying about dreams. . . . Now let me tell you a fairy tale or two to make you feel a little better."

—Apuleius

　　Fairy tales are often the first stories children hear. They have been used for centuries to enchant and entertain children and are unparalleled sources of adventure. Some scholars propose that part of the appeal of fairy tales is that they help children learn to deal with conflicts, both internal and external. In *From the Beast to the Blonde,* Mariana Warner explores real-life themes in fairy tales such as rivalry between women, marital relationships, neglect, incest, death, murder, and prejudice. In *The Witch Must Die,* Sheldon Cashdan explores the themes of vanity, gluttony, envy, lust, greed, and so on. In *Fairy Tales and Society,* Ruth B. Bottigheimer discusses fairy tales from the point of view of history, folklore, literature, and psychology. In *The Uses of Enchantment,* child psychologist Dr. Bruno Bettelheim identifies ways in which fairy tales, "educate, support, and liberate the emotions of children." Most fairy tales contain elements that lend themselves to a variety of studies. One of the most interesting aspects of many fairy tales is the role that women play. The predominant adult female roles can be divided into three general categories: good mothers (often dead), bad mothers (usually stepmothers), and witches (usually wicked).

In "Snow White and Rose Red" and "The Goose Girl," the good mothers are alive and help their daughters achieve happiness. Snow White and Rose Red are good girls who love their good mother and are in tune with nature. They are safe from all wild creatures. After they befriend a brown bear who is freezing to death, the bear later saves them from an evil, ungrateful dwarf. Upon the death of the dwarf, the bear is released from the dwarf's curse and becomes his true self—a handsome prince. Rose Red weds the prince, and Snow White marries his brother. The two young princesses take their good mother with them to the palace, where she lives happily the rest of her life. In "The Goose Girl," the good mother is a widowed queen who sends her lovely daughter to marry a prince in a far away land. Dressing her daughter in fine clothes and jewelry and giving her magnificent presents for her future husband, the good mother puts her on a fairy horse and gives her a magic handkerchief. When the princess loses the magic handkerchief, her evil waiting maid steals her identity and presents herself to the prince. The impostor princess has the fairy horse beheaded and the real princess is required to tend a flock of geese. Through the intervention of the fairy horse, whose head talks even though it has been severed from his body, the impostor is discovered and cast out in disgrace. The real princess marries her prince who later becomes king. The fairy horse is restored to life, and the new king, his queen, their children, and the fairy horse live happily ever after. Good mothers who are present provide their children with a nurturing environment and training that assures their future happiness.

In many fairy tales, when a good mother dies (the absent mother), she is replaced by a bad mother—a stepmother—who treats the good mother's child or children most cruelly. Beautiful Cinderella is forced to do the domestic work for her stepmother and her ugly stepsisters, but she is saved by her fairy godmother. Snow White's vain, evil stepmother orders a servant to take Snow White to the forest and kill her, but the servant disobeys and abandons her instead. Eventually she becomes the housekeeper for the seven dwarfs. When the mirror continues to vaunt the beauty of Snow White, the evil stepmother finally succeeds in poisoning her. She is saved by a handsome prince who asks her to marry him. When the wicked stepmother attends their wedding, she is so furious when she discovers that the prince's bride is none other than Snow White that she goes into a rage and dies. In most of the stories of wicked stepmothers, the young heroines are rewarded for their goodness and kindness, and the stepmothers are punished for their wickedness. Goodness is triumphant.

Witches, often wicked ones, instead of wicked stepmothers, are central to many fairy tales. Witches who are particularly malevolent usually die traumatic deaths. In "Hansel and Gretel" Gretel tricks the cannibalistic, old witch and kills her by sliding her into an oven. In the *Wizard of Oz,* Dorothy melts the Wicked Witch of the West by dousing her with water. Other witches may cause great suffering or may extract great prices for their services, but when their acts are not essentially evil, they do not die. The witch in "Rapunzel" is not punished because she, unlike the evil queen in "Snow White and the Seven Dwarfs," kept Rapunzel in the tower, not to destroy her, but to protect her. In "Sleeping Beauty," the witch (bad fairy) delivers a death curse, but a good fairy modifies it to a sleeping curse. In "Jorinda and Jorindel," the witch turns young girls into birds and then cages them in her castle, and to prevent their being rescued, no man is allowed to come near the castle. Through a magic flower, Jorindel rescues Jorinda and the other girls. The witch loses her power, and, once again, love and goodness triumph over wickedness.

Fairy tales in which good mothers, evil stepmothers, and good and bad witches play a major role demonstrate certain principles that may be of value in forming a child's perception of reality and may demonstrate to them that the qualities of goodness, honesty, and love will be rewarded, and that the qualities of hate, greed, excessive pride, possessiveness, and so on may result in disillusionment, destruction, or death.

—Fern Blair

Thinking and Discussing

1. Which of these fairy tales are unfamiliar to you?

2. Think of some fairy tales that you know that are not mentioned in this essay. What role does the adult female play?

3. What is your favorite fairy tale? Why?

4. Do you think that some of the stereotyping in society comes from fairy tales? Explain.

Writing Suggestions

Choose one of the following prompts and write a five-paragraph division and classification essay.

1. Discuss the dress of groups of campus instructors. You may want to discuss the way the dress affects the class atmosphere or the statements that instructors make by their attire.

2. Students in a particular discipline or in a particular class.

3. Restaurants in your hometown.

4. Superstitious people.

5. Chat rooms.

6. Sports fans.

7. Various kinds of eaters.

8. Various kinds of vacation destinations.

9. Modes of transportation.

10. Instructors.

Argumentation and Persuasion

A paper developed by argumentation and persuasion is one in which the writer states a point of view on one side of an arguable topic—one that has no absolute answers and is disputable—and then explains it. The purpose of an argumentative or persuasive paper is to convince readers to act or think in a certain way. The writer advances his or her point and tries to get the readers to agree or take a certain action.

Like other types of development, argumentative and persuasive papers must deal with a specific topic that can be fully developed within a limited space. First, select a topic and then choose a specific issue related to that topic. Define the issue and put it into one sentence, either a statement or a question. You may not include the definition in your final draft, but it will help keep you on track as you develop your idea about the issue. After choosing a topic and defining a related issue, decide on the position that you are going to take and put it into a statement. This statement in a paragraph is the *topic sentence,* and in an essay it is the *thesis statement.* The statement must be an *arguable* one—capable of being argued rationally in more than one way. It must be more than an opinion or an observation. An arguable statement may be questioned or challenged.

▶ **Appeals** Depending upon what you hope to accomplish, you may develop the paper by support that appeals to the intellect or to the emotions or a combination of the two. Traditionally, writers use three types of appeals—*logic, emotions,* and *ethics*—to convince readers to accept an idea, adopt a solution, take a certain course of action, or change their opinions about an issue. These appeals have advantages and disadvantages, and careful writers choose the appeals that are appropriate to the audience, the topic, and the purpose.

Note: These appeals are often used in their Greek forms. *Logic* is derived from *logos:* speech, word, reason, account. *Pathos* expresses the concept of emotional appeal: something that arouses feelings of pity, sympathy, tenderness, or sorrow. The word *ethics* comes from *ethos:* meaning character or fundamental values peculiar to a person or a people.

Logical Appeals Although you may use other types of appeals, generally, college writing relies heavily on logical appeals. Logical appeals provide evidence for decision making, but they often require readers to read critically and carefully. Use reasoned arguments and present evidence such as *test results, statistics, expert testimony,* and *surveys* to support your point.

Emotional Appeals Marketing and advertising rely heavily on emotional appeals. Because emotional appeals are based on people's deep seated desires and needs, they can produce immediate results, but because of their nature they can produce unexpected or undesired results. Emotional appeals include *desire for recognition; need to achieve power, money, fame, and so on; need to belong, to be part of the in-group; desire to endure when lesser people cannot;* and *fear of defeat, loss of face, and threats to self or others.*

Ethical Appeals   Sermons, editorials, and political speeches rely heavily on ethical appeals. Ethical appeals can be most convincing if the audience and writer share the same value system, but if they do not share the same value system, these appeals are of little value. Ethical appeals include *religion*—the desire to follow the rules; *patriotism*—the desire to place country above self; *ideals*—the desire to be a good parent, role model, citizen, professional, and so on; and *humanitarianism*—the desire to do good for others.

▶ **Logical Fallacies**   Do not use arguments that are based on false or invalid inferences. Learn to recognize the following logical fallacies so that you can challenge them when you find them in the works of other writers and avoid using them in your own work.

Ambiguity   (*equivocation*) Using terms that may be interpreted in more than one way.

Beth can be trusted to tell whatever she knows.

(Is Beth an honest person, or is she a gossip?)

Attacking the Person   (*name calling*) Attacking the person who presents the issue instead of dealing with the issue itself.

People who oppose gun control are boors.

(Attack the issue of gun control, not the level of refinement of the people who oppose it.)

Everyone Is Doing It   (*jumping on the bandwagon*) Assuming that something is right because other people are doing, thinking, or saying it is right.

All the students cheated on the last test.

(Just because other people cheated on a test does not make cheating acceptable.)

Circular Statements   (*begging the question*) Treating a question as if it has been answered.

He broke this window because he has broken windows before.

(Just because he has broken windows in the past does not mean that he broke this window.)

Irrelevant Point   (*red herring*) Sidetracking a major issue by drawing attention to a minor or irrelevant one.

We the Board of Trustees refuse to approve a cost of living salary increase for the teachers because some of them refused to actively support the bond issue.

(The issue is the cost of living increase. The bond issue is irrelevant.)

One-Step Downfall   (*slippery slope*) Assuming that if one event is allowed to occur, it will be the first step in a total downfall.

Once a person smokes marijuana, it's only a matter of time until he or she becomes a heroin addict.

(Smoking marijuana does not necessarily lead to the use of other drugs.)

Either Or   Offering only two alternatives when there are others.

Son, you must eat at least one green vegetable each day. Eat broccoli or cabbage.

(Broccoli and cabbage are not the only green vegetables.)

False Analogy   Assuming that because two things are alike in some ways that they are alike in all ways.

Crack cocaine should be legalized because alcohol is legal.

(They may both be addictive drugs, but there are more differences than similarities.)

False Authority   Assuming that an expert in one field is an expert in another.

I'm betting on Also Ran in the Kentucky Derby because Mayor McDonald picked him to win.

(Mayor McDonald may be an expert in running a city, but that ability does not make him an expert in picking a winning horse.)

False Cause   Assuming that because one event follows another, the first one is the cause of the second one.

We have had so much rain that all my flowers are dead.

(The rain may or may not have caused the flowers to die. There are other possibilities.)

Guilt by Association   Trying to make one person responsible for the beliefs or actions of others.

Pat is an arrogant, unpleasant person who belongs to the Grow More Garden Club, and I will not join that club of arrogant, unpleasant people.

(Just because Pat is arrogant and unpleasant does not mean that all the people in the garden club are arrogant and unpleasant.)

Hasty Generalization   Drawing a conclusion based on too little evidence. Hasty generalizations, unlike sweeping generalizations, can be supported. They may require several examples to support the point being made. Some statements require more support than others.

Last year an elderly person hit my parked truck and did $3,000 worth of damage to it. Last month another elderly person bashed into the rear of my car while I was stopped at a stoplight, and yesterday another elderly person ran a red light and almost hit my dog and me while we were crossing the street. Therefore, I am convinced that elderly drivers are a serious threat to other people.

(This conclusion may be true, but three examples of reckless driving by elderly people are insufficient to support the conclusion that all elderly drivers are menaces on the highway. A large-scale investigation would have to be made to collect sufficient evidence to support this generalization.)

Illogical Conclusion   (*does not follow*) Reaching a conclusion that does not follow logically from what has already been said.

Brandy is a champion field dog; therefore, he will be a champion show dog.

(The requirements for a champion show dog are different from the requirements for a field champion. Qualifying in one area does not mean he will qualify in another area.)

Oversimplification   Leaving out relevant points about an issue.

People with beautiful white teeth are fortunate.

(There's more to having beautiful white teeth than good fortune.)

Sweeping Generalization   (*absolute statements*) Making statements that cannot be supported. Stereotypes of racial, religious, gender, nationality, or other groups are sweeping generalizations.

Women are notoriously bad drivers.

(Not true. Many women are excellent drivers.)

Paragraph Developed by Argumentation and Persuasion   In the following paragraph, the student writer responds to the following prompt: "Write a paragraph (about 150 words) in which you advance the idea that educational standards in the United States have (or have not) been lowered in part by social forces not directly linked to the educational system."

Student Argumentation and Persuasion Paragraph

See You in Court

Educational standards in the United States have been lowered in part by social forces not directly linked to the educational system. The school system must accept some responsibility, but not all. One good example of a social force that affects the school system is the growing eagerness of people to file lawsuits to seek retribution for real or imagined grievances. A child sued his parents over disciplinary actions and won. A single Native American family threatened a school district with a lawsuit over a mascot, and the mascot was changed. Shortly after the mascot was changed, the family moved from the district. With the public in general so anxious to sue for almost any reason, educators worry about any acts or conditions that might result in a lawsuit. Students may sue a school because they don't like the grades they earned. Parents may sue the school because they feel that their child was not properly taught and because he or she was not properly taught did not earn a promotion. A student may sue a school because he or she was expelled for inappropriate conduct. What is the solution to this problem? In an attempt to stem the tide of lawsuits, educators assign inflated grades, give students social promotions, and lower the standards of conduct and expectations.

—Christopher M. Lamm

Note: You may use more than one method of paragraph development in a single paragraph. The preceding paragraph on educational standards includes division and definition.

Thinking and Discussing

1. From your own experience, do you agree or disagree with Lamm that educational standards in the United States have been lowered in part by social forces not directly linked to the educational system?

2. Give examples of your experiences that support or do not support some of his ideas.

3. Is the title appropriate? What would you suggest as an alternative title?

Writing Suggestions

Choose one of the following suggestions and write an argumentative and persuasive paragraph.

1. Choose a current local or state political issue and write a paragraph that could be used in a voters' pamphlet. You may be for or against the issue.

2. Write a paragraph for a voters' pamphlet in which you support one candidate over another. The candidate may be running for a state, county, city, or school position.

3. Defend or dispute the use of a particular expletive. You may want to defend your use of the word, or you may want to repudiate other people's use of it.

▶ **Essay Developed by Argumentation and Persuasion**   Like other essays, argumentative and persuasive essays contain the same elements—an *introduction*, a *middle* (supporting body paragraphs), and a *conclusion*.

- In the introduction, establish your tone and attitude toward the subject.

- In the middle, present your argument, provide background information, respond to opposing points of view, present reasons in support of your point, and anticipate possible objections to your case.

- In the conclusion, summarize your argument, reaffirm your stand, and call for action.

Opposing Point of View   In addition to these three elements, the essay must include the opposing arguments and dispute them by showing that they are not true, not fair, not logical, not important, or not pertinent. If you cannot dispute an opposing argument, concede that point, gracefully, but when possible, try to show weaknesses or limitations of that point; but do not present it unfairly or ridicule it. The placement of opposing arguments is a tactical problem. Generally, if they are weak, present them after you have presented your arguments; but, if they are strong, you may want to present them before you begin presenting your arguments.

Arrangement of the Elements   There is no one best way to organize an argumentative essay, but the following three organizational plans are ones that are commonly used.

Model 1

Introduction: Thesis statement and three points

First Point and evidence

Second Point and evidence

Third Point and evidence

Refutation of opposing arguments for points 1, 2, and 3

Conclusion

Model 2

Introduction: Thesis statement and three points

First point, evidence, and refutation of opposing argument

Second point, evidence, and refutation of opposing argument

Third point, evidence, and refutation of opposing argument

Conclusion

Model 3

Introduction: Thesis statement and three points

Summary of opposing arguments

First point and evidence

Second point and evidence

Third point and evidence

Conclusion

The following essay was written by a student who had only a few days earlier been involved in the World Trade Organization demonstration in Seattle. In this essay he establishes his attitude toward the subject and toward the readers, introduces the topic, establishes his thesis, and presents his three points. He writes with a "fresh from the battlefield fervor" and uses logical, emotional, and ethical appeals—although he relies heavily on emotional appeals. Some of the support is slanted, and his argument could have been stronger had he presented more opposing arguments and refuted them.

Student Argumentative and Persuasive Essay

A World of Hurt

The World Trade Organization's (WTO) assembly on U. S. soil was doomed from the start. Not by deciding to come to Seattle on that fateful week, but even from coming into existence as a spin-off of the General Agreement on Tariffs and Trade. These three capitalized letters (WTO) and apocalyptic images are forever etched into the membrane of Seattle's consciousness. For many, the events that took place during the week of November 29–December 3, 1999 were stupid and unnecessary. "Those damn kids just wanted to cause trouble." But for those who bothered to scratch the surface and were exposed to the horrors that seeped out, it was one of the most important fights for humanity in recent decades. To understand why people fought, we must look at the source of the protest, the strong and violent resistance of the police, and the media's coverage of the melee.

The WTO's main objective is to not hamper the free flow of trade. To accomplish this goal, atrocities against humanity and the environment are sanctioned. WTO caters to big corporations in an attempt to globalize the economy. But by globalizing the economy, the organization hampers the growth of new businesses and consolidates the power within corporations that have a large enough base to spread across the globe. This is a threat to all: All corporations will be bound by no single set of rules, and in countries where they can violate human rights, they will. It threatens the safety of humanity by not regulating standards for safe working environments— or even sanitary ones. Countries that tolerate the beating and raping of its workers are happy as long as trade is not affected. Many people in the United States seem to think the violation of human rights is acceptable as long as the atrocities are not happening here, but the main offices of those factories are based here. We buy their products and thereby create the demand for more products. For the WTO protesters, inhuman working conditions are not acceptable.

The resistance that met protesters was that of over-zealous, over-worked police officers—dressed to the nines in assault gear—who simply were not prepared or trained to deal with such a situation. The actions of a few protesters resulted in assault on many. If someone breaks a window on one side of the street, should the police mace everyone within a four-block radius? No, of course, not. But this is what happened. People on the frontlines, surrounded by peaceful protesters, did not know why they were being attacked. The media focused on the acts of violence, letting the world know that the protesters were violent and were getting what they deserved.

The news stations' cameras were set on tripods and aimed directly at scenes of violence and destruction. No coverage was given to the cause of the peaceful fight that was taking place. No concern was shown for the injustice being done, just that the big corporations—the ones that owned the news stations and networks—were being unfairly attacked. Biased news reporting was the story once again.

The time has come to look beyond ourselves and see that everything is relative, and every cause has an effect on everybody, eventually. The next time a protest comes under question will you be among the ones who scratch the surface and take a stand to protect the environment and the rights of human beings, or will you do nothing and just chalk up the protest to a generation of bored, unruly students who have nothing better to do with their time than disrupt a world-wide business meeting? Apathy is humanity's worst enemy; it kills.

—Carlos Lopez

Thinking and Discussing

1. What do you know about the World Trade Organization?

2. Did you gain insight into the problems of WTO?

3. Did you change your mind about some of the ideas you had before you read this essay?

4. Did the essay make you want to learn more about WTO?

5. Although Lopez fails to include opposite viewpoints, does this seriously detract from his message? If so, how?

6. Does the fact that he participated in the demonstrations give him credibility?

Writing Suggestions

Choose one of the following prompts and write a five-paragraph argumentative or persuasive essay.

1. Violent television shows contribute to violence in society.

2. High schools are or are not adequately preparing students for college.

3. Animals have rights.

4. Animal research is essential to the development of new therapies.

5. Interracial adoptions prevent adoptees from appreciating and understanding their birth culture.

6. Write a critical review of a book, an article, or essay that you have read recently.

7. Choose a recent opinion piece in a newspaper or magazine and write a refutation of it.

8. Choose a local political issue (school, city, county, state) and write an essay supporting it or repudiating it.

9. Identify a problem in your college and write an essay in which you try to persuade the college to recognize the problem and remedy it.

10. Write a letter in essay form to a higher being in which you try to persuade the deity to recognize and remedy a human condition problem.

Narration and Description

Most of the essays you write in college will be expository or argumentative essays. You will rarely be asked to develop an essay using narration or description exclusively; however, sometimes you will want to use narration and description in developing other types of essays.

▶ **Narration**   Narration is storytelling. It is often used in histories, biographies, travel books, novels, and so on. It is a type of composition that relates the details of a real or fictitious event, and the series of events—usually related in the order that they happened—are used to support a point. The art of telling a good story lies chiefly in the process. You want to introduce your topic, arouse and partly satisfy the curiosity of the reader, and create an air of suspense by occasionally suspending the action of the story. When you use narration, you use a story to make your point. Keep in mind that you are telling the story for a reason—to make your point. The point you are making by using a story is the important part of the essay—not the story.

To use narration effectively,

- make your point

- include only material that advances your point

- usually, present the information in the time order in which the events happen

- choose a verb tense (present or past) and use it consistently throughout the story (If you are summarizing a story, use the present tense.)

Paragraph Developed by Narration   You may use a short story, an incident, or a short account of an interesting or humorous incident to develop a topic sentence into a paragraph. The story or incident should illustrate the idea in the topic sentence and make it more specific. In the following example, Cicero tells a story that supports the point (topic sentence) he makes in his first sentence: Riches do not bring happiness.

Professional Narration Paragraph

Dionysius and Damocles

Dionysius, the tyrant of Sicily, showed how far he was from being happy, even whilst abounding in riches and all the pleasures which riches can procure. Damocles, one of his flatterers, was complimenting him one day upon his power, his treasures, and the magnificence of his royal state, and affirming that no monarch ever was greater or happier than he. "Have you a mind, Damocles," said the king, "to taste this happiness, and know by experience what my enjoyments are, of which you entertain so high an appreciation?" Damocles gladly accepted the offer. Then the king ordered that a royal banquet should be prepared, and a gilded couch placed for him, covered with rich embroidery, and sideboards loaded with gold and silver plate of immense value. . . . Damocles fancied himself amongst the gods. In the midst of all his happiness he sees, let down from the roof, exactly over his head as he lay indulging himself in state, a glittering sword hung by a single hair. The sight of destruction, thus threatening him from on high, soon put a stop to joy and reveling. . . . He hastened to escape from his dangerous situation, and at last begged the king to restore him to his former humble condition, having no desire to enjoy any longer so dreadful a kind of happiness.

—Cicero

Thinking and Discussing

1. Chart the sentences in the paragraph. Using a 1 for the topic sentence, 2s for major support sentences, and 3s for minor support sentences.

2. If you could trade places with someone else, which person would you choose?

3. If you could put your problems in a bag and then play "grab bag" with others, would you want to retrieve your own bag?

Writing Suggestions

Write a narrative paragraph about a humorous trivial incident that revealed a hidden side of you, a friend, or a family member, such as

1. A fight with a vending machine

2. Forgetting a date

3. Doing the wrong assignment

4. Calling the wrong person

5. Forgetting the name of a friend or family member

6. Showing up for an appointment at the wrong time or on the wrong day

7. A fortunate accident

8. Being in the wrong place at the right time

9. Looking over a four-leafed clover that you had overlooked before

10. A lesson learned outside the classroom

Essay Developed by Narration   See professional models in Part 7.

▶ **Description**   Description is the delineation of a person or thing. It appeals to the senses by showing how the subject looks, sounds, feels, smells, and tastes. Narration deals with successive facts; whereas description deals with objects that exist at the same time. Description is often used with another mode (manner of development) to gain the attention or sympathy of the reader or to make events more intelligible. Often it is used to give variety to another mode presenting scenes of striking interest to the imagination.

When you use *description,* you are trying to convey your perceptions to the readers by painting mind pictures with your words. You are creating these pictures to support your point—not for the sake of creation. As you create these pictures, do not rely solely on words that appeal to the sense of sight; use words that appeal to the other senses (taste, touch, smell, and sound). To use description effectively,

- include only material that advances your point

- present the information according to a plan (spatial or relationship)

- use transitional terms to let the readers know the type of organization you are using

  - Spatial: in the middle, on the left, near the top, on the far side, and so on

  - Relationship: first, then, finally, furthermore, most important, equally important, and so on

Paragraph Developed by Description   Although description is rarely used to produce long literary works, it is often used to develop one-paragraph compositions. You may use sensory details to develop a paragraph about a point or an impression.

Describing Things   Since it is impossible to express in words all that the eye can take in if a thing were actually observed, fully develop a few objects, briefly point out others, and suggest the rest by some general terms. You may describe things or you may describe characters. In the following paragraph, Longfellow uses sight and sound to describe the beauty of a snow scene.

Professional Descriptive Paragraph

The first snow came. How beautiful it was, falling so silently all day long, all night long, on the mountains, on the meadows, on the roofs of the living, on the graves of the dead! All white save the river, that marked its course by a winding black line across the landscape; and the leafless trees, that against the leaden sky now revealed more fully the wonderful beauty and intricacies of their branches. What silence, too, came with the snow, and what seclusion! Every sound was muffled, every noise changed to something soft and musical. No more tramping hoofs, no more rattling wheels! Only the chiming sleigh-bells, beating as swift and merrily as the hearts of children.

—Henry Wadsworth Longfellow

Describing Characters   There are two kinds of character descriptions. An *individual* character description delineates a real or imaginary person by a multiplicity of traits. A *general* character description presents one trait only, common to a whole class of people. Both descriptions should present the individual, or the class of persons described, by striking traits that will enable the reader to form a distinct idea of the person or the class of people.

Following are two types of description. In the first example, Welty paints a vivid word picture of Phoenix Jackson as she begins her long trek to secure essential medicine for her little grandson. In the second example, Marshall describes one minister who exemplifies the class of clergymen who are "good and easy."

Professional Descriptive Paragraphs

from A Worn Path

Far out in the country there was an old Negro woman with her head tied in a red rag. . . . She was very old and small. . . .carried a thin, small cane made from an umbrella. . . . wore a dark striped dress reaching down to her shoe tops, and an equally long apron of bleached sugar sacks, with a full pocket: all neat and tidy, but every time she took a step she might have fallen over her shoelaces, which dragged from her unlaced shoes.

—Eudora Welty

from Comedy of Convocation

The Good and Easy Clergyman was a more agreeable type, and one which he had frequent opportunities of studying. . . .His voice and manner were so tender that he seemed to be always on the point of making everybody an offer of marriage. . . . Sometimes his eye would kindle, and you would have said he was going to launch a rebuke against some popular sin; but good taste came promptly to the rescue, and the sinner's sensibility was greatly spared. He considered [his sermons] in every aspect, and drew such ravishing pictures of the "devoted mother," or "the Christian at home," or "the good parent's reward," that people said his sermons were as good as a novel; and so they were. He was quite sure he never once alluded to hell during his whole career.

—Marshall

Writing Suggestions

Use one of the following topics and write a descriptive paragraph.

1. A homeless person or a famous person
2. A courteous robber or some other criminal
3. Your room
4. Your special place
5. The route you take to school
6. A crime scene
7. Your favorite painting
8. An accident scene
9. Your least or most favorite instructor
10. Your pet

Writing Suggestions

Write a five-paragraph essay on one of the following topics. Be sure that you have a reason for writing the essay. Do not tell a story for the sake of telling a story, and do not describe something just for the sake of describing it.

1. An incident in your life that taught you a lesson.

2. An incident that changed your thinking about something or one that gave you new insights into yourself.

3. An event that was a blessing in disguise.

4. Describe your life after you win the lottery. You may choose the amount you win.

5. Something you once valued but no longer value.

6. Your life ten years from now.

7. Describe your ideal person of the opposite sex. Include appearance, personality, and some other major point that you consider important.

8. The greatest event (concert, sports, theatrical performance, and so on) that you have ever attended.

9. A particular place that is special to you. You may use a combination of narration and description.

10. An incident in which another person greatly affected your life.

PART 3

Understanding Sentences

I always write a good first line, but I have trouble in writing the others.

MOLIÈRE, MASCARILLE,
in Les Precieuses Riddicules, Sc. 11.

Understanding Subjects and Verbs

A *sentence* contains a subject and a verb and makes a complete statement. The *subject part* of the sentence is that part about which something is being said. The *main subject* is the principal word or group of words in the subject. The *verb* is that part of the sentence that says something about the subject. The *main verb* is the principal verb and its helping verbs, if any. It shows the action of the subject or links the subject to another part of the sentence. The main verb carries the principal meaning in the sentence. If a sentence does not contain a main subject or a main verb or does not make a complete statement, it is a sentence fragment. If a sentence contains more than one complete statement, it is a run-together sentence. Sentence fragments and run-together sentences are major sentence skills errors. To rid your writing of these errors and to use subjects and verbs correctly, you need to recognize subjects and verbs and know how they function.

Understanding Verbs

When you are trying to decide if a word is a verb or not, put *I, you, he, she, it,* or *they* in front of it, and if the sentence makes sense, the word is a verb.

SENTENCE	CHECK	RESULT
The girls enjoyed the play.	*They* enjoyed the play.	Makes sense
Fred sings and dances.	*He* sings and dances.	Makes sense
Linda looks happy.	*She* looks happy.	Makes sense
The play is a tragedy.	*It* is a tragedy.	Makes sense

▶ **Action Verbs** *Action verbs* may be physical or mental. The action of a physical verb is visible. The action of a mental verb is not visible. Following are a few examples of action verbs:

Physical   *cry   drink   jump   hit   blow   make   perform   drop*

The umpire shouts. The pitcher drops the ball. The catcher laughs.

Mental   *know   imagine   enjoy   hate   love   think   like   believe*

The crowd enjoys the show. The fans dislike the pitcher.

EXERCISE 1

In each of the following sentences, put two lines under the action verb.

I sit astride life like a bad rider on a horse. —Ludwig Wittgenstein

By night an atheist half believes in God. —Edward Young

1. Early adult literature recounted myths and legends, including ballads, sagas, and epics.

2. Children too enjoyed these forms of literature.

3. Bede and others wrote instructional material expressly for children.

4. John Newberry published "Little Goody Two Shoes" in 1766.

5. In 1884–1885 William Caxton printed *Aesop's Fables* and Malory's *Morte d'Arthur*.

6. Other books of the same period taught the alphabet, numbers, and prayers.

7. The first English literature for children related dreary, religious tales.

8. In 1719 Daniel Defoe's *Robinson Crusoe* brought excitement to English literature.

9. Crusoe, an English sailor, survived for several years on a small tropical island.

10. Johanthan Swift's *Gulliver's Travels* satirized English courts, political parties, and statesmen.

▶ **Linking Verbs** Linking verbs function as main verbs. A *linking verb* links the subject to a noun, pronoun, or adjective that renames or describes the subject. Think of a linking verb as an equal sign.

Sue is a *carpenter.* (The noun *carpenter* renames the subject—Sue. Sue = carpenter)

The butler became a prime *suspect.* (The noun *suspect* renames the subject— butler. butler = suspect)

The mob remains *hostile.* (The adjective *hostile* describes the subject—mob. mob = hostile)

The police officers look stern. (The adjective *stern* describes the subject— officers. officers = stern)

The most common linking verbs are

- some form of the verb *be*

- verbs that can be perceived through the five senses

- verbs that indicate a state of being

Frequently Used Linking Verbs

Be	*am, are, is, was, were, be, being, been*
Sense	*feel, look, smell, sound, taste*
State of Being	*appear, become, believe, grow, prove, remain, stay, seem, turn*

EXERCISE 2

In each of the following sentences, put two lines under the linking verb.

Wanda is the winner. Her mother looked pleased.

1. Francis felt happy.

2. Those boys are my brothers

3. That kitten appears contented.

4. A tomato is a fruit.

5. She became a physician.

6. This apple tastes sour.

7. That music sounds terrible.

8. That tiger appears vicious.

9. Peanuts are legumes.

10. My dog is a field champion.

Note: Many linking verbs may also be used as action words. If a form of *seem* cannot be substituted for the verb, then it is probably functioning as an action verb. If a form of *seem* can be substituted for the verb, it is probably functioning as a linking verb.

ACTION	LINKING
She felt (*seem*) the material. No	He feels (*seems*) ill. Yes
They looked (*seemed*) *for* evidence. No	They looked (*seemed*) unhappy. Yes
He appeared (*seemed*) before the judge. No	He appeared (*seemed*) uneasy. Yes
She remained (*seemed*) in the study. No	She remained (*seemed*) calm. Yes

EXERCISE 3

In each of the following sentences, put two lines under the verb.

1. I smell honeysuckle.
2. He sounded the alarm.
3. They tasted the brew.
4. She stayed in the car.
5. She smelled the gas fumes.

6. The detective looked for evidence.
7. He felt the heat.
8. She turned to say goodbye.
9. They looked for the lost child.
10. The vine grew over the fence.

▶ **Main Verbs**   The main verb in a sentence may be a *one-word verb*, a *compound verb*, or a *verb phrase*. A compound verb has two or more verbs that are connected by a joining word (usually *and* or *or*) and have the same subject. A verb phrase has a main verb and one or more helping verbs.

One-Word Verb   The man / staggered in front of the car. The car / swerved.

Compound Verb   The driver / braked and stopped. The pedestrian / staggered and fell.

Verb Phrase   The police / have been called. The officer / will make a full report.

Note: Sometimes the parts of a verb phrase may be separated by words such as *always, never, not, hardly, scarcely, just, only,* and so on. Although these words appear next to a main verb, they are not part of it.

Separated Verb Phrases   Shelly / cannot help you. She / has just received bad news.

▶ **Helping Verbs**   *Helping verbs* combine with main verbs to make a statement about the subject. Helping verbs are forms of the *be* verbs, *do* verbs, *have* verbs, *condition* verbs, and *combinations* of these verbs.

He *can* drive the car. She *has* tried to get help. They *might have* been friends.

I *have been* helping them. You *should have* told me about your problem. He *must have* been here.

 **Forms of Helping Verbs**

Be	*am, are, is, was, were, be, being, been*
Do	*do, does, did, done, doing*
Have	*have, has, had, having*
Condition	*can, could, may, might, must, need [to], ought [to], shall, should, will, would*

Combinations:

have	**+ be**	*have been, has been, had been*
condition verbs	**+ be**	*can be*
condition verbs	**+ have**	*can have*
condition verbs	**+ have + be**	*can have been*

EXERCISE 4

Complete each sentence by adding the main verb (or some form of it) in parentheses and one or more helping verbs.

(write) I *will* write to you later.

(send) At a young age, the Grimm Brothers *were* sent to live with their grandfather.

1. (publish) *Grimm's Fairy Tales* __________________ in 1812–1815.

2. (write) In the nineteenth century novelists __________________ quality literature for children.

3. (include) Fantasy __________________ in much of the literature.

4. (enjoy) In 1926 children __________________ A. A. Milne's *The House at Pooh Corner.*

5. (read) When you were a child, __________________ you __________________ *Winnie the Pooh?*

6. (buy) The Smiths __________________ several Pooh books for their new baby.

7. (publish) *The Hobbit* __________________ in 1937.

8. (open) The *Nutcracker Ballet* _____________________ next Thursday.

9. (buy) My neighbors _____________________their tickets.

10. (see) I _____________________ already _____________________ it.

 ### Be, Do, and Have Verbs

The helping verbs *be, do,* and *have* may be used alone or in a verb phrase as the main verb of a sentence. They change form to show the time of the action or condition of the subject.

BE	DO	HAVE
I am busy.	I do my homework.	I have your number.
They are ready.	He does the dirty work.	She has the flu.
He is handsome.	She did all the work.	She had a cold.
He was here.	She will do her job.	They have bought a new car.
She is having a bad day.		
He will be here soon.		
They were walking.		

 ### Condition Verbs

The *condition* verbs cannot be used alone as the main verb of a sentence because they require a helping verb. They help other verbs express the meaning of *ability, advisability, necessity, obligation, permission,* or *possibility.*

You can call.	You could have called.	You may call later.
I might answer your call.	You must call your mother.	I shall call you tomorrow.
I will call you every day.	You should call your father	He will call you later.
Your call would be welcomed.		

EXERCISE 5

In each of the following sentences, put two lines under the verb.

I am in front of you.   I was here first.   You should have been here earlier.

1. You do the driving.

2. He should have been careful.

3. He is at the dentist's office.

4. They must have been late.

5. I have a headache.

6. They had a quarrel.

7. He might have been hurt.

8. I shall go next week.

9. They may be the next victims.

10. He must have done something wrong.

EXERCISE 6

In each of the following sentences, put two lines under the verb and identify the type by using O for one-word-verbs, C for compound verbs, and VP for verb phrases.

______   1. Some mountains are extremely steep and form high peaks.

______   2. Other mountains are lower and have more gently rounded peaks.

______   3. A series of mountains may be called a range.

______   4. A group of ranges is commonly called a chain.

______   5. Some very old mountain ranges, such as the Appalachians, were pushed up more than 250 million years ago.

______   6. Is the minimum height of a mountain 980 feet?

______   7. The world's highest mountain range stretches between India and Tibet.

______   8. The Brooks Range, the northernmost section of the Rocky Mountains, is located in Alaska.

______   9. Do the Rocky Mountains run from northwestern Canada to the southwestern United States?

______   10. The Andes in South America and the Rockies in North America, the two largest mountain ranges in the world, form a great mountain chain.

EXERCISE 7

Write eight sentences, two with a one-word verb, two with a compound verb, two with a verb phrase, and two with a separated verb phrase. Double underline the verbs.

Note: Do not be misled by verbs that have their forms changed by adding *-ing* or *to*. When a new word is formed by adding *-ing* to the end of a verb, that word cannot serve as a sentence's main verb unless it is used with one or more helping verbs.

Incomplete Verb   She ˄ playing tennis.   They ˄ leaving.   Business ˄ booming.

Complete Verb   She is playing tennis They are leaving. Business is booming.

When the word *to* is placed in front of a verb, that verb cannot serve as the verb of a sentence.

To + a Verb   He wants to go.   To win is his goal.   I have a plane to catch.

He came to hear her.

Sometimes the word *to* in front of the verb is left out, but it is still understood to be before the verb.

Help me [to] *do* the dishes.   The aspirin helped [to] *alleviate* the pain.

EXERCISE 8

In each of the following sentences, put two lines under the verb.

1. Linda wanted to become a scientist.

2. Being a physician was her sister's goal.

3. Writing her college application letter was a difficult task.

4. Helen offered to help her write it.

5. Declining her offer, Linda asked Mr. Dale to assist her in the task.

6. Mr. Dale had been helping other students write their letters of application.

7. He tried to work with all the college-bound students.

8. He helped many students get into college.

9. Often he would be working with several students at the same time.

10. Being a full-time track coach and a part-time writing coach kept him busy.

EXERCISE 9

Write sentences using each term in parentheses. Put two lines under the verbs in your sentences.

1. (verb + -ing word) ____

2. (verb + -ing word) ____

3. (to + a verb expression) ____

4. (to + a verb expression) ____

5. (to + a verb expression, omitting the *to*) ______________________

Separating Complete Subjects and Complete Verbs

When sentences are long or complicated, the task of finding the subject and verb may be simplified by identifying the two main parts of a sentence—the *complete subject* and the *complete verb*. The *complete subject* is the main subject and all the words associated with it. The *complete verb* is the main verb and all the words associated with it. To find the two parts of a sentence, examine the purpose of the sentence. The purpose of a sentence is to *make a statement, ask a question, give a command,* or *make a request.*

Statement   Cabeza de Vaca was the first European to cross North America.

Question   Did he wander for eight years before finally reaching northwest Mexico?

Command or Request   For more information about de Vaca, read his account of the journey.

EXERCISE 10

Classify each of the following sentences according to its purpose. Use S for statements, Q for questions, and C for commands or requests.

1. What does the name *Cabeza de Vaca* mean? ______

2. It means "the head of a cow." ______

3. That is a strange name. ______

4. How did he get this name? ______

5. One of his ancestors helped the Spanish troops by marking a crucial mountain pass with the head of a cow. ______

6. Read the story about the way the king showed his gratitude to the man. ______

7. He ennobled the family and changed their name to Cabeza de Vaca. ______

8. For an interesting description of buffalo, read de Vaca's colorful account. ______

9. What happened to de Vaca after he returned to Spain? ______

10. He became governor of Paraguay. ______

▶ **Statement Sentences** In most statement sentences, the *complete subject* is the first part, and the *complete verb* is the second part. To separate the complete subject and the complete verb in a statement sentence, put a slash mark in front of the first verb in the sentence. In the following sentences, the complete subjects are underlined, and the complete verbs are double underlined.

The colonists in Paraguay / revolted.

They / shipped de Vaca back to Spain in chains.

EXERCISE 11

In the following sentence statements, put a slash mark between the complete subject and the complete verb and put two lines under the main verb.

1. The solar system is made up of the sun and nine planets.

2. All the planets circle the sun.

3. Moons orbit many planets.

4. Europa, one of the four brightest satellites of Jupiter, is named after a Phoenician princess.

5. She was abducted and taken to Crete by the Greek god Zeus.

6. It was originally sighted by Galileo.

7. Titan is the name of the largest satellite of Saturn.

8. It is the largest satellite in the solar system.

9. In Greek mythology the Titans were a family of gods.

10. They were overthrown and supplanted by the family of Zeus.

Here and There   *Here* and *there* are not usually the subject of a statement sentence. In sentences beginning with the words *there* or *here* followed by a form of the verb *be*, the subject follows the verb. To more easily separate the complete subject and the complete verb in these kinds of sentences, revise them. Move or drop *here* and *there*, and when necessary, relocate the verb.

Here statement	*Here* is the glass.	**Relocated *here***	The glass / is here.
There statement	*There* is no place like home.	**Dropped *there***	No place / is like home.

EXERCISE 12

Revise the following sentences. Put a slash mark between the complete subject and the complete verb, and put two lines under the main verb.

1. There is a cloud of comets at the outer edge of the solar system.

2. There are seven large moons in the solar system.

3. There are four planets (Mercury, Venus, Earth, and Mars) closer to the sun than the others.

4. Here they are known as the Earthlike planets.

5. There are gas giants (Jupiter, Saturn, Uranus, and Neptune) beyond Mars.

6. Here is a copy of a book about the solar system.

7. Here are a few questions from students.

8. Here you can see Saturn through a telescope.

9. Here is one of the most beautiful things that can be seen through a telescope.

10. There is a beautiful system of rings surrounding Saturn.

▶ **Question Sentences**   To separate the complete subject and complete verb of a question, turn it into a statement. The statement may sound awkward, but it will help you find the two parts of the sentence.

Question Was de Vaca tried?   **Statement** De Vaca / was tried.   **Solution** Was de Vaca tried?

Question Did they exile him?   **Statement** They / did exile him.   **Solution** Did they exile him?

EXERCISE 13

Turn each of the following questions into statements and then separate the complete subject and complete verb by putting a slash mark in front of the first verb. Put two lines under the main verb.

1. Are you sugar sensitive?

2. As a child did you hide candy?

3. As an adult how often do you eat sweets?

4. Do you eat an entire container full of sweets and then hide the container?

5. Have you lied about how much sweet food you eat?

6. Do you hide your sweet treats from others?

7. Do you eat sweets such as sugar, jelly, or honey straight from the container?

8. Can people be addicted to sugar?

9. Do you turn to sweets for solace?

10. Do you often eat sweets as snacks between meals?

> ► **Command or Request Sentences**   Every command or request statement has the same subject—*you*. It may be stated or implied. When it is implied, write *you* in parentheses before the verb.

Stated   <u>You</u> / should <u><u>cover</u></u> your mouth when you cough.

Implied   (<u>You</u>) / <u><u>Cover</u></u> your mouth when you cough.

EXERCISE 14

Use a slash mark to separate the complete subject and the complete verb in the following sentences. If the subject is implied, add *you* in parentheses. Put two lines under the main verb.

1. Please pass the chocolate.

2. Try to control yourself.

3. Have your credit card ready.

4. You should spend two hours on homework for every in-class hour.

5. You can expect a call from my lawyer in a few days.

6. Buy now and pay later.

7. You can become a good writer.

8. Stop by my office sometime tomorrow.

9. Drop and roll if you are in flames.

10. Be calm during an emergency.

Understanding Subjects

The subject is what the sentence is about. It is the *who* or *what* that is doing the action or being the condition of the verb. The whole subject is called the *complete subject*. The *main subject* is the principal word or group of words in the subject. The subject may be a noun or a noun substitute.

> ► **Nouns**   A *noun* is a naming word that names *people*, *places*, *things*, or *ideas*. There are thousands of nouns in the English language. Following is a list of types of nouns, their description, and examples of them.

Kinds of Nouns

TYPE	DESCRIPTION	EXAMPLES
Specific	names of specific people, places, or things	John Galt, London, Monday
General	names of general people, places, or things	man, city, day
Sensible	things perceptible by the senses	rain, honey
Not Sensible	things not perceptible by the senses	attitude, memory
Collective	names of groups	team, jury
Countable	items that can be counted	hours, cups
Uncountable	material that cannot be counted	sand, water

Specific From 1892 to 1943 <u>Ellis Island</u> was the major entry station for immigrants to the United States.

General Before they're <u>plumbers</u> or <u>writers</u> or <u>unemployed</u> or <u>journalists</u>, before everything else, <u>men</u> are <u>men</u>. —Marguerite Duras

Sensible <u>Wine</u> makes a man more pleased with himself. —Samuel Johnson

Not Sensible <u>Procrastination</u> is the thief of time. —Edmund Young

Collective A <u>committee</u> is an animal with four back legs. —John Le Carré

Countable The red-letter <u>days</u> now become . . . dead-letter <u>days</u>. —Charles Lamb

Uncountable (also called *mass nouns*) Aunt Jemima pancake <u>flour</u> was invented in 1889.

Noun Indicators To simplify identifying nouns, look for *noun indicators*. These words (*a, an, the, this, some, all, every,* and so on and possessives such as *my, your, ours, Ted's,* and so on) signal that a noun is coming.

a house	*Betty's* boots	*all* children
an opportunity	*no* value	*every* student
the law	*some* peace	*such* examples

Note: Sometimes another word or words come between the indicator and the noun.

The *first* <u>duty</u> in life is to be as artificial as possible. —Oscar Wilde

The *only* <u>rules</u> comedy can tolerate are those of taste, and **the** *only* <u>limitations</u> those of libel. —James Thurber

 **Subjects**

Most English independent clauses (sentences) and dependent clauses contain a subject and a verb and are used to make statements or ask questions. Make sure all clauses contain a subject.

No   <u>Megan</u> ordered a large steak *because was hungry.* (dependent clause missing a subject)

Yes   <u>Megan</u> ordered a large steak *because <u>she</u> was hungry.*

In sentences that make a statement, usually the subject comes before the verb.

<u>Jane</u> <u>will come</u> to your house. The <u>dog</u> <u>barked</u>. (The dog did bark.)

In sentences that ask a question, usually part of the verb comes before the subject.

<u>Will</u> <u>Jane</u> <u>come</u> to your house? <u>Did</u> the <u>dog</u> <u>bark</u>?

Do not put a personal pronoun next to the subject.

No   My little dog **he** is lost.   **Yes**   My little dog is lost.

No   My aunt and uncle **they** are in New York.   **Yes**   My aunt and uncle are in New York.

When the sentence is a command or polite request, the subject is **you.** It may be stated or implied.

Stated   <u>You</u> close the door.   **Implied**   Close the door. (You) close the door.

Some English clauses have a filler word in the subject position, and the subject comes later. When you are writing this kind of sentence, always include the filler word.

No   Are many thorns on roses.   Many thorns on roses.

Yes   **There** are many thorns on rose stems.

No   Is time for me to study.   Time for me to study.

Yes   **It** is time for me to study.

Although in some languages a sentence may begin with a word that is not grammatically linked to the sentence, in English the subject must clearly state what the sentence is about.

No   Handsome man I am attracted to him.

Yes   I am attracted to that handsome man.

 **Singular and Plural Nouns**

A noun that refers to one person or thing is *singular* in number: one picture, one child, one lake. A noun that refers to more than one person or thing is *plural* in number: two pictures, two children, two lakes.

Countable nouns usually have a singular form and a plural form: week, weeks.

Uncountable nouns usually have only a singular form: rain, snow, sugar.

A and ***an*** can only refer to singular nouns.

No   **a** rivers   **an** islands   **Yes**   **a** river   **an** island

The can refer to either singular or plural nouns.

Yes   **the** river   **the** rivers   **the** island   **the** islands

A and ***an*** are not used with uncountable nouns.

No   **A** rain is falling.   **Yes**   **The** rain is falling.

The makes a noun more specific. *A* and ***an*** do not.

The boy ate **a** pie. (a single item, not specific)

The boy ate **the** pie. (a specific pie)

The baby has **an** apple. (a single item, not specific)

The baby has **the** apple. (a specific apple)

 **Specific Nouns (Proper Nouns)**

No article or the article *the* is used before specific nouns. Usually, *singular specific nouns* take no article.

No   **The** William Faulkner is a famous writer.   **Yes**   William Faulkner is a famous writer.

Usually, *plural specific nouns* take the article *the.*

No   Santa Cruz Islands were discovered in 1595.

Yes   **The** Santa Cruz Islands were discovered in 1595.

 **General Nouns (Common Nouns)**

Singular countable nouns take *a, an,* or *the*. These nouns cannot stand alone.

No   Baby is crying.   **Yes**   A baby is crying.   **Yes**   The baby is crying.

Plural countable nouns take no article or the article *the*. Do not use an article before a plural countable noun that refers to persons or things as a group or in general.

No   The golfers are competitive people.   **Yes**   Golfers are competitive people.

Use *the* to refer to something specific.

No   Golfers ate in the clubhouse.   **Yes**   The golfers ate in the clubhouse.

▶ **Pronouns**   *Pronouns* are words used in place of a noun. They may be used to replace a noun, refer to a noun in general, or point to a noun.

Personal Pronouns   Personal pronouns replace specific nouns. They include *I, me, we, us, my, mine, our, ours, you, your, yours, he, she, it, its, him, his, her, hers, they, them, their,* and *theirs.*

Reggie is a student. He attends college. (The pronoun *he* replaces the noun *Reggie.*)

Diamonds are beautiful. They are expensive. (The pronoun *they* replaces the noun *diamonds.*)

Independent Pronouns (*indefinite pronouns*)   Independent pronouns do not refer to any specific person or thing but refer to a noun in general. They include *all, another, any, anybody, anyone, both, each, either, everybody, everyone, few, many, most, neither, nobody, none, no one, one, other, several, some, somebody, someone,* and *such.*

Everyone likes him. (The pronoun *everyone* refers to people in a general way.)

Someone should call the police. (The pronoun *someone* refers to a person in a general way.)

Pointing Pronouns   Pointing pronouns point to persons or things. *This, that, these,* and *those* are pointing pronouns.

This is my new coat. (The pronoun *this* points to the noun *coat.*)

That is a haunted house. (The pronoun *that* points to the noun *house.*)

▶ **Noun Clauses**   A noun clause can be used as the subject of a sentence. A *noun clause* is a group of related words that has a subject and a verb and begins with one of the following words: *how, that, what, whatever, when, where, whether, which, whichever, who, whoever, when, whenever, whose,* and *why.*

Whoever wins the election / must have a party for the workers.

Why this is important / should be clear. How to solve the problem / was our concern.

▶ **Verb + -ing and To + a Verb Words and Phrases**   A verb ending in *-ing* (a *gerund*) or *to + a verb* expression (an *infinitive*) may be the subject of a sentence.

-ing word subjects	Swimming /is good exercise. Clear thinking / precedes clear writing. Getting her phone number / was his objective.
To + a verb subjects	To succeed is his goal. To see is to believe. To see the show / is an experience.

▶ **Main Subjects**   The **main subject** of a sentence is the principal word or group of words in the subject part of the sentence. The **complete subject** of a sentence is the main subject plus the words associated with it.

The first **attempt** to abandon Hansel and Gretel / fails.

The second abandonment **plan** / is more successful.

The main subject may be a *one-word* subject, a *compound* subject (two or more words connected by a joining word) a *noun clause* subject (a subordinate clause used as a noun), or a *verb form* subject.

One-word subjects	The man / staggered in front of the car. The car / swerved. The poor, starving children / are prisoners in a cannibalistic witch's cottage.
Compound subjects	The dog and the cat / fought. The boy and girl / played. Hansel and Gretel / hear their parents' plans for abandonment.
Noun clause subjects	Where he put the key / is a mystery. Whoever wants to know the heart and mind of America had better learn baseball. . . . —Jaques Barzun

Verb form subjects   Dieting / takes willpower. Earning an "A" / requires hard work.

To meditate / is therapeutic. To discipline the child / seems useless.

To find the main subject of a sentence, first find the verb, and then ask WHO? or WHAT? is doing the action of the verb. The answer will be the subject.

Mountains are made of many different rocks. WHAT are made? mountains

Edmund Hillary and Tenzing Norkay became the first explorers to reach the summit of Mt. Everest, WHO became? Edmund Hillary and Tenzing Norkay

Lake Titicaca (TIT-i-**KAH**-kuh) lies in the Andes Mountains. WHAT lies? Lake Titicaca It is the largest navigable lake in the world. WHAT is? it (pronoun for *lake*)

Recognizing Prepositional Phrases

A *preposition* is a word that is used to show the relationship (space, time, cause, and so on) of a noun or a noun substitute to another word in the sentence. A *prepositional phrase* is a group of words beginning with a preposition and usually ending with a noun or pronoun.

The silk **rug** *under* the coffee *table* is from Bahrain. (relationship of rug to table)
Out of the Attic was written *by Doug Johnson*. (relationship of book to the author)

Frequently Used Prepositions

about	*before*	*during*	*through*
above	*behind*	*for*	*to*
across	*below*	*from*	*toward*
after	*beneath*	*in*	*under*
against	*beside*	*into*	*underneath*
along	*between*	*of*	*until*
among	*beyond*	*off*	*up*
around	*by*	*on*	*upon*
at	*down*	*over*	*with*

You need to recognize prepositional phrases so that you will not confuse the noun or pronoun in them with the subject of the sentence. Generally, crossing out prepositional phrases simplifies the task of finding subjects.

The golfer's ball went through the trees, over the water, and into the sand trap.

The golfer jumped into his cart, raced across the fairway, took his sand wedge from his bag, walked into the sand trap, and took aim at the ball.

EXERCISE 15

Put one line under the main subject and two lines under the main verb. Use the WHO? or WHAT? method to find the subject. You may find it helpful to put a slash mark between the complete subject and the complete verb and to cross out prepositional phrases.

Through cultural conditioning attitudes and values / are transmitted to the members of a society.

WHO or **WHAT** are transmitted? Answer: attitudes and values

Members of a society / are shaped by the customary beliefs and social forms of their society.

WHO or **WHAT** are shaped? Answer: Members

1. People's accumulated knowledge and experiences guide their behavior.

2. We are to a large degree the products of the particular place and time in which we were raised.

3. Many assumptions and beliefs are the result of cultural conditioning.

4. Some of these ideas are deeply embedded in people's way of thinking. They may not even be aware of them.

5. Inherited cultural assumptions may include unexamined assumptions. These unexamined assumptions may be neither true nor laudable.

6. Unexamined cultural assumptions bias people's thinking and prevent them from thinking critically.

7. Critical thinkers will examine the source and validity of their cultural assumptions.

8. Many cultural assumptions, especially the ones involving the roles of men and women, should be critically examined.

9. Non-critical thinkers hold to their assumptions and believe in them despite evidence to the contrary.

10. For these non-critical thinkers, evidence does not alter their assumptions. They force the evidence to conform to their beliefs.

EXERCISE 16

The following sentences are examples of biased cultural assumptions. In each sentence, fill in the subject with the word that reflects common beliefs and put two lines under the main verb.

1. ___________________ make better nurses than men.

2. The _________________ should be the major breadwinner.

3. ___________________ are naturally passive.

4. ___________________ are naturally aggressive.

5. ___________________ may be sexually promiscuous, but not females.

6. Real _________________ do not cry.

7. ___________________ should be seen and not heard.

8. Rich _________________ are unhappy.

9. ___________________ cannot buy happiness.

10. ___________________ should be physically punished for their crimes.

Review Exercises

Finding Subjects and Verbs

Put two lines under the main verb in a sentence and fill in blank spaces with an appropriate verb. Use the WHO or WHAT method to find the main subject.

The problems of many fairy tale heroines are caused by an ogress—a female monster.

A fairy tale ____is____ / a fanciful tale of legendary deeds and creatures.

One-Word Main Verb   Few young female fairy tale heroines / control their own lives.

Compound Main Verb   Family members /often mistreat them, abuse them, or abandon them.

Verb Phrase   Are they victimized by people and circumstances? (question)
They/ are victimized by people and circumstances. (statement)
Are they victimized by people and circumstances? (solution)

Separated Verb Phrase   They / are often rescued by some magical figure or by a male.

Note: In some sentences you may find it helpful to first identify the complete subject and complete verb and separate them with a slash mark and cross out prepositional phrases.

REVIEW EXERCISE 17

1. Often fairy tale heroines are victimized by a family member.

2. In many cases the father causes the problem by his actions or permits the injustices to occur.

3. Where was Cinderella's father? Did he know about his daughter's mistreatment?

4. In another famous fairy tale, Beauty is forced to live with a beast. Her father ___________________ stolen a rose from the beast's garden.

5. Her father ___________________ a choice. He can die or send his daughter to live with the beast.

6. Did Beauty willingly go to the castle of the beast? "Oh yes, I would do anything to please my father."

7. A boastful miller lies about his daughter's ability to spin straw into gold.

8. His boast almost ___________________ his daughter her life and almost ___________________ her to give her first child to Rumpelstiltskin.

9. Rumpelstiltskin spins the straw into gold for the miller's daughter.

10. Snow White's father is another absent father. He never seems to be around and never hears the conversations between the new queen and her mirror.

REVIEW EXERCISE 18

1. Beauty and a good heart ___________________ to be the necessary ingredients for a fairy tale heroine.

2. Marrying a handsome prince will enable her to live happily ever after.

3. In one story an old fairy casts an evil spell on a beautiful princess.

4. The fairy is a jealous, ugly, old, evil woman.

5. In the same story another female disobeys the king's orders to destroy all spinning wheels.

6. This woman is old and insubordinate.

7. The old woman allows the young princess to play with a spindle.

8. The old woman is foolish.

9. The princess pricks her finger and goes to sleep for a hundred years.

10. With just one kiss, a handsome young prince _____________________ Sleeping Beauty and brings to life all the inhabitants of the castle.

REVIEW EXERCISE 19

1. Nursery rhymes and fairy tales are part of children's early cultural conditioning.

2. Most people do not forget childhood rhymes and fairy tales.

3. Often these rhymes and fairy tales contain elements of truth about the human condition.

4. They also reflect the attitudes and values of society.

5. An examination of females in nursery rhymes and fairy tales reveals some interesting patterns.

6. Certain females are odious (**OH**-di-uhs) or evil.

7. Other females are young and beautiful but have problems. The problems can only be solved by magical intervention or by the acts of a male.

8. The story of Cinderella is an old one.

9. It first appeared in a centuries-old Chinese book.

10. Even in this story, she has a wicked stepmother.

REVIEW EXERCISE 20

1. Most fairy tale stepmothers are wicked hags or evil witches.

2. These hags or witches are usually older women.

3. In general, older women are not well-treated in children's literature. Think about some of your childhood nursery rhymes.

4. "Old Mother Hubbard went to the cupboard to get her poor dog a bone."

5. The ending of the rhyme is strange. The dog is happy, well-fed, well-dressed, and has the old woman for his servant.

6. "The dame made a curtesy,/ The dog made a bow;/ The dame said, 'Your servant,'/ The dog said, 'Bow-wow!'"

7. The old woman in the shoe is not a paragon of motherhood.

8. She whips her children and then sends them to bed hungry.

9. Jack Sprat's wife is obese. He has to wheel her around in a wheelbarrow.

10. Peter, the pumpkin eater, solves the problem of a runaway wife by incarcerating her.

REVIEW EXERCISE 21

1. Children's literature and myths convey social attitudes, concepts, and many biases.

2. The word *Cinderella* is often used to describe a sports team.

3. A Cinderella team _____________________ success after being unsuccessful for a long time.

4. There are many foolish people. Their goose lays golden eggs. They kill the goose and eat it. Then they wonder about their lost source of income.

5. Some of the elements of myth and children's literature moved into the realms of the collective unconscious.

6. Carl Jung (**yoong**), a Swiss psychiatrist, _____________________ the term *collective unconscious.*

7. He _____________________ the term to mean mental patterns.

8. According to his theory, under certain conditions, these patterns become archetypes.

9. An archetype _____________________ a model or type. Other things are often patterned after an archetype.

10. A prototype or pattern of human life may be a character, an action, or a situation.

1. A sacrificial scapegoat is made to bear the blame of others.

2. According to the Bible, on the Day of Atonement, Aaron confesses all the sins of the children of Israel over the head of a live goat and sends the goat into the wilderness.

3. Symbolically, the goat takes all their sins with him.

4. The punishment of Adam may be an archetype of all people's struggles and sorrows.

5. Samuel Taylor Coleridge's *The Rime of the Ancient Mariner* is probably based on the archetype of Adam's fall.

6. Archetypes represent primordial sin, retribution, and death.

7. The works of Melville and Hawthorne come from archetypes.

8. Melville admired Hawthorne's exploration of the darker side of people and dedicated *Moby Dick* to him.

9. Melville recognized a kindred spirit in Hawthorne.

10. Great literature is often grounded in archetypal patterns.

1. According to Jung, certain images may have symbolic meanings.

2. Archetypal images abound in literature.

3. These images may include water, sun, colors, and geometric shapes.

4. Water is the most common symbol for the unconscious.

5. The sea may be representative of timelessness and eternity, infinity, death, and rebirth.

6. The flowing of rivers is often connected to transitional phases of the life cycle.

7. The sun, fire, and, sky are closely related.

8. Creative energy, laws of nature, and consciousness are related to the sun.

9. A father is symbolic of creative energy.

10. The color black is often associated with chaos, death, and the unconscious.

REVIEW EXERCISE 24

1. Red may represent blood, sacrifice, passion, or disorder.

2. The circle or sphere may be connected to wholeness, unity, and life.

3. These images, however, do not always function as archetypes.

4. Many myths and their elements _____________________ archetypes.

5. The forms of the archetypal woman may include Earth Mother, Terrible Mother, and Soul-Mate.

6. Ships may be compared to people's voyage through time and space.

7. Hero archetypes may fall into the categories of transformation and redemption.

8. The sacrifice of a hero may be considered an archetype.

9. Superman may fit the pattern of a super savior.

10. A hero-savior often _____________________ long, difficult journeys and performs impossible deeds.

Identifying and Correcting Sentence Fragments

A *complete sentence* includes a subject, a complete verb, and makes sense by it-self. A *sentence fragment* is an incomplete sentence that is punctuated as if it were a complete sentence. Many instructors consider the sentence fragment to be the most serious of all sentence skill errors. Learn to recognize fragments and correct them so that you can rid your writing of them. If your readers cannot tell where one idea ends and another one begins, they may have difficulty under-standing what you have to say. In each of the following examples, the meaning is not clear and may be interpreted in more than one way.

Fragment   John scored two touchdowns. *Although his hand was broken.* He did not tell the coach.

Problem   John scored two touchdowns although his hand was broken. or Although his hand was broken, John did not tell the coach.

Fragment   *When war came with Japan.* The Japanese seized three Alaskan islands. *Planning to use them as bases.* The U.S. government began work on a number of military installations.

Problem   Was Japan going to use the islands as bases, or was the United States going to use them as military installations?

Fragment   The area of Alaska is 586,400 square miles. *Nearly a fifth of the size of the rest of the United States.* Texas is ranked second.

Problem   Which state is nearly a fifth of the size of the rest of the United States?

Note: Do not confuse a short sentence with a sentence fragment. A complete sentence may be short or long. The length of a sentence has nothing to do with fragmentation.

Sentence fragments may be caused by

- missing verbs

- missing subjects

- dependent clauses

- modifiers

- transitions

To rid your writing of sentence fragments and write smooth sentences, you need to be able to correct them in several different ways. Often, the type of error will dictate the type of correction. Correct a sentence fragment by

- adding a missing verb, a missing subject, or both

- changing a verb form

- dropping a dependent word

- attaching the fragment to the sentence in front of it or the one after it

- rewriting the passage

Missing-Verb Fragments

A complete sentence must have a verb that tells what the subject is doing, has done, will do, or its condition. These fragments may be caused by the careless omission of a verb, when a writer mistakenly thinks that the verb in the first part of a compound sentence can serve as the verb in the second part of the sentence, by an incomplete verb, or by a list following a complete sentence. When a fragment has no verb, add a verb, attach it to an adjoining sentence, or add the verb and form a new sentence.

▶ **Careless Omissions**   Sometimes verbs are carelessly omitted because the writer mistakenly thinks that the verb in one sentence can serve as the verb in a following sentence.

> Two serious disputes arose between the United States and Britain over Alaskan affairs.
>
> *The first* ∧ *about seal hunting in the Bering Sea.*
>
> *The other* ∧ *about the boundaries between the United States and Canada.*
>
> Two disputes arose between the United States and Britain over Alaskan affairs.
>
> The first was about seal hunting in the Bering Sea. (verb added = two sentences)
>
> The first was about seal hunting in the Bering Sea, and the *other* was about the boundaries between the United States and Canada. (verb added, sentences joined = compound sentence)

▶ **Compound Sentences**   The verb in the first part of a compound sentence cannot serve as the verb in the second part. It must have its own verb.

No   Small amounts of gold were found in Alaska in 1861, *but enormous amounts* ∧ *in the Klondike in the Yukon Territory in 1896.*

Yes   Small amounts of gold were found in Alaska in 1861. Enormous amounts were found in the Klondike in the Yukon Territory in 1896. (two sentences)

Yes   Small amounts of gold were found in Alaska in 1861, but enormous amounts were found in the Klondike in the Yukon Territory in 1896. (compound sentence)

Yes   Although small amounts of gold were found in Alaska in 1861, enormous amounts were found in the Klondike in the Yukon Territory in 1896. (complex sentence)

▶ **Lists**   A list that follows a complete sentence is sometimes incorrectly punctuated as a separate sentence, but it is not. It does not have a verb. Use a colon or a dash to attach the list to the sentence in front of it.

No   Rockwood Park appeals to many people. *Golfers, hikers, walkers, and skaters.*

Yes   Rockwood Park appeals to many people: golfers, hikers, walkers, and skaters.

No   The campground has many facilities. *Showers, a canteen, a washroom, and full hookups.*

Yes   The campground has many facilities—showers, a canteen, a washroom, and full hookups.

▶ **Incomplete Verbs**   Do not be misled by a verbal. A verbal is part of a verb acting as a noun or modifier. It is formed from a verb but cannot be used alone as the main verb in a sentence. It requires a helping verb. Verbals include

- present participles formed by adding *-ing* to a verb (watch*ing*)

- past participles formed by adding *-ed* to a regular verb (rain*ed*)

- past participles formed by adding *-ed, -d, -t, -en, -n* (rain*ed*, sav*ed*, deal*t*, eat*en*, spok*en*) to an irregular verb

- infinitives formed by putting the word *to* before a verb (*to run*)

▶ **Verb + *-ing* and Verb + *-ed* Words**   To correct *-ing* and *-ed* fragments, add a verb or a subject and a verb, change the verb form, or attach it to a complete sentence.

Fragment   The baby ran to its mother. *Crying loudly.*

Attached   The baby ran to its mother, crying loudly.

Subject and verb added   The <u>baby</u> <u>was</u> crying loudly.

Fragment   The accident happened suddenly. *The car totally wrecked.*

Attached   The accident happened suddenly, the car totally wrecked.

Verb added   The car <u>was</u> totally wrecked.

Fragment   After he left her, she sobbed. *Her heart broken.*

Attached   After he left her, she sobbed, her heart broken.

Verb added   Her heart <u>was</u> broken.

Being   When the word *being* causes the sentence fragment, change it to another form of the verb *to be* (*am, are, is, was, were*).

Fragment   *It being the only show in town.*

Verb form changed   It <u>was</u> the only show in town.

Fragment   *They being the best in the business.*

Verb form changed   They <u>were</u> the best in the business.

▶ **To + a Verb Expressions**   Do not add an explanatory *to + a verb* expression after the period in a sentence.

Their parents gave them permission. *To go trick or treating.*

Their parents gave them permission to go trick or treating.

<hr>

EXERCISE 25

Revise each of the following items to eliminate fragments caused by missing or incomplete verbs.

1. Indiana has long been called the Hoosier State. To some people it means "hill dweller." To others "highlanders."

2. The symbol "&" for ampersand means "and." One of the few survivors of Latin shorthand.

3. Martin Luther, a Protestant reformer of the sixteenth century, being one of the first persons to have a candlelit tree at Christmas.

4. Cigarettes invented by Turkish soldiers when their communal smoking pipe was destroyed by canon fire.

5. They rolled cigarettes. Using the paper that they used for firing their guns.

6. Paper money was first used in China in the ninth century. Copper being scarce and not enough coins being minted.

7. Kansas has many nicknames. Central State, Cyclone State, and Grasshopper State.

8. Anthony being the only candidate.

9. Katie called her mother. To let her know she was well and happy.

10. He opened his door to his friends. And his pocketbook to the poor.

Missing-Subject Fragments

These fragments are often caused by writers mistakenly thinking that the subject in the first part of a compound sentence can serve as the subject of the second part of the sentence. Each sentence must have its own subject. To find the subject of a sentence, first find the verb and ask "WHO?" or "WHAT?" is doing the action of the verb. If you cannot find *who* or *what* the verb is about, then the sentence is not complete. When a sentence fragment is caused by a missing subject, add an appropriate one to make it a complete sentence or attach it to an adjoining sentence, forming either a simple sentence with a compound verb or a compound sentence.

Alaska needed a state flower. *And chose the forget-me-not.* WHO chose? No one chose.

Alaska needed a state flower. <u>It</u> chose the forget-me-not. (two sentences)

Alaska <u>needed</u> a state flower and <u>chose</u> the forget-me-not. (compound verb)

Alaska needed a state flower, and <u>it</u> chose the forget-me-not. (compound sentence)

The Alaska-Canada Highway was officially opened November 20, 1942. *And was opened to the public in 1948.* WHAT was opened? Nothing was opened.

The Alaska-Canada Highway was officially opened November 20, 1942. <u>It</u> was opened to the public in 1948. (two sentences)

The Alaska-Canada Highway <u>was</u> officially <u>opened</u> November 20, 1942, and <u>was opened</u> to the public in 1948. (compound verb)

The Alaska-Canada Highway was officially opened November 20, 1942, and <u>it</u> was opened to the public in 1948. (compound sentence)

Note: Sometimes a sentence that gives a command or makes a polite request may look like it does not have a subject, but it does. *You* (either stated or implied) is the subject.

Dependent-Clause Fragments

A complete sentence must make sense by itself. A dependent clause fragment has a subject and a complete verb, but it begins with a word that makes it dependent on a sentence next to it to complete its meaning. It does not make sense by itself. When it is punctuated as a sentence, it becomes a sentence fragment. To identify dependent clause fragments, look for a group of words beginning with a dependent word. See Part 2: Building Complex Sentences (p. 28) for a list of frequently used dependent words and the relationships they express.

Correct dependent clause fragments by dropping the dependent word at the beginning of the clause or attaching the clause to an adjoining sentence. Dropping the dependent word from the dependent clause is an easy way to correct this fragment.

Because Rockwood offers many attractions. It is a popular destination.

~~Because~~ Rockwood offers many attractions. It is a popular destination.

Since the campground has many facilities. It is usually filled.

~~Since~~ The campground has many facilities. It is usually filled.

Sometimes dropping the dependent word makes the sentence choppy, or it does not say exactly what you want to say. In these cases, attach the fragment to an adjoining sentence. Decide whether it logically belongs to the sentence in front of it or to the one following it.

Fragments   *When Arizona was admitted to the Union.* Its constitution contained a radical measure. *That allowed judges to be recalled by popular vote.* It was deleted. *Because the president of the United States objected to it. After Arizona became the forty-eighth state.* It immediately amended its constitution to provide for the recall of judges.

Revised   *When* Arizona was admitted to the Union, its constitution contained a radical measure *that* allowed judges to be recalled by popular vote. It was deleted *because* the President of the United States objected to it. *After* Arizona became the forty-eighth state, it immediately amended its constitution to provide for the recall of judges.

Fragments may begin with the word *that,* or the words *who, whom, whose, which* when they are not used to form a question.

> This building is owned by Mr. Wilson. *Who is, I wish to add, a most successful business man.*

> This building is owned by Mr. Wilson, who is, I wish to add, a most successful business man.

EXERCISE 26

Revise the following items to eliminate fragments caused by missing subjects or dependent clauses.

1. George Eastman invented the first Kodak camera in 1888. And chose the name Kodak, which has no meaning. It simply satisfied trademark laws. And was easy to spell.

2. Roman soldiers probably invented the military salute. Raised their right hand. And showed that they did not have a weapon concealed in it.

3. We have Christmas dinner at home. But go out for New Year's Eve dinner.

4. Before the development of elementary vocal language. Primitive people used a combination of basic noises and simple signs to communicate with each other.

5. Because their vocal language was limited. They used facial expressions and bodily gestures to supplement grunts and growls.

6. For example, today we still use sign language for specific purposes. And use it in everyday situations—such as waving goodbye or signaling a greeting.

7. Although we may not think about it. Sign language is used in many other ways. To give directions to actors and to signal information during the production of radio and television shows.

8. When people want to add emphasis to spoken language. They often use the language of silence.

9. Although many gestures mean about the same thing in many places. Others have different meanings in different parts of the world. In most parts of the world, a hand wave says "goodbye," but not the meaning in the East.

10. Another example of sign language. In Mediterranean countries, head shaking means "yes." Elsewhere is signaled by head nodding.

Modifying Fragments

Modifying fragments usually give additional information, but they should not be punctuated as separate sentences. Attach them to the appropriate adjoining sentence, or for the sake of clarity and effective sentence construction, you may find that rewriting the passage is the best way to correct the fragment.

The modifiers may be *adverbs, adjectives, prepositional phrases, appositives,* or *transitions.*

▶ **Adverbs**   An adverb answers the questions *how* (quietly), *when* (never), *where* (everywhere), or *how often* (daily).

Fragment   Tina drove her father's new Porsche to the party. *Very carefully.*

Attached   Tina drove her father's new Porsche to the party, very carefully.

Rewritten   Tina very carefully drove her father's new Porsche to the party.

Fragment   The woman asked her husband to stop and ask for directions. *Repeatedly.*

Attached   The woman asked her husband to stop and ask for directions, repeatedly.

Rewritten   The woman repeatedly asked her husband to stop and ask for directions.

▶ **Adjectives**   An adjective answers the question *what kind* (large), *which one* (that girl), *how many* (several).

Fragment   Jeanette is a wonderful friend. *A kind, thoughtful, and generous person.*

Attached   Jeanette is a wonderful friend, a kind, thoughtful, and generous person.

Rewritten   Jeanette, a kind, thoughtful, and generous person, is a wonderful friend.

Fragment   Marty is his own worst enemy. *Witty but unwise.*

Attached   Marty is his own worst enemy, witty but unwise.

Rewritten   Marty, witty but unwise, is his own worst enemy.

▶ **Prepositional Phrases**   A *prepositional phrase* is a group of words beginning with a preposition and usually ending with a noun or pronoun. A *preposition* shows the relationship of a noun or pronoun to some other word in the sentence.

Fragment   My friend's house is on a golf course. *On the twelfth green next to the cart path.*

Attached   My friend's house is on a golf course on the twelfth green next to the cart path.

Fragment   The first Spanish settlement was a trading post. *At the place that is now Tucson.*

Attached   The first Spanish settlement was a trading post at the place that is now Tucson.

Rewritten   Spain's first settlement in the New World was a trading post on the site of present-day Tucson.

▶ **Appositives**   An *appositive* is a noun or pronoun—often with modifiers—set by another noun or pronoun to give added information about it. Use commas, not periods, to set them off.

Fragment   The Grand Canyon of the Colorado River is in the northwest corner of Arizona. *An enormous gorge twelve miles wide and a mile deep.*

Set off with commas   The Grand Canyon of the Colorado River is in the northwest corner of Arizona, an enormous gorge twelve miles wide and a mile deep.

Fragment   *Peanut. A toy fox terrier with a bad attitude. Was an effective guard dog.*

Set off with commas   Peanut, a toy fox terrier with a bad attitude, was an effective guard dog.

Transition Fragments

Sometimes transitional expressions (*again, also as a result, besides, for example, instead, specifically, such as,* and so on) lead to sentence fragments.

Fragment   Heraldo wanted a new car. *Specifically, a high performance sports car.*

Rewritten   Heraldo wanted a new car, specifically, a high performance sports car.

Fragment   Her frequent calls were annoying. *Especially, when I was doing homework.*

Rewritten   Her frequent calls were annoying, especially, when I was doing homework.

EXERCISE 27

Revise the following items to eliminate fragments caused by modifiers or transitions.

1. Sign language has a variety of uses. Especially, in broadcasting and at gaming tables.

2. In broadcasting. A finger pointing to the throat means "cut."

3. At the card table. To identify cheaters, a dealer will place his or her fingertips on the table.

4. Sign language. A substitute for speech. Is derived from gestures and facial expressions that accompany speech.

5. It is used where silence is a rule or to overcome language barriers. As among Trappist monks and as among Plains tribes.

6. American Sign Language is a system of communication for those who are hearing-impaired that employs manual signs. Also called *Ameslan.*

7. Sign language for persons who are deaf was systematized in France. In the eighteenth century.

8. Sign language is often taught along with other systems. Specifically, the manual alphabet and lip reading.

9. Melinda is an excellent interpreter. Quick, accurate, and clear.

10. Semaphore. A visual system for sending information by means of two flags. Uses an alphabetic code based on the position of the signaler's arms.

Intentional Fragments

You have probably noticed sentence fragments in the work of professional writers and wondered why they use them. Journalists, creative writers, and advertisement writers use sentence fragments intentionally for special effects such as emphasizing a point, imitating casual conversation, or making a selling point. Generally, intentional fragments are not acceptable in college or business writing.

Emphasis   All the dogs howled. *Even the puppies.*

Imitation of conversation   *Want the facts? Okay, right here.*

Selling point   Forage, fish, then enjoy a lamp-lit four-course meal. *Fireside or alfresco. Guaranteed to give you that feel-good glow.*

EXERCISE 28

Write ten different types of sentence fragments and then correct them.

Review Exercises

Revise each item to eliminate sentence fragments, using the way you think is most appropriate. Try to use several different ways in each exercise. Since most sentences can be corrected in a variety of ways, answers will vary.

REVIEW EXERCISE 29

1. Sled dog racing was part of the culture of several groups of people. Such as the Inuits and the northern Indians of North America and the people of Scandinavia.

2. The first formally recorded race occurred in 1908. A run of 408 miles from Nome to Candle and back.

3. Recognized as the world's most famous sled dog race. The Iditarod Trail Sled Dog Race runs from Anchorage to Nome, Alaska.

4. The first winner was Dick Wilmarth. Taking 20 days, 15 hours, 49 minutes, and 41 seconds to complete the race.

5. Rick Swanson (U.S.) won the race five times. In 1977, 1979, 1981, 1982, and 1991.

6. In 1993 Jeff King (U.S.) won the race. With a record breaking time of 10 days, 15 hours, 38 minutes and 15 seconds.

7. Martin Buser won the 1994 race. In a record of 10 days, 13 hours, and 2 minutes. His second win in 3 years.

8. Buser won the race. And received $50,000 in prize money. And a pickup truck valued at about $25,000.

9. Rick Mackey finished second, and Jeff King third.

10. The Iditarod Trail Headquarters. Located at Mile 2.2 Knik Road, Wasilla, Alaska. Open noon to 6 P.M. Wednesday through Sunday from June 1 through August 31.

REVIEW EXERCISE 30

1. A jilted bride in Sidney, Australia, was probably the prototype for Miss Havisham. The aged recluse of Charles Dickens' novel *Great Expectations.*

2. After the young Australian girl was left standing at the altar on her wedding day. She was heartbroken. And became a hermit. Never leaving her own home.

3. The door to the hall was locked. The wedding decorations and food left there to rot.

4. Pip. The main character in *Great Expectations.* Describes his first meeting with Miss Havisham. The description paralleling the tragic life of the young Australian girl.

5. "I saw the bride within the bridal dress had withered like the dress. And like the flowers, and had no brightness left. But the brightness of her sunken eyes. I saw that the dress had been put upon the rounded figure of a young woman. And that the figure upon which it now hung loose. Had shrunk to skin and bone." [Note: Punctuation errors were not part of the original text.]

6. Dickens completed the novel in 1861. Five years after the Australian girl's fiancé failed to attend his own wedding.

7. Remember little Jack Horner who sat in a corner? According to one legend. Little Jack was taking a huge Christmas pie from his employer Richard Whiting to Henry VIII.

8. Supposedly. The pie contained deeds to twelve manors.

9. Perhaps he sat in the corner. Perhaps not. Anyway, Little Jack put his hand in the pie. Pulled out the deed to the Manor of Mells in Somerset—the plum. And said, "What a good boy am I."

10. According to the records. A Tom Horner—not Jack—became the owner of Mells. His descendants say he bought the manor from the king. And that the rhyme is slander.

REVIEW EXERCISE 31

1. Verdi's *La Traviata* is based on the real-life story of Rose Plessis. Later known as Marie Duplesis.

2. Fifteen-year old Rose, who ran away from her home near Normandy, France. Arrived in Paris hungry and penniless. And turned to prostitution.

3. Alexandre Dumas, a young writer who was the son of the man who wrote *The Three Musketeers*. Was captivated by her beauty. He fell in love with her. And bankrupted himself to pay for her medical bills.

4. Because Marie suffered from chronic tuberculosis. She told Dumas: "You will have a sorry mistress. A woman who is nervous, ill, sad, and gay. With a gaiety sadder than grief. A woman who spits blood and spends 100,000 francs a year." [Note: Punctuation errors were not part of the original text.]

5. Despite her illness that grew increasingly worse. And despite her marriage to another man. The young writer remained faithful to her until her death.

6. She died February 3, 1847. When she was twenty-three years old.

7. Her casket was covered with white camellias. Her favorite flowers.

8. Shortly after her death. Dumas began the novel *La Dame aux Camelias*.

9. Later rewriting it as a play.

10. The play was Verdi's inspiration for the opera. Which gave Maria musical immortality.

REVIEW EXERCISE 32

1. A mammal is a warm-blooded animal. With a backbone or spinal column.

2. It has certain characteristics. Such as a covering of hair on the skin and milk-producing glands in the female.

3. The largest mammal in the world. The blue whale.

4. The heaviest blue whale ever captured. A female whale taken in the Southern Ocean in 1947. Weighing in at 209 tons and measuring 90 feet and 6 inches long.

5. The African bush elephant is the largest living land animal. Averaging about 10 feet and 6 inches at the shoulder and weighing 6.3 tons.

6. The cheetah. Over a short distance—up to 1,800 feet—is the fastest animal on land.

7. The fastest land animal over a sustained distance—3,000 feet or more. The pronghorn antelope is the winner.

8. The slowest mammal. For example, the three-toed sloth. Can attain a ground speed of 6 to 8 feet a minute. But in a tree, can speed up to 15 feet a minute.

9. The sleepiest winners the armadillos, opossums, and sloths. Sleeping up to 80 percent of their lives.

10. Dall's porpoises take the prize for sleeplessness. Supposedly, never sleeping.

REVIEW EXERCISE 33

The Puritans lived harsh lives. Practically all their waking hours devoted to work. Having little leisure time. They regulated their lives and the lives of their neighbors by strict rules and regulations. Severely punishing anyone who broke the laws. One day was allowed for rest from work. Not only were they allowed to rest. They were required to rest. They could not take a walk in the woods. Could not whistle or read any book except the Bible. Because they might be arrested. They could not even have a friendly conversation in the streets. They were forbidden to participate in any type of recreation. Such as fishing, shooting, sailing, rowing, or riding for pleasure. Playing games or dancing a serious offense. On one occasion a female servant was threatened with banishment from the Plymouth Colony. Because she had committed the terrible offense of smiling in church. The penalties imposed for the most trivial offenses were severe indeed. A writer in 1868 described some of their practices. [Note: Punctuation errors were not part of the original text.]

Their laws for reformation of manners are very severe . . . For being drunk. They either whip [the culprit] or impose a fine of five shillings . . . For cursing and swearing. They bore through the tongue with a hot iron. For kissing a woman in the street. Though [the kiss is] but in way of civil salute, [they] whip or [impose a fine on the offender]. Stealing is punished with restoring fourfold the value of the stolen property. If they [the thieves] are able [to pay that amount]. If not. They are sold. Stocks are used to punish lesser offenses. Public whippings given to punish offenses which the Puritans consider serious ones. For more serious offenses. Ears, noses, and arms are cut off. And bodies branded with hot irons. Most of the Puritans believe in witches and witchcraft. Live in terror of witches. Often charging harmless old women with witchcraft. And hanging them for the offense of talking to themselves.

Identifying and Correcting Run-Together Sentences

Run-together sentences occur when two or more complete sentences (independent clauses) are treated as one single sentence. The sentences are allowed to run together without the necessary connections. Often these sentences are the result of carelessness rather than lack of understanding. Remember, an independent clause contains a subject and a verb and expresses an idea by itself. To prevent misreading and to show the relationship between independent clauses, join them correctly.

> **Run-Together Sentence**　The Alabama Capitol has a magnificent **dome it** is one of the best examples of its style.

> **Run-Together Sentence**　Montgomery is the capital of **Alabama, Birmingham** is its most populous city.

Note: The term *run-together* is used because often students confuse the term *run-on* with a stringy sentence—a string of compound sentences.

A run-together sentence may be caused by a

- fused sentence

- comma splice

To rid your writing of run-together sentences and write clear effective sentences, you need to be able to revise them in a variety of ways. Often, the meaning of the sentence will dictate the way it should be revised. Correct a run-together sentence by

- adding a comma, a connecting word, or both

- adding a semicolon or a semicolon and a bridge word

- separating clauses into two sentences

- turning two clauses into one clause

- turning one clause into a dependent clause

A *fused sentence* (also called a *run-on sentence* or a *comma fault*) occurs when two or more sentences (independent clauses) are joined with no punctuation. These sentences may or may not include a joining word (*for, and, nor, but, or, yet, so*).

A *comma-splice sentence* consists of two or more sentences (independent clauses) joined by a comma. A comma splice usually occurs when a writer mistakenly thinks that a comma alone can show where one idea ends and another one begins.

In the following examples, the word at the end of one sentence and the one at the beginning of the second sentence are boldfaced.

Fused   In this building Alabama voted to secede from the **Union and** the Confederacy was born.

Comma Splice   Alabamans chose Jefferson Davis to be their **president, he** took the oath of office.

 Linking independent clauses with a comma is not acceptable in American usage, but British usage commonly links independent clauses with a comma.

EXERCISE 34

Identify the types of run-together sentences in the following sentences. Use **F** for fused sentences and **CS** for comma splices.

1. The average American eats about 525 pounds of food a year and about 20 percent of that food is sugar. _______

2. The people of England, Scotland, and Ireland consume large amounts of sugar, the average person eats over 100 pounds of sugar a year. _______

3. Beekeeping was important in medieval Europe for the beeswax was needed for church candles. _______

4. At that time honey was plentiful for it was simply a byproduct of the beekeeping. _______

5. During the Reformation, the Church declined and with this decline, the supply of honey declined. _______

6. Honey was no longer plentiful, more people began to use sugar. _______

7. White sugar robs the body of vitamin B and it causes tooth decay. _______

8. You should not eat too much white sugar it is not good for you. _______

9. Sugar cane and sugar beets are used to produce sugar but these products do not produce naturally white sugar. ______

10. The sugar needs to be treated to make it white and to do this the ashes of burned beef bones are added to the sugar to make it white. ______

Linking Clauses with Commas and Connecting Words

When the two clauses in a run-together sentence are equally important and fairly closely related, join them with a comma and a connecting word (*for, and, nor, but, or, yet, so*).

No   Montgomery is the capital of **Alabama Birmingham** is its most populous city. (*fused*)

No   Montgomery is the capital of **Alabama but** Birmingham is its most populous city. (*fused*)

No   Montgomery is the capital of **Alabama, Birmingham** is its most populous city. (*comma splice*)

Yes   Montgomery is the capital of **Alabama, but** Birmingham is its most populous city. (*sentence*)

EXERCISE 35

Revise the run-together sentences, adding commas and connecting words as needed.

1. Are legendary lands and beasts merely travelers' tales or are they attempts to explain something?

2. In the West, dragons represented evil in the East they were usually benevolent creatures.

3. Chinese dragons came in different colors: black representing destruction, yellow representing luck, and azure heralding the birth of great men and, according to legend, two azure dragons appeared the night Confucius was born.

4. Chinese dragons could change their shapes they could shrink to the size of caterpillars or grow so large that they blotted out the sky.

5. Many of them resided at the bottom of the sea and they lived in pearl palaces.

6. Dragon bones were popular elements of traditional Chinese medicine, these bones were more than likely fossils of prehistoric animals.

7. In the West, treasures were often guarded by man-eating dragons, these dragons flew at night and spit fire or poison.

8. They differ in size, color, and attitude but dragons exist in the legends of many lands.

9. Dinosaurs disappeared from the earth 70 million years ago but human being did not appear until a few million years ago so dragon legends cannot be folk memory of a time when huge animals existed.

10. Possibly, ancient human beings discovered fossilized bones of dinosaurs and they thought that at one time some gigantic lizardlike creature ruled the earth.

Linking Clauses with Semicolons

When you want to emphasize the equality of two closely related clauses in a run-together sentence, link them with a semicolon.

No   The Alabama Capitol has a magnificent **dome it** is one of the best examples of its style. (*fused*)

No   The Alabama Capitol has a magnificent **dome and** it is one of the best examples of its style. (*fused*)

No   The Alabama Capitol has a magnificent **dome, it** is one of the best examples of its style. (*comma splice*)

Yes   The Alabama Capitol has a magnificent **dome; it** is one of the best examples of its style. (*sentence*)

When the two independent clauses of a run-together sentence are equally important, you may add a semicolon and a transitional expression such as *consequently* or *therefore* to show the relationship of the two clauses. (See p. 53.)

No   Alabamans voted to secede from the **Union they** chose Jefferson Davis as their president. (*fused*)

No   Alabamans voted to secede from the **Union and** they chose Jefferson Davis as their president. (*fused*)

No   Alabamans voted to secede from the **Union, they** chose Jefferson Davis as their president. (*comma splice*)

Yes Alabamans voted to secede from the **Union; subsequently,** they chose Jefferson Davis as their president. (*sentence*)

No Robert E. Lee declined the field command of U.S. **forces he** accepted command of the Army of Virginia. (*fused*)

No Robert E. Lee declined the field command of U.S. **forces but** he accepted command of the Army of Virginia. (*fused*)

No Robert E. Lee declined the field command of U.S. **forces, he** accepted command of the Army of Virginia. (*comma splice*)

Yes Robert E. Lee declined the field command of U.S. **forces; however,** he accepted command of the Army of Virginia. (*sentence*)

Note: When you add a transitional expression, generally put a comma after it.

EXERCISE 36

Revise the run-together sentences, adding necessary semicolons and transitional words as needed.

1. Before 1603 the shield of Britain's royal coat of arms was supported by a lion and a dragon after James I united Scotland and England, the dragon was replaced by a unicorn.

2. Ancient writers wrote about the unicorn's abilities they also wrote about its problems.

3. The unicorn was so strong that it could impale and carry away three elephants on its horn however, it was unable to shake them off and usually died of starvation.

4. During the Renaissance, assassination by poison was a common hazard cups made of "unicorn horn" were used as protection against the deadly drinks.

5. Venomous insects would not cross a line that had been drawn with a unicorn horn, poisonous plants would burst and die when they came near the magic horn.

6. These magic horns were enormously expensive, supposedly, Queen Elizabeth's crown jewels contained one valued at $500,000.

7. Queen Elizabeth's valuable horn was probably the tusk of a narwhal, this small whale grows one tooth to a great length and is twisted and pointed like the horn of the legendary unicorn.

8. According to one writer, there was only one way to tame a unicorn, a virgin had to convince the unicorn to lay its head on her lap. The trusting unicorn placed his head on the maiden's lap and slept, the unicorn hunters fell upon the sleeping animal and killed it with darts.

9. In 400 B.C. a Greek writer described a unicorn, the description appears to be that of a rhinoceros.

10. The legend could also have been born when hunters saw the profile of a long-horned antelope with one horn broken off, they thought it was an animal that had only one horn.

Separating Clauses into Sentences

Turning the two clauses into two sentences is one of the easiest ways of correcting a run-together sentence. When the two independent clauses are not equally important or are not about the same idea, they may be turned into two sentences.

No Abraham Lincoln was born in a log cabin in **Kentucky his** father moved the family from Kentucky to Illinois. (*fused*)

No Abraham Lincoln was born in a log cabin in Kentucky **and his** father moved the family from Kentucky to Illinois. (*fused*)

No Abraham Lincoln was born in a log cabin in **Kentucky, his** father moved the family from Kentucky to Illinois. (*comma splice*)

Yes Abraham Lincoln was born in a log cabin in **Kentucky. His** father moved the family from Kentucky to Illinois. (*sentence*)

No Lincoln had less than two years of formal **education he** was almost totally self-educated. (*fused*)

No Lincoln had less than two years of formal **education so** he was almost totally self-educated. (*fused*)

No Lincoln had less than two years of formal **education, he** was almost totally self-educated. (*comma splice*)

Yes Lincoln had less than two years of formal **education. He** was almost totally self-educated. (*sentence*)

Turning Two Clauses into One Clause

Sometimes you can rewrite the run-together sentence and reduce it to one clause by dropping the subject in the last part. The resulting sentence has one subject and a compound verb.

No Jefferson Davis too was born in **Kentucky he** moved to Mississippi. (*fused*)

> **No** Jefferson Davis too was born in **Kentucky but** he moved to Mississippi. (*fused*)

> **No** Jefferson Davis too was born in **Kentucky, he** moved to Mississippi. (*comma splice*)

> **Yes** Jefferson Davis too was born in Kentucky **but** moved to Mississippi. (*sentence*)

> **No** Lincoln settled in New **Salem he** clerked in a store, split rails, and served as a postmaster. (*fused*)

> **No** Lincoln settled in New Salem **and he** clerked in a store, split rails, and served as postmaster. (*fused*)

> **No** Lincoln settled in New **Salem, he** clerked in a store, split rails, and served as a postmaster. (*comma splice*)

> **Yes** Lincoln settled in New Salem **and** clerked in a store, split rails, and served as a postmaster. (*sentence*)

Turning One Clause into a Dependent Clause

When one of the clauses is less important than the other, you may turn that clause into a dependent clause by adding a dependent word to it. Generally, a dependent clause is set off with a comma, when it comes at the beginning of the sentence, but not when it comes at the end.

> **No** Lincoln was chosen to run against Stephen Douglas for a seat in the U.S. **Senate he** began his campaign with his famous "House Divided" speech. (*fused*)

> **No** Lincoln was chosen to run against Stephen Douglas for a seat in the U.S. **Senate and** he began his campaign with his famous "House Divided" speech. (*fused*)

> **No** Lincoln was chosen to run against Stephen Douglas for a seat in the U.S. **Senate, he** began his campaign with his famous "House Divided" speech. (*comma splice*)

> **Yes** *When* Lincoln was chosen to run against Stephen Douglas for a seat in the U.S. **Senate, he** began his campaign with his famous "House Divided" speech. (*sentence*)

> **No** Lincoln was defeated by **Douglas their** debates brought him national recognition. (*fused*)

No   Lincoln was defeated by **Douglas but** their debates brought him national recognition. (*fused*)

No   Lincoln was defeated by **Douglas, their** debates brought him national recognition. (*comma splice*)

Yes   *Although* Lincoln was defeated by **Douglas, their** debates brought him national recognition. (*sentence*)

EXERCISE 37

Revise the run-together sentences, separating clauses into two sentences, turning two clauses into one clause, or turning one clause into a dependent clause.

1. Well-sealed bottles have been sea-going messengers for many years they can bob safely through rough seas and hurricanes that can wreck ships.

2. These seemingly fragile objects made of glass are extremely seaworthy and, for most practical purposes, glass lasts forever.

3. In 1954 bottles were salvaged from a ship sunk 250 years earlier, the contents of the bottles were unrecognizable but the bottles themselves were in good shape.

4. Many people have experimented with dropping bottles into the ocean and they have found that it is impossible to predict the direction a bottle will take.

5. Two bottles dropped off the Brazilian coast took two entirely different routes, one bobbed east for 130 days and landed on a beach in Africa, the other bobbed northwest for 190 days and landed in Nicaragua.

6. The longest recorded bottle voyage was that of a bottle named the Flying Dutchman, it was launched in the southern Indian Ocean it had a message inside that could be read without breaking the bottle.

7. It was found and it was reported and it was thrown back into the water.

8. Six years after it began its journey, it landed on the west coast of Australia and during its journey, it covered 16,000 miles it averaged six nautical miles a day.

9. Benjamin Franklin was the postmaster general for the American colonies and he became interested in charting the currents in the Atlantic.

10. He wondered why whaler captains were crossing the Atlantic more quickly than the British mail ships, he thought it might have something to do with the currents, he dropped bottles into the Gulf Stream and gathered and recorded information about the currents from the bobbing bottles and the information he obtained about the currents has changed very little since his time.

Review Exercises

Revise each item to eliminate run-together sentences, using the way you think sounds best. Try to use several different ways in each exercise.

REVIEW EXERCISE 38

1. De Soto was probably the first white man to visit the area that became Alabama he passed through the area (1539–1540) on his last expedition to the New World.

2. He was entertained by the powerful Indian chief Tuscaloosa (TUS-kuh-**LOOH**-suh), "the Black Warrior," Tuscaloosa's capital was a large walled city.

3. It was built of wood and mud and it was large enough to hold eighty thousand people.

4. The white men were royally entertained by the Indians however, a fight broke out later between the two groups and the guests killed a great many of the host people.

5. The word *Alabama* comes from a Choctaw word it may mean "to open or clear the thicket."

6. English traders from the east came to Alabama from time to time but it was not settled until 1702 French settlers established themselves in Mobile Bay.

7. Other countries and other states laid claim to Alabama however, in 1813 it became the undisputed possession of the United States.

8. It became part of the Mississippi Territory and in 1819 it was admitted to the Union.

9. After the Revolutionary War was over, English settlers of all classes began pouring into the area the land was cheap and there were fertile river valleys.

10. Native Americans lived in these fertile valleys and they resisted the newcomers.

REVIEW EXERCISE 39

1. In the War of 1812 the Creeks joined the British and wiped out hundreds of settlers they were led by the powerful Shawnee chief Tecumseh (ti-**KUM**-suh).

2. They fought valiantly however, Andrew Jackson and his soldiers put down the uprising.

3. The Cherokee people lived in the area too they were members of the largest eastern tribe.

4. The Cherokees adopted many of the ways of the white settlers they raised crops, owned slaves, and raised cattle.

5. A Cherokee language alphabet was perfected by the Cherokee scholar Sequoia (si-**KWOI**-uh), his "talking leaf" had eighty-five letters and they represented all the sounds in the language.

6. By the sixteenth century they had an advanced agricultural culture however soon after 1750, half the tribe died in a smallpox epidemic.

7. Later, they established themselves as the Cherokee Nation and they had a constitution that provided for an elected republican government.

8. Gold was discovered on their lands, they were forcibly removed to what is now Oklahoma.

9. Chief John Ross led them on this "trail of tears" and thousands of them died along the way.

10. Today the Cherokees constitute the largest U.S. tribe, over 94,000 live in Oklahoma and more than 5,000 live on a reservation in North Carolina.

REVIEW EXERCISE 40

1. Alabama is called the Cotton State for cotton was once the state's major source of income.

2. Before the Civil War most of the cultivated land was planted in cotton vast numbers of slaves were brought in to do the work.

3. Farmers found that cotton was hard on the soil it robbed it of nutrients.

4. The farmers learned how to keep the soil fertile they began to plant other crops and began to rotate them.

5. They found that corn used up the nitrogen in the soil but peanuts put it back.

6. Peanuts owe their popularity to the African American scientist George Washington Carver he discovered many new ways to use peanuts, including making soap and ink.

7. Eli Whitney, a Yankee schoolteacher who had gone to Georgia for his health, revolutionized cotton production he invented the cotton gin.

8. By using this machine, workers could pick the seeds from raw cotton fiber three hundred times as fast as they could by hand. People began growing more cotton the crops increased from 2,000,000 pounds in 1791 to 177,000,000 in 1872.

9. Eli Whitney's invention brought about an economic revolution it made cotton "king" of the South.

10. England's cotton mills were increasing, the English wanted to buy all the cotton the United States could produce so the people of Alabama raised as much cotton as they could.

REVIEW EXERCISE 41

1. Alabama is part of what is known as the Old South, it is bounded on the north by Tennessee.

2. It is also one of the states known as the Deep South the other Deep South states are Georgia, Louisiana, Mississippi, and South Carolina.

3. It is bounded on the east by Georgia and it is bounded on the south by Florida and the Gulf of Mexico and on the west by Mississippi.

4. All of Alabama except the northern part lies in the coastal plain of the Gulf of Mexico and in the north the Cumberland Plateau rises as high as 1,800 feet and it is deeply cut by the Tennessee River and its branches.

5. Cheaha Mountain (2,407 feet) is the highest mountain in Alabama, other mountains in the state include Raccoon and Lookout.

6. The state bird is the yellowhammer it is commonly called the flicker it is a member of the woodpecker family.

7. The state song is "Alabama" and it was adopted in 1931.

8. The state motto is "We Dare Defend Our Rights" and its nickname is "Heart of Dixie."

9. The state flower is the camellia the state tree is the Southern (longleaf) pine.

10. Alabama's Tuskegee Institute was founded by Booker T. Washington in 1881 and in 1896 botanist George Washington Carver became the director of its Department of Agriculture.

Learning More About Pronouns

A pronoun takes the place of a noun. The noun that the pronoun replaces is called the *antecedent.*

The house is small. (noun) It is on the corner. (pronoun)

The pronoun *it* replaces the noun *house,* which is the antecedent.

Recognizing Forms of Pronouns

Pronouns take different forms. The forms they take show how they relate to other words in the sentence. Pronouns may serve as *subjects,* as *objects,* or as *possessives.*

▶ **Subject Forms** Subjects are nouns or noun substitutes that tell who or what a sentence is about.

We are ready. (*We* is the subject.) <u>Morgan</u> and <u>he</u> are late. (<u>He</u> is part of a two-word subject.)

▶ **Object Forms** An object is a noun, pronoun, or group of words functioning as a noun to which the action of the verb applies.

Meg called *me.* (*Me* is the object of the verb *called.*)

Randy gave *her* a ring. (*Her* is the object of the verb *gave.*)

He bought a diamond for *her.* (*Her* is the object of the preposition *for.*)

Locating *them* was a difficult task. (*Them* is the object of the *verb* + *-ing* word *locating.*)

Allen asked Sam to locate *them.* (*Them* is the object of the *to* + *a verb* expression *to locate.*)

▶ **Possessive Forms** Possessive forms indicate who owns something.

My truck is red. (*I* own the red truck.) *Their* house is white. (*They* own the house.)

His truck is black. (*He* owns the black truck.) The fault is *hers.* (*She* has the fault.)

Use the following chart to choose the correct pronoun forms.

Pronoun Forms

SUBJECT FORMS	OBJECT FORMS	POSSESSIVE FORMS
I	me	my, mine
we	us	our, ours
you	you	your, yours
he	him	his
she	her	hers
it	it	its
they	them	their, theirs
who	whom	whose

Understanding Common Pronoun Errors

▶ ***Than* or *As* Implied Comparisons**   When an implied comparison ends with a pronoun, you can determine the correct form of the pronoun to use by completing the comparison. Sometimes the meaning of the sentence dictates the choice of the pronoun.

Tanya is *as* tall as (I, me). (tall as *I* am tall, not tall as *me* am tall)

Betty is prettier *than* (she, her). (prettier than *she* is pretty, not prettier than *her* is pretty)

Cindy likes cats better *than* (he, him).
Cindy likes cats better than *he*. (more than he likes cats) (one meaning)
Cindy likes cats better than *him*. (better than she likes him) (another meaning)

You know the instructor better than (*I, me*).
You know the instructor better than *I*. (better than I know the instructor) (one meaning)
You know the instructor better than *me*. (better than you know me) (another meaning)

EXERCISE 42

Underline the correct pronoun in the parentheses. If a sentence can have two different meanings, explain both meanings.

1. They like bears better than (she, her).

2. My twin is three inches taller than (I, me).

3. She is also heavier than (I, me).

4. George cares more about Linda's sister than (she, her).

5. Sara is more aggressive than (him, he).

Write five sentences using implied comparisons, including two that may have two different meanings.

▶ **Compound Constructions**   Sometimes a sentence has a compound pronoun subject or compound pronoun object. When you use a compound construction, you will need to choose the correct pronoun form. A compound construction does not change the form of the pronoun. A subject form is still used as a subject, and an object form is still used as an object. Do not switch or mix the two. To choose the correct pronoun form in a compound construction, drop the other part of the sentence.

Problem   Kate and (*I, me*) wrote a play.

Drop   "*I* wrote a play." or "*Me* wrote a play."

Answer   Kate and *I* wrote a play.

Problem   The theater invited Kate and (*I, me*).

Drop   "The theater invited *I*." or "The theater invited *me*."

Answer   The theater invited Kate and *me*.

EXERCISE 43

Underline the correct pronoun in the parentheses.

1. My friend and (I, me) were late for the game.

2. The coach told my friend and (I, me) to arrive early for future games.

3. Carl and (he, him) are never late.

4. The coach called Carl and (he, him) his best players.

5. (She, Her) and (he, him) are engaged.

6. After (he, him) and (she, her) are married, they will rent an apartment.

7. The landlord agreed to let (he, him) and (her, she) choose the paint for the walls.

8. They have asked Beth and (me, I) to help decorate the place.

9. The newlyweds invited their friends, including Tom, Jon, and (I, me) to the open house.

10. Call (I, me) after you and (he, him) return.

▶ **Pronouns Ending in -*self* and -*selves***   Use -*self* pronouns to refer to the subject of the sentence or clause or to emphasize a preceding noun or pronoun.

She hurt *herself.* (The pronoun *herself* refers to the pronoun *She.*)

Harry *himself* recognized his error. (The pronoun *himself* emphasizes the noun *Harry.*)

Do not use -*self* pronouns in place of *I* or *me.*

No   Cliff and *myself* played tennis.   **Yes**   Cliff and *I* played tennis.

No   They called Cliff and *myself.*   **Yes**   They called Cliff and *me.*

EXERCISE 44

Underline the correct pronoun in the parentheses.

1. Sue, Betty, and (I, me, myself) were ready for the test.

2. The instructor complimented them and (I, me, myself) on the quality of our work.

3. Ted wanted to learn more about (I, me, myself).

4. If (she, her, herself) can come to the party, (I, me, myself, I myself) will take her home.

5. (He, Him, Himself, He himself) injured (he, him, himself, he himself) when he tripped and fell.

6. (She, Her, Herself) is the subject of an investigation.

Write four sentences using *myself, himself, herself,* and *themselves.*

▶ **Added Explanatory Words**   When a noun or noun phrase uses different words to identify the noun or pronoun it follows, use the same form as the word it identifies. To choose the correct form, drop the other part of the construction.

Two famous boxers, Sugar Ray Leonard and (*he, him*), fought great fights.

~~Two famous boxers, Sugar Ray Leonard and~~ *He,* not *him,* fought great fights.

Have you read about these boxers, Sugar Ray Robinson and (*he, him*)?

Have you read about ~~these boxers, Sugar Ray Robinson and~~ *him,* not *he.*

EXERCISE 45

Underline the correct pronoun in the parentheses.

1. In our book club, only two members, Isabel and (I, me), had read the novel.

2. They asked us, Isabel and (I, me), to summarize the plot of the novel.

3. The best athletes in school, Tom and (he, him), ran for class president.

4. The class elected the two athletes, Tom and (he, him), co-presidents.

5. A husband and wife team, Mark and (she, her), won the chili cooking contest.

6. The judges awarded them, Mark and (she, her), both first and second prize.

7. Only two people, Molly and (I, me), met the qualification standards.

8. They interviewed us, Molly and (I, me), yesterday.

9. Two members of my family, my aunt and (I, me), brought a picnic lunch for everyone.

10. Two ladies, Dolly Madison and (she, her), served as White House hostesses. Harriet Lane and (she, her), the two popular hostesses, presided over the social functions at the White House for President Jefferson, a widower and President Buchanan, a bachelor.

▶ **The Possessive Form of Pronouns Before Words Ending in -*ing***   Use the possessive form of pronouns before verbs ending in -*ing* that are used as nouns.

Bill's parents objected to *his,* not *him,* boxing.

Mother disapproved of *their,* not *them,* going to the dance.

▶ **Subject Pronouns Following Linking Verbs**   Use the subject form of pronouns after linking verbs. Linking verbs connect a subject to a word that renames it. The most common linking verb is the verb *be* (*am, are, is, was, were, be, being, been*). Other linking verbs are the *sense* verbs (*look, smell, taste, sound, feel*) and the *seem* verbs (*appear, become, remain,* and so on)

> The man most likely to succeed is *he*. (*He* renames *the man*, the subject.)

> The winners of the lottery are *he* and *I*. (*He* and *I* rename *the winners*, the subject.)

> Who called? It was *I*. (*I* renames *it*, the subject.)

> It is *he*. (*He* renames *it*, the subject.)

Note: In everyday speech and informal writing, you may use the object form in constructions such as the last two examples (It was *me*. It is *him*.), but in your academic writing always use the subject form.

EXERCISE 46

Underline the correct pronoun in the parentheses.

1. (Him, His) being tardy irked his instructors.

2. It was (I, me) who suggested that Jim take this class.

3. (Them, Their) squabbling is a common occurrence.

4. The neighbors were annoyed by (them, their) constant battling.

5. The guilty person was (him, he).

6. (You, Your) teasing the dog may cause him to bite you.

7. The best-qualified candidate is (she, her).

8. It was (I, me) who called the police.

9. (You, Your) helping others is a mark of your good character.

10. (Him, His) cooking for her was a new experience.

Review Exercises

Underline the correct pronoun in the parentheses and make any necessary corrections in the use of pronouns. If a sentence may be interpreted in two ways, indicate both meanings. Mark correct sentences with a C.

REVIEW EXERCISE 47

1. Johann Sebastian Bach, who became one of the greatest composers in the world, began copying works of famous organists when (he, himself, he himself) was a young boy.

2. His older brother was jealous of (he, him) because the younger boy was more talented than (he, him).

3. Our music teacher told my sister and (I, me) stories about Bach's personal life.

4. Her and me were surprised to learn that he had twenty children.

5. Bach (he, himself) never thought of himself as a genius.

6. Our music teacher invited my three friends and (I, me, myself) to a Bach concert.

7. He asked us if either she or I knew that George Frederick Handel, the man who wrote the *Messiah,* showed an interest in musical toys at a young age.

8. Handel's father, wanting his son to be a lawyer, strongly objected to (him, his) studying music.

9. When Handel was only nineteen years old, he applied for a position as an organist in a church, and the elders who hired him realized that the great organist they were seeking was (he, him).

10. Handel and Bach had much in common. Both Bach and (him, he) were blind when they died.

REVIEW EXERCISE 48

1. Amy likes the music teacher better than (I, me). Handel better than (he, him).

2. Betty and she knew that George Frederick Handel wrote many successful operas.

3. The story of (him, his) fighting a duel when he was a young man is interesting.

4. An oversized button on his coat prevented (him, his) being run through by his opponent's sword.

5. The other students and (I, me, myself) asked the instructor why he began writing oratorios.

6. To earn money for (him, himself) and his family, Handel began writing oratorios because the opera houses were empty during Lent.

7. The word *oratorio* was new to (me, I).

8. My music teacher explained to my friend and (I, me) that an oratorio is similar to an opera, except there is no acting, no costumes, and no scenery.

9. Gus and (I, me, myself) are particularly fond of Handel's *Water Music.*

10. Our music teacher is fond of Mozart, and it was (her, she) who told us the story of his life.

REVIEW EXERCISE 49

1. It was me who told her that Mozart wrote a concerto when he was only four.

2. Molly, John, and myself met the new music instructor yesterday.

3. Is it he who is the resident Mozart expert?

4. Have the department members approved (him, he, his) teaching a seminar devoted to Mozart?

5. The instructor and (they, them) will limit the enrollment to students who are music majors.

6. My fellow students and (me, I, myself) were impressed with her knowledge.

7. Melinda and I have been studying the lives of great composers. She knows more about the earlier composers than (I, me).

8. Who is responsible for monitoring the enrollment? It is (him and them, he and they, him and they), and if anyone can teach the course successfully, it is (he, him).

9. Henry asked them if they would approve (him, his) auditing the class.

10. Several nonmusic majors audited the class, including (he, him) and (I, me).

Understanding Common Pronoun Reference Errors

Pronouns (*I, you, he, she, it, they, whom, this, that, one,* and so on) take the place of nouns. The nouns that the pronouns replace are called *antecedents.* The relationship of the antecedent and the pronoun is called *pronoun reference.*

▶ **Ambiguous Antecedents**   A pronoun reference is ambiguous if the pronoun seems to refer to more than one antecedent. Rewrite ambiguous sentences and make each pronoun clearly refer to one specific antecedent.

Ambiguous	He took the saddle off the horse and put <u>it</u> in the barn. (What did he put in the barn—the saddle or the horse?)
Clear	He took the saddle off the horse and put the horse in the barn.
Ambiguous	Bill told Harry that <u>his</u> class had been canceled. (Whose class had been canceled—Bill's class or Harry's class?)

Clear	Bill said, "Harry, your class has been canceled."
Clear	Bill said, "Harry, my class has been canceled."

► ***This, That, Which,*** **and** ***It* Problems**   Rewrite sentences to eliminate the vague use of *this, that, which,* or *it*.

Not Clear	The dog growled and bared its teeth. <u>This</u> frightened the mail carrier.
Clear	The dog growled and bared its teeth. This <u>behavior</u> frightened the mail carrier.
Not Clear	The golfer hooked and sliced his first two balls. <u>That</u> made him unhappy.
Clear	The golfer hooked and sliced his first two balls. The <u>bad shots</u> made him unhappy.
Not Clear	Jean's car has a cracked windshield and a bad paint job <u>that</u> she needs to replace.
Clear	Jean's car has a bad paint job and a cracked windshield <u>that</u> she needs to replace.
Clear	Jean's car has a cracked windshield <u>that</u> she needs to replace.
Not Clear	Betty tried to use a paring knife to peel an orange, but <u>it</u> was too dull.
Clear	Betty tried to peel an orange with a paring knife, but <u>it</u> was too dull.

EXERCISE 50

Revise the following sentences and make the pronoun references clear.

1. Cindy said to Cher that <u>she</u> had taken first place in the talent show.

2. When the dog bit the cat, she hit <u>it</u> with a folded newspaper.

3. When Tess put a pie in the oven, <u>it</u> burst into flames.

4. The lines were long, and numerous forms had to be completed. <u>This</u> frustrated the applicant.

5. The Pilgrims landed at Plymouth Rock in 1620, <u>which</u> is still celebrated.

6. After taking the skin off the fish, he put <u>it</u> in the refrigerator.

7. The skyscrapers seemed to reach the sky; trolley cars rattled down crooked streets; sailboats were gliding over the bay. <u>It</u> was impressive.

8. After washing their new cars, Joe and Jack asked their girlfriends to polish <u>them</u>.

9. Ted's sweater is missing a button and has a hole <u>that</u> needs to be replaced.

10. Hank had many spelling errors and wrong words in his letter of application. <u>That</u> resulted in his not getting an interview.

▶ ***They, It,* and *You***   Rewrite sentences to eliminate vague uses of *they, it,* or *you.*

Not Clear   Bill lives on a horse farm in Kentucky. <u>It</u> is famous for beautiful women and fast horses.

Clear   Bill lives on a horse farm in Kentucky. The <u>state</u> is famous for beautiful women and fast horses.

Not Clear   <u>It</u> says in the newspaper that there was an earthquake in Mexico.

Clear   The <u>article</u> in the newspaper says that there was an earthquake in Mexico.

Not Clear   <u>They</u> said on the news that tomorrow would be sunny.

Clear   The <u>weather forecaster</u> said that tomorrow would be sunny.

Not Clear   In many of <u>your</u> recreational parks in this state, <u>you</u> have pet restrictions. (Do *you* the reader own recreational parks, and do *you,* the reader, have pet restrictions?)

Clear   Many recreational parks in this state have pet restrictions.

▶ **Repeated Subject**   Do not write a sentence in which a pronoun repeats the subject.

No   My sister <u>she</u> is an expert sailor.

Yes   My sister is an expert sailor.

No   The soldier who was wounded in Vietnam <u>he</u> finally received his Medal of Honor.

Yes   The soldier who was wounded in Vietnam finally received his Medal of Honor.

EXERCISE 51

Rewrite the sentences so that all pronoun references are clear. In some sentences you may need to change the verb form.

1. Many people say that when <u>you</u> are pregnant <u>you</u> have a special glow.

2. In yesterday's *Chronicle* <u>it</u> said that domestic violence is a major problem here.

3. She is a conscientious, hardworking student, but <u>it</u> doesn't always result in high marks.

4. My friend Annette <u>she</u> drives a snowplow.

5. In a recent food report <u>it</u> says <u>you</u> should eat butter, not margarine.

6. My instructor <u>he</u> never takes attendance.

7. Our college has developed a new plan for solving the parking problem. <u>They</u> will give an annual $50 rebate to each student who does not buy a parking permit.

8. The Boy Scout, the one with all the awards, <u>he</u> helped the elderly lady across the street.

9. The *Progressive Grocer* is an annual report of the grocery industry. <u>They</u> say that Saturday and Thursday are the most popular days to buy groceries.

10. <u>You</u> have students graduating from high school who cannot fill out a simple job application form.

▶ ***Who, Which,* and *That*** Use *which* and *that* to refer to places, things, or unnamed animals. Use *which* in nonessential clauses, and use *that* in essential clauses. Set off nonessential clauses with commas, but not essential ones.

> **Place**   The restaurants <u>that</u> I like best are the ones with authentic ethnic food. (*essential clause*)

> **Thing**   The Statue of Liberty, <u>which</u> was given to America by the French, was designed by Bartholdi. (*nonessential clause*)

> **Unnamed Animal**   The dog <u>that</u> won the national championship is from Ohio. (*essential clause*)

> Use *who* to refer to people or to animals that have names. You may use *who* in essential or nonessential clauses.

> **Person**   Benjamin Franklin, <u>who</u> began working as a printer when he was only twelve years old, began publishing his own paper by the time he was twenty-three. (*nonessential clause*)

Person   The trainer <u>who</u> trained my dog is my friend. (essential clause)

Named Animal   Brandy, <u>who</u> is a field champion, is my dog. (nonessential clause)

EXERCISE 52

Fill in the blanks with the correct word (*who, which,* or *that*) and add the appropriate commas.

1. A Dutch oven ___________________ is one of the most useful outdoor cooking pots is made of cast iron and has a flat top that will hold a layer of live coals.

2. A double skillet is a matched pair of skillets—one shallow and one deep—___________________ can be locked together with a tongue-and-slot hinge.

3. An outdoor cook ___________________ knows how to use these utensils is usually a good camp cook.

4. Jerky is meat ___________________ is not cooked, but dried at a low temperature.

5. Someone once said, "An electric knife sharpener is the best friend of the man ___________________ sells knives and the worst enemy of the man ___________________ uses them."

6. Rufus ___________________ is an Abyssinian cat likes asparagus and cantaloupe.

7. The only house cats ___________________ have never been fully domesticated are Abyssinians.

8. Joel Chandler Harris is remembered for his charming stories about Uncle Remus and animals ___________________ act like men and women.

9. The publication of *The Jungle* ___________________ was written by Upton Sinclair about the life of a poor immigrant ___________________ is a worker in the Chicago stockyards led to the passage of the first Pure Food and Drug Act.

10. Willa Cather ___________________ wrote exquisite descriptions of life on the American deserts and plains is best known for her novel *My Antonia* ___________________ is a story about pioneer farm life.

Review Exercises

Revise each sentence so that the pronoun reference is clear or underline the correct pronoun in the parentheses and add the necessary commas, delete unnecessary pronouns, and change verbs when necessary.

REVIEW EXERCISE 53

1. James Fenimore <u>he</u> introduced Natty Bumppo in *The Pioneers.*

2. Cooper entered Yale when he was thirteen but was expelled for "unruly conduct" and later went to sea. After <u>that</u> he became a shipbuilder and an expert seaman.

3. In 1817 an editor in Boston received a packet of unsigned poems. He was impressed with them and showed them to his literary friends who said <u>it</u> was a joke.

4. <u>It</u> was not a joke. <u>It</u> meant that for the first time an American had written excellent poetry.

5. William Cullen Bryant had written the poems and left them in a drawer. Years later his father found them and sent them to the Boston editor. The best of the poems was "Thanatopsis." <u>He</u> is considered to be America's first nature poet.

6. In 1850 Nathaniel Hawthorne's masterpiece *The Scarlet Letter,* drawn in part from the Puritan past and his own family tradition, was published. <u>This</u> made him famous.

7. One of Hawthorne's ancestors had been a judge in the Salem witch trials, and a "witch" had placed a curse on him, <u>which</u> caused the house to be haunted.

8. Judge Joseph Crater (who, that) disappeared in 1930 was declared legally dead in 1939. <u>It</u> has not been officially closed because reports of his reappearance still occur.

9. As a young woman, Emily Dickinson fell deeply in love with a man who returned her love, but either he was already married or her stern father forbade her to marry him, <u>which</u> caused her to become a strange recluse. Ms. Dickinson she wore nothing but white and hid herself from even her best friends.

10. The author (who, which, that) wrote the *Call of the Wild,* wrote *The Sea Wolf.* Jack London <u>he</u> also wrote the novel *White Fang* (which, that) later was made into a movie.

REVIEW EXERCISE 54

1. After beating the eggs until they reached a stiff peak, she poured <u>it</u> into a mold and baked it.

2. Becky told Gladys that <u>her</u> roommate had not paid her share of the rent.

3. The county passed an ordinance that discriminated against people with children or pets, and <u>they</u> wondered why they were not reelected.

4. In *The Great Hunger,* author Cecil Woodham-Smith <u>he</u> recounts the story of the Irish Potato Famine of the 1840s (which, that) caused the deaths of over a million people.

5. The Salton Sea, the largest inland surface body of water in California, is a productive sport fishery. The most significant water quality problem is the increasing salinity concentration. <u>This</u> occurs naturally because <u>it</u> lies in a closed basin without an outlet.

6. William Sydney Porter took his pen name, O. Henry, from the name of products (which, that) he had seen in his brother's drug store.

7. "Muckracking"—a term (which, that) means just what it says, raking muck—came into being about 1908.

8. The muckrakers were writers (who, that, which) uncovered scandals, decried sweatshops, and lambasted the corruption and graft of public officials and wealthy people.

9. In Cortez, Colorado, a concrete monument marks the spot where Arizona, Colorado, New Mexico, and Utah touch. Although developed as a trading center for the ranchers of the area, oil and tourism have added dimensions to <u>its</u> economy.

10. This brand of coffee contains chicory <u>which</u> she does not like.

REVIEW EXERCISE 55

1. After disjointing the chicken, she dipped <u>them</u> in batter and fried them.

2. Poi is a staple food of Hawaii made from taro root. The taro plant is grown for its large underground tuber (which, that) is easily digested. The taro root must be cooked because it is too acrid to be eaten raw. To make <u>it,</u> the root must be cooked, pounded to a paste, and then fermented.

3. The "Dutch" in Pennsylvania Dutch has nothing to do with Holland Dutch because the people we know as Pennsylvania Dutch are of Germanic origin. <u>It</u> is a corruption of the word *Deutsche* (which, that) means "German."

4. The kitten (who, which, that) was lost has a white nose and a white tip on its tail.

5. Edgar Allan Poe, the poet (who, which, that) could read, draw, dance, and recite poetry when he was six years old, died when he was only forty years old.

6. Julia Ward Howe wrote the words to "Battle Hymn of the Republic," and sometime after it was published, Union soldiers sang it to celebrate the news of the victory at Gettysburg. She is best remembered for <u>this</u>.

7. Marty told his father <u>he</u> was responsible for the accident.

8. Samuel Clemens took his pen name, Mark Twain, from his experiences on the the river. The expression (which, that) means "exactly two fathoms" was the announcement of the depth of the water.

9. In <u>your</u> small towns everyone seems to know everyone else's business.

10. The chef sliced the potatoes and arranged <u>them</u> in layers in the baking dish.

Using *I, We, You,* and *He, She, It, They*

When you plan a writing project, you have three points of view, or approaches, from which to choose: first, second, or third person point of view. The first person point of view (*I, we*) focuses on the writer. The second person point of view (*you*) focuses on the reader. The third person point of view (*he, she, it, they*) focuses on the subject.

▶ **First Person Point of View: *I***   Use *I* for informal writing and whenever it is appropriate for you or your opinions to be part of a piece of writing. Generally, do not use *I* in scientific reports and expository essays.

When *I* read "Salvation" by Langston Hughes, *I* identified with his disillusionment because *I* had a similar experience as a youngster.

When faced with the problem of using *I* or using wordy or clumsy constructions, either use *I*, or, better yet, reword the sentence.

Wordy   It is believed that Diablo Valley College nurtures academic growth.

Improved   *I* believe that Diablo Valley College nurtures academic growth.

Better   Diablo Valley College nurtures academic growth.

Clumsy   It is the opinion of this writer that people are recklessly wasting natural resources.

Improved   *I* believe that people are recklessly wasting natural resources.

Better   People are recklessly wasting natural resources.

Note: Some instructors do not allow students to use *I* in college papers. Other instructors feel that the use of *I* is appropriate in some situations. Find out your instructors' preferences and respect them.

▶ **First Person Point of View: *We***   Use *we* when you are working with another writer or writers or when you are speaking for a group.

After *we* completed our joint research project, *we* were pleased with our cooperative work.

As members of this community, *we* want to have a voice in budget matters.

▶ **Second Person Point of View: *You***   Use *you* to address your readers directly: Use it to give advice, to give orders or directions, or to explain how to do something or how something works. Do not use *you* to refer to people in general.

Yes   Now *you* can clean the bathtub or shower without having to stoop or bend.

Yes   If *you* want to be successful in college, *you* need to learn to write well.

Yes   When *you* finish reading this report, will *you* please fill out the attached questionnaire.

Yes   *You* just add milk and butter to the all-natural ingredients and pour the mixture into a pan.

No   In many college classes *you* cannot use *I* in *your* expository essays.

Yes   In many college classes students cannot use *I* in their expository essays.

No   My English instructor limits the number of "be" verbs *you* can use in a paragraph.

Yes   My English instructor limits the number of "be" verbs students can use in a paragraph.

Note: This book uses *you* to address *you,* the reader, directly.

EXERCISE 56

Fill in the blanks with the appropriate pronouns (*I, we, you*) or revise sentences to rid them of inappropriate pronouns.

1. If _________________ wake up in the morning with aching joints, _________________ may need a new mattress.

2. _________________ believe that we should have more student parking spaces in the lot.

3. When _________________ spoke to the dean on behalf of the student body, _________________ told him that _________________ need additional funds.

4. If _________________ want to neutralize offensive odors in a house, use Lemon Mist spray.

5. To become a better golfer, _________________ should take lessons from a professional.

6. When we finish this chapter you know the instructor will give us a pop quiz.

7. In high school, I thought you had to be pretty to be popular, but in college I found out that you can be popular without being pretty.

Write three sentences using *you* incorrectly or reread some of your paragraphs or essays to see if you have misused *you*. Revise the sentences, getting rid of any inappropriate uses of *you*.

▶ **Third Person Point of View: *He, She, It, They*** The third person point of view (*he, she, it, they*) is the most common approach in college writing, and, generally, that is the one you will use in most of your academic writing.

 **Using It**

It can be used in three ways in English: as a *personal pronoun,* as an *expletive,* or as part of an *idiomatic expression* of distance, time, or weather.

Sandy's essay is due today, but she has not finished writing *it.* (*personal pronoun*)

It is not a good idea to play golf during a thunderstorm. (*expletive*—a subject filler)

It is too far to walk to the restaurant.   *It* is 5 o'clock. *It* is raining.   (*idiomatic expressions*)

When *it* is acting as an expletive or as part of an idiomatic expression, do not omit it.

No   *Is* necessary to take careful notes.   **Yes**   *It is* necessary to take careful notes.

No   *Was* raining this morning.   **Yes**   *It was* raining this morning.

Learning More About Verbs

Regular and Irregular Verbs

The English language contains **regular** and **irregular** verbs. Except for the verb *be*, the main verb of a sentence has four forms: *base, past, present participle,* and *past participle.* All other forms are derived from these four forms.

▶ **Regular Verbs**   The other principal forms of regular verbs are formed by adding letters to the base verb and adding helping verbs. Present participles are formed by adding *-ing* to a verb (cry*ing*, laugh*ing*, throw*ing*). Past participles are formed by adding *-ed, -d, -t, -en,* or *-n* to the base verb (ask*ed*, love*d*, deal*t*, eat*en*, see*n*).

Main Verb Forms of Regular Verbs

Base: I jump.   **Past:** I jumped   **Present Participle:** I am jumping.   **Past Participle:** I have jumped.

Note: A *participle* is a verb form. Although participles are formed from verbs, they cannot be used alone as verbs. When a participle is accompanied by a helping verb, it acts as a verb and is considered to be part of the verb. When a participle is used alone with no helping verb, it acts as an adjective or as a noun.

▶ **Irregular Verbs**   Irregular verbs do not follow the same forms as the regular verbs. Sometimes the *past* and *past participle* are the same, and sometimes they are not. When they are the same, the dictionary lists two parts, but when they are different it lists three parts.

stand, v (*stood*)   buy, v (*bought*)   swim, v (past *swam*, pp *swum*)
sing, v (past *sang*, pp *sung*)

Note: When you are not sure which form of the verb to use, consult a dictionary. When the dictionary lists only the base form of a verb, it is a regular verb.

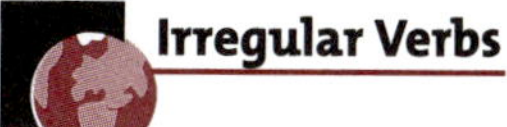 **Irregular Verbs**

See Appendix A for a list of irregular verbs.

Understanding Simple Tenses

Verbs change form to show the time of their action or the idea they express. *Tense* is the form a verb takes to indicate when an action occurs or when a condition exists. The time expressed by the verb is its tense. The simple tenses are *present*, *past*, and *future*.

 The simple present and simple past tenses need no helping verbs to form the verb, except for the negative and interrogative forms. Other verb forms require helping verbs.

Simple Present　　They **walk** to school.

Simple Past　　They **walked** to school.

▶ **Present Tense**　Use the present tense to show an action or condition taking place in the present. Form the present tense by adding *-s* or *-es* to base verbs that have third person subjects that are one person or thing, the pronouns *he*, *she*, and *it*, and independent pronouns such as *everyone* and *everybody*. Do not add the *-s* endings when the subject is not third person singular.

	SINGULAR		PLURAL	
First Person (speaking)	I	learn	we	learn
Second Person (spoken to)	you	learn	you	learn
Third Person (spoken about)	he/she/it	learns	they	learn
	man	learns	men	learn
	one	learns		

 Remember to add the *-s or -es* to verbs that are third person singular.

No   My dog bark at strangers.   **Yes**   My dog bark**s** at strangers

No   He never bite anyone.   **Yes**   He never bite**s** anyone.

Special Present Tense Usage   Use the present tense for specific occasions: to show a regular occurrence, to signal a future time (using words like *end, begin, arrive,* and *depart*), to state a general or an ongoing truth or belief, or to discuss a literary work.

Regular occurrence   A security officer *opens* the gate every morning at 8 o'clock.

Future time   Retired people often *leave* cold climates in the fall.

General belief   Robert E. Lee *is* among the world's great soldiers.

Literature   In *The Awakening,* Kate Chopin *presents* an unconventional heroine.

▶ **Past Tense**   Use the *past tense* to show an action or condition that has already taken place. Form the past tense by adding **-ed** or **-d** to the present tense form of a regular verb or by changing the form of an irregular verb.

William Penn's family *wanted* him to give up his Quaker faith. He *refused* to give up his faith.

Patrick Henry *delivered* his famous speech in 1775. He *was* a popular attorney.

Note: The *-ed* and *-d* attached to the base form are often sounded softly or even omitted in speech. In your writing be sure that you do not omit these endings.

No He **ask** her to dance.   **Yes** He **asked** her to dance.

No She **want** Teddy for her partner.   **Yes** She **wanted** Teddy for her partner.

 In English sentences the time of the action referred to by each verb must be indicated, even when the time is obvious.

No   Last Christmas I receive a new backpack from my friend.

Yes   Last Christmas I receiv**ed** a new backpack from my friend.

▶ **Future Tense** Use the future tense to show that an action will take place. Form the future tense by adding *will* or *shall* in front of a present tense verb to show that a future action will definitely happen, to show an intention, or to show a probability.

Future	Some prescription drugs **will keep** asthma attacks to a minimum.
Intention	The instructor **will post** the grades on her office door.
Probability	The need for shelters for the homeless **will** probably **escalate** this winter.

EXERCISE 57

Put two lines under the correct verb in the parentheses.

1. A cold (affect, affects) the air passages in the head, neck, and chest.

2. Call your doctor if your fever (last, lasts) more than three or four days.

3. Last week a young mother (call, calls, called) her doctor and (ask, asks, asked) her about giving babies aspirin tablets.

4. Her doctor (tell, tells, told) her to never give an aspirin to anyone under eighteen years of age because the aspirin could cause brain and liver damage.

5. In Amy Tam's book *The Joy Luck Club,* she (interlock, interlocks, interlocked) sixteen intricate stories.

6. Richard Wagner (is, was) known for his romantic operas.

7. In 1911 six Americans each (pay, pays, paid) $300,000 for the *Mona Lisa,* and everyone (becomes, became) the proud owner of a clever work of art by master forger Yves Choudion.

8. The students in the drama class will (practice, practices, practiced) in the theater once a week.

9. This morning I (complete, completes, completed) my homework.

10. This year my friend (wash, washes, washed) his car every Saturday morning.

# Progressive Tenses and Perfect Tenses

Progressive tenses show continuing action. Use the appropriate form of the verb *be* plus the present participle.

Present progressive shows actions or conditions that are ongoing.

subject + am/is/are + present participle (taking place now)

I	am	working now.
Bill	is	working now.
They	are	working now.

Past progressive shows ongoing actions or conditions in the past, often with specific limits.

subject + was/were + present participle.

| Bill | was | working yesterday. |
| They | were | working yesterday. |

Future progressive shows recurring actions or conditions that will take place in the future.

subject + will + be + present participle (recurring in past, may still be)

| Bill | will | be | working tomorrow. |

The perfect tenses designate actions that were or will be finished before other actions or conditions. Use the appropriate form of the helping verb *have* plus the past participle.

Present perfect progressive shows a past action or condition that may continue in the present.

subject + have/has + been + past participle

| Bill | has | been | working all week. |
| They | have | been | working all week. |

Past perfect progressive shows a past recurring action or condition has ended.

subject + had + been + present participle

| Bill | had | been | working all week until he became ill. |

Future perfect progressive shows an ongoing action or condition that will be completed at a specific time in the future.

subject + will + have + past participle

By the end of this week, Bill   will   have   worked for the company for ten years.

Avoiding Non-Standard Verb Usage

In some dialects the Standard English usage of -s and -ed word endings, the verbs *has* and *have, do* and *does,* and the forms of the verb *to be (am, are, is, was, were, be, being, been)* are not observed. If you are accustomed to using these non-standard forms, you will need to learn to recognize them so that you can avoid using them in all situations except in informal settings in which a particular dialect is acceptable. Remember, if you want your ideas to be understood and respected by the greatest number of people, use Standard English constructions to express them. To help you recognize errors, read your work aloud and sound each syllable distinctly. In this way you can identify many of these kinds of errors. Grammar checkers catch some, but not all of them.

▶ **Omitted -s Endings**   Do not omit the required -s endings when you are forming the present tense verbs that have third person singular subjects.

No	Willie *want* more sugar in his coffee.	**Yes**	Willie *wants* more sugar in his coffee.
No	Everyone *need* a friend.	**Yes**	Everyone *needs* a friend.
No	She *go* on a diet often.	**Yes**	She *goes* on a diet often.

▶ **Added -s Endings**   Do not add the -s endings to verbs when the subject is not third person singular.

No	I *takes* pride in my work.	**Yes**	I *take* pride in my work.
No	The children *needs* to be fed.	**Yes**	The children *need* to be fed.
No	Their dogs *howls* at night.	**Yes**	Their dogs *howl* at night.

▶ **Omitted -ed Endings**   Do not omit the -ed or -d endings on verbs when you are forming the past tense or past participle of regular verbs.

No	She *advise* me to take this course.	**Yes**	She *advised* me to take this course.
No	He *has ask* for my advice.	**Yes**	He *has asked* for my advice.
No	I *use* to love you.	**Yes**	I *used* to love you.
No	I am *suppose* to work tonight.	**Yes**	I am *supposed* to work tonight.

EXERCISE 58

In the following sentences correct the errors in *-es /-s* and *-ed/-d* endings and the forms of the verbs. Some sentences contain more than one error.

1. The *New York Times* refer to the Bird Cage Theater in Tombstone, Arizona, as the wildest, wickedest night spot between Basin Street and the Barbary Coast.

2. Between 1881 and 1889 the Bird Cage Theater was the most famous honky-tonk in America, and for over nine years, never close its doors.

3. The ladies of Tombstone never enter the Bird Cage Theater.

4. In fact, they refuse to walk on the same side of the street that it was on.

5. The name of this infamous theater was derive from the fourteen gilded bird cage compartments suspend from the ceiling, overhanging the casino and dance hall.

6. "She's Only a Bird in a Gilded Cage," one of the nation's most popular songs of the day, was inspire by the ladies of the night—as they were called—who occupied the gilded cages.

7. Today, visitors to Tombstone still sees the hand-painted stage curtain and the original stage that retain its faded luster of a bygone era.

8. When the mines in the area flood, the Bird Cage were seal and boarded up.

9. All its fixtures and furnishings was left intact.

10. For almost fifty year the Bird Cage, with its colorful trappings, was close and untouched. It became a historic landmark of the American West when it was open to the public in 1934.

▶ **Omitted Necessary Verbs** Do not leave out necessary helping verbs or linking verbs.

No When we ʌ on vacation, we always eat at family style restaurants.

Yes When we *are* on vacation, we always eat at family style restaurants.

No Sometimes we eat at fast-food restaurants because they ʌ inexpensive.

Yes Sometimes we eat at fast-food restaurants because they *are* inexpensive.

No We ʌ been going to the same restaurants for years.

Yes We *have* been going to the same restaurants for years.

EXERCISE 59

Correct the errors in *-es/-s* and *-ed/-d* verb endings and add missing verbs. Some sentences contain more than one error.

1. Dennis been the coach here for ten years.

2. Melissa want to know if I be willing to help her with her homework.

3. Liz a charming hostess who put everyone at ease.

4. I ask Mildred if she be ready to go shopping by 10 o'clock.

5. Maria begin serving her early bird specials at 7 o'clock, but you be there before 6:30 if you wants to enjoys one of these extraordinarily delicious meals.

6. We been staying at the Oasis Resort every spring for the past three years, but this year we be going to the Coconut Villa.

7. Elmo, who write for a local weekly newspaper, seldom has difficulty meeting his deadlines, but he usually work many hours on each article.

8. I ask the instructor to explain the problem, but she refuse to do so and told me I was suppose to ask questions during class time, not after class.

9. Although Mary occasionally get low marks, she always try her best.

10. The other instructors gives fewer assignments than my English instructor do. She certainly believe in the old saying "Practice make perfect."

▶ *Has* **and** *Have*   Use *has* with third person singular subjects. Use *have* for all other subjects.

	SINGULAR	PLURAL
First Person	I have	we have
Second Person	you have	you have
Third Person	he/she/it has	they have
	sister has	sisters have
	somebody has	both have

No   My sister *have* a problem with her mother-in-law.

Yes   My sister *has* a problem with her mother-in-law.

▶ **Do** and **Does**   Use *does* with third person singular subjects. Use *do* with all other subjects.

	SINGULAR	PLURAL
First Person	I do	we do
Second Person	you do	you do
Third Person	he/she/it does	they do
	person does	people do
	anybody does	many do

No   Hadley *do* not know me.   **Yes**   Hadley *does* not know me.

No   I *does* my math homework first.   **Yes**   I *do* my math homework first.

EXERCISE 60

Correct the errors in the usage of *has/have* and *does/do*. Some sentences contain more than one error.

1. My neighbors and the golf course marshal has heated discussions.

2. The marshal do not understand why the neighbors are upset.

3. Some golfers does not respect private property.

4. Many of them seem to think that it is okay to retrieve their balls that has landed in someone's backyard.

5. The "No Trespassing" sign do not deter them.

6. For the golfers who does not have a ball retriever, they just walk into people's yards to retrieve their balls.

7. Another complaint the neighbors has is the failure of golfers to yell warnings.

8. Some does, but many does not yell the word *fore* when they hit an errant ball.

9. The vocabulary of golf have many strange words such as *bogey, birdie,* and *eagle.*

10. A person do not have to be a great golfer to enjoy playing golf.

▶ ***To Be* Verbs: *Am, Are, Is, Was, Were, Be, Being, Been***

Use *am* (present tense) and *was* (past tense) with first person singular
subjects.

Use *is* (present tense) and *was* (past tense) with third person singular subjects.

Use *are* (present tense) and *were* (past tense) with all other subjects.

	SINGULAR		PLURAL	
First Person	I	am/was	we	are/were
Second Person	you	are/were	you	are/were
Third Person	he/she/it	is/was	they	are/were
	mother	is/was	mothers	are/were
	nobody	is/was		

Do not use the verb *been* alone as the verb of a sentence. Always use the
helping verbs *has, have,* or *had* with it.

No   We been friends for five years.   **Yes**   We have been friends for five
years.

Do not use the verb *be* alone as the verb of a sentence. Use another form of
the *to be* verb or add an appropriate helping verb.

No   I be on the dean's list.   **Yes**   I am on the dean's list.

No   I be on the dean's list next month.   **Yes**   I will be on the dean's list next
month.

EXERCISE 61

Correct the usage errors in the *to be* verbs.

1. Americans be suffering from an energy crisis.

2. About 50 percent of all complaints to doctors be about fatigue.

3. Gerry be addicted to coffee and been drinking several cups of coffee every day for years.

4. The caffeine in the cups of coffee were raising her blood pressure.

5. I been drinking green tea for years.

6. Supposedly, the antioxidants in tea is good for the body.

7. Exercise are a well-known energy booster.

8. Many people in America is fatigued because they not be getting enough sleep because they is suffering from sleep apnea.

9. Sleep apnea are a condition that causes a person to stop breathing as often as several times an hour.

10. If you been fatigued all the time, you may want to consult your physician to determine if you be suffering from sleep apnea.

EXERCISE 62

Correct the usage errors in *have/has, do/does,* and *am/are/is/was/were/be/being/been.* Some sentences contain more than one error.

1. Our coach, who have been here for years, do not have any difficulty recruiting athletes.

2. When we was shopping for a new car, the salesperson were most helpful.

3. When you called me I were getting ready to go to the store.

4. I has many friends in high places.

5. My cousin's children does not have good table manners, yet she have impeccable manners.

6. When we was in Nova Scotia, we played golf at the Highlands Golf Links.

7. My dog that just had puppies are having a hard day today.

8. My other dog is great. He be chasing the neighbor's cats all day.

9. The cats been trying to catch the birds that come to our bird feeders.

10. Hal were my best friend in high school, but now he do not even send a Christmas card to me.

Review Exercises

Correct the errors in verb usage. Most sentences contain more than one error. Mark correct sentences with a C.

REVIEW EXERCISE 63

1. We was suppose to go bowling, but when we call the alley, we found that it were closed.

2. The baby were sleepy, but he refuse to take a nap.

3. My cousin be eating three sandwiches every day for lunch, but she do not gain weight.

4. My sister drive a new car, but my brothers have old ones, even though they makes more money than she do.

5. I be concerned about the health of my parents because they lives in a distant city and has no one to check on them daily.

6. As soon as we get one thing fix on the car, we knows something else will go wrong.

7. The hardwood floors in my kitchen gets hard usage, and even though I cleans them with a mild solution of vinegar and water, they still does not look good.

8. Although they does not get married until next June, they announce their engagement in December.

9. The children at the beach be having fun, but the adult who was supervising them were not.

10. Do Karen know that she need to gets a permit if she going to carpool with us?

REVIEW EXERCISE 64

1. Cary do not attend his music class today because he have a cold, but he call one of his classmates and ask her to take notes for him.

2. As a little boy, Beethoven live in fear of his father who were a penniless, ill-natured alcoholic singer.

3. The Beethoven family were poor, and little Ludwig seldom have enough clothes to keep him warm.

4. The violin, one of the most important solo instruments, belong to the family of stringed instruments.

5. The English horn, descend from old English instruments called hornpipes, are not a horn, but the alto member of the oboe family.

6. The accordion consist of a small pair of hand bellows with a keyboard on one side.

7. The carillon—sometimes call a glockenspiel—are often used in the orchestra.

8. The trumpet, according to the Bible, be the instrument that will summon people to the Last Judgment.

9. The bass drum be one of the most important percussion instruments of the orchestra.

10. The banjo are a stringed instrument that may come from Africa.

REVIEW EXERCISE 65

1. Liqueurs be spirits that been sweetened, flavored, and colored.

2. The recipe for liqueurs usually remain a well-kept secret.

3. The alchemy of liqueurs are in the selection and blending of the ingredients.

4. The word *liqueur* come from the Latin word *liquefarce,* which means "to make liquid," or "dissolve."

5. Liqueurs has an alcohol content of over 24 percent by volume.

6. The proof can vary from 49 to 110.

7. There be varying degrees of sweetness within the liqueur family.

8. The cremes are distinguish by a syrupy sweetness.

9. The word *cordial* been use to describe fruit-flavored liqueurs.

10. Many years ago people use to make their own liqueurs. In the seventeenth and eighteenth centuries, English ladies serve liqueur in little cordial pots.

Making Words Agree

Some words have matching forms to show grammatical relationships. Words are in agreement when they match grammatically. Subjects and verbs and pronouns and antecedents must agree.

Making Subjects and Verbs Agree

A subject and verb must agree in number. The **subject** of a sentence is a noun or a noun substitute, and it is what the sentence is about. The **verb** of a sentence shows the action or condition of the subject. **Number** is the form of a word that indicates whether the subject is one person or thing or more than one person or thing. To make subjects and verbs agree in number, use a singular verb when the subject is one person or thing and use a plural verb when the subject is more than one person or thing.

The *s* is the key to making subjects and verbs singular or plural. An *-s* or *-es* at the end of a singular subject makes it plural. The reverse is true for verbs. An *-s* or *-es* at the end of a verb makes it singular.

The girl sings in the church choir. (singular subject, singular verb)

The girls sing in the church choir. (plural subject, plural verb)

A light opera is an operetta. (singular subject, singular verb)

Aida and *Carmen* are famous operas. (plural subject, plural verb)

In a sentence the letter *-s* can go with the subject to make it plural, or it can go with the verb to make it singular. It cannot go with both. Visualize the letter *-s* traveling down the sentence highway. When it approaches the subject and verb, it can go with one or the other—not both.

s >>>The little   < dog needs / dogs need > a home.

s >>> Hoping to improve their performance,   > good instructors encourage / a good instructor encourages > students.

▶ **Present Tense Verb Endings**   Add *-s* or *-es* to present tense verbs (except *be* and *have*) when the subject is *he, she, it,* or any one person or thing.

The driver needs to renew his license.   She always renews her license on time.

Somebody sends out reminder notices prior to renewal time.

Note: Do not add *-s* or *-es* to present tense verbs when the subject is *I, we, you,* or *they.*

I want (not *wants*) a gold bracelet for Christmas.   **We** need (not *needs*) a new car.

You talk (not *talks*) too much.   **They** cry (not *cries*) when they are hurt.

▶ *Be* and *Have* **Verbs**   Use the following forms for *be* and *have* verbs:

		SINGULAR			PLURAL	
		BE	HAVE		BE	HAVE
First Person	I	am/was	have	**we**	are/were	have
Second Person	you	are/were	have	**you**	are/were	have
Third Person	he/she/it	is/was	has	**they**	are/were	have

Note: *Person* is the form a noun or pronoun takes to show who or what acts or experiences an action.

▶ **Words Between Subject and Verb**   When words come between the subject and the verb, make the verb agree with the subject—not the intervening words. These words often appear in phrases that begin with the following expressions:

accompanied by	in addition to	of the
along with	including	together with
as well as	not to mention	with

When subjects are followed by such phrases, the number of the subject does not change.

The flickering <u>light</u> of the candles <u>was</u> (not *were*) a welcome sight.

The <u>sound</u> of the raindrops on the roof <u>puts</u> (not *put*) the children to sleep.

The <u>instructor</u>, as well as the students, <u>was</u> (not *were*) in the classroom.

The <u>students</u>, as well as the instructor, <u>were</u> (not *was*) in the classroom

---

EXERCISE 66

Put one line under the subject and two lines under the verb in parentheses that agrees with it. If you have trouble finding the subject, choose one of the verbs in the parentheses and ask WHO or WHAT the action is about. The answer will be the subject.

1. Over 95 million people in America (use, uses) the Internet to get health care information.

2. Sandy, as well as her parents, (seek, seeks) advice from alternative medical practitioners.

3. An avalanche of alternative medical information, including hundreds of websites, (is, are) yours for the click of your mouse.

4. Sam, like many careful web browsers, (steer, steers) clear of information coming from people in chat rooms.

5. The information that one gets in chat rooms (is, are) often not reliable.

6. Rob, as well as many other students, (want, wants) online information to be dated.

7. The Health on the Net Foundation (have, has) developed a Code of Conduct for health care sites.

8. The code of conduct for medical and healthy websites (is, are) designed to promote reliability and credibility.

9. Currently, over 2,800 sites on the Internet (follow, follows) the code.

10. Cancers that are related to smoking (account, accounts) for more than one-third of cancer deaths.

▶ **Subjects Joined by *And*** When you join subjects with *and,* generally use a plural verb.

> Lakes **and** trees line (not *lines*) the fairways.

> Coffee **and** tea are (not *is*) breakfast drinks.

▶ **Exceptions** When you use *and* to join **subjects that stand for one idea,** use a singular verb.

> Peanut butter **and** jelly is (not *are*) my favorite sandwich spread.

When you put ***each* or *every* in front of subjects** joined by *and,* use a singular verb.

> *Every* twist and turn in the road brings (not *bring*) back memories.

▶ **Subjects Joined by *Or*** When you join subjects with *or* or with *either/or* or *neither/nor,* the verb may be singular or plural. Use a singular verb if both subjects are singular. Use a plural verb if both subjects are plural. When one subject is singular and the other is plural, use the verb that agrees with the subject that is nearer to it.

> **Singular**   John **or** Mary delivers (not *deliver*) the mail on Tuesday.
>
> **Plural**   Either poodles **or** toy fox terriers are (not *is*) exceptional pets.
>
> **Mixed**   Neither the twins **nor** their cousin comes (not *come*) to the family reunion.
>
> **Mixed**   Neither my cousin **nor** his twin sisters come (not *comes*) to the family reunion.

Note: Usually, you can avoid these awkward mixed constructions by rewording the sentence.

> **Better**   My cousin is not coming to the family reunion, and neither are his twin sisters.

EXERCISE 67

Put two lines under the correct verb in parentheses.

1. Every man, woman, and child (need, needs) to be immunized.

2. Peaches and cream (is, are) my favorite dessert.

3. "Every age, every culture, every custom and tradition (has, have) its own character." —Herman Hesse

4. The stars and stripes (is, are) our national symbol.

5. Either the police officer or the witnesses (is, are) not telling the truth.

6. "Every human benefit and enjoyment, every virtue and every prudent act (are, is) founded on compromise and barter." —Edmund Burke

7. Neither the salesmen nor the manager (like, likes) to deal with disgruntled customers.

8. "Honesty and frankness (make, makes) you vulnerable. Be honest and frank anyway." —Angeles Arrien

9. "Every burned book or house (enlighten, enlightens) the world; every suppressed or expunged word (reverberates, reverberate) through the earth from side to side." —Ralph Waldo Emerson

10. Either Bat Masterson or Doc Holiday (was, were) involved in the O.K. Corral shoot-out.

▶ **Independent (Indefinite) Pronouns** Use a singular verb with most independent pronouns, such as *another, anyone, everyone, one, each, either, neither, anything, everything, something, nothing, nobody,* and *somebody.*

Everyone deserves (not *deserve*) an education.

Nobody wants (not *want*) to be a failure.

Use a plural verb with the following independent pronouns: *both, many, few, several* and *others.*

Several of the students look (not *looks*) tired.

Others appear (not *appears*) rested.

Note: Use a singular verb after a word or series of words that begin with *every* or *many a.*

Many a student <u>has</u> failed a course because he or she did not take notes.

Every man, woman, and child <u>was</u> counted.

When you are using the independent pronouns *some, all, any, more, most,* and *none,* use the verb that agrees with the noun in the "of phrase" that follows the pronoun. The *of* may be stated or implied.

<u>Some</u> of the *popcorn* <u>refuses</u> (not *refuse*) to pop.

<u>Some</u> of the *children* <u>walk</u> (not *walks*)to school.

All the *sugar* <u>is</u> (not *are*) in the bowl.

All the *pickles* <u>are</u> (not *is*) in the jar.

EXERCISE 68

Put two lines under the correct verb in the parentheses.

1. Each of the kittens (have, has) two white feet.

2. All the coffee (have, has) been used.

3. Everyone in the cast (deserve, deserves) a round of applause.

4. Everything in his pockets (was, were) stained with ink.

5. Many a pizza delivery person (has, have) become lost in our neighborhood.

6. Neither of the dogs (eat, eats) table scraps.

7. Neither of the instructors (was, were) in the classroom.

8. Every nook and cranny in the house (was, were) filled with junk.

9. All of the diamond rings and gold bracelets (look, looks) stunning on her.

10. Many of the students (arrive, arrives) late every day.

▶ **Group Names and Number** Use a singular verb when a group name refers to the unit. Use a plural verb when a group name refers to the members of the group. When you are in doubt about which form to use, mentally substitute the words *it* or *they* for the group name. Use a singular verb with the imagined *it* and a plural verb with the imagined *they.*

The unit   Our football <u>team</u> (*it*) <u>is</u> first in the league.

Members   Our football <u>team</u> (*they*) <u>are</u> not allowed to use tobacco products.

When you use *the* number, always use a singular verb. When you use *a* number, always use a plural verb.

The number   The <u>number</u> of students receiving parking tickets <u>has</u> increased.

A number   A <u>number</u> of instructors <u>were</u> absent yesterday.

▶ **Inverted Subject-Verb Order**   Generally, the verb follows the subject, but not always. When the subject follows the verb as in questions and sentences beginning with *there is* or *there are,* be sure that the verb agrees with the subject. First, find the verb and ask WHO? or WHAT? is doing the action of the verb.

Are teddy bears cuddly? The verb is *are.* What are? Bears *are.* <u>Are</u> teddy <u>bears</u> cuddly?

There is a cute brown bear on the shelf. The verb is *is.* What is? Bear *is.*

There <u>is</u> a cute brown <u>bear</u> on the shelf.

▶ **Linking Verbs**   When you use a linking verb to connect a subject to its complement, be sure that you use the verb that agrees with the subject—not the complement. Think of the linking verb as an equal sign between the subject and the complement. To choose the correct verb, ignore the complement—the last part of the equation.

Her greatest asset (is, are) her eyes. asset = eyes

Drop the last part of the equation: asset = ~~eyes~~. Asset is singular and takes the singular verb *is.*

EXERCISE 69

Put two lines under the correct verb in the parentheses.

1. The jury (was, were) discussing the case.

2. The number of careless errors in Vic's paper (was, were) surprising.

3. Where (is, are) your uncle and aunt?

4. A number of students (was, were) absent.

5. There (is, are) self-centered people in my class.

6. The jury (has, have) been selected.

7. The female firefighters (is, are) a credit to the department.

8. Betty (has, have) many friends.

9. There (appear, appears) to be a problem with the electrical wiring.

10. There are a number of students who (think, thinks) the exam was too difficult.

▶ **Titles of Works, Company Names, and Verb + -*ing* Words**   Use singular verbs with titles of works and organization names even when the name is plural.

> <u>A Tale of Two Cities</u> is (not *are*) an excellent novel.

> <u>Weber & Sons</u> replaces (not *replace*) broken windows.

Use singular verbs with verb + -*ing* words (*swimming, painting, donating, working,* and so on) used as subjects.

> <u>Working</u> with students in foreign countries is challenging.

EXERCISE 70

Put two lines under the verb in the parentheses that agrees with the subject.

1. *Wind in the Willows* (is, are) Fran's favorite book.

2. Contributing canned goods to food drives (help, helps) feed needy people.

3. Carpanito Brothers (sell, sells) fresh fruit and vegetables.

4. The Girl Scouts of America (is, are) a nonprofit organization.

5. Playing golf in thunderstorms (is, are) not a good idea.

6. "The Oxen" (was, were) written by Thomas Hardy.

7. "Easter Wings" (has, have) a distinctive visible shape.

8. Taking vitamins on an empty stomach sometimes (cause, causes) nausea.

9. Brennans in New Orleans (is, are) a famous restaurant.

10. The United States (try, tries) to live up to commitments to other governments.

Review Exercises

Correct each sentence, making the subject and verb agree. Put two lines under the main verb and one line under the main subject. Mark correct sentences with a C.

REVIEW EXERCISE 71

1. The raindrops on the roof makes a pleasant sound.

2. The child, as well as his parents, were walking dangerously close to the edge of the cliff.

3. The best flavored sticks of cinnamon come from Vietnam.

4. Everyone have heard of John Paul Jones.

5. A number of his battles are recounted in history books.

6. *American Folklore and Legends* paint interesting pictures of American life.

7. Some of my classmates has never heard of John Paul Jones.

8. Neither Terry nor his roommates know that John Paul Jones is considered the father of our navy.

9. There is many great stories about this naval giant.

10. He adopts his surname in his early twenties after he kills a mutineer.

REVIEW EXERCISE 72

1. Smith Brothers make the best sourdough bread in town.

2. The curtains above the door looks like tattered sails.

3. There is two distinct types of savory.

4. Summer savory and winter savory are both pungent and strong.

5. Everyone of the cooks use basil in pasta sauce.

6. The school board is discussing dress codes for students.

7. The number of people at the dinner table varies.

8. There is a few pieces of cake on the tray.

9. Her favorite pieces of jewelry is her gold bracelets.

10. Neither Gladys nor Don and Jeanette likes to walk in the rain.

1. Rum, the beverage distilled from fermented sugar cane products, were an important part of early American commerce.

2. Completing all the assignments on time are difficult for many students.

3. Each of the twins have a new car.

4. Everyone of the students want good grades.

5. There are over five hundred varieties of sage.

6. The fresh or dried leaves of sage is widely used in the cuisine of many countries.

7. Ali Baba, the sailor in *Arabian Nights,* introduce the word *sesame* into fiction.

8. Some of the money was missing.

9. Some of the quarters was missing.

10. The number of missing quarters are not known.

Making Pronouns and Antecedents Agree

A **pronoun** is a word that takes the place of a noun. When a pronoun refers to a preceding noun or pronoun (*antecedent*), they should agree in **person, gender,** and **number.**

▶ **Person**   Agreement in **person** seldom presents a problem.

    First Person   I will buy the book **myself.**

    Second Person   **You** should have brought **your** own book.

    Third Person   Len will not lend you **his** book.

▶ **Gender**   When the antecedent is masculine, use masculine pronouns (*he, him, his*). When the antecedent is feminine, use feminine pronouns (*she, her, hers*).

When the antecedent is neither masculine nor feminine, use neuter pronouns (*it, its*).

Beth is president of **her** company.

Tom is the top salesperson in **his** company.

Our **neighborhood** is proud of **its** Christmas decorations.

When the antecedent may be either masculine or feminine, use both masculine and feminine pronouns (*him or her, he or she, his or hers*) or change the antecedent to a plural word and use a plural pronoun (*them, they, their*).

No   A **lawyer** will often refuse to give **his** friends free legal advice.

Yes   A **lawyer** will often refuse to give **his or her** friends free legal advice.

Yes   **Lawyers** will often refuse to give **their** friends free legal advice.

▶ **Number**   To make antecedents and pronouns agree in **number,** use singular pronouns (such as *he, him, his, she, her, it, me, myself,* and *oneself*) to refer to singular antecedents, and use plural pronouns (such as *we, us, they, them,* and *their*) to refer to plural antecedents.

Singular   **Abigail Adams,** like many women of **her** time, had little formal education.

Plural   The **Washingtons** had a set menu of coffee, tea, and cake for **their** Friday receptions.

▶ **More than One Antecedent**   When a pronoun has two or more antecedents joined by *and,* generally, use a plural pronoun.

George Washington and **James Madison** were good fathers to **their** stepchildren.

When a pronoun has two or more singular antecedents joined by *or* or *nor,* use a singular pronoun.

Either **Brandy** or **Britt** will win first place for **her** original recipe.

When a pronoun has two or more antecedents and one is singular and one is plural, use a pronoun that agrees in person and number with the nearer antecedent, or recast the sentence.

Neither **Suzy** nor the **boys** answered **their** telephone.

Neither the **boys** nor **Suzy** answered **her** telephone.

The **boys** did not answer **their** telephone, nor did **Suzy** answer **her** telephone.

▶ **Group Name Antecedents**   When the group name refers to the group as a unit, use a singular pronoun. When it refers to members of the group, use a plural pronoun.

Hint: When you can substitute the word *it* for the group name, use a singular pronoun. When you can substitute the word *they* for the group name, use a plural pronoun.

Singular	The **jury** (*it*) delivered **its** verdict.		**Plural**	The **jury** (*they*) ate **their** lunch.
Singular	The **team** (*it*) won **its** first game.		**Plural**	The **team** (*they*) drove **their** own cars.

EXERCISE 74

Fill in the blanks with the appropriate pronouns.

1. When Dolly Madison's house caught fire, ___________________ would not be rescued until ___________________ had rescued ___________________ husband's papers.

2. Elizabeth Monroe and Louisa Adams were highly intelligent First Ladies, but ___________________ did not care for official society.

3. Will everyone who dislikes speeding tickets please raise ___________________ right foot.

4. The homeowners' association has revised ___________________ list of rules.

5. Our team won ___________________ first game of the season.

6. The jury ate ___________________ lunch in silence.

7. Usually, a police officer will not draw ___________________ gun unless ___________________ is forced to do so.

8. Neither the children nor their father voiced ___________________ opinions on the matter.

9. The basketball team will be wearing ___________________ new uniforms at today's game.

10. Will everyone please park ___________________ car in the designated area.

▶ **Independent Pronoun Antecedents**   Independent (*indefinite*) pronouns refer to persons or things in general. Most indefinite pronouns are always singular—even the ones that seem to have plural meanings.

Commonly Used Singular Indefinite Pronouns

anybody	anyone	anything	each
everybody	everyone	everything	either
nobody	one	something	neither
somebody	someone	nothing	
	no one		

A phrase following a singular antecedent does not change the number of the antecedent.

No   **Each** <u>of the boys</u> rode **their** bicycle.

Yes   **Each** <u>of the boys</u> rode **his** bicycle.

No   **Neither** <u>of the girls</u> brought **their** books.

Yes   **Neither** <u>of the girls</u> brought **her** books.

▶ **The *Every* Problem**   Using plural pronouns to refer to singular indefinite pronouns is a common problem. The tendency is to consider these words plural and to use plural pronouns to refer to them. This practice is not acceptable in college writing. You may correct the agreement problem by replacing the plural pronoun with *he or she*, make the antecedent plural, or rewrite the sentence to eliminate the problem.

No   Will *everyone* please take *their* seats.

Yes   Will *everyone* please take *his or her* seat.

Yes   Will all the *people* take *their* seats.

Yes   If *you* are standing, please take *your* seat.

The indefinite pronouns **both** and **many** are always plural.

No   *Both* of the students completed *his or her* assignments.

Yes   *Both* of the students completed *their* assignments.

The indefinite pronouns ***all, any, more, most, none,*** and ***some*** may be singular or plural depending on the context. If the last word in the "of phrase" is singular, use a singular pronoun. If it is plural, use a plural pronoun.

Plural   *None* <u>of the students</u> are in *their* seats. (*None* refers to the plural noun *students.*)

Singular   *All* <u>of the research</u> is still in *its* original draft form. (*All* refers to the singular noun *research.*)

The "of phrase" may be stated or implied.

Plural   *Some* ⌃ team members *are* naturally athletic. (*Some* refers to the plural noun *members.*)

EXERCISE 75

Fill in the blanks with the appropriate pronouns.

1. Everybody should write a letter to _____________________ representative.

2. Neither organization wanted to accept responsibility for _____________________ budget deficit.

3. Many of the students park _____________________ cars and take public transportation to school.

4. Some of the students prefer to form _____________________ own carpool.

5. Some of the work on the parking lot resulted in certain inconveniences, but _____________________ has solved many of the parking problems.

6. Both of the students need to get _____________________ annual parking permit.

7. Everyone wanted to see _____________________ picture in the yearbook.

8. No one should park in the carpool zones if _____________________ does not have a carpool permit.

9. None of my students made poor marks on _____________________ research papers.

10. Will everyone please submit _____________________ essay on time.

Review Exercises

In the following exercises fill in the blanks with the appropriate pronouns.

REVIEW EXERCISE 76

1. Neither the cat nor the dogs will sleep in _________________ bed.

2. If anybody wants to take a makeup exam, _________________ should go to the testing center.

3. Either the musicians or the female vocalist did not understand _________________ contract.

4. Each of the girls was pretty in _________________ own way.

5. Each of the students was working on _________________ own research project.

6. Most of the boys in the photography class planned to give _________________ best work as a gift.

7. Neither Jennifer nor Jeannette wore _________________ diamonds to the dance.

8. Everyone of the women had been told to not carry _________________ money in _________________ handbag.

9. Some of the students were not in _________________ room when the instructor arrived.

10. The team discussed _________________ new game plans.

REVIEW EXERCISE 77

1. Neither Rose nor Laura brought _________________ children to the party.

2. The club sent notices to _________________ members who had not paid the dues.

3. Everyone added _________________ e-mail address to the list.

4. If somebody calls, take a message and tell _________________ I will return the call tomorrow.

5. Either Lynn or Linda will show __________________ dog this weekend.

6. Both of the dogs have __________________ own special diet.

7. Most of the dogs in the show have __________________ own grooming tables.

8. A dentist often does not charge __________________ family for routine dental work.

9. Most of the sugar was still in __________________ original container.

10. A nurse must always be alert when __________________ is on duty.

1. Both General Lee and General Grant were fond of __________________horses.

2. Each of these men distinguished __________________ in the Mexican War.

3. Many Civil War buffs have done __________________ master's thesis on these two generals.

4. Everyone has __________________ opinion about which man was the best general.

5. Neither President Harrison nor President Taylor finished __________________ term in the White House.

6. Neither Andrew Jackson nor Millard Fillmore brought __________________ wife to the White House.

7. James Buchanan, as well as other single or widowed presidents, asked one of __________________ relatives to serve as __________________ hostess.

8. If anybody wants to know more about these two presidents, __________________ can read about them in books about the lives of American presidents.

9. One book club discusses only American historical figures at __________________ monthly meeting.

10. Some of the members of the club were asked for copies of __________________ reports.

Using Modifiers: Adjectives and Adverbs

A *modifier* is a word or group of words that acts as an adjective or adverb. Both *adjectives* and *adverbs* are words that describe or limit other words, phrases, or clauses. Some people think that all adverbs end in *-ly*—and most of them do—but not all of them. (He talked *well*. She spoke *often*.) Some adjectives end in *-ly* also (*sickly* baby, *lonely* lady). Generally, words ending in *-ful, -ish, -less,* and *-like* are adjectives (success*ful* man, self*ish* child, thought*less* act, life*like* portrait). The way a word is used—not the form—determines whether it functions as an adjective or as an adverb.

> The baby looked *happy*. (*happy,* adjective modifying the noun *baby*)

> The baby *happily* reached for the bottle. (*happily,* adverb modifying the verb *reached*)

> To decide whether to use an adjective or an adverb, identify the expression that is being limited. Use an adjective when the expression being modified is a *noun* or *pronoun*. Use an adverb when the expression being modified is a *verb*, an *adjective*, or another *adverb*.

Function of Modifiers

Understanding the function of modifiers will help you build better sentences because English sentences often contain modifying words, phrases, and clauses that make the meaning of the sentence clearer and more specific. Modifiers are classified according to their function: *adjectives, adverbs, nouns,* and *pronouns.*

Adjective Modifiers   The function of an adjective is to describe, limit, or qualify a noun. An adjective shows what the noun is like, its condition, or which one it is. An adjective modifier may be placed before a noun or any word or group of words used as a noun or after a linking verb.

> The *black* dog barked. The dog is *black.*

Note: The words *a, an,* and *the* are adjectives that designate or limit a noun.

Adverb Modifiers   The function of an adverb is to tell

when (time) *how* (manner, condition, or reason)

where (place) *how much* (extent or number)

why (cause or reason)

An adverb can modify a verb, an adjective, or another adverb. Generally, a single-word adverb precedes an adjective or another adverb, but often follows a verb.

Noun Modifiers   In addition to being modified by an adjective, a noun may be modified by another noun. Both types of modification are common in the English language.

round pan, *pie* pan good partner, *business* partner

smart officer, *police* officer wet towel, *paper* towel

When an adjective and a noun modify another noun, the adjective appears first.

The handsome police officer, not *the police handsome officer.*

The soggy paper towel, not *the paper soggy towel.*

Pronoun Modifiers   A noun may be modified by a pronoun.

Which class are you taking? (*Which* modifies the noun *class.*)

I like *this* instructor. (*This* modifies the noun *instructor.*)

The following words may be used both as pronouns and as adjectives.

all	either	one	these
another	few	other	this
any	many	several	those
both	more	some	what
each	neither	that	which

Using Adjectives

Adjectives give added information about nouns and pronouns by specifying *the condition, which one, how many, which size, what color,* and so on.

Seven children are in the pool. (*how many*)

The *old, deserted* house stands on the corner. (*condition*)

I need a *white* blouse. (*what color*)

Use **adjectives** to describe, limit, qualify, or specify nouns or pronouns.

He was *charming.* (The adjective *charming* modifies the pronoun *he.*)

Bitter memories flooded his mind. (The adjective *bitter* modifies the noun *memories.*)

He remembered her *sad* eyes. (The adjective *sad* modifies the noun *eyes.*)

Using Adverbs

Adverbs answer the questions "*How?*" "*Why?*" "*Where?*" "*When?*" and "*To what extent?*"

The old man walked *rather slowly.* (*how*)

He *recently* had a stroke. (*when*)

He was *unusually* tired. (*to what extent*)

Use adverbs to describe the action of verbs or to modify adjectives or other adverbs.

▶ **Adverbs Modifying Verbs**   When the expression being modified is a *verb,* use an adverb.

Caleb *quietly* closed the door. (The adverb *quietly* modifies the verb *closed.*)

The old man walked *slowly.* (The adverb *slowly* modifies the verb *walked.*)

The child *quickly* grabbed the candy bar. (The adverb *quickly* modifies the verb *grabbed.*)

▶ **Adverbs Modifying Adjectives**   When the expression being modified is an *adjective,* use an adverb.

Sue is *fairly* successful. (The adverb *fairly* modifies the adjective *successful.*)

The *extraordinarily* handsome man smiled. (The adverb *extraordinarily* modifies the adjective *handsome.*)

The little man was *unusually* strong. (The adverb *unusually* modifies the adjective *strong.*)

▶ **Adverbs Modifying Other Adverbs**   When the expression being modified is another *adverb,* use an adverb.

The student responded *very* quickly. (The adverb *very* modifies the adverb *quickly*.)

He spoke *quite* loudly. (The adverb *quite* modifies the adverb *loudly*.)

She replied *rather* quickly. (The adverb *rather* modifies the adverb *quickly*.)

Choosing Between Adjectives and Adverbs

When you have to decide whether to use an adjective or an adverb, ask yourself what the word modifies. If it modifies a noun or pronoun, choose the adjective. If it modifies a verb, choose the adverb. Some verbs may be used as either *linking* verbs or *action* verbs. For example, the word *look* may be used as a *linking* verb or as an *action* verb. When a verb shows action, it is called an *action* verb. When a verb links the subject of a sentence to a word or phrase that renames or describes the subject, it is called a *linking* verb.

Suzy looked sad. (The adjective *sad* is correct because it modifies the noun *Suzy*.)

Curt looked quickly at the paper. (The adverb *quickly* is correct because it modifies the verb *looked*.)

Note: Linking verbs, especially the *sense* verbs, are often followed by an adjective. Action verbs are often followed by an adverb.

Many of the *linking* verbs in the following list may also be used as *action* verbs.

Common Linking Verbs

BE	SENSE	SEEM
am	feel	appear
are	look	believe
is	sound	become
was	smell	grown
were	taste	remain
be		prove
being		stay
been		

When you do not know whether a verb is acting as a linking verb or as an action verb, substitute the word *seem*—which is always a *linking* verb—for it. If the sentence is not greatly changed and the meaning is about the same, the verb is a *linking* verb and takes an adjective form. If the revised sentence does not make sense, the verb is an *action* verb and takes an adverb form.

seems

Sue looks sad.   Sue ~~looks~~ sad.

It has about the same meaning and makes sense. *Looks* in this sentence is a *linking* verb and takes the adjective *sad*.

seems

Tom looks quickly at the paper.   Tom ~~looks~~ quickly at the paper.

It does not make sense. *Looks* in this sentence is an *action* verb and takes the adverb *quickly*.

seemed

Adam appeared happy.   Adam ~~appeared~~ happy.

It makes sense. *Appeared* in this sentence is a linking verb and takes the adjective *happy*.

seemed

Ed appeared suddenly.   Ed ~~appeared~~ suddenly.

It does not make sense. *Appeared* in this sentence is an action verb and takes the adverb *suddenly*.

EXERCISE 79

Underline the correct word (*adjective* or *adverb*) in the parentheses.

1. The racer ran (fast, fastly).

2. She looked (sleepy, sleepily).

3. She looked (sleepy, sleepily) at me.

4. I helped the (elder, elderly) person across the street.

5. Doug wrote the poem (slow, slowly).

6. My sister wants her children to behave (proper, properly).

7. The children (quick, quickly) ran to the playground.

8. The situation proved to be (dangerous, dangerously).

9. The adjuster handled the matter (poor, poorly).

10. At the beginning of her speech, she spoke (slow, slowly).

EXERCISE 80

Underline the correct word (*adjective* or *adverb*) in the parentheses.

1. The patient looked (unhealthy, unhealthily).

2. The accused shoplifter looked (innocent, innocently) at the detective.

3. All the people in the building remained (calm, calmly).

4. His alibi sounded (suspicious, suspiciously) to me.

5. She looked at him very (cool, coolly).

6. Why are you looking so (sad, sadly)?

7. His bragging grew (increasing, increasingly) worse as he grew older.

8. The dog appeared (content, contentedly) in his new doghouse.

9. The screeching sound of a violin sounded (terrible, terribly).

10. Poison perfume smells (great, greatly).

▶ ***Bad*** **and** ***Badly***   These words are often confused. *Bad* is an adjective modifying nouns and pronouns. Use it to describe how something is like when the verb is functioning as a linking verb.

seems

The food tastes (bad, badly).   The food ~~tastes~~ bad.   The food tastes bad.

Note: The verbs of sense—*feel, smell, taste, sight, sound*—are followed by an adjective (not an adverb) modifying their subjects.

She feels *bad*.   The soup smells *good*.   The apple tastes *good*.
He looks *bad*.   It sounds *good*.

Badly is an adverb modifying verbs, adjectives, and adverbs. Use it to describe how something is done when the verb is functioning as an action verb.

seems

She writes poetry (*bad, badly*). She ~~writes~~ poetry bad. She writes poetry badly.

▶ ***Good* and *Well*** These words are often troublesome. Always use the modifier *good* as an adjective.

seems

Joy perfume smells (*good, well*).   Joy perfume ~~smells~~ good.   Joy perfume smells good.

Never use *good* to modify a verb.

No   We played *good*.   **Yes**   We played *well*.

No   We worked *good* together.   **Yes**   We worked *well* together.

Well is usually an adverb, but it can be an adjective. Use it as an adverb to mean "to perform an action capably."

You write (*well, good*).   You write capably.   You write *well*.

Use *well* as an adjective to mean "to be in good health," "to be well-dressed or well-groomed," "to be in a satisfactory condition," "to be advisable or prudent."

Health   Lana looks *well*.   **Satisfactory**   She dresses *well*.
Prudent   It is *well* that you stayed.

EXERCISE 81

Underline the correct word (adjective or adverb) in the parentheses.

1. The students did (well, good) on their last exam.

2. The cooked cabbage smelled (bad, badly).

3. The writing teams worked very (good, well) together.

4. She looks (good, well) in her new suit.

5. The coach felt (bad, badly) about the referee's call.

6. These new shoes do not fit (good, well).

7. She cooks (bad, badly).

8. This food tastes (good, goodly).

9. I feared that you had been hurt (bad, badly).

10. It is (good, well) that you had your cellular phone with you.

Comparing Adjectives and Adverbs

Adjectives and adverbs are compared according to the degree of the qualities they express.

▶ **One- and Two-Syllable Words**   Generally, add *-er* to the base form of one- and two- syllable adjectives and adverbs when comparing two things. Add *-est* to the base form when comparing three or more things.

> She is *pretty.* (base form)
>
> She runs *faster* than her sister. (comparing two people or things)
>
> She is the *prettiest* girl in the class. (comparing three or more people or things)

▶ **Words with More Than Two Syllables**   For adjectives of more than two syllables and adverbs ending in *-ly*, generally, use *more* or *less* to compare two things, and use *most* or *least* to compare three or more things.

> He is **qualified.** (base)
>
> He is the *most* **qualified** man in the company. (three or more things compared upward)
>
> He is the *least* **qualified** man in the company. (three or more things compared downward)
>
> He talks **softly.** (base)
>
> He talks *more* **softly** than his friend. (two things compared upward)
>
> He talks *less* **softly** than his boss. (two things compared downward)

▶ ***Other* or *Else***   Be sure to include the word *other* or *else* when you compare one thing with a group of which it is a part.

> **No**   Sam made a higher score than anyone in his class.
>
> He is a member of his class, so he cannot have a higher score than himself.
>
> **Yes**   Sam made a higher score than anyone *else* in his class.

▶ **Irregular Forms**   Some comparative forms of adjectives and adverbs are formed in irregular ways. Since these words are not formed in the usual way, you need to memorize them.

Irregular Forms

	BASE	TWO THINGS	THREE OR MORE THINGS
Adjectives	good	better	best
	bad	worse	worst
	a little	less	least
	many, some, much	more	most
Adverbs	badly	worse	worst
	well	better	best

▶ **Double Comparisons**   Avoid double comparisons. Do not combine *more* and *most* or *less* and *least* with the endings *-er* or *-est*.

No   He is *more taller* than his dad.   **Yes**   He is *taller* than his dad.

No   She is the *most cutest* baby in nursery.   **Yes**   She is the *cutest* baby in the the nursery.

▶ **Illogical Expressions**   Do not use illogical expressions such as *most unique, rather unique, very flat, truly perfect,* and so on. Something is unique, flat, perfect and so on, or it is not.

No   She has *a most* unique accent.

Yes   She has a unique accent.   **Yes**   She has a most unusual accent.

EXERCISE 82

In the following sentences, make the necessary corrections in the comparisons.

1. Which dessert do you like best, cake or pie?

2. I like pie more better than I like cake.

3. Key lime pie has a most unusual tangy taste that I like.

4. Although closely related to the lemon, the lime is usually smallest.

5. Cardamom, often called grains of paradise, is more fragrant than all spices.

6. Saffron, the world's more expensive herb, is made from the tiny stigma of autumn crocuses.

7. This most unique herb was used in medicines in ancient times.

8. Many gourmets think morels are more tastier than any mushroom.

9. Of the three types of ham, Westphalia, Virginia, and Parma, I like the Westphalia better.

10. I put pecans and walnuts in fudge, but I like pecans best.

Review Exercises

Make the necessary corrections in the use of adjectives and adverbs or underline the correct forms. Mark correct sentences with a C.

REVIEW EXERCISE 83

1. Shallots, a member of the onion family, are grown extensive in Europe.

2. Use rosemary sparingly in salad dressings.

3. The finer caviar is gray beluga. It is better than any caviar.

4. The leaves of lemon thyme are particular suited to fish and many sauces.

5. Tarragon is indispensably in many sauces.

6. Sweet woodruff makes even cheap wine taste well.

7. It imparts an unusually fine flavor to fruit punches.

8. Sage goes particularly good with pork dishes.

9. Kobe beef raised in Japan are better than any beef.

10. Pickled lemon rinds are a most essential ingredient in many Moroccan dishes.

REVIEW EXERCISE 84

1. Burnet tastes like cucumbers, and its leaves taste well in salads.

2. Chicory is sometimes added to coffee to make it taste bitterly.

3. Capers are used extensive in sauce for fish.

4. True cinnamon is light brown and more delicate flavored than the cassia variety.

5. Use caraway seeds in sauerkraut because in this dish they taste better than any seeds.

6. Cumin, with its slight bitter taste, is used in curry powder.

7. Cardamom is frequent misspelled with an ending *-n* instead of an *-m*.

8. When you use herbs and spices, trust your own palate, it will serve you good.

9. The English especial like to plant thyme (tiem) along their garden paths.

10. Montezuma was probably one of the greater chocolate enthusiasts in history.

REVIEW EXERCISE 85

1. You look good today even though you just returned from the hospital.

2. Sunflowers, which Van Gogh painted so magnificent, contain tasty seeds.

3. Pumpkin seeds taste badly before they are roasted.

4. The most wide used spices are cinnamon, nutmeg, cloves, allspice, and ginger.

5. Large amounts of herbs may make your food taste badly.

6. You look good in your new outfit.

7. You sang well in church this morning.

8. I can't understand her because she speaks too rapid.

9. Rosemary, one of the older known herbs, is mentioned in all ancient writings about food.

10. Of the two types of savory, winter and summer, I like summer the best.

REVIEW EXERCISE 86

1. Indian cooks saute their spices to release their most unique aromas.

2. Wild rice is not real wild rice at all. It is the seed of an aquatic grass.

3. It tastes wonderfully and is in short supply.

4. Snails are undoubted the most renowned French delicacy.

5. We could not hear very good because the people in front of us were talking.

6. The twins thought their older brother had treated them unfair.

7. Since it was raining, I drove real careful.

8. The dessert tasted deliciously.

9. The music not only sounded badly, it was bad.

10. The baby looked sleepily and nodded her head slowly.

Improving
Sentences

If you're going to write, don't pretend to write down. It's going to be the best you can do, and it's the fact that it's the best you can do that kills you.

—DOROTHY PARKER
Interview in Writers at Work

Putting Modifiers Where They Belong

Every modifier should be so placed that the reader may connect it immediately and unmistakably with the word that it modifies. *To modify* means "to limit" or to make more definite the meaning of a word. Adjectives modify nouns or pronouns by telling *what kind,* pointing out *which one,* or telling *how many.* Adverbs modify verbs, adjectives, or other adverbs. They may tell *how, when, where,* or *to what extent.* A modifier may be a single word, a phrase, or a clause. Place the modifier as near as possible to the word it is intended to modify—*the headword*—to clarify the meaning of the word or make the meaning more definite. If the modifier is placed too far from the headword, the effect of the modifier may be lost or diverted to another word. When the headword intended to be modified is missing, the meaning of the sentence may be ambiguous or confusing.

Revising Misplaced Modifiers

When the modifier is not properly placed as near as possible to the intended headword, it is called a *misplaced modifier.*

No   We have a variety of float tubes for fishing enthusiasts with step-in or slide-in options.

Yes   For fishing enthusiasts, we have a variety of float tubes with step-in or slide-in options.

No   He drove down the highway toward her house that had recently been paved.

Yes   He drove toward her house down the highway that had recently been paved.

No   I saw a student in my classroom that I know.

Yes   In my classroom I saw a student that I know.

▶ **Limiting Modifiers**   The placement of *limiting modifiers* such as *almost, even, ever, exactly, hardly, just, merely, only,* and *simply* can change the meaning of a sentence. Place the limiting modifier as near as possible to the word you intend to modify.

She spent *almost* a thousand dollars. (*She* did spend money—almost a thousand dollars.)

She *almost* spent a thousand dollars. (She *almost* spent a thousand dollars, but she didn't.)

▶ **Two-Way Modifiers**   If a modifier is placed in such a position that it can refer to either the preceding or the following part of the sentence, it can be confusing because the reader cannot be sure which of the two possible meanings is intended. These modifiers may be revised in two ways, depending on meaning. To make the meaning clear, put the modifier where it refers to only a single term.

No   Tell Ruthie *when she comes home* I want to see her.

Yes   When she comes home, tell Ruthie I want to see her.

Yes   Tell Ruthie I want to see her when she comes home.

EXERCISE 1

In each sentence correct the misplaced modifier by either moving it closer to its headword or revising the sentence so the connection between the headword and the modifier is clear.

1. Morgan saw a leather coat in the store that he liked.

2. We saw a little boy riding a merry-go-round horse with a pacifier in his mouth.

3. Marvin's broken leg during the night began to hurt in the cast.

4. I asked my supervisor when I should report for work last week.

5. Ted invited Laura to go to the movies in an e-mail.

6. The driver told the passenger to fasten his seat belt.

7. Arrange the flowers and candles on the table with your friend Mandy.

8. A Double-Dutch Fudge carton of ice cream is melting on the sink.

9. The baby is her little girl in the playpen.

10. Students who attend class often receive higher marks.

Revising Dangling Modifiers

When the modifier does not clearly modify a word in the sentence, it is called a *dangling modifier.*

No To hold the plank in place, one foot should be placed on it.

Yes To hold the plank in place, put one foot on it.

Yes Hold the plank in place by putting one foot on it.

No On entering the museum, the Jan Vermeer masterpiece is seen.

Yes On entering the museum, one can see the Jan Vermeer masterpiece.

Yes As you enter the museum, you can see the Jan Vermeer masterpiece.

EXERCISE 2

Correct the dangling modifiers in the following sentences by adding a missing headword, changing the subject of the main clause, or rewriting the sentence.

1. Squatting and grooming themselves, the zoology students studied the baboons.

2. Cooking a gourmet dinner for my new boyfriend, my former boyfriend rang the doorbell.

3. In early childhood my grandfather took me to many ball games.

4. Although bent with age, one can see that the old man was handsome in his younger days.

5. The zipper in my pants always sticks when hurrying to dress for school.

6. Playing balderdash, the game took over an hour.

7. Absorbed in an interesting experiment, the time passed quickly.

8. When only a teenager, my father taught me to play the stock market.

9. Being an extrovert, my friend is always comfortable with strangers.

10. Left alone on the Fourth of July, the puppy was frightened by the fireworks.

Review Exercises

The sentences contain misplaced and dangling modifiers. Revise each sentence so that the meaning is clear.

REVIEW EXERCISE 3

1. Having rained all night, the Coopers found they had four feet of water in their living room.

2. They had just bought a new computer and a new puppy, which they had not yet unpacked.

3. They had lived in the house that floods near the river for five years.

4. The neighbors waved as they went by in their boat.

5. They had asked us before we left to call them.

6. My wife said during the worst part of the flood the rescue workers found our cat.

7. The river was described by the news commentator that was over its banks.

8. After living in the house for five years, the rescue routine was familiar.

9. Living constantly with the fear of flooding, their anxiety increased.

10. While watching the unfolding disaster on television, Nan's pet pig ate a bag of chips.

REVIEW EXERCISE 4

1. A car drove down the street with a Just Married sign on it.

2. The Jeep is on the road that he wrecked.

3. Jan listened while the professor lectured attentively.

4. He showed the ring to his girlfriend that he bought at a garage sale.

5. He asked his friend to borrow his car.

6. Everyone stared at the stunningly beautiful woman and her boyfriend wearing a sequined gown.

7. She was wearing several gold bracelets on her arm that she had purchased in Turkey.

8. He worked hard to earn a living for his family without complaint.

9. She gazed at the handsome model with glazed eyes.

10. Joan and Bill discussed having a baby frequently, but they never did.

Using Parallelism

Parallelism in sentence structure exists when two or more sentence elements of equal rank are similarly expressed. Stating ideas in parallel form adds clarity and smoothness to a sentence. Faulty parallelism occurs when equal and closely related ideas are not expressed in the same grammatical form.

Making Words, Phrases, and Clauses Parallel

Whether you are working with words, phrases, or clauses, make sure they are expressed in the same grammatical form. Match one part of speech with the same part of speech—nouns with nouns, verbs with verbs, and so on.

No   The girls *giggled, smiled,* and *were flirting* with the boys.

Yes   The girls *giggled, smiled,* and *flirted* with the boys. (matched *past tense verbs*)

Match *verb + -ing* words and phrases with *verb + -ing* words and phrases.

No   Martha enjoys *golfing, sailing,* and *to go fishing.*

Yes   Martha enjoys *golfing, sailing,* and *fishing.* (matched *-ing words*)

Match *to + a verb* words and phrases with *to + a verb* words and phrases.

No   *To increase her strength* and *trying to develop her muscle tone,* Fran followed her trainer's advice.

Yes   *To increase her strength* and *to develop her muscle tone,* Fran followed her trainer's advice. (matched *to + a verb phrases*)

Match phrases with similarly constructed phrases.

No   She went *to the post office, to the grocery store,* and *stopped at the garage.*

Yes   She went *to the post office, to the grocery store,* and *to the garage.* (matched *prepositional phrases*)

Match clauses with similarly constructed clauses.

No   Fred plays golf once a week *if the weather is nice* and *because George can join him.*

Yes   Fred plays golf once a week *if the weather is nice* and *if George can join him.* (matched *adverb clauses*)

Often faulty parallelism may be corrected in more than one way.

No   *To drive carefully* and *driving defensively* are essential elements of safe driving.

Yes   *To drive carefully* and *to drive defensively* are essential elements of safe driving.

Yes   *Driving carefully* and *driving defensively* are essential elements of safe driving.

In parallel constructions repeat an introductory word or phrase whenever necessary to make the meaning clear.

No   The thief denied *that he had broken into the store* and *he had stolen the jewels.*

Yes   The thief denied <u>*that*</u> *he had broken into the store* and <u>*that*</u> *he had stolen the jewels.*

Making Paired Items and Items in a Series Parallel

▶ **Items Linked with Connecting Words**   Present paired items or items in a series in parallel form and link them with a connecting word (*for, and, nor, but, or, yet, so*).

No   The boys were *tall, tan,* **and** looked *handsome.*

Yes   The boys were *tall, tan,* and *quite handsome.*

No   Students *who take careful notes* **and** the ones *who attend class regularly* usually make high marks.

Yes   Students *who take careful notes* **and** *who attend class regularly* usually make high marks.

EXERCISE 5

Revise each sentence, using parallel structures to express parallel elements.

1. Alan enjoys working crossword puzzles and to read historical novels.

2. Bicycling across the country and to visit the capital of each state are two of his goals.

3. The chef carefully and with a great deal of accuracy measured the ingredients.

4. She gazed at the picture of her first boyfriend, lovingly and with longing.

5. Taking good notes and the frequent review of them is essential in college.

6. They considered two aspects of the proposal—cost and the amount of time.

7. She knew that he was rich, but she did not know about his being a millionaire.

8. Before the students took the exam, they were worried, nervous, and felt anxious.

9. The first time they met they were close, confident, and felt comfortable with each other.

10. Our dog is well-trained, obedient, and is a good friend.

▶ **Items Linked with Paired Joining Words**   Paired items are often linked by certain pairs of joining words called *correlatives* (*either . . . or, neither . . . nor, both . . . and, not only . . . but [also]*). These pairs of words add to the clarity of writing in two ways: They tell the readers that the related ideas are to be considered together, and they often reduce the number of words needed to express an idea.

> **No**   To earn high marks Sue tried both taking good notes and to review them often. (15 words)

> **Yes**   To earn high marks Sue tried *both* taking good notes *and* reviewing them often. (14 words)

> **No**   The overweight French poodle was put on a strict diet, and the skinny Doberman pincer was put on a strict diet also. (22 words)

> **Yes**   *Both* the overweight French poodle *and* the skinny Doberman pincer were put on a strict diet. (16 words)

Always put each part of these two-part connecting words before the item it introduces.

No   She *both* uses abbreviations *and* codes when she takes notes. (No item is parallel with *uses*.)

Yes   She uses *both* <u>abbreviations</u> *and* <u>codes</u> when she takes notes. (*Abbreviations* and *codes* are parallel.)

EXERCISE 6

Revise the following sentences, using paired joining words correctly.

1. The students did not like the enrollment procedures, and neither did the counselors.

2. You must do your work or you will be fired.

3. She both changed her schedule and her major.

4. Dallas both collects blue vases and ceramic frogs.

5. Jon both studied geography and cartography in college.

6. Lenny not only likes golfing but also fishing.

7. Sammy won first prize in the talent show, and he also won first prize in the science fair.

8. The waiter was both efficient and treated us with courtesy.

9. The rain contributed to the hazardous road conditions and so did the mud slide.

10. You may either eat a hamburger or a hot dog for lunch.

Making Contrasting Ideas Parallel and Complete

When you use *than* or *as* to compare ideas, make the ideas parallel and complete.

No   Baking a cake is easier *than* a pie. (*Baking a cake* cannot be compared with *pie.*)

Yes   Baking a cake is easier *than* baking a pie. (*Baking a cake* is compared with *baking a pie.*)

No   Playing basketball can be *as* challenging as football. (*Playing basketball* cannot be compared with *football.*)

Yes   Playing basketball can be *as* challenging as playing football. (*Playing basketball* is compared with *playing football.*)

No Her test scores were higher *than* her roommate's. (*incomplete*)

Yes Her test scores were higher *than* her roommate's test scores. (*complete*)

EXERCISE 7

Correct the faulty parallelism in each of the following sentences.

1. He was told to report to the locker room and that he would be issued his uniform.

2. When we took the achievement test, we were told that we should bring our own SCANTRON and to have a number 2 pencil.

3. Candidates for this program may qualify either by taking an examination or they can take a specific course.

4. My brothers are good students as well as athletic.

5. When Mary chose her new dog, she had to decide whether to buy a purebred puppy or she would rescue a dog from the pound.

6. He had to decide whether to buy a new car or repairing the old one would be too expensive.

7. Working crossword puzzles is more fun than jigsaw puzzles.

8. Her physician recommended she wear a leg brace and using crutches.

9. Knowing how to take notes and to budget time are important skills for college students.

10. Betty's bikini is briefer than Ann's.

Review Exercises

The sentences contain faulty parallelism. Revise them to make the parallelism correct and logical.

REVIEW EXERCISE 8

1. The new employee soon proved herself to be not only capable but also a woman who was aggressive.

2. Playing golf is more satisfying than tennis.

3. Before becoming a teacher, Mr. Smith had been a dog trainer, a tour guide, and drove a truck.

4. My dentist advised brushing my teeth after each meal and to floss them at least once a day.

5. Swimming in a river is more dangerous than to swim in a swimming pool.

6. Tony is not only president of the Black Student Union but also his church's youth group.

7. The team both experienced the agony of defeat and the thrill of victory.

8. The tacos were fresh, hot, and had a delicious taste.

9. The instructor either returns essays on Friday mornings or Monday mornings.

10. To begin writing an essay is often harder than finishing it.

REVIEW EXERCISE 9

1. Early settlers came with hope of being free and happy and to make a new life for themselves.

2. My math classroom is more cheerful than English.

3. Have you compared your college grades with your high school?

4. The beauty contestant was slim, svelte, and had a beautiful face.

5. Trudy likes to train dogs, to groom dogs, and showing them.

6. Jeannette told me that her new play was informative, timely, and would hold my interest.

7. The guest lecturer spoke with warmth and in a passionate manner.

8. The handbag Kathy bought at K-Mart looks as good as Nordstrom's handbags.

9. All the students tried to listen attentively, to take careful notes, and ask pertinent questions.

10. The baby's latest accomplishments are rolling over and to play with his toes.

Revising Awkward or Confusing Sentences

Avoiding Distracting Shifts

Unnecessary shifts in *tense, number, person, mood, voice,* and from *direct to indirect quotations* create awkward or confusing sentences.

▶ **Shifts in Tense**   *Tense* is the indication of the time of the action of the verb. It changes form to establish *present time, past time,* or *future time* of the action being described.

Unnecessary Shifts in Tense   When you have established a particular time, do not slip into another time without a reason. Time shifts within or between sentences can create awkwardness and confusion.

No   North Dakota fascinated (*past tense*) Lewis and Clark, and they spend (*present tense*) much time exploring the region. (*unnecessary tense shift*)

Yes   North Dakota fascinated (*past tense*) Lewis and Clark, and they spent (*past tense*) much time exploring the region. (*consistent tense*)

No   In 1838 the first known European ventured (*past tense*) into what is now North Dakota. A French fur trader comes (*present tense*) in search of buffalo robes. (*unnecessary tense shift*)

Yes   In 1838 the first known European ventured (*past tense*) into what is now North Dakota. A French fur trader came (*past tense*) in search of buffalo robes. (*consistent tense*)

Necessary Shifts   In certain situations, however, shifts in time are necessary. Shifting to the present tense is acceptable when you are *discussing works of literature, expressing a general truth,* or *indicating habitual action.*

Literature   *Gone with the Wind* was written (*past tense*) by Margaret Mitchell. It is (*present tense*) a famous movie. In this movie, Scarlett O'Hara says (*present tense*), "Death and taxes and childbirth! There's never any convenient time for any of them."

General truth—something that is always true   My friend visited (*past tense*) his family in South Dakota, and while he was (*past tense*) there, they toured Pierre, which is (*present tense*) the state's capital.

Habitual action—something that usually happens They also went (*past tense*) to Capital Lake. Each fall, thousands of migratory birds visit (*present tense*) Capital Lake.

Shifting to the past tense is acceptable when you are *discussing historical events, giving biographical data,* or *identifying prior events*—ones that happened prior to the time of the main action.

Historical events George Washington is known (*present tense*) as "The father of his country." He was (*past tense*) the first president of the United States.

Biographical data Will Rogers is remembered (*present tense*) for his salty political and social comments. He was born (*past tense*) in Oolagah Indian Territory, present-day Oklahoma.

Prior event The Post-Rogers Memorial in Barrow, the northernmost settlement in Alaska, commemorates (*present tense*) the death of Will Rogers and his pilot Wiley Post, who were killed (*past tense*) in a 1935 plane crash near Barrow.

Note: For the sake of vividness, a narrative may be written in the present tense; however, beginning writers often use this tense as a cheap substitute for better means of attaining vividness. If you do use the present tense, use it throughout the paragraph or essay. Do not carelessly shift from present to past.

EXERCISE 10

Revise the following sentences, making them consistent in *tense.*

1. Paleo-Indians were South Dakota's earliest inhabitants. These early inhabitants are hunter-warriors, but eventually they develop more stable communities.

2. By A.D. 900 these Plains Villagers have large settlements with fortifications and are farming their lands.

3. In the mid-seventeen hundreds, the Plains Villagers are driven out by the tribes of the Great Sioux Nation—Dakota, Lakota, and Nakota.

4. Exploration of the area by Europeans began in 1743, and by the 1850s, Eastern land companies begin establishing towns.

5. The Dakota Territory is created in 1861; however, most of the settlement was confined to the southeastern area.

6. As encroachment on Sioux land increases, tension increased on both sides. To ease the tension, a treaty is signed that ensured the Great Sioux Nation all lands west of the Missouri.

7. In 1874 Lt. Col. George Armstrong Custer lead an expedition into the Black Hills, and there they discover gold. By the way, the slopes of these hills have a dark appearance because they had a thick cover of Ponderosa Pine, and for this reason, the Indians call them the Black Hills.

8. Gold miners and settlers poured into the region, and the natives are driven out. In an all-too-familiar pattern, the treaty that guaranteed certain rights to the Great Sioux Nation was broken.

9. Although the Lakota and Northern Cheyenne joined forces and annihilate Custer and his men at Montana's Little Big Horn River in 1876, they lost the later battles and are eventually forced to give up more land, including the Black Hills.

10. By this time the railroads have reached the territory, and they brought thousands of farmers—mostly from Northern Europe. In 1889 the territory is divided into North and South Dakota, and they are admitted to the Union.

▶ **Shifts in Number and Person**   **Number** indicates whether a person or thing is one (singular—*cat, it*) or more than one (plural—*cats, they, them*). Pronouns must agree in number with their antecedents (the words to which they refer). If a word or idea is singular, all references to it must be singular; if it is plural, all references to it must be plural. Do not use plural pronouns to refer to singular nouns; do not use singular pronouns to refer to plural nouns.

Shift	A *student* should review *their* notes often. (*plural pronoun referring to singular noun*)
Consistent	A *student* should review *his* or *her* notes often. (*singular noun and pronoun*)
Consistent	*Students* should review *their* notes often. (*plural noun and pronoun*)

Person indicates who is speaking (first person—*I, we*), who is spoken to (second person—*you*), and who or what is spoken about (third person—*he, she, it, they*). Keep person consistent. Most errors in person are caused by shifts between second-person and third-person pronouns.

Shift	When a *person* is in love, *you* have a special glow. (*shift from third person to second person*)

> **Consistent**   When *you* are in love, *you* have a special glow. (*second person*)
>
> **Consistent**   When a *person* is in love, *he* or *she* has a special glow. (*third person*)

EXERCISE 11

Revise the following sentences, making them consistent in *number* and *person*.

1. A person should not take dietary supplements on the basis of your personal fitness trainer's recommendation.

2. Many arthritis sufferers take the nutritional supplements *glucosamine* and *chondroitin* and believe it will cure their arthritis.

3. The average American woman does not get enough calcium in their diet.

4. Many people may be failing to absorb the calcium tablets they take because he or she may be taking the wrong kind.

5. If a person who is taking prescription medication wants to take vitamin supplements, they should first consult their physician.

6. Linda takes vitamin E because they may cut your risk of having a heart attack.

7. Some people think that bottled water is better than the water you get from the tap.

8. If people buy bottled water, you may be paying as much as $3 for a bottle of water that costs one-third of a cent when it comes from your taps.

9. If a person's bottled water label says "distilled" or doesn't give the source, you are probably drinking tap water that has been stripped of its nutrients.

10. Some companies claim its water is "calcium enriched."

EXERCISE 12

Revise the following sentences, making them consistent in *number* and *person*.

1. Deadwood is located in the Black Hills of South Dakota and is well known for your Wild West era.

2. If one takes a look at history, you will learn that "Wild Bill" Hickok, Calamity Jane, Wyatt Earp, and Doc Holiday walked the single dusty street of this gold-rush town.

3. If you are interested in any of these characters and the part they played in Deadwood, one might want to visit this old town.

4. A person can learn a great deal of history about the Wild West days if you study the lives of some of the legendary characters of this period.

5. If you study the life of James Butler "Wild Bill" Hickok, one learns that, like others of his kind, he was an American frontier scout and a marshal.

6. You may want to read some of the dime novels of the 1800s in which one encounters characters such as Buffalo Bill, Ned Buntline, and Deadwood Dick.

7. If you visit Deadwood's Boot Hill, one can see the graves of "Wild Bill" Hickock, Calamity Jane, and Deadwood Dick.

8. One can still visit Deadwood's historic 1876 Main Street Saloon No. 10, and you probably know that this is where "Wild Bill" was shot and killed.

9. If you know your history, one knows that "Wild Bill" was playing poker in the saloon when he was shot from behind by a drifter named Jack McCall.

10. If you like historical reenactments, from Memorial Day weekend through mid-August, one can see the reenactment of the assassination of "Wild Bill" and the trial of Jack McCall.

▶ **Shifts in Mood**   **Mood** is the form of the verb that shows the intent of the writer, and it may be used to

■ make a statement or ask a question (*indicative mood*)

■ give a command or make a request (*imperative mood*)

■ indicate a wish or a condition contrary to fact (*subjunctive mood*)

The indicative mood is the most commonly used form. Sometimes, however, the imperative mood is most effective—particularly in "how to" writing. Just remember to be consistent and do not carelessly slip from one form to another.

Shift	Take an aspirin and you should call me in the morning. (*imperative to indicative*)
Consistent	Take an aspirin and call me in the morning. (*imperative*)
Shift	Taking a short, fast walk is an easy form of exercise and do it at least once a day. (*indicative to imperative mood*)
Consistent	Taking a short, fast walk is an easy form of exercise and should be taken at least once a day. (*indicative*)

EXERCISE 13

Revise the following sentences, making them consistent in *mood*.

1. To use chopsticks, place one of them between your thumb and index finger, and you should hold the other one between your middle finger and your ring finger.

2. To avoid brain strain, cover your eyes with your hands for twenty seconds, and you should look only at the task in front of you.

3. After you awake in the morning, lift your arms toward the ceiling, and then you should stretch your toes toward the foot of the bed.

4. Your dog's teeth need to be brushed often and use special doggy toothpaste.

5. I have an 8 o'clock class, and I should leave home at 7 o'clock.

6. Form a single line along the wall, and you should have your papers with you.

7. Avoid contact with poison ivy, and you should avoid poison oak also.

8. Properly cooking abalone is important, and you should never overcook it.

9. Knowing two basic things about poker is essential: You should know the value of hands and the principles of betting.

10. Organizing your time is important, and always remember to schedule your time wisely.

The uses of the subjunctive mood occur primarily in formal English and usually apply to only one verb form—*were*. The subjunctive *were* is usually used after *if* or *as though*.

I wish I <u>were</u> (not *was*) in Vale, Colorado. (*wish*)

If I <u>were</u> (not *was*) in Vale, I would ski every day. (*statement contrary to fact*) I am not in Vale.

The instructor talked to me as though she <u>were</u> (not *was*) my best friend. (*statement contrary to fact*) She is not my best friend.

▶ **Shifts in Voice**   **Voice** is the form that shows whether the subject of a verb is acting or is acted upon. It may take the *active* or *passive* form. A verb is in the *active voice* when it expresses an action performed by its subject. A verb is in the *passive* *voice* when it expresses an action performed upon its subject. In general, use the active voice because it is more straightforward and more effective than the passive voice. (*See* Part 4: Emphasizing Ideas, p. 243.)

To avoid awkwardness and possible confusion, avoid voice shifts within a sentence. Note that a shift in voice results in a shift in subject.

Shift	The e-mail was received, and she read it eagerly. (*passive to active*)
Consistent	She received e-mail and read it eagerly. (*active*)
Shift	Today, I read the report to the committee that was written by you last week. (*active to passive*)
Consistent	Today, I read the report to the committee that you wrote last week. (*active*)
Shift	A serious error was made by the young officer, and the captain suspended him. (*passive to active*)
Consistent	A serious error was made by the young officer, and he was suspended. (*passive*)

EXERCISE 14

Revise the following sentences, making the *voice* consistent. Use the active voice to emphasize the *doer* of the action, and use the passive voice to emphasize the *receiver* of the action.

1. It was once believed by psychologists that only bigots used stereotypes, but recent studies reveal the fact that we all use stereotypes.

2. Stereotypes are used by many people, but they do it unknowingly.

3. Historically, theories about stereotypes were concerned with unabashed racism and sexism, but today more subtle and insidious types of stereotyping are being considered by psychologists.

4. Through the ages some kind of love potion has been sought by both sexes of all races.

5. When people use stereotypes, they take in the gender, the age, the skin color, and then the information is processed by the mind and responded to by sending such messages as *hostile, slow, weak, unintelligent, ineffectual,* and so on.

6. Classical music is not liked as much by me as I like jazz.

7. The bank was robbed by several people, and one of the robbers wrote a book about the robbery.

8. When Anne was promoted, her co-workers congratulated her.

9. The children carefully examined their Halloween candy, but no suspicious sweets were found.

10. Since Jane knew that efficiency was essential in her new job, a time management course was taken by her.

▶ **Shifts Between Direct Quotations and Indirect Quotations**   A *direct quotation* is the exact words of a speaker or writer and is enclosed in quotation marks.

> **Direct**   Sally said, "I was late for class, and may I borrow your notes?"

An *indirect quotation* is a report of the words of a speaker or writer, but it does not repeat the exact words, and it is not enclosed in quotation marks. It is usually introduced by the word *that* or in questions by *whether, who, what, why, how,* or *if.*

> **Indirect**   Sally said that she was late for class and asked if she could borrow my notes.

To prevent confusion, avoid shifts between direct and indirect quotations within a sentence. Notice that direct and indirect quotations take different verb tenses.

> **Shift**   The instructor wanted to know whether the students had finished the first part of the test and are you ready for the second part?
>
> **Consistent**   The instructor asked the students, "Are you finished with the first part of the test, and are you ready for the second part?"
>
> **Shift**   The instructor asked the students, "Are you finished with the first part of the test?" and whether they were ready for the second part.
>
> **Consistent**   The instructor wanted to know whether the students had finished the first part of the test and whether they were ready for the second part.
>
> **Shift**   The student asked what could he do to prepare for the test.
>
> **Consistent**   The student asked what he could do to prepare for the test.
>
> **Consistent**   The student asked, "What can I do to prepare for the test?"

EXERCISE 15

Revise the following sentences, eliminating shifts between *direct* and *indirect quotations*. If a sentence begins with an indirect quotation, make the rest of the sentence consistent. If a sentence begins with a direct quotation, make the rest of the sentence consistent.

1. He asked me whether I would take notes for him and will I drop them off at his house?

2. Sally said that she would call Liz and "I expect you to call Kathy."

3. The shopper asked, "Is the fish fresh?" and whether the vegetables were organically grown.

4. The student cook asked, "Do I use the stems or the leaves of fresh herbs?" and wondered what the term *sprig of herbs* means.

5. The instructor told him that, generally, cooks use only the leaves, but "They use the tender stems of some herbs such as cilantro and parsley."

6. Becky Pate of *Cooking Light* says that ketchup is her favorite condiment and that "I truly appreciate how long and how many tomatoes it takes to create this delectable sauce."

7. If you spend a great deal of time at your computer, the American Occupational Therapy Association (AOTA) says, "Position the monitor directly in front of you, eighteen to twenty inches from your forehead" and that the top of the screen should be at eye level.

8. AOTA also say that you should sit up straight with your head, shoulders, and hips in alignment and "Keep both feet flat on the floor (or on an angled footrest)."

9. The instructor asked the students if they knew that farmers' markets were once a universal element of everyday life in America and "Do you know that in 1918 more than half of all American cities with populations of 30,000 or more had public markets?"

10. He said, "Clarence Saunders introduced the first self-service grocery store in 1918 at his Piggly Wiggly in Memphis, Tennessee," and that this new type of one-stop, self-service grocery store heralded the end of traditional public markets.

Recognizing and Revising Mixed Sentences

Sentences are mixed when the first and the second part are mismatched (*mixed construction*), or when the subject part and the verb part do not make sense together (*illogical connection*).

▶ **Mixed Constructions**   When you begin a sentence with one grammatical strategy and then shift to another, the result is a mixed sentence. The most common causes of mixed construction are the result of writers mistakenly thinking that a *preposi-*

tional phrase, a *dependent clause,* or an *independent clause* can logically serve as the subject of a sentence. Correct mixed constructions by

- adding a subject

- changing the phrase to one that can serve as subject

- creating compound or complex sentences

A **prepositional phrase** cannot serve as the subject of a sentence.

No   By observing speed limits is the best way to avoid getting a speeding ticket.

Yes   You can avoid getting a speeding ticket by observing the speed limits. (Subject *you* is added.)

Yes   Observing speed limits is the best way to avoid getting a speeding ticket. (Prepositional phrase is changed to a *verb* + *-ing* word phrase, which can serve as subject.)

A **dependent clause** cannot serve as the subject of a sentence.

No   Because she missed the bus was the reason she was late for her first class.

Yes   She was late for her first class because she missed the bus. (Subject *she* is added.)

Yes   Because she missed the bus, she was late for her first class. (Dependent clause is followed by an independent clause, creating a complex sentence.)

Yes   Missing the bus caused her to miss her first class. (Dependent clause is changed to a *verb* + *-ing* word phrase that can serve as subject.)

An **independent clause** cannot serve as the subject of a sentence.

No   He practiced his putting was the best way to improve his golf game.

Yes   Practicing his putting improved his golf game. (Independent clause is changed to a *verb* + *-ing* word phrase that can serve as subject.)

Yes   He practiced his putting, and it improved his golf game. (Independent clause is connected to another independent clause, creating a compound sentence.)

Yes   Because he practiced his putting, he improved his golf game. (Independent clause has been changed to a dependent clause, creating a complex sentence.)

▶ **Illogical Connections** An illogical connection (*faulty predication*) occurs when the subject part of a sentence and the verb part do not make sense together. Common causes of illogical connections between subjects and verbs are the use of *is when, is where, the reason . . . is because,* and incorrect subject complements.

    Is when **or** ***is where*** are often mistakenly used in definitions and summaries. A definition must have a noun or noun phrase on both sides of the word *is.*

No Love **is when** you have an intense affectionate concern for another person.

Yes <u>Love</u> **is** *<u>an intense affectionate concern</u> for another person.*

No *Unnatural Exposure,* by Patricia Cornwell, **is where** a scientist tries to create an epidemic. (*Unnatural Exposure* is a novel, not a *where.*)

Yes <u>*Unnatural Exposure*</u> **is** <u>a novel</u> in which a scientist tries to create an epidemic.

When the expression ***the reason . . . is because*** appears in a sentence, leave out either the word *because* or the phrase *the reason is.* They are redundant for *because* means "for the reason that."

No **The reason** she did not go **was because** she had no money.

Yes The reason she did not go was *that* she had no money.

Yes She did not go *because* she had no money.

When the *subject complement* does not logically relate to the subject, the sentence is faulty. A *subject complement* is a word or phrase that follows a linking verb and describes, explains, or identifies the subject. It can be an adjective or a noun.

    Nouns usually follow only the verb *be* (*am , are, is, was, were,* and verbs ending in *be* or *been*).

<u>Mexico City</u> is the world's largest *city.*   <u>Miss Wiggly</u> was my kindergarten teacher.

Adjectives follow the verb *be* or one of the other linking verbs: *feel, look, smell, taste, remain, sound, appear, become,* and so on.

These <u>apples</u> are *rotten.*   That <u>boy</u> looks *tired.*

Revise faulty sentences by providing a subject complement that logically relates to the subject.

No My pet peeve is drivers who change lanes without signaling. (*The peeve is not the drivers.*)

Yes   My pet peeve is drivers changing lanes without signaling. (*The peeve is the changing lanes.*)

EXERCISE 16

Revise each of the following mixed sentences so that the parts fit together grammatically and logically. Revisions will vary because each sentence may be revised in more than one way.

1. Some people think that the reason people swear is because they have limited vocabularies.

2. By using sunscreen is the best way to prevent sunburn.

3. By building a fire was the way the campers could cook their dinner.

4. By working as a cocktail waitress was the way she earned money to pay her college expenses.

5. A special place is where you feel at peace with yourself and the world.

6. Because she did not water the tomato plants is the reason they died.

7. The high point of the recital was Elizabeth at the piano.

8. The windows covered with frost made it difficult to see the mountain.

9. An anger management problem is when you cannot control your temper.

10. People who argue that the crime rate is not related to violence on television are fallacious in their reasoning.

Review Exercises

Revise the following sentences, making them consistent in *tense, number,* and *person.* Mark correct sentences with a C.

REVIEW EXERCISE 17

1. I took a human relations class in which you were introduced to basic human relations theory and skills.

2. General psychology is an introduction to the basic principles and concepts of psychology, and it emphasized an understanding of human behavior at home, school, and in the workplace.

3. The early childhood program gives you two options: One can earn a Certification of Completion or an Associate of Applied Science Degree.

4. A special culinary arts program is offered at some technical schools, and they train people for the hospital food industry.

5. When a student is enrolled in the aesthetician program, you learned about skin care and make-up techniques.

6. Cozy was enrolled in the cosmetology program, and she is learning about shampoos, cuts, styles, perms, and hair coloring.

7. The medical assistant program is one of the most popular programs, and they teach you how to perform a variety of patient-related tasks.

8. An emergency dispatcher specializes in police, fire, and medical skills, and they learn to work with state-of-the art equipment.

9. If a student wants to do so, they can take a course to learn how to get a divorce.

10. If one wants to enroll in one of these programs, you must have a high school diploma or a GED.

REVIEW EXERCISE 18

1. The world's largest sculpture is in progress in the Black Hills of South Dakota.

2. When they are complete, the in-the-round figure of Chief Crazy Horse astride his pony will be 561 feet high and 641 feet long.

3. They represent all the tribes of the North American Indians. The Crazy Horse Memorial is begun by Korczak Ziolkowski at the request of Lakota Chief Henry Standing Bear and other Lakota chiefs.

4. When Chief Standing Bear invited Ziolkowski to come to the Black Hills and carve Crazy Horse, he writes, "My fellow chiefs and I would like the white man to know the red man has great heroes, too."

5. The chiefs learn about Korczak's work when he wins the first prize at the 1939 New York World's Fair.

6. He accepted the chiefs' invitation and arrives in the Black Hills on May 3, 1947.

7. He begins working on the mountain in 1949 when he is almost forty years old and had only $174.

8. Knowing that the project would take longer than his lifetime, he developed a scaled model, and he and his wife write three books containing detailed plans to be used to continue the project after his death.

9. During the thirty-three years that he worked on the sculpture, he battles financial problems, racial prejudice, and advancing age. They felt that you should not accept federal funding for the monument.

10. He wants it to be a nonprofit, educational, cultural project built by the public.

11. Twice he turned down 10 million dollars in potential federal funding.

12. Ziolkowski is born September 6, 1908, to parents of Polish descent.

13. When he was one year old, he becomes an orphan and subsequently grows up in foster homes.

14. He has no formal training in art, sculpture, architecture, or engineering.

15. He is completely self-taught.

Revise the following sentences, correcting any unnecessary shifts in *mood, voice,* and *direct* and *indirect quotations.*

1. As we walked along the trail, a snake was seen.

2. Taking a brisk walk is a simple way of exercising, you should do it every day.

3. Carolyn said that she was going to have a baby and that I hope I have twins.

4. The student asked, "Is the essay due Monday?" and whether she could turn it in one day late.

5. When you are baking bread, spoon the flour into a measuring cup and you should level it off with a knife.

6. The chef salted the meat with sea salt and freshly ground black pepper was added.

7. The sixtieth anniversary edition of *Gourmet* was received today, and Suzy read it eagerly.

8. It was once believed by people that tomatoes were poisonous, and some even believed that they were an aphrodisiac.

9. Our history professor said, "People of the fifties enjoyed a period of unprecedented prosperity" and that we should study that period to understand how millions of people were propelled into the middle class.

10. James Cagney epitomized the screen gangster, but in none of his films is the expression "You dirty rat" used by him.

REVIEW EXERCISE 20

Revise the following mixed sentences so that the parts fit together grammatically and logically.

1. Because French author Charles Perrault incorrectly used the word *verre* (glass) instead of *vair* (fur) is the reason that Cinderella's slippers became glass.

2. Snakes are charmed by tapping of their feet and swaying of their body and pipe is the way snake charmers perform this feat.

3. By digesting the fat in their humps is the way camels can go for several days without food or water.

4. The "thumbs down" signal was when a Roman emperor signaled to a gladiator to kill his fallen opponent.

5. There are many theories about the disappearance of the dinosaurs, and some people have theorized that the reason is because of lack of room in Noah's Ark.

6. By doing all your homework and attending class regularly is the way to succeed in college.

7. A bogey is when golfers shoot a hole of golf in one stroke over par, and a birdie is when they shoot one stroke under par.

8. Because she is such a dynamic instructor explains why her classes are always full.

9. An example of support of government action is flying the flag.

10. Many schools have done away with winners and losers, and the reason is because self-esteem in children is thought to be more important than achievement.

Writing Effective Sentences

Effective sentences create a definite impression in the minds of readers. Sentences that contain few specific details and rely upon vague general words to get their point across are ineffective sentences.

Using Specific Language

Vague words and phrases prevent writers from precisely expressing the ideas they have in mind. Interesting writing is rich in images—things that can be experienced through the senses. *Concrete adjectives, picture verbs* and *verb + -ing words* contribute to the effectiveness of a sentence.

▶ **Concrete Adjectives**   Adjectives vary in the their degree of specificity. Vague adjectives refer to ideas or conditions that are too general to appeal to the senses. Concrete adjectives name things that the readers can *see, hear, smell, taste,* or *touch.* Choose adjectives that say precisely what you mean—ones that enable the readers to appreciate them through the senses.

Vague   My girlfriend has pretty hair and a nice smile.

This sentence will neither create a definite impression in the minds of the readers, nor will it stir their emotions. It contains no concrete detail. What makes her hair pretty? Does she have long, blond, silky tresses? Does she have blue-black ebony curls that barely cover her ears? Does she have an infectious smile that makes everyone around her happy? Does she have a warm smile that puts people at ease? Notice the strong adjectives in the following passage:

The air was raw and pointed, but not far below freezing; and the flakes were large, damp, and adhesive. The whole city was sheeted up. . . . High up overhead the snow settled among the tracery of the cathedral towers. Many a niche was drifted full; many a statue wore a long white bonnet on its grotesque or sainted head. The gargoyles had been transformed into great false noses, drooping towards the point.

—Robert Louis Stevenson, "A Lodging for the Night"

▶ **Strong, Active Verbs—Picture Verbs**   Your writing will be more vivid and interesting when you use verbs that are specific and active. The forms of the verb *to be* (*am, are, is, was, were, be, being, been*)—although common and necessary—are weak and colorless. They do nothing to create a mind picture. Vague verbs such as *walk, talk, act, move, sleep,* and so on are too general to create a vivid image. Using verbs that picture a precise action—one the readers can visualize—makes a sentence vivid.

Weak The baby walked across the room.

Strong The baby toddled across the room.

Weak The child talked about the new puppy.

Strong The child jabbered about the new puppy.

Weak Black smoke was coming out of the engine.

Strong Black smoke belched out of the engine.

As you increase your English vocabulary, try to learn a variety of colorful verbs because well-chosen verbs make sentences more precise and powerful.

▶ **Verb + -*ing* Words as Nouns**   A *verb + -ing* word (*gerund*—a verb form ending in *-ing* that is used as a noun) has an advantage that a noun does not have: It names both the noun idea and implies the action. Sometimes you can achieve greater effectiveness in a sentence through the use of a *verb + -ing* word. In the following sentences, the nouns simply present a general picture, but the verb + -ing words suggest physical activity.

His *dance* was an excellent exhibition of control and timing.

His *dancing* was an excellent exhibition of control and timing.

The audience applauded Black Ice's *rap.*

The audience applauded Black Ice's *rapping.*

EXERCISE 21

Rewrite the following sentences and make them more effective by using concrete adjectives, picture verbs, and verb + -ing words.

1. The bird flew into the tree. ____

2. The boy sat on the tree branch. ____

3. She was sleeping. ____

4. The river was high. ____

5. Kelly sang a song. ____

6. She has a secret. ____

7. The dog ate dinner. ____

8. The class was interesting. ____

9. She read a good book recently. ____

10. She spoke to her friend. ____

Emphasizing Ideas

▶ Main Ideas

To emphasize the main idea in a sentence, either put it at the beginning of the sentence (*cumulative sentence*) or at the end (*periodic sentence*). Most of the sentences you read and write are cumulative sentences. In a cumulative sentence the basic thought is clear to the reader before the full structure of the sentence is expressed. Build a cumulative sentence by starting with the main clause and then adding modifying words, phrases, and clauses.

> Every individual has a place to fill in the world, and is important in some respect, whether he chooses to be so or not.
>
> —Hawthorne

When you want to create suspense, use a periodic sentence. In a periodic sentence the main idea is not given until the end of the sentence is reached. Build a periodic sentence by piling up words, phrases, and clauses at the beginning of the sentence and presenting the main idea at the end of it.

> It is an axiom in political science that unless a people are educated and enlightened it is idle to expect the continuance of civil liberty or the capacity for self-government.
>
> —Texas Declaration of Independence

EXERCISE 22

Revise the following sentences, making them more emphatic.

1. Because he was dying of tuberculosis, Doc Holiday lived a dangerous life, gambling and fighting.

2. Although Doc Holiday was a dentist, gambling and fighting were his chief interests, taking precedence over everything else.

3. Although he was thought of as a drunken killer, Doc Holiday never appeared to be drunk even when he was drinking four quarts of whiskey a day.

4. Doc's wife was as wild as he, but she took care of him when he was ill or in danger, nursing him during long bouts of coughing or breaking him out of jail.

5. When Kate and Doc were in Tombstone, they had a fight that ended their relationship forever because she falsely accused Doc of robbing a stagecoach.

6. Although The Earp brothers did not particularly like Doc, he was always loyal to them and saved Wyatt Earp's life more than once.

7. Write two *cumulative sentences.*

8. Write two *periodic sentences.*

▶ **Paired Items or Items in a Series**   When paired items or items in a series serve the same purpose in a sentence, present them in the same grammatical form to draw attention to them and to add clarity and smoothness to the sentence. (*See* Part 4: Using Parallelism, p. 220.)

politics
The committee reviewed all aspects of the problem: *ethics, cost,* and ~~*political*~~

collecting stamps
Hal's hobbies include *restoring old cars* and ~~*stamp collection*~~

lifted weights
To become more physically fit, Pat *ran five miles a day, ate sensibly,* and ~~*lifting weights*~~

▶ **Active and Passive Voice of Verbs**   If the subject performs the action of the verb, that verb is in *active voice.* If the subject is acted upon, the verb is in *passive voice.* Many inexperienced writers unconsciously overuse the passive, thinking that it sounds more formal or more scholarly. It does not. As the name indicates, the passive is a weak rather than a strong voice, and careful writers use it sparingly. Generally, use the active voice because it is more emphatic than the passive voice. The use of the passive voice detracts from the smoothness, interest, and emphasis of a sentence.

ACTIVE VOICE	PASSIVE VOICE
The car struck the stop sign.	The stop sign was struck by the car.
The police officer filed a report.	A report was filed by the police officer.
The catcher dropped the ball.	The ball was dropped by the catcher.

In some situations, however, you will want to use the passive voice. The passive voice is appropriate when

- the action is more important than the actor (Germ theory was discovered by Louis Pasteur.)

- the actor is unknown or unimportant (The final examination schedule was published Monday.)

- a writer wants to conceal the identity of the actor or eliminate the actor (The car was left unlocked, and it was stolen.)

- a writer wants to eliminate a vague pronoun subject (*They* sold hot dogs and popcorn at the ball game. Hot dogs and popcorn *were sold* at the ball game.)

- a writer wants to avoid beginning a sentence with *it* or *there*—neither of which is particularly strong (*There* are many ways to vary sentences. Sentences *can be varied* in many ways.)

Active Voice: Someone **did** something.

Passive Voice: Something **was done** by someone.

In the passive voice the object in the sentence is shifted to the subject position. The active verb is replaced by some form of *be* (*am, are, is, was, were, being, been*) plus a past participle (a verb form indicating past or completed action).

ACTIVE VOICE	PASSIVE VOICE
The boy hit the ball.	The ball was hit *by* the boy.
The president vetoed the bills.	The bills were vetoed *by* the president.
I like cake.	Cake is liked *by* me.
The dog bit the cat.	The cat was bitten *by* the dog.

EXERCISE 23

Revise the following sentences, changing the *passive* constructions to *active* ones whenever you think it improves the sentence. If you think the passive is preferable, mark the sentence with a C.

1. All the ingredients for the dish were assembled by the chef.

2. His trial was held on Friday, and he was convicted.

3. The batter was hit by the baseball.

4. In college they expect students to study at least two hours for each class.

5. The car was wrecked by Megan.

6. Gunpowder was invented by the Chinese.

7. A decision was made to eliminate four positions.

8. A box of trash was dumped on our lawn.

9. The scenery in Alaska was enjoyed by all the members of the family.

10. We were invited by our professor to see his collection of old medicine bottles, which had been arranged in neat rows on shelves in his basement.

Writing Concise Sentences

A concise sentence—one that clearly makes the writer's point in as few words as possible—is clear and compact. A wordy sentence contains useless words and phrases and needs to be revised. Make your sentences concise by eliminating *meaningless words, filler words, roundabout expressions,* and *needless repetition.*

▶ **Meaningless Words**   Words that have no meaning add nothing to a sentence (*in a very real sense, in the process of, in my opinion, I think, it seems, as a matter of fact,* and so on).

The first chapter in the book is a masterpiece ~~in itself.~~

~~It is important to note that~~ the two courses cannot be taken concurrently.

~~In my opinion, I think~~ your haircut is cute.

~~For all intents and purposes,~~ the two courses are similar.

▶ **Filler Words**   Words that have no precise meaning and general words that are almost meaningless are empty words (*kind, type, area, factor, tendency, quality, good, bad, nice, important, exists, basically, entirely, barely, completely, very, definitely,* and so on). They occupy space but add nothing to the sentence.

Professor Johnson ~~is the kind of instructor who~~ makes students want to learn.

Professor Johnson makes students want to learn.

His lectures are ~~very definitely good.~~

His lectures are well prepared and clearly delivered.

Students are ~~favorably~~ impressed by his warmth and wit.

Students appreciate his warmth and wit.

~~A great many~~ students ~~always~~ flock to his classes.

Students flock to his classes.

▶ **Roundabout Expressions**   Excessive addition of words that do not provide further meaning or the addition of too many minor details detract from the point of the sentence.

~~There were~~ five ~~of the~~ students ~~in the class who~~ made As.

Five students made As.

The instructor divided ~~or separated~~ the students into ~~peer response~~ groups ~~with each group having between~~ four or five ~~in number.~~

The instructor divided the students into groups of four or five.

▶ **Needless Repetition**   Although repetition can be used for emphasis, needless repetition slows down the movement of thought and adds no additional information.

The students cooperated ~~together~~ with the instructor.

Garvin is tall, ~~good looking,~~ and handsome.

Modern college students ~~of today~~ face many problems.

The skyline was visible ~~to the eye.~~

Note: Do not confuse long compositions with wordiness. A long piece of writing may contain no wordy sentences, whereas a short composition may contain many. Length has nothing to do with wordiness.

EXERCISE 24

Revise the following sentences, eliminating *unnecessary words.*

1. My English teacher who teaches beginning English composition is too picky, and in the opinion of many of her students, they think this quality makes her an ineffective teacher.

2. When she finds three or four run-together sentences in her students' essays, which they may have spent hours writing, she stops reading and stamps "Rewrite" on the essays and gives them back to the students in her class.

3. Many of the students in her class think that she does not respect her students because she always insists that they follow certain rules and are not allowed to write the kind of essays in which they can fully express their own creative style.

4. Other English teachers who teach English are not as fussy as Ms. Prim N. Proper—the nickname that her students always use invariably behind her back when she isn't present.

5. Her comments on written compositions are often of an offensive nature.

6. It seems to me that in a very real sense, she seems to want to make students feel bad about themselves or their writing ability by writing comments such as "not logical," "irrelevant information," "wordy," and "unnecessary shift."

7. The most interesting instructor in the English Department is Coach Smith, an interesting former priest, who coaches the swim team at a summer camp when he is not teaching at the college during the summer.

8. I first met Coach Smith four long years ago when he was coaching the swim team at summer camp and I was attending summer camp when my parents, who were thinking about getting a divorce decided that they would go on a second honeymoon to try to repair their marriage, thought it would be in my best interest to attend summer camp.

9. Often, he would quite readily join a group of campers to discuss their future hopes, dreams, plans, and aspirations for the coming years.

10. As a matter of fact, in light of the fact that he was a former priest, many of the campers often visited him in his office at one time or another, and he always gave them the type of good advice that they needed.

Writing Unpretentious Sentences

Sometimes beginning writers produce work that is artificial and cumbersome because they are trying too hard to sound like great writers. This pretentious style is the result of mistakenly thinking that big words, unusual words, and padded sentences are the marks of great writing. To avoid writing pretentious sentences, never use a big or unusual word when a small or simple one will do, and express ideas clearly and simply, using as few words as possible.

Pretentious   Illumination is required to be extinguished upon vacating these premises.

—Sign in a government building

Revised   Turn out the lights when you leave.

Pretentious   The septuagenarian male biped perambulated across the black-paved asphalt strip.

Revised   The seventy-year-old man crossed the road.

Pretentious   His ocular orbs were semi-occluded.

Revised   His eyes were half shut.

Pretentious   The diminutive antiquated female with refined habits and gentle manners slipped on the frozen precipitation on the surface of the concrete walkway, which precipitated the abrupt contact between her torso and the strong, hard conglomerate construction and suffered a fractured tibia.

Revised   The little old lady slipped on the icy sidewalk and broke her leg.

Review Exercises

REVIEW EXERCISE 25

Rewrite the following sentences and make them more effective by using concrete adjectives, picture verbs, and verb + -ing words.

1. She talked to her sister. ____

2. Wally walked home.____

3. She is a nice person. ____

4. The dog barked at the mail carrier. ____

5. The party was good. ____

6. Lupe is pretty. ____

7. Jorge likes her. ____

8. They are good friends. ____

9. It was a hot day. ____

10. The snow is falling. ____

REVIEW EXERCISE 26

Revise the following passage, making sentences more emphatic when necessary by placing the main idea at the beginning of the sentence or at the end.

Roman Emperor Elagabalus, who ruled from A.D. 218 to 222 and was known as Elagabalus the Horrible, was fond of animals. Having his chariot pulled by wild animals such as tigers or lions was a favorite mode of transportation, and having a wheelbarrow pulled by naked women was his favorite way of arriving at state functions. On one occasion he invited the seven fattest men in Rome to dine with him, and the men were sent sprawling to the floor when he had slaves puncture the air pillows on which they sat. Another famous dinner party trick that he enjoyed was to feed his guests food made of marble, ivory, or glass, which they were required to eat. On another occasion he smothered his guests to death, showering them with rose petals. Sometimes he served real food, laced with spiders and dung, which etiquette compelled the guests to eat. He particularly liked to surprise his courtiers with frogs, scorpions, and poisonous snakes that he sent to them as gifts. He often ordered an expensive bath to be built and then destroyed it after he had taken one bath in it. When guests ate too much food and fell asleep, waking up in a room full of lions, leopards, and bears was common punishment meted out by the young emperor. Romans did not approve of his practical jokes or high living, and on the orders of his grandmother, his guards killed the eighteen-year-old emperor and dumped his body into the Tiber River.

REVIEW EXERCISE 27

Revise the following sentences, changing the *passive* constructions to *active* ones whenever you think it improves the sentence. If you think the passive is preferable, mark the sentence with a C.

1. The Kodiak Islands have been inhabited by the Alutiiq people for more than 7,500 years.

2. At one time the numerous coastal communities of the islands were inhabited by more than 20,000 Alutiiq.

3. The islands were invaded by the Russians in the late 1700s.

4. Diseases unknown to the native people were introduced by the Russians.

5. Entire villages were wiped out by Russian warfare and disease.

6. Currently, more than 800 archaeological sites are being explored in an effort to piece together the prehistoric and historic life of the ancient Alutiiq.

7. In 1995 the Alutiiq Heritage Foundation was founded by eight Kodiak area native corporations.

8. The culture of the Alutiiq continues to be studied, preserved, and protected.

9. Traditional Alutiiq dances are still performed by dancers in an authentic underground earthen hut, expressing thousands of years of cultural and spiritual values.

10. These dances have been well received.

REVIEW EXERCISE 28

Revise the following sentences, eliminating unnecessary words.

1. It seems there are many myths about the human mind and the human body.

2. It is important to note that many of these fictitious myths are the kind of stories that people like to talk about to other people.

3. According to one myth that has been around for a long time, people who fall from great heights are dead before they even hit the ground.

4. This was proven to be untrue or false by a German airplane pilot who jumped out of his shell-torn airplane without a parachute or anything else when he was 18,000 feet up in the sky.

5. After he fell 18,000 feet from the sky, he landed unhurt and was still conscious.

6. It seems that a great many people believe that they are double-jointed, and, on the surface, it may look like some contortionists and people who are advanced in the practice of yoga may appear to be double-jointed.

7. The fact of the matter is that no one has been born who is truly double-jointed.

8. Their genes that they inherited from their parents and constant exercise that they do may make these people's joints a lot more elastic than the joints of other people.

9. Now, here's one of those myths that you probably have heard all of your life, and it supposedly had its origin in the Garden of Eden—men have one rib fewer than women.

10. As a matter of fact, men and women have the same number of ribs—twelve; however, you may be interested to learn that some women have one vertebra fewer than men.

Writing Varied Sentences

Vary the length and structure of your sentences to achieve greater interest and emphasis.

Varying Sentence Length and Openings

Most English sentences—both spoken and written—begin with the subject. When ideas are presented in a string of subject-verb sentences, they may be clear—but monotonous. To avoid monotony, begin some sentences with a *modifier* (*a single word, a phrase,* or *a clause*) or a *transposed appositive*. A *modifier* acts as an adjective or an adverb. It describes, limits, or qualifies another word or group of words. Generally, put a modifier as close as possible to the word or group of words it modifies.

▶ **Single-Word Modifiers**

Skagway, Alaska, was the original starting point of the Chilkoot Pass. (*subject first*)

Originally, Skagway, Alaska, was the starting point of the Chilkoot Pass. (*single-word modifier first*)

Chilkoot Pass was treacherous and dangerous and was the quickest route to the Klondike. (*subject first*)

Treacherous and dangerous, Chilkoot Pass was the quickest route to the Klondike. (*single-word modifiers first*)

▶ **Phrase Modifiers**

Thousands of gold seekers swarmed into Skagway during the icy winter of 1897. (*subject first*)

During the icy winter of 1897, thousands of gold seekers swarmed into Skagway. (*prepositional phrase first*)

The population of Skagway swelled from one family to more than 20,000 people within three months. (*subject first*)

Within three months the population of Skagway swelled from one family to more than 20,000 people. (*prepositional phrase first*)

They purchased their gear and supplies to prepare for their dangerous trek. (*subject first*)

To prepare for their dangerous trek, they purchased their gear and supplies in Skagway. (*to + a verb phrase first*)

They risked their lives every day, going over treacherous mountains and down raging rivers. (*subject first*)

Going over treacherous mountains and down raging rivers, they risked their lives every day. (*-ing + verb phrase first*)

▶ **Clause Modifiers**

Prospectors were required to have almost a ton of food and gear when they attempted the trip to the Yukon. (*subject first*)

When they attempted the trip to the Yukon, prospectors were required to have almost a ton of food and gear. (*clause first*)

Many prospectors formed partnerships because it was almost impossible for one man to haul everything. (*subject first*)

Because it was almost impossible for one man to haul everything, many prospectors formed partnerships. (*clause first*)

▶ **Transposed Appositives**

An *appositive* is a noun or pronoun—often with modifiers—put beside another noun or pronoun to explain or identify it. An *appositive phrase* is a phrase consisting of an appositive and its modifiers.

Dawson City, the northernmost community on the Klondike Highway, is situated at the confluence of the Yukon and Klondike Rivers. (*subject first*)

The northern most community on the Klondike Highway, Dawson City, is situated at the confluence of the Yukon and Klondike Rivers. (*transposed appositive first*)

Dawson City, once known as the "Paris of the North," is located 144 miles south of the Arctic Circle. (*subject first*)

Once known as the "Paris of the North," Dawson City is located 144 miles south of the Arctic Circle. (*transposed appositive first*)

Practice beginning sentences in a variety of ways by revising each of the following sentences according to the instructions in the parentheses.

1. George Carmack, Dawson Charlie, and Skookum Jim discovered gold on August 16, 1896. (Begin with a prepositional phrase.)

2. Bonanza Creek, a tributary of the Klondike River, was the site of their discovery. (Begin with a transposed appositive.)

3. Dawson City, situated at the confluence of the Yukon and Klondike Rivers, is just 144 miles south of the Arctic Circle. (Begin with a transposed appositive.)

4. Dawson City was booming and bustling for it was the center of excitement of one of the world's most famous gold strikes. (Begin with two single-word modifiers.)

5. Miners from Dawson City arrived in Seattle and San Francisco with nearly $2 million in the summer of 1897. (Begin with a prepositional phrase.)

6. More than sixty thousand men and women passed through Seattle and Alaska's Chilkoot and White passes on their way to the Klondike by the next spring. (Begin with a *verb + -ing* phrase.)

7. Dawson City became known as the "Paris of the North" because it had a large population, telephone service, and running water. (Begin with a clause.)

8. Attractions in Dawson City are numerous today. (Begin with two or more single-word modifiers.)

9. The Canadian government operates a free ferry service for transporting passengers and vehicles across the Yukon River to the Top of the World Highway. (Begin with a *to + a verb* phrase.)

10. Mining operations continue in the area, although Dawson City's economy is based more on tourism than gold mining. (Begin with a clause.)

Combining Choppy Sentences

Avoid the choppy style caused by a series of short, jerky sentences. Aside from being monotonous, choppy sentences give undue emphasis to unimportant ideas. Combine choppy sentences to form one long sentence, putting the most important ideas in independent clauses and less important ideas in subordinate constructions. Skillful use of complex sentences is the mark of mature style.

Choppy   Carcross is a small town in Alaska. It was originally called Cariboo Crossing. Its name today is a combination of the first two syllables in the original name.

Combined	Carcross, *a small town in Alaska that was originally called Cariboo Crossing*, derived its current name from the first two syllables of its original name.
Combined	*Originally called Cariboo Crossing*, Carcross, a small town in Alaska, derived its current name from the first two syllables of its original name.
Choppy	Carcross Desert is north of Carcross. It runs along the Klondike Highway. It is the smallest desert in the world. It covers 650 acres.
Combined	*Located north of Carcross along the Klondike Highway*, the 650-acre Carcross Desert is the smallest desert in the world.
Combined	Carcross Desert, *which is located north of Carcross along the Klondike Highway*, covers 650 acres and is the smallest desert in the world.
Combined	Just north of Carcross, *along the Klondike Highway*, lies the 650-acre Carcross Desert, the smallest desert in the world.
Choppy	It was created by retreating glaciers. They left a sandy lake bottom. Winds from Lake Bennet constantly blow across the area. It shifts the sand. Vegetation is limited.
Combined	*Created by retreating glaciers that left a sandy lake bottom*, Carcross Desert has limited vegetation because winds from Lake Bennet constantly shift the sand.
Combined	Carcross Desert, *created by retreating glaciers that left a sandy lake bottom*, has limited vegetation because winds from Lake Bennet constantly shift the sand.

EXERCISE 30

Use various means of subordination (*subordinate clauses, appositives, phrases,* and so on) and combine the choppy sentences in each group into one long, smooth sentence.

1. She was known as Klondike Kate. She symbolized the life and times of the Klondike. Her name was Kathleen Eloisa Rockwell. She was born in 1876 in Junction City, Kansas.

2. She was a teenage chorus girl. She joined a vaudeville company. She traveled west by train from New York to Spokane, Washington.

3. She disliked her new job. She was required to encourage men to buy as many drinks as they could drink. She decided to quit. It was not the kind of job she had expected.

4. She could not leave. She had no money. She was in debt for her train ticket. She accepted her fate. Eventually, she learned to like the job.

5. Kate read headlines about the Klondike gold rush. She decided to go North. She quit the show. She and four other entertainers began their journey to the Klondike. Midway, her fellow travelers turned back.

6. Kate was determined. She continued on her way. She was doing her "buck and wing dancing"—tap dancing—to earn money.

7. Kate arrived in Dawson City in 1900. She worked at the Palace Grand. She had red hair. She could sing. She could dance. She was very popular. She was especially popular with the miners.

8. In Dawson City she worked as a variety entertainer. She worked as a dance hall girl.

9. She had a relationship with Alexander Pantages. He was the owner of Dawson's Orpheum Theater.

10. The relationship ended. She sued him for breach of promise. She sued him for $25,000. She left Dawson City.

Revising "Stringy" Sentences

► **Excessive Coordination**

In everyday conversation, ideas are often strung together one after another with connecting words—usually *and, for,* and *so;* however, when ideas are strung together in this manner in writing, it is monotonous and boring. Break up a stringy sentence by

- subordinating ideas

- dividing it into more than one sentence

- turning it into a simple sentence that contains compound verbs

Stringy   Chicken is a small town in Alaska, *and* it is located near the Alaska-Yukon border, *and* it is the setting for Ann Purdy's novel *Tisha.*

Revised   Chicken, a small town in Alaska that is located near the Alaska-Yukon border, is the setting for Ann Purdy's novel *Tisha.*

Stringy   Ann Purdy was a young woman, *and* she went to Chicken, Alaska, to teach school, *and* she helped her Athabaskan students, *and* she fell in love with a local man, *and* she made Chicken her home.

Revised   When Ann Purdy was a young woman, she went to Chicken, Alaska, where she taught school, helped her young Athabaskan students, fell in love with a local man, and made Chicken her permanent home.

Stringy   The early miners wanted to name their town Ptarmigan after a chickenlike type of grouse that inhabited the area, *but* they had to abandon the idea, *for* none of them could spell Ptarmigan, *so* they named the town Chicken.

Revised   Although the early miners wanted to name their town Ptarmigan after a chickenlike type of grouse that inhabited the area, they had to abandon the idea. Because none of them could spell Ptarmigan, they named the town Chicken.

 If you are told that your sentences are too long and need to be limited, revise any sentence that contains more than three clauses.

▶ **Excessive Subordination**   Stringy sentences may also be the result of excessive subordination. If a sentence contains more than two subordinate words such as *after, since, because, when, who, which,* or *that,* the meaning of the sentence may not be clear and should be revised.

Stringy   The Yukon Transportation Museum, *which* is located off the Alaska Highway at Kilometer Post 2475.7, *which* is near the Whitehorse Airport, exhibits many modes of transportation, *which* include snowshoes, dog sleds, stage coaches, boats, aircraft, and military vehicles *that* were used during the construction of the Alaska Highway.

Revised   The Yukon Transportation Museum, located off the Alaska Highway at Kilometer Post 2475.7 near the Whitehorse Airport, exhibits many modes of transportation that were used during the construction of the Alaska Highway. The exhibit includes snowshoes, dog sleds, stage coaches, boats, aircraft, and military vehicles.

Stringy   *The Queen of the Yukon, which* is the sister plane of *The Spirit of St. Louis, which* was the plane flown by Charles A. Lindbergh *when* he flew the first nonstop solo transatlantic flight, is also displayed.

Revised   *The Queen of the Yukon,* the sister plane of Charles A. Lindbergh's *The Spirit of St. Louis,* the plane in which he flew the first nonstop solo transatlantic flight, is also displayed.

EXERCISE 31

Revise the following stringy sentences, getting rid of excessive coordination and subordination.

1. The step from high school to college is a big one, *and* it took a long time for me to get used to it *because* everything was so different, *but* now I am accustomed to being on my own, *and* I enjoy it.

2. The campus is large, *and* it has many trees, *and* the paths are well-marked, *but* at night I have trouble finding my way *because* the lighting is poor, *and* I often get confused *because* I have a poor sense of direction.

3. *Although* I was still in high school, I enrolled in college in a special program designed for high school students *because* I was bored *since* the courses I was taking in high school were too easy, *and* I wanted to get a taste of college life.

4. I did not enjoy my first college class *because* it was very different from my high school classes, *and* the expectations were different, *and* the instructor even gave us a list of things he expected from his students, *which* I did not like.

5. *Although* my instructor was knowledgeable and friendly, he did not accept late work, *which* I did not think was fair *because* students have other responsibilities, *and* they cannot always meet an instructor's deadlines.

6. *Since* he did not accept late work, I expected him to give extra credit assignments *that* I could count on to raise my grade, *but* he would not do this *although* I told him *that* I needed extra credit *because* I had been unable to complete all the assignments.

7. *When* I sat down to write my first college composition, I immediately developed writer's block *because* I had never had to do preplanning or prewriting or revising, *which* seemed like a waste of time to me *because* I always just wrote one draft and submitted it, *and* I usually got high marks.

8. I was accustomed to being free to express my ideas creatively, *and* I did not like his rules for writing different kinds of essays, *so* I wrote the essay in my usual style, *but* he said it did not meet the requirements of the assignment *because* it was not an expository essay, *and* he said it was a first person narrative, *and* I had to redo it.

9. I am now a full-time college student, *and* I have learned to adapt to the requirements of instructors, *so* I go to class on a regular basis, *and* I am seldom late, *and* I complete all the assignments on time.

10. *Although* I did not like my first college instructor *because* he was strict, *and* I felt he was unfair, I did learn a few things from him, *which* I guess have helped me with my subsequent college courses, *and when* I see him on campus, he remembers me, *and* he asks how I am doing in my classes.

Review Exercises

REVIEW EXERCISE 32

Begin sentences in a variety of ways, revising them according to the instruction in the parentheses.

1. Barrow is 340 miles north of the Arctic Circle on the edge of the Arctic ice pack and is the northernmost settlement in Alaska. (Begin with an appositive.)

2. The sun does not go below the horizon for eighty-two days from early May to early August. (Begin with a prepositional phrase.)

3. The sun does not rise above the horizon for fifty-one days between November and January. (Begin with a prepositional phrase.)

4. Barrow is the main trade center of northern Alaska and has government and military facilities. (Begin with a transposed appositive.)

5. The Eskimos of Barrow continue to follow their traditional way of life, but a more modern way of life is the trend. (Begin with a dependent clause.)

6. Hunting, fishing, whaling, and crafting art objects are still important to the people, but the discovery of the North Slope oil has brought about many changes. (Begin with a dependent clause.)

7. They still use Husky sled dogs for transportation, but snowmobiles have become popular. (Begin with a to + a verb phrase.)

8. Sir John Barrow, a British geographer and second secretary of the admiralty, promoted scientific voyages in the Arctic. (Begin with a transposed appositive.)

9. John Ross and William Parry were searching for the Northwest Passage when they explored the Arctic in 1818. (Begin with verb + -ing phrase.)

10. Sir John Barrow was a venerable man who helped found the Royal Geographical Society in 1830. (Begin with a one- or two-word modifier.)

REVIEW EXERCISE 33

Combine the choppy sentences in each group into one long, smooth sentence. Use various means of subordination (*subordinate clauses, appositives, phrases,* and so on).

1. Prudhoe Bay is an inlet of the Arctic Ocean. Oil was discovered there in 1968.

2. The Trans-Alaska Pipe Line was completed in 1977. Oil is transported from the Prudhoe Bay oil fields to Valdez. Valdez is about 800 miles south of Prudhoe Bay.

3. The pipeline is an amazing engineering feat. It crosses three mountain ranges. It crosses three fault lines.

4. It is able to withstand an earthquake measuring up to 8.5 on the Richter scale. It is able to withstand temperatures as low as minus 80 degrees Fahrenheit. The pipeline cost $9.7 billion. It is 789 miles long.

REVIEW EXERCISE 34

Revise the following stringy sentences, getting rid of excessive *coordination* and *subordination*.

1. On March 9, 1942, the U.S. Army Corps of Engineers began working on the Alaska Highway, which would be a direct land route between the United States and the Alaska Territory, which originated as an emergency passage for American troops during World War II after the Japanese occupied the Aleutian Islands, which extend southwestward from the Alaska Peninsula.

2. Although more than 11,000 troops worked on the road, civilians were hired to help, and Canada supplied the right-of-way and materials, for it wanted to be able to use the road after the war ended.

3. The workers built 133 bridges, and they dug more than 8,000 culverts, and although that winter was the worst one in recorded history, they completed the highway in eight months.

4. In 1943 the highway became public, and more than 16,000 civilian workers labored on the road for the next seven years, for they were trying to turn it into a road that could be traveled all year.

5. The Alaska Highway is 1,523 miles long, and it starts at Dawson Creek, British Columbia, and goes through the Yukon Territory, and it goes on through Delta Junction to Fairbanks.

6. Although the road is maintained daily, its condition can change rapidly when the weather changes, so when people drive this famous highway, they should take their time, and they should drive with their headlights on, and they should always be alert for bumps and holes in the road.

7. Fairbanks, which is near the geographical center of Alaska and which is named after Charles Warren Fairbanks who was a U.S. Senator from Indiana and who later became Theodore Roosevelt's vice president, is a major visitor center and the northern terminus of the Alaska Railroad.

8. Where Fairbanks now stands, in 1901 Captain E. T. Barnette founded a trading post when a riverboat captain refused to take him any farther up the Chena River because the water level was too low, and the next year gold was discovered nearby, and gold prospectors began pouring into the area.

9. When the Alaska Highway was completed and when military personnel flooded into Fairbanks, the place experienced a second surge of growth, and the discovery of oil in Prudhoe Bay, which is about 390 miles north of Fairbanks, triggered a third wave of development.

10. Fairbanks has a variety of winter sports, which includes aurora viewing, cross-country and downhill skiing, curling, ice hockey, and its semiprofessional baseball team, which is the Alaska Goldpanners, plays its Midnight Sun Game every June 21 at 10:30 P.M., and the game is played without artificial lighting.

PART 5

Using the Right Words

There is no greater impediment to the advance of knowledge than the ambiguity of words.

—THOMAS REID
Essays on the Intellectual Powers of Man, Essay 1

Fairly or unfairly, television is blamed for many things, and many educators blame poor usage and spelling on television. It may or may not have directly influenced usage and spelling, but it certainly seems to have done so indirectly. When people get most of their information from television rather than reading, their ability to use words correctly and precisely may be affected, particularly when the words sound alike or when they are frequently misused or misspelled for the sake of catchy advertising, such as using *nite* for *night* and *rite* for *right.*

Understanding Commonly Confused Words

People who think that they are poor spellers are often not poor spellers at all. They may have trouble choosing the right word when two or more words sound or look alike. This is a usage problem, not a spelling problem. As you study the list of words that are often confused, put a check mark by the ones that give you trouble. If you do not have a problem with certain words, skip them. Concentrate on the ones that you misuse or do not know. To help you sort out words and choose the right form,

- pronounce words carefully and spell them correctly

- learn the difference between ownership words and contractions

- recognize unacceptable words

- associate words with their meanings through memory tricks or memorization

Working with Spelling, Ownership, and Contraction Problems

Misspelling is a common problem—*lite* for *light* or *thru* for *through.* If you have a problem with these commonly misspelled words, flag them and memorize the correct spelling. The misuse of the apostrophe is another common problem. The apostrophe is used to mark the omission of letters from contractions (*didn't, can't, they're*) and to show possession (*student's book*). Although the apostrophe is used to show ownership, the possessive form of personal pronouns (*mine, his, your, our,* and so on) shows ownership without the use of an apostrophe. Writers who do not have a clear understanding of the way possessives and contractions are formed and the difference between the two, often use a possessive word when they mean to use a contraction and vice versa— *you're* (a contraction) for *your* (possessive). If you misuse words because you confuse contractions and possessives, study Part 6: Using Apostrophes (pp. 339–341).

WORDS	DEFINITIONS	EXAMPLES
1. *all right*	proper or satisfactory condition	The patient is *all right.*
alright	unacceptable (misspelled)	
2. *a lot of*	large number or large extent	He has *a lot of* money.
alot of, alota	unacceptable (misspelled)	
3. *could've*	contraction of *could have,* not *could of*	I *could've* danced all night.
should've	contraction of *should have,* not *should of*	I *should've* known better.
would've	contraction of *would have,* not *would of*	You *would've* known better.
4. *its*	possessive form of *it*	What is *its* name?
it's	contraction of *it is*	*It's* your turn.
5. *may be* (**MAY BEE**)	action or being	Your dog *may be* lost.
maybe (**MAY**-bee)	possibly or perhaps	*Maybe* you should offer a reward.
maby	unacceptable (misspelled)	
6. *their*	possessive form of *they*	The police came to *their* house.
there	at or in that place	The children were *there.*
they're	contraction of *they are*	*They're* knocking on your door.
7. *threw*	past tense of *throw*	He *threw* the ball.
through	in one side and out the other	He drove *through* the tunnel.
thru	unacceptable (misspelled)	
8. *where*	at or in what place	I will be *where* you can find me.
were	past tense form of *be*	*Were* you out of town?
we're	contraction of *we are*	*We're* supposed to meet.
9. *whose*	possessive form of *who*	*Whose* car are you driving?
who's	contraction of *who is*	*Who's* on first?
10. *your*	possessive form of *you*	I like *your* new car.
you're	contraction of *you are*	*You're* my favorite instructor.

Fill in the blanks with the appropriate form of the words in parentheses.

1. (all right, alright) Is it _____________________ for people of the same sex to get married in some states?

   "The day will come when men will see the U.N. and what it means clearly. Everything will be _____________________." —Dag Hammarskjold

2. (a lot, alot) "To be happy with a man you must understand him _____________________ and love him a little. To be happy with a woman you must love her _____________________ and not try to understand her at all." —Helen Rowland

3. (have, of) "Alive today he [Shakespeare] would undoubtedly _____________________ written and directed motion pictures, plays, and God knows what. Instead of saying, 'This medium is not good,' he would _____________________ used it and made it good." —Raymond Chandler

4. (its, it's) Who said "It_____________________ not over until the fat lady sings"?

   "The same costume will be indecent ten years before _____________________ time, shameless five years before _____________________ time, daring one year before _____________________time, smart/dowdy one year after _____________________ time . . . quaint fifty years after _________ time, charming seventy years after _____________________ time, romantic one hundred years after _____________________ time." —James Laver, *Taste and Fashion*

5. (May be, Maybe, Maby) "A man _____________________ a tough, concentrated, successful money-maker and never contribute to his counry anything more than a horrible example." —Robert Menzies

   "The proverb warns that 'You should not bite the hand that feeds you.' But _____________________ you should, if it prevents you from feeding yourself." —Thomas Szasz

   "There _____________________ other reasons for a man's not speaking in publick [thus] than want of resolution: he may have nothing to say." —Samuel Johnson

6. (their, there, they're) "The brotherhood of men does not imply _____________________ equality. Families have _____________________ fools and _____________________men of genius . . ." —Aldous Huxley

"However big the fool, _________________ is always a bigger fool to admire him." —Nicholas Despreaux

Beans are an important food staple because _________________ often used as a meat substitute.

7. (threw, through, thru) "A merciless fate _________________ me into this maelstrom, but the gale of the world carried away me and my work." —Draza Mihajlovic

"The many faces of intimacy: the Victorians could experience it _________________ correspondence, but not _________________ cohabitation; contemporary men and women can experience it _________________ fornication, but not _________________ friendship." —Thomas Szasz

8. (where, were, we're) "_________________ justice is denied, _________________ poverty is enforced, _________________ ignorance prevails, and _________________ any one class is made to feel that society is in an organized conspiracy to oppress, rob, and degrade them, neither persons nor property will be safe." —Frederick Douglas

"And I saw the dead, small and great, stand before God; and the books _________________ opened . . ." —Bible: Revelation 20:12

9. (whose, who's) "San Franciso is a mad city inhabited for the most part by perfectly insane people _________________ women are of remarkable beauty." —Rudyard Kipling

"Never play cards with a man called Doc. Never eat at a place called Mom's. Never sleep with a woman _________________ troubles are worse than your own." —Nelson Algren

What is the title of the song that contains the following lines: "I wonder _________________ kissing her now. I wonder _________________ teaching her how"?

10. (your, you're) "Crime is terribly revealing. Try and vary _________________ method as you will, _________________ tastes, _________________ habits . . . and _________________ soul is revealed in _________________ actions." —Agatha Christie

Many country western songs are about lost loves. One such song contains the following lines: "_________________ someone else's love; _________________ no longer mine."

EXERCISE 2

Write sentences using each of the following words. You may use more than one of the words in a sentence: *all right, a lot, should've, its, may be, there, they're, threw, through, were, we're, who's, your, you're.*

Choosing Appropriate Forms

Many confusing word problems are caused by the writer not knowing which form to choose when the sounds of the words are the same or similar or the words closely resemble each other.

WORDS	DEFINITIONS	EXAMPLES
11. *a*	before words beginning with a consonant sound	Len saw *a* leprechaun.
	before a word beginning with a *u* but sounds like a *y*	I saw *a* **u**nicorn.
an	before words beginning with a vowel sound	Anne ate *an* **a**pple.
		He has *an* **u**mbrella.
	before words beginning with a silent *h*	Harry is *an* **h**onest man.
12. *accept* (ak-**SEPT**)	receive, admit, regard as true	I *accept* your apology.
except (ik-**SEPT**)	exclude, leave out, other than	Everyone came *except* you.
13. *affect* (uh-**FEKT**)	influence, change, cause	The sun *affected* her skin.
effect (i-**FEKT**)	result, brought about by a cause	The *effect* was a sunburn.
effect	bring about, to execute	The sunscreen *effected* a change.
14. *aggravate*	worsen	Scratching *aggravates* sores.
irritate	annoy	He *irritates* his sister.
15. *altar*	table or stand in a church	They stood before the *altar*.
alter	change, modify, or adjust	We will *alter* our plans.
16. *born*	brought into life	Where were you *born*?
borne	carried, endured	She has *borne* tragedy.

17. *brake*	stopping device, reduce speed	The car needs new *brakes*.
break	separate into pieces by sudden force	She *broke* the crystal vase.
18. *capitol*	government building	Is that the *capitol*?
capital	town or city of seat of government	Salem is the *capital* of Oregon.
	wealth, money, assets	Tim invested his *capital* wisely.
	major importance	That is a *capital* idea.
19. *pass*	move on or ahead, by, past; hand over	Kyle did not *pass* the test.
passed	past time of *pass*	Fran *passed* the test.
past	over, not current, happened or was earlier	She made errors in the *past*.
	pass by, go beyond	He walked *past* the school.
20. *to*	preposition—in a direction toward	Tania went *to* town.
	part of to + a verb phrase	We have *to leave* now.
too	also, in addition	Tom wanted to go *too*.
	more than enough, excessive	He ate *too* much candy.
two	cardinal number equal to 1 + 1	Lars ate *two* large cookies.

EXERCISE 3

Fill in the blanks with the appropriate form of the words in parentheses. Sometimes you may have to add an *s* or an *ed*.

11. (a, an) "American public opinion is like _______________ ocean—it cannot be stirred by _______________ teaspoon." —Hubert H. Humphrey

Note: When using the letter *a*, pronounce it as *ay*. Pronounce it as *uh* for all other purposes, except for emphasis.

12. (accept, except) "No democracy can long survive which does not _______________ as fundamental to its very existence the recognition of the rights of minorities." —Franklin D. Roosevelt

13. (affect, effect) "Pain and fear and hunger are _____________________ of causes which can be foreseen and known: but sorrow is a debt which someone else makes for us." —Freya Stark

    "A teacher _____________________ eternity; he can never tell where his influence stops." —Henry Adams

    "The State is the _____________________ of political freedom." —Emma Goldman

14. (aggravate, irritate) "When grief is fresh, every attempt to divert only _____________________." —Samuel Johnson

    Osteoporosis is _____________________ by smoking and excessive alcohol consumption.

15. (altar, alter) "The man who never _____________________ his opinion is like standing water, and breeds reptiles of the mind." —William Blake

16. (born, borne) "Man, _____________________of woman, has found it a hard thing to forgive her for giving him birth. The patriarchal protest against the ancient matriarch has _____________________ strange fruit through the years." —Lillian Smith

17. (brake, break) "Inanimate objects are classified scientifically into three major categories—those that don't work, those that _____________________down and those that get lost." —Russell Baker

18. (capital, capitol) "_____________________ is money, _____________________ is commodities." —Karl Marx

Note: Use *capitol* for a government building and *capital* for all other purposes.

19. (passed, past) "By the time a person has achieved years adequate for choosing a direction, the die is cast and the moment has long since _____________________which determined the future." —Zelda Fitzgerald

20. (to, too, two) "Friends love misery, in fact. Sometimes, especially if we are _____________________ lucky or _____________________ successful or _____________________ pretty, our misery is the only thing that endears us _____________________ our friends." —Erica Jong

    "_____________________ cheers for democracy: one because it admits variety and _____________________ because it permits criticism." —E. M. Forester

Note: Pronounce the word *tooh* before a consonant sound and *tuh* before a vowel sound.

EXERCISE 4

Write sentences using each of the following words. You may use more than one of the words in a sentence: *a, accept, affect, irritate, altar, born, break, capitol, pass, passed, to.*

Pronouncing Words Carefully

The following words are often confused because they are carelessly pronounced. Pronouncing them carefully may help you sort them out. Some of the examples contain sentences or memory tricks that may be helpful to you. On the other hand, you may want to make up your own sentences or memory tricks. In the examples if one word is a verb and the other is a noun, the word is followed by (n.) to indicate a *noun*—a word used to name a person, place or thing—or a (v.) to indicate a *verb*—a word that shows action or being.

WORDS	DEFINITIONS	EXAMPLES
21. *advice* (ad-**VIES**)	opinion about a course of action	Mr. Nice gave me good *advice* (n.).
advise (ad-**VIEZ**)	offer advice, recommend, inform	He *advised* (v.) me to tell the truth.
22. *angel* (**AYN**-juhl)	immortal, spiritual being	Do you have a guardian *angel* (n.)?
angle (**ANG**-guhl)	to fish with a hook and a line	Cal *angles* (v.) for crappies.
	to use a scheme or trick	Al *angled* (v.) for a promotion.
	geometric figure, space	An *angle* (n.) of 90° is a right *angle*.
23. *breath* (breth)	air inhaled and exhaled	Bad *breath* (n.) is offensive.
breathe (breeth)	inhale or exhale air	Dan's dog *breathes* (v.) on him.
24. *chose* (chohz)	to make a choice (past tense)	Cindy *chose* the rose.
choose (choohz)	to make a choice (present tense)	Did you *choose* a blues CD?
25. *cloths* (klothz)	pieces of cloth	The shop *cloths* are dirty.
clothes (kloohz)	wearing apparel, garments	Woo wears expensive *clothes*.
26. *later*	more late	Pater will arrive *later*.
latter (**LAT**-uhr)	the second of two	Matt chose the *latter* of the two.

27. *lead* (leed)	to go first (present tense)	Reed will *lead* (v.) this expedition.
led (led)	to go first (past tense)	Ned *led* (v.) the other expedition.
lead (led)	heavy metal, graphite in pencil	Pig *lead* (n.) is crude *lead* (n.).
28. *lose* (looz)	not find, mislay	Cruze, did you *lose* your book?
	fail to win	Did you *lose* the game?
loose (loos)	not tightly fastened	The baby's tooth is *loose*.
	not close together	The car skidded on the *loose* gravel.
	free	The moose is *loose*.
29. *quit* (kwit)	depart, leave, give up, relinquish	Kit *quit* her job.
quiet (**KWIE**-it)	silent, still, peaceful	The library is a *quiet* place.
quite (kwiet)	altogether, completely, actually	You are *quite* right.
30. *than*	introduces a second element	I'd rather switch *than* fight.
then	that time; next	I scan a book; *then,* I read it.

EXERCISE 5

Fill in the blanks with the appropriate form of the words in parentheses. Sometimes you may need to add an *s* or an *ed* to a word.

21. (choose, chose) (*Choose* rhymes with *lose,* and *chose* rhymes with *rose.*)

    "People do not _________________ their careers; they are engulfed by them." —John Dos Passos

    "I _________________ my wife as she did her wedding gown, not for a fine glossy surface, but such qualities as would wear well." —Oliver Goldsmith

22. (later, latter) (*Later* rhymes with *cater,* and *latter* rhymes with *matter.*)

    "Corruption is worse than prostitution. The _________________ might endanger the morals of an individual, the former invariably endangers the morals of the whole country." —Karl Kraus

    "No memory of having starred/Atones for _________________ disregard,/ Or keeps the end from being bad." —Robert Frost

23. (lead, led, lead) (*Lead*—present tense—rhymes with *deed*. *Led*—past tense—rhymes with *bed*. *Lead*—metal—rhymes with *bed*.)

    The _________________ in a pencil may be soft, medium, or hard.

    "The mass of men _________________ lives of quiet desperation." —Henry David Thoreau

    Harriet Tubman, one of the most successful "Conductors" on the Underground Railroad, _________________ more than three hundred slaves to freedom.

24. (cloths, clothes) (*Cloths* rhymes with *Roths*, and *clothes* rhymes with *hose*.)

    Ground _________________ are used to keep moisture away from people or things.

    "_________________ make the poor invisible. . . . We have the best-dressed poverty in the world." —Michael Harrington

25. (loose, lose) (*Loose* rhymes with *goose*, and *lose* rhymes with *booze*.)

    "Cry 'Havoc!' and let _________________ the dogs of war." —William Shakespeare

    "When people are taken out of their depths they _________________their heads, no matter how charmingly a bluff they may put up." —F. Scott Fitzgerald

26. (quiet, quite, quit) (*Quiet* rhymes with *diet*. *Quite* rhymes with *right*. *Quit* rhymes with *pit*.)

    John Philip Sousa, who _________________ the Marine Corps, wrote "The Stars and Stripes Forever."

    "We do not _________________ forgive a giver. The hand that feeds us is in some danger of being bitten." —Ralph Waldo Emerson

    "The best doctors in the world are Dr. Diet, Dr. _________________, and Dr. Merryman." — Jonathan Swift

27. (than, then) (*Than* rhymes with *man*, and *then* rhymes with *hen*.)

    "Like other parties of the kind, it was first silent, _________________ talky, _________________, argumentative, _________________ disputatious, _________________ altogether inarticulate, and _________________drunk." —Lord Byron

    "The fact that a believer is happier _________________ a skeptic is no more to the point _________________ the fact that a drunken man is happier _________________ a sober one." —George Bernard Shaw

28. (advice, advise) (*Advice* rhymes with *lice,* and *advise* rhymes with *revise.*)

    "The physician can bury his mistakes, but the architect can only _________________ his

    clients to plant vines." —Frank Lloyd Wright

    "I always pass on good _________________. It is the only thing to do with it." —Oscar Wilde.

29. (angel, angle) (The end syllable of *angel* rhymes with the first syllable of *jello. Angle* rhymes with

    dangle.)

    "Modesty is the only sure bait when you _________________ for praise." —Lord Chesterfield

    "Make friends with the _________________, who though invisible are always with you." —

    Saint Francis de Sales

    "To knock a thing down, especially if it is cocked at an arrogant _________________, is a deep

    delight to the blood." —George Santayana

30. (breath, breathe) (*Breath* rhymes with *death,* and *breathe* rhymes with *seethe.*)

    "And the Lord God formed man of the dust of the ground, and _________________ into his

    nostrils the _________________ of life." —Bible: Genesis 2:7

    "The Air is precious to the red man, for all things share the same _________________. . . .

    The white man does not seem to notice the air he _________________." —Attributed to Chief

    Seattle

EXERCISE 6

Write sentences using the following words. You may use more than one of these words in a
sentence: *advise, angel, breathe, chose, cloths, later, lead* (leed), *lose, past, quite* (kwiet), and *then.*

Sorting Out More Confusing Sets of Words

WORDS	DEFINITIONS	EXAMPLES
31. *all ready*	totally prepared	He was *all ready* for the big game.
already	previously	I have *already* done my homework.

32. *among*	group of more than two	Divide the candy *among* the four children.
between	just two	Divide the popcorn *between* the two girls.
33. *amount*	refers to uncountable quantity	He has a great *amount* of intelligence.
number	refers to things that can be counted	A large *number* of people were there.
34. *altogether*	entirely	She does not *altogether* approve of him.
all together	every one in the same place	The family was *all together* at Christmas.
35. *conscious*	(**KOHN**-shuhs) aware, awake	After the accident, he was not *conscious*.
conscience	(**KOHN**-shuns) sense of right/wrong	He has a guilty *conscience*.
36. *desert*	(**DEZ**-urt) a dry region	The Sahara is a vast *desert*.
desert	(di-**ZURT**) to leave	Do not *desert* a faithful friend.
dessert	(di-**ZURT**) a sweet concoction	Pie is his favorite *dessert*.
37. *coarse*	crude	The suspect used *coarse* language.
	rough	Sandpaper has a *coarse* surface.
course	a playing area	Golf *courses* attract ducks and geese.
	a unit of study	How many *courses* are you taking?
	route or pathway	Which *course* has the least traffic?
38. *fewer*	small number of countable things	He has *fewer* friends than she.
less	small number of uncountable things	She has *less* enthusiasm than he.
39. *good* (adj.)	positive or desirable	We have a *good* baseball team.
good (n.)	valuable or useful part or aspect	There is much *good* in most people.
well (adv.)	in a good manner	He played *well*.
well (adj.)	in a satisfactory condition	Do you not feel *well*?
	(*good,* adjective or noun,	
	never an adverb	
	well, adverb or adjective)	
40. *hanged*	past tense of *hang,* executed	Roy Bean ordered many men to be *hanged*.
hung	past tense of *hang,* other purposes	She *hung* the picture at eye-level.

41.	*hear*	perceive sound	I *hear* the sound of the wind in the trees.
	here	at or in this place	Do you live *here?*
		(Memory trick: The word *hear* has the word *ear* in it.)	
42.	*knew*	past tense of *know,* to be aware	He *knew* all the answers for the test.
	new	still fresh, never used, not old	The *new* waitress has a *new* uniform.
43.	*principal*	sum of money	He pays interest on the *principal.*
		school leader	My school *principal* was not my pal.
		most important	I was her *principal* headache.
	principle	rule of conduct, basic truth	Do you value the *principle* of free speech?
44.	*sometime*	a time in the future	He promised to call her *sometime.*
	sometimes	occasionally	*Sometimes* he forgets his promises.
	some time	a period of time	She had not heard from him in *some time.*
45.	*we + a noun*	used as subject	*We students* are not ready for the test.
	us + a noun	used as object	Let *us students* take the test later.
46.	*weather*	state of the atmosphere	I like rainy *weather.*
	whether	introduces an alternative	I wonder *whether* or not it will rain today.
47.	*who*	used as subject	I wonder *who* called.
	whom	used as object	The boy *whom* I met today is from Ohio.
			To *whom* shall I send the bill?

EXERCISE 7

Fill in the blanks with the appropriate form of the words in parentheses. Sometimes you may need to add an *s* or an *ed* to a word.

31. (all ready, already) "[To] consult [is] to seek another's approval of a course

_______________________ decided on." —Ambrose Bierce

Are you _______________________ for the final examination?

32. (among, between) "While gossip _____________________ women is universally ridiculed as low and trivial, gossip _____________________ men . . . is called theory or idea or fact." —Andrea Dworkin

    "There is a fine line _____________________ loving life and being greedy for it." —Maya Angelou

33. (amount, number) "It seems to me that there must be an ecological limit to the _____________________ of paper pushers the earth can sustain." —Barbara Ehrenreich

    "To be good . . . is quite easy. It merely requires a certain _____________________ of sordid terror." —Oscar Wilde

34. (altogether, all together) "Talk that does not end in any kind of action is better suppressed _____________________." —Thomas Carlyle

    "Never the time and the place/ And the loved ones _____________________!" —Robert Browning

35. (conscious, conscience) "A man's _____________________ and his judgment are the same thing." —Thomas Hobbes

    "The greatest of faults, I should say, is to be _____________________ of none." —Thomas Carlyle

36. (desert, dessert) "The Mojave is a big _____________________ and a frightening one." —John Steinbeck

    Rats _____________________ a sinking ship.

    "Drama is like a plate of meat and potatoes; comedy is rather like the _____________________, a bit like meringue." —Woody Allen

37. (coarse, course) "For the first time, the weird and the stupid and the _____________________ are becoming our cultural norm." —Carl Bernstein

    "I have fought the good fight, I have finished my _____________________, I have kept the faith." —2 Timothy 4:7

    "In Washington, success is just a training _____________________ for failure." —Simon Hoggart

    Capitalize school subjects and classes only when the subjects themselves are proper nouns or when they are the titles of specific _____________________.

38. (fewer, less) "I grow daily to honour facts more and more, and theory _____________________ and _____________________." —Thomas Carlyle

    "The best thing that could happen to motherhood already has. _____________________ are going into it." —Victoria Billings

39. (good, well) "One cannot think ___________________, love ___________________, sleep

    ___________________, if one has not dined ___________________." —Virginia Woolf

    "Though language forms the preacher,/ 'Tis' ___________________ works make the man." —

    Elize Cook

40. (hanged, hung) "He that is born to be ___________________ shall never be drowned." —French

    Proverb

    The boxes for animal crackers are topped with a string so that they can be ___________________

    on a Christmas tree.

41. (hear, here) "If you are not too long, I will wait ___________________ for you all my life."

    —Oscar Wilde

    "To read a poem is to ___________________ it with our eyes; to ___________________ it is to

    see it with our ears." —Octavio Paz

42. (knew, new) "I would not talk so much about myself if there were anybody else whom I

    ___________________ as well." —Henry David Thoreau

    "To the old, the ___________________ is usually bad news." —Eric Hoffer

43. (principal, principle) "It's always easier to fight for one's ___________________ than to live up to

    them." —Alfred Adler

    "All animals, except man, know that the ___________________ business of life is to enjoy it."

    —Samuel Butler

    One who holds the position of highest rank in an elementary school or high school is the

    ___________________ or head teacher.

    Use this formula to compute interest on a sum of money: ___________________ × rate

    × time.

44. (sometime, sometimes, some time) "Clearly, ___________________ ago makers and consumers

    of American junk food passed jointly through some kind of sensibility barrier . . ." —Bill

    Bryson

    "___________________ they will give a war and nobody will come." —Carl Sandburg

    "I must have a prodigious quantity of mind; it takes me as much as a week,

    ___________________, to make it up." —Mark Twain

45. (we + a noun, us + a noun) ___________________ Americans are proud of our country. Don't tug on Superman's cape; don't spit in the wind; and don't mess in the affairs of ___________________ Americans.

46. (weather, whether) "The ___________________ is like the government, always in the wrong." —Jerome K. Jerome

    "Life is an end in itself, and the only questions as to ___________________ it is worth living is ___________________ you have had enough of it." —Oliver Wendell Holmes, Jr.

47. (who, whom) "There are three wants which never can be satisfied: that of the rich, ___________________ wants something more; that of the sick, ___________________ wants something different; and that of the traveler, ___________________ says, 'Anywhere but here.'" —Ralph Waldo Emerson

    "It is human to hate the man ___________________ you have hurt." —Tacitus

    "Man is the only animal for ___________________ his own existence is a problem which he has to solve." —Erich Fromm

EXERCISE 8

Write sentences using the following words. You may use more than one of these words in a sentence: *already, among, number, altogether, conscience, dessert, coarse, less, good, hanged, hear, new, principal, sometime, some time, weather, a noun + we, who, whom, a noun + us.*

Review Exercises

Fill in the blanks with the letter or letters of the meaning of the words.

REVIEW EXERCISE 9

______ 1. *alright*   a. proper or satisfactory condition   b. misspelling   c. definitely okay

______ 2. *alot*   a. misspelling   b. large number   c. large extent

_____ 3. *could've*   a. contraction of *could have*   b. contraction of *could of*

_____ 4. *it's*   a. possessive of *it*   b. contraction of *it is*   c. misspelling

_____ 5. *maybe*   a. possibly or perhaps   b. action or being   c. misspelling

_____ 6. *their*   a. at or in that place   b. possessive form of *they*   c. misspelling

_____ 7. *thru*   a. in one side and out the other   b. misspelling   c. past time of throw

_____ 8. *where*   a. at or in one place   b. past time form of *be*   c. form of *we are*

_____ 9. *who's*   a. possessive form of *who*   b. misspelling   c. contraction of *who is*

_____ 10. *you're*   a. possessive form of *you*   b. contraction of *you are*   c. misspelling

REVIEW EXERCISE 10

_____ 1. *an*   a. before a beginning vowel sound   b. before a beginning consonant sound

_____ 2. *accept*   a. exclude   b. receive   c. admit   d. other than

_____ 3. *affect*   a. influence or change   b. cause   c. result   d. bring about

_____ 4. *aggravate* a. irritate   b. annoy   c. misspelled   d. worsen

_____ 5. *alter*   a. change   b. modify   c. stand in a church   d. adjust

_____ 6. *borne*   a. brought to life   b. carried   c. endured

_____ 7. *brake*   a. separate into pieces by force   b. a stopping device   c. reduce speed

_____ 8. *capital*   a. government building   b. wealth   c. major importance   d. seat of government

_____ 9. *past*   a. move on ahead   b. go through   c. time before   d. push aside

_____ 10. *too*   a. also   b. more than enough   c. a number   d. toward

REVIEW EXERCISE 11

_____ 1. *advice*   a. opinion about a course of action   b. recommend   c. inform

_____ 2. *angle*   a. spiritual being   b. fish with a hook and a line   c. try to use a scheme or trick   d. geometric figure

______ 3. *breath*   a. air inhaled and exhaled   b. breeze   c. inhale or exhale air

______ 4. *choose*   a. make a choice (past time)   b. make a choice (present time)

______ 5. *clothes*   a. pieces of cloth   b. wearing apparel   c. garments

______ 6. *latter*   a. more late   b. the second of two   c. step stool

______ 7. *lead*   a. go first (present time)   b. go first (past time)   c. heavy metal

______ 8. *loose*   a. not find, mislay   b. fail to win   c. not tightly fastened   d. not close   e. free

______ 9. *quiet*   a. depart   b. relinquish   c. silent   d. still   e. altogether   f. actually

______ 10. *then*   a. introduces a second element   b. that time   c. next in time, space, or order

REVIEW EXERCISE 12

______ 1. *all ready*   a. totally prepared   b. previously

______ 2. *between*   a. refers to groups of more than two things   b. refers to just two things

______ 3. *amount*   a. refers to things that can be counted   b. refers to uncountable things

______ 4. *all together*   a. everyone in the same place   b. entirely

______ 5. *conscious*   a. aware   b. sense of right and wrong   c. awake

______ 6. *desert*   a. dry region   b. leave   c. a sweet concoction

______ 7. *course*   a crude   b. rough   c. playing area   d. pathway

______ 8. *fewer*   a. small number of countable things   b. small number of uncountable things

______ 9. *well*   a. positive   b. desirable   c. in a good manner   d. satisfactory condition

______ 10. *hung*   a. execution   b. suspended   c. held up

______ 11. *here*   a. perceive sound   b. at or in this place

______ 12. *knew*   a. past tense of *know*   b. be aware   c. still fresh   d. never used

______ 13. *principle*   a. sum of money   b. rule of conduct   c. school leader   d. most important

______ 14. *sometimes*   a. time in the future   b. occasionally   c. a period of time

______ 15. *whether*   a. state of the atmosphere   b. introduces an alternative

Improving Spelling

Spelling problems may be caused by one or several situations: pronouncing words carelessly, not knowing how to make words plural, not knowing how to add suffixes, or not knowing when to put *i* before *e*. Most weak spellers make specific kinds of spelling errors, and they keep making them over and over.

Many people erroneously think that big unusual words are the ones that are often misspelled. It's not the big, uncommon words such as *eleemosynary* or *saprophytic* that cause writers to stumble. When writers need to use one of these words, they look them up in a dictionary because they do not use these words often and know that they do not know how to spell them. It is often the small everyday words such as *your, lose, past, judgment,* or *writing* that cause the most grief.

If you think of yourself as being a weak speller, get help from the best instructor you know—yourself. Begin keeping a list of words that you misspell. Keep your list up to date. Add new misspelled words, but be sure to cross words off your list when you no longer misspell them. Group errors by types.

Pronunciations	Omitted or added sounds that are the result of careless pronunciation
Plurals	Plurals formed incorrectly
EI/IE	Misuse of *ei* and *ie*
Prefixes	Prefixes added incorrectly
Suffixes	Suffixes added incorrectly

Once you begin to see your tendencies to make certain types of errors, you can begin to systematically work on them. You will probably soon see that you have a few specific problems that you can correct and that you are not a weak speller in all areas.

Pronouncing Words Carefully to Improve Spelling

Mispronunciation is responsible for many errors in spelling. Careless pronunciations result in omitted sounds in some words and added sounds in other words. If you mispronounce a word, more than likely you will misspell it.

▶ **Omitted Sounds** Sometimes sounds of letters or combinations of letters are left out, and sometimes whole syllables are left out.

EXERCISE 13

In this exercise, the careless omission of the sound of the letter *a* may cause spelling problems. Pronounce each word carefully. Be sure to pronounce the boldfaced letters. Then, write each word three times.

1. accidentally

2. dialect

3. finally

4. laboratory

5. liable

6. quandary

7. probably

8. temperament

9. temperature

10. valuable

In the following exercises, the careless omission of the sound of a missing letter or a missing ending of a word may cause spelling problems. Pronounce each word carefully, and be sure to sound the boldfaced letters. Write each word three times.

EXERCISE 14

11. remember

12. arctic

13. ask**ed**

14. candi**d**ate

15. gran**d**father

16. supposed to

17. used to

18. bachelor

19. gaiety

20. capital

EXERCISE 15

21. mathematics

22. poem

23. together

24. length

25. strength

26. recognize

27. auxiliary

28. criminal

29. dilapidated

30. easily

EXERCISE 16

31. miniature

32. primitive

33. vigilant

34. ruin

35. attack

36. vulnerable

37. government

38. attacked

39. chocolate

40. sophomore

EXERCISE 17

41. description

42. prompt

43. impromptu

44. pumpkin

45. February

46. surprise

47. library

48. attempt

49. congratulate

50. formerly

EXERCISE 18

51. quantity

52. representative

53. sent

54. strictly

55. tempt

56. continuous

57. regular

58. usually

59. vacuum

60. probably

▶ **Added Sounds** The following words are often carelessly mispronounced and/or misspelled because an extra letter has been added or a similar sounding letter has been substituted for the correct letter.

EXERCISE 19

Pronounce each word carefully, and be sure that you do not include the sound of the added boldfaced letter. Write each word three times.

61. athlete, not ath**e**lete

62. drowned, not drown**d**ed

63. equipment, not equip**e**ment

64. grievous, not griev**e**ous

65. mischievous, not mischiev**e**ous

66. pronunciation, not proneunciation ____________ ____________ ____________

67. similar, not simular ____________ ____________ ____________

Making Nouns Plural

Nouns are naming words. They are used to name persons, places, things, events, or ideas. Nouns that name particular persons or things are *specific nouns* (also called *proper nouns*), and nouns that do not name particular persons or things are *general nouns* (also called *common nouns*). Most nouns have two forms: *singular form* (refers to one thing) and *plural form* (refers to more than one thing). Learning a few simple rules will enable you to correctly change single form nouns to plural form nouns. To apply these rules, remember that the vowels are *a, e, i, o, u,* and sometimes *y,* and the consonants are the other letters of the alphabet.

▶ **Most Words**   Add *s* to form the plural of most nouns.

> pictures desks computers lamps fans tissues crates

Add *es* to form the plural of nouns that end in a hissing sound—words that end in *s, ch, sh, x,* and *z* —to make them easier to pronounce.

> brushes glasses watches waxes patches boxes taxes topazes

▶ **Words Ending in *y***   Change *y* to an *i* and add *es* when the *y* is preceded by a consonant.

> story>stories glory>glories armory>armories army>armies navy>navies

Keep the *y* and add *s* when the *y* is preceded by a vowel or when the word is a proper name.

> toys boys days rays bays plays keys

> Flannerys O'Reillys Kellys

▶ **Words Ending in *o***   Add *s* when the *o* is preceded by a vowel.

> ratio trios radios rodeos zoos

For nouns ending in *o* preceded by a consonant, the plural forms are so variable that you should consult a dictionary whenever in doubt.

Generally, add *es* when the *o* is preceded by a consonant.

> heroes tomatoes echoes potatoes

Exceptions   memo>memos piano>pianos solo>solos cello>cellos
ditto>dittos hobo>hobos silo>silos photo>photos
typo>typos taco>tacos soprano>sopranos

EXERCISE 20

Fill in the blanks with the plural forms of the words.

1. chair _________________   11. mosquito_________________

2. dress _________________   12. hero_________________

3. box _________________   13. candy_________________

4. bush _________________   14. bench_________________

5. fly _________________   15. match_________________

6. lady _________________   16. valley_________________

7. salary _________________   17. genius_________________

8. monkey _________________   18. video_________________

9. enemy _________________   19. party_________________

10. rodeo _________________   20. O'Mally_________________

EXERCISE 21

Write sentences using the plural forms of the following words. You may use more than one of
these words in a sentence: *city, holiday, country, wash, fox, annex, allergy, voter, tendency.*

▶ **Words Ending in *f* or *fe***   For most words that end in *f* or *fe*, add an *s* to form plurals.

beliefs cliffs gaffs reefs giraffes carafes

For some words that end in *f* or *fe*, change the *f* or *fe* to *v* and add *s* or *es* to form
plurals.

leaf>leaves wife>wives knife>knives loaf>loaves thief>thieves wolf>wolves

Add only *s* to a word that ends in *ff.* tariff>tariffs

▶ **Words That End in *is*** Change *is* to *es* when a noun ends in *is.*

crisis>crises diagnosis>diagnoses oasis>oases

▶ **Irregular Plural Forms** The plural of a few words is formed by irregular methods. Memorize the ones you do not already know.

mouse>**mice** man>**men** woman>**women** child>**children** foot>**feet**

locus>**loci** datum>**data** bacterium>**bacteria** tooth>**teeth**

▶ **Words That Are Both Singular and Plural** Put *a, several,* or *a number* in front of a word that is both singular and plural to show whether the noun is one thing or more than one thing.

deer>**a** deer>**two** deer moose>**a** moose>**several** moose quail>**one** quail>**ten** quail

Note: The plural of some of these words is formed by adding *s* or *es.* When in doubt, consult a good up-to-date dictionary.

elk>**elks** or **two (or more) elk** fish> **fishes** or **two (or more) fish**

▶ **Plurals of Compound Words** To form the plural of most compound words, add *s* or *es* to the most important word—usually, the last word, but not always.

checkbooks stonewalls bookcases mothers-in-law commanders-in-chief vice-presidents

EXERCISE 22

Write the plurals of the following words.

1. chief _________________

2. wife _________________

3. prognosis _________________

4. welfare state _________________

5. goose _________________

6. moose _________________

7. ox _________________

8. cupful _________________

9. drive-in _________________

10. stonewall _________________

Learning a Few Spelling Rules

▶ **The *ie/ei* Combination**   The following old jingle works for most situations:

i before *e*   retrieve belief grief field cashier niece thief

except after *c*   conceive receive deceit deceive ceiling receipt perceive

or when the sound is *ay*   neighbor weigh sleigh eight beige

Major exceptions *-ie*   conscience efficient financier proficient science species sufficient

                 -ei   counterfeit foreign forfeit either height heir leisure neither seize sleight weird

---

EXERCISE 23

Add either *ei* or *ie* in the blank in each of the following words.

1. for_____gn
2. br_____f
3. f_____nd
4. l_____sure
5. bel_____f

6. rec_____pt
7. w_____rd
8. bel_____ve
9. s_____ze
10. th_____f

11. perc_____ve
12. ach_____ve
13. retr_____ve
14. p_____ce
15. gr_____f

16. rel_____ve
17. conc_____ve
18. anc_____nt
19. caff_____ne
20. ch_____f

▶ **Adding Prefixes**   A *prefix* is one or more letters or syllables added to the beginning of a word to make a new word. The syllables *a-*, *de-*, *dis-*, *in-*, *im-*, *mis-*, *non-*, and *un-* are common prefixes.

When a prefix is added to a word, the spelling of the word itself remains the same, even when the first letter of the word it is added to is the same.

a + miss = **am**iss   dis + solve = dissolve   dis + satisfy = dissatisfy

mis + spell = misspell   mis + spent = misspent   im + material = immaterial

un + necessary = unnessary   mis + fortune = misfortune   for + bid = forbid

in + numerable = innumerable   un + able = unable   dis + service = disservice

▶ **Adding Suffixes**   A *suffix* is one or more letters or syllables added to the end of a word to make a new word or another form of a word.

Spelling That Does Not Change   Do not change the spelling of most words that end in a *consonant* when you add a suffix that begins with a *consonant.*

kin<u>d</u> + <u>n</u>ess = kindness   trus<u>t</u> + <u>w</u>orthy = trustworthy   kin<u>d</u> + <u>l</u>y = kindly

▶ **Words Ending in Silent *e***   Drop the silent *e* before a suffix that begins with a vowel.

us<u>e</u>>us**ing**   writ<u>e</u>>writ**ing**   hav<u>e</u>>hav**ing**   com<u>e</u>>com**ing**   separat<u>e</u>>separat**ion**   desir<u>e</u>>desir**ous**

Exceptions   Do not drop the silent *e* if dropping it creates a word that can be confused with another word or if it creates a nonsensical word.

dy<u>e</u> + ing = dying (cease living)   dy<u>e</u> + ing = dy<u>e</u>ing (to color)

courag<u>e</u> + ous = courageous—not *couragous*   b<u>e</u> + ing = b<u>e</u>ing—not *bing*

mil<u>e</u> + age = mileage—not *milage*   sho<u>e</u> + ing = shoeing—not *shoing*

Keep the silent *e* before a suffix that begins with a consonant.

lik<u>e</u> + <u>l</u>y = likely   lov<u>e</u> + <u>l</u>y = lovely   requir<u>e</u> + <u>m</u>ent = requirement

Exceptions   judg<u>e</u> + <u>m</u>ent = judgment   tru<u>e</u> + <u>l</u>y = truly   acknowledge + <u>m</u>ent = acknowledgment

---

EXERCISE 24

Combine each of the following words and suffixes, dropping the silent *e* when necessary.

1. arrange + ment _______________

2. nine + ty _______________

3. complete + tion _______________

4. notice + able _______________

5. ice + y _______________

6. replace + able _______________

7. grade + ing _______________

8. mutate + ion _______________

9. nine + th _______________

10. due + ly _______________

▶ **Words Ending in *y***   In words ending in *y* preceded by a consonant, generally, change the *y* to *i* before any suffix except one beginning with *i*.

> happy + ness = happiness   try + ed = tried   mercy + ful = merciful

> **Exceptions**   dry + ness = dryness   shy + ly = shyly

In words ending in *y*, keep the *y* if it is preceded by a vowel or if the suffix begins with *i*.

> play + ful = playful   employ + ed = employed   joy + ful = joyful

> study + ing = studying   hurry + ing = hurrying   funny + ier = funnier

> **Exceptions**   day + ly = daily   gay + ly = gaily

EXERCISE 25

Combine each of the following words and suffixes, changing *y* to *i*, keeping the final *y*, or dropping it as necessary.

1. ally + ance ___________________

2. buy + ing ___________________

3. justify + cation ___________________

4. wry + ly ___________________

5. rosy + ness ___________________

6. pity + ful ___________________

7. bully + ing ___________________

8. convey + or ___________________

9. angry + ly ___________________

10. betray + al ___________________

▶ **Doubling Final Consonants**   Double the final consonant of a word before a suffix that begins with a vowel when it meets the following three conditions:

- the word has one syllable or is stressed on the last syllable

- it contains only one vowel in the last syllable

- it ends in a single consonant

> drop + ing = dropping   flat + est = flattest   step + ed = stepped
> rob + er = robber   o-**mit** + ing = omitting   re-**fer** + ed = referred
> oc-**cur** + ence = occurrence

Do not double the final consonant if the accent shifts to a different syllable in the new word.

prefer + ence = prefer**ence**   **defer** + ence = defer**ence**

Note: Keep the last letter of the first word when you combine two words, even if it is the same letter as the beginning letter of the second word.

boo**kk**eeper   gran**dd**ad   roo**mm**ate

EXERCISE 26

Combine each of the following words and suffixes, doubling the final consonant before the suffix when necessary.

1. hum + ing _________________

2. refer + ence _________________

3. confer + ence _________________

4. occur + ence _________________

5. stir + ed _________________

6. occur + ed _________________

7. rot + en _________________

8. tip + ing _________________

9. prefer + ential _________________

10. slip + ed _________________

▶ *-able, -ible* **Endings**   Generally, add *-able* if the *root* (the part of the word that carries the basic meaning) is a complete word.

accept + able = accept**able**   comfort + able = comfort**able**   consider + able = consider**able**

Exceptions   irrit**able**   inevit**able**   prob**able**

Drop the *e* before adding *-able* when the root ends in *e*.

desire + able = desir**able**   debate + able = debat**able**   excuse + able = excus**able**

Exceptions   Keep the final *e* to retain the soft sound of *c* or *g* preceding the *e*.

noti**c**e + able = notice**able**   marria**g**e + able = marriage**able**

Generally, add *-ible* if the root is not a complete word.

divis + ible = divis**ible**   feas + ible = feas**ible**

Exceptions   contempt**ible**   digest**ible**   flex**ible**   respons**ible**

EXERCISE 27

Add *-able* or *-ible* to each of the following words.

1. accept _________________

2. change _________________

3. desire _________________

4. eat _________________

5. notice _________________

6. plaus _________________

7. incred _________________

8. love _________________

9. sale _________________

10. audi _________________

► **-sede, -ceed, and -cede Endings**   Only one word ends in *-sede* (super**sede**). Only three words end in *-ceed* (ex**ceed,** pro**ceed,** suc**ceed**). All other words that end with the sound of *seed,* such as *con**cede,*** pre**cede,** inter**cede,** end with *-cede.*

Review Exercises

Rewrite the words correctly, adding omitted letters, leaving out extra ones, and changing incorrect ones.

REVIEW EXERCISE 28

1. finlly _________________

2. probly _________________

3. granfather _________________

4. use to _________________

5. simular _________________

6. crimnal _________________

7. easly _________________

8. minature _________________

9. choclate _________________

10. suprise _________________

REVIEW EXERCISE 29

1. mischieveous _______________

2. lenth _______________

3. drownded _______________

4. stricly _______________

5. vunerable _______________

6. mathmatics _______________

7. captal _______________

8. formely _______________

9. libary _______________

10. Febuary _______________

Write the plural form of each of the nouns in the following exercises.

REVIEW EXERCISE 30

1. beauty _______________

2. quiz _______________

3. bias _______________

4. fantasy _______________

5. midriff _______________

6. belief _______________

7. fish _______________

8. flourish _______________

9. policy _______________

10. justice of the peace _______________

REVIEW EXERCISE 31

1. ox _______________

2. salmon _______________

3. wolf _______________

4. shelf _______________

5. tendency _______________

6. attorney at law _______________

7. tomato _______________

8. belief _______________

9. irony _______________

10. ratio _______________

Rewrite the following words, adding *ie* or *ei* or combining base words and suffixes.

REVIEW EXERCISE 32

1. gr _____ ve   5. counterf _____ t   8. bit + en _________________

2. s _____ ge   6. inter + (seed sound) _____________   9. effic _____ nt

3. n _____ gh   7. grand + dad _____________   10. cancel + ed _______________

4. debate + (able or ible)

REVIEW EXERCISE 33

1. mean + ness _______________   5. miss + spell _______________   9. w_____ld

2. use + able _______________   6. argue + ment _______________   10. n_____ghbor

3. funny + ier _______________   7. prefer + able _______________

4. final + ly _______________   8. profit + able _______________

Choosing Appropriate Language

Several different kinds of English exist. In general, however, there are two broad categories of English: *standard* and *non-standard*. Standard English is the language most widely recognized as acceptable English. It is the language used by the greatest number of people who speak English, and it serves as a model for others to follows. It is the language that reaches the greatest audience. Non-standard English is the form of English that is not acceptable to the majority of English speakers, and, therefore, the audience is limited. Two main differences between the two languages appear in the use of pronouns and certain verb forms.

STANDARD	NON-STANDARD
He dressed *himself.*	He dressed *hisself.*
The dog *ran* away.	The dog *run* away.
She *doesn't* respect him.	She *don't* respect him.

To effectively reach the largest possible audience, always use Standard English.

Choosing Appropriate Levels of Standard English

The choice of words and phrases in a piece of writing is called *diction. Diction* means "say." The words and phrases you use to say what you have to say depend on the subject, the needs of the audience, the purpose, and your attitude (tone) toward the material and the audience. The level of diction may be *formal, informal,* or *college writing*—a level between the two.

▶ **Formal Diction** *Formal diction,* sometimes referred to as "literary" English, is grammatically correct and is aimed at an educated audience. Generally, the tone is objective and dignified. Writers generally use formal diction in formal reports, research papers, scholarly works, and addresses on serious or solemn occasions. In formal writing the sentences are often long, contain words not used in ordinary conversation, and contain few contractions and no slang.

▶ **Informal Diction** *Informal diction* is the language of conversation. It is the language most English-speaking people use most of the time. Informal English is less rigid than formal English. In informal writing, sentence lengths vary. It contains less difficult vocabulary and sounds conversational. Although *colloquialisms, regionalisms,* and *slang* are common in conversation, generally, you should not use them in written work, except to reproduce speech or dialect.

Colloquial Expressions Everyday speech that includes contractions, shortened words, vague words, and jargon used in particular fields.

Contractions	*didn't*/did not *can't*/cannot *isn't*/ is not *wasn't*/was not
Shortened words	*gym*/gymnasium *phone*/telephone *TV*/television *cab*/taxicab
Vague words	*nice* *good* *bad* *okay*
Jargon	*hacker high-tech interface downsize feedback boot menu*

Regional Expressions   Words, usage, and pronunciation that are characteristics of a form of language that is identifiable with a geographic area and are different from the standard form.

STANDARD	REGIONAL
think	allow, calculate, reckon
I blame him for it.	I blame it on him.
completely	plumb
carry	tote or pack
paper bag	poke
identical to	identical with
at home	to home
He stood in line.	He stood on line.

Slang   New meanings given to standard words and made-up words (*bro, hood, groovy, cool, hip*). It may be vivid and colorful, but it is extremely informal. It is usually short-lived, and meanings are neither constant nor consistent. Someone or something that was *the cat's pajamas* in the thirties might be *cool* today. Sometimes the word *bad* means "good," and other times it means "not good." Slang does not accurately communicate meaning. If you are not sure of the appropriateness of a word, check a dictionary and do not use it if it is labeled *slang*.

▶ **College Writing**   Most of your *college writing* will fall somewhere between formal and informal diction, depending on the assignment. Generally, assignments dealing with personal experiences will be more informal in style, whereas research papers, essay answers to examination questions, literary criticism, and so on require a more formal style. Colloquial and regional expressions, slang, and other nonstandard usage are generally inappropriate in college writing.

Unacceptable Expressions   Some of the following words and expressions may be acceptable in informal situations or in certain regions, but you should avoid using them in your college writing.

although, while	Do not use *while* for *although* if there is any chance of confusion.
	Although (not *while*) it was not raining, Sue bought an umbrella.

A.M., P.M.	Use after specific times, not as alternatives for morning and evening.
as to	Do not use *as to* as a substitute for *about*.
	The police questioned the suspect *about* (not *as to*) his recent activities.
at, to	Do not use *at* and *to* after *where*.
	Where are you going? (not Where are you going *to*?)
	Where is it? (not Where is it *at*?)
being as, being that	Not acceptable. Use *because* or *since*.
	Because (not *being as*) I overslept, I was late for class.
better	Do not substitute *better* for *had better*.
	We *had better* (not *better*) study for the test.
but, however, yet	Do not combine these words; use them separately.
	They won the battle; *however* (not *but however*), they lost the war.
center around	Do not use *center around*; use *center on*.
	The Ritalin controversy *centers on* (not *around*) misdiagnosis of teenagers.
could of, would of	*Could've, would've, should've* sound like *could of, would of, should of*, but they are not.
should of	They are contractions of *could have, would have*, and *should have*.
	Do not use contractions in your college writing.
	They *would have* (not *would've*) danced all night if they *could have* (not *could've*).
different from	He is *different from* his twin in temperament.
different than	Often used in speech to mean unlike, but it is not acceptable in college writing.
got to	Not acceptable. Use *have to, has to*, or *must*.

have got	I *have to* (not *have got to*) read *The Sound and the Fury* this weekend.
if, whether	Use *whether,* not *if,* in indirect questions or to express a doubt.
	I wonder *whether* (not *if*) the author treats Pat Garrett too kindly in sagas.
	"I am not sure *whether* [not *if*] I am dreaming or remembering." —Eugene Ionesco
irregardless	Unacceptable form of *regardless.*
	Positions in Congress are based on length of service, *regardless* of ability.
inside of, outside of	The *of* is not necessary. He stepped *inside* (not *inside of*) the building.
is when, is where	Do not use these words in definitions.
	Wrong: Self-love *is when* a person wants to promote his or her own well-being.
	Right: Self-love is the desire to promote one's own well-being.
	Wrong: A sand trap *is where* golfers face a hazard.
	Right: A sand trap is a hazard on a golf course.
kind of, sort of	Not acceptable. Instead, use *rather* or *somewhat.*
	The Saga of Billy the Kid is a *rather* (not *kind of*) interesting book.
lots, lots of, a lot of	Do not use these expressions; instead, use *many, much,* or *a great deal.*
most	Do not use *most* for *almost.*
	Almost (not *most*) all the students had read "How to Mark a Book."
plus	Do not use *plus* as a substitute for *and.*
	The baby ate all his vegetables *and* (not *plus*) a jar of peaches.

rarely ever	In college writing, use *rarely* or *hardly ever.*
	She *rarely* calls me, and I *hardly ever* call her.
real, really	*Real* means "genuine," and *really* means "actually."
	Do not use *real* and *really* as intensifiers.
	Rhonda is (not *real*) pretty and has a (not *really*) pleasant disposition.
reason is because	Unacceptable. Use *that* with reason, not *because.*
	The reason he was late is *that* (not *because*) he couldn't find a parking space.
reason why	Unacceptable. Use one or the other.
	I understand the *reason* (not *reason why*) that caused you to be late.
	I understand *why* (not *reason why*) you were late.
right	Do not use *right* as an intensifier.
	Brandy performed *extremely* (not *right*) well in the dog show.
since	Do not use *since* for *because* if there is any chance of confusion.
	Because (not *since*) he lost his beloved, he plays sad music. (In this sentence *since* could mean either "from the time that he lost his beloved" or "on account of losing his beloved."
supposed to, used to	Be sure to keep the final *d* in these words.
	He *used* (not *use*) to practice when he *was supposed* (not *suppose*) to do so.
sure	Do not substitute *sure* for *surely* or *certainly.*
	Certainly (not *Sure*) I will come to your party.
thusly	Not acceptable. Do not substitute *thusly* for *thus.*
	"*Thus* [not *thusly*] is his cheek the map of days outworn." —Shakespeare
try and, sure and	Not acceptable. Use *try to* and *sure to.*

	I will *try to* (not *try and*) be on time.
type	Do not substitute *type* for *type of.*
	That *type of* (not *type*) sunscreen is most effective.
unique	Do not use with qualifiers such as *more, most,* or *very.*
	The Lowes found a *unique* (not *most unique*) table at a flea market.
wait on	Use *wait on* to indicate service, but do not substitute it for *wait for.*
	If the orderly cannot *wait on* me, I will *wait for* (not *wait on*) you.
where	Do not substitute *where* for *that.*
	I read *that* (not *where*) Amazon.com is selling kitchen gadgets.

EXERCISE 34

Underline the non-standard and informal language in the following sentences and then rewrite them, using language that is more appropriate for college work.

1. As a fact, I remember of seeing him.

2. The judge prohibited Melissa to drive an automobile for six months.

3. She don't like him, and he better get use to it.

4. I should of returned my library book today.

5. I've got to be more punctual, but I sort of loose track of time.

6. Henry was suppose to remind me, but he has alot of things on his mind.

7. The reason why I ordered a hamburger was because the steak was way too high.

8. A diner is a place where you can get good food that is different than the food in fast-food joints.

9. Jim, who is hip to the happenings in our chemistry class, told me that the instructor wants for us to finish our lab experiment tomorrow.

10. Recently, I read where Groucho Marx said, "Finding a four-leaf clover is a sign that you have been down on your hands and knees."

Avoiding Offensive Language

Writers who want to reach the largest possible audience and who do not want to anger or alienate their readers, do not use terms and epithets that insult, belittle, or demean other people.

▶ **Derogatory Terms**   Avoid using *racial, ethnic, religious, age, class, regional, physical ability,* or *sexual orientation* terms that are derogatory. Although some of these terms change according to what is considered politically correct at a given time, generally, try to choose words that you would not find offensive if you were a member of that group.

Offensive	Non-Offensive
Chinaman	Chinese man
Bohunk	person from east-central Europe
redneck	white, rural laborer
handicap	disability
queer	gay or homosexual

EXERCISE 35

Revise the following sentences, replacing offensive expressions with non-offensive words.

1. Derogatory: My neighbor is a *WASP.*

2. Derogatory: Some people think all people from the South are *rednecks* or *crackers.*

3. Racist: Some of her best friends are *Wops.*

4. Homophobic: Lizzy's delightful new neighbor, a movie producer, is a *queer.*

5. Discriminatory: She is a *JAP* (Jewish American Princess).

6. Discriminatory: Her father is a well-known *Jew* lawyer.

7. Discriminatory: He tried to *welsh* on his bet.

8. Homophobic: Laura wrote an article about the financial discrimination that *lesbos* and *homos* face.

9. Derogatory: The young man in the wheel chair is a *cripple.*

10. Discriminatory: The *decrepit old* man was *deaf.*

▶ **Sexist Language** Avoid using sexist language that degrades or discriminates against either sex. Terms such as *hunks, chicks, studs, babes,* and *biddies* demean others and detract from your objectivity and sensitivity. Probably the most common form of sexist language is the result of using male terms generically.

Sexist	Nonsexist
policeman	police officer
man-sized portion	large portion
men at work	people at work

Using the generic term *he* or *him* when the person could be male or female is particularly problematic because the correction can result in an awkward or ungrammatical construction. To avoid this problem, use the third person plural or the phrase *he or she*—not *he/she.*

Sexist	To earn high marks *a student* must complete all *his* homework.
Awkward	To earn high marks *a student* must complete all *his/her* homework.
Improved	To earn high marks *a student* must complete all *his or her* homework.
Ungrammatical	To earn high marks *a student* must complete all *their* homework.
Improved	To earn high marks *students* must complete all *their* homework.

EXERCISE 36

Revise the following sentences, avoiding sexist language and awkward or grammatically incorrect constructions.

1. My wife is a chick; my mother-in-law is an old hen; my neighbor is an old biddy.

2. The mailman frequently delivers my mail to my neighbor.

3. A pizza delivery boy is expected to be familiar with the neighborhood.

4. A prospective fireman must pass a rigorous physical test before he can be hired.

5. When you punish your child, be sure that he understands why you are punishing him.

6. In 1674 an English Puritan said that slave hunters were the enemies of mankind.

7. When I choose a physician, I always interview him to be sure that he is a good listener.

8. Man cannot live by bread alone.

9. Who is the chairman of the finance committee?

10. Do you often write to your congressman?

Avoiding Ineffective Words

▶ **Jargon**   Jargon is the specialized or technical language of a trade, a profession, or similar group. When you use specialized or technical words and phrases outside the group that understands them, consider your purpose and your audience. An educator may use educational jargon in a letter or article written for other educators, but that jargon would not be appropriate for a general audience. When you are writing for a general audience, define or explain the meaning of any technical words.

EXERCISE 37

Write a paragraph for a group that uses a specialized language—one that you understand, such as a hobby, a sport, a business, a trade, or a craft. After you have written the paragraph for a specialized audience, rewrite it for a general audience.

▶ **Pretentious Language**   Avoid using an overblown or stuffy word when a plain one is effective.

Plain Word	Pretentious Word
table napkin	napery
bathroom	lavatory
knives	cutlery
brother or sister	sibling
dog	canine
old	superannuated
think	cogitate
convert	transmogrify

EXERCISE 38

Revise the following sentences, substituting simple, straightforward words and expressions for the pretentious ones. Use a dictionary to help you translate unfamiliar words.

1. He is a *penurious* person.

2. She *perambulated* across the street.

3. Ghosts have been *observed* in the *cemetery*.

4. The medication she *ingested* caused *alopecia*.

5. Will you please *bifurcate* this plant.

6. I work for an *eleemosynary* organization.

7. When did your *ancient canine expire?*

8. Your lovely new blouse is *besmirched*.

9. Bess is the most *disputatious* person I know.

10. He is a *vainglorious* person.

▶ **Worn-Out Expressions**   Worn-out expressions, sometimes called clichés, are expressions that have lost their vigor because they have been overused. Avoid using these expressions because they add nothing to your writing, and many of them no longer make sense. *Hitting the nail on the head* or *being dead as a doornail* tells your readers nothing and will probably confuse rather than clarify.

Common Worn-Out Expressions

accidents will happen

add insult to injury

after all is said and done

bite off more than you can chew

easier said than done

few and far between

in no uncertain terms

to make a long story short

out of the frying pan into the fire

what goes around comes around

a penny for your thoughts

rush to judgment

viselike grip

straight as an arrow

EXERCISE 39

Revise the following sentences, substituting simple, straightforward language for the worn-out expressions.

1. My best friend and I had an argument, but today we decided to *bury the hatchet.*

2. Good friends are *few and far between.*

3. Although she has a few faults, she *is a diamond in the rough.*

4. I may not be a *budding genius,* but I know when to *come in out of the rain.*

5. My other friend called and said that her dog was *at death's door.*

6. *To make a long story short,* I finally went to her house and found that the dog had eaten too many doggy biscuits but was *none the worse for wear.*

7. I told her *in no uncertain terms* that if she wanted her pet to live to *a ripe old age* she should *last but not least* put him on a diet.

8. Both Virignia and Belinda are *good as gold* and are *true blue friends.*

9. *Beyond the shadow of a doubt,* Belinda has more *trials and tribulations* that anyone I know.

10. *After all is said and done,* I am glad I have two good friends with whom I can be *fair and square.*

Review Exercises

Revise the passages, using language that is appropriate for college writing.

REVIEW EXERCISE 40

1. In 1434 this Portugee dude by the name of Gil Eannes decided he'd explore Africa's west coast. 2. Being as there were a bunch of strange tales about this area, sailors didn't want to go irregardless of the promises made to them by Eannes' boss, Prince Henry the Navigator. 3. They were hale and hearty, the type men who were used to trials and tribulations—not wimps or male bimbos. 4. The reason why they were real afraid was because they had heard some scary tales about this part of the world. 5. Sure, they had heard about sailors being wiped out by sea monsters, deep-sixed in sinister whirlpools, or pushed off the edge of the world. 6. To make a long story short, they were afraid they'd not survive the trip, but, however, when they came to what they figured would be the end of the world, they found a lovely coastline. 7. They didn't see no sea monsters plus no boiling whirlpools. 8. After fifteen attempts and dog gone near fifteen years, these Portugee sailors sailed beyond what was once reckoned to be the edge of the world. 9. Last but not least, they explored the coastline for another thirty miles, and this is where they went ashore and spotted a plant that looked kind of familiar—rosemary. 10. They picked a bunch of the stuff for good ole Prince Henry and headed for home, being plumb downright proud of theirselves.

REVIEW EXERCISE 41

1. Being that America has been discovered numerous times, one wonders why its discovery by Columbus—a Johnny-come-lately— was different than the other discoveries. 2. After all is said and done, historical eggheads agree that America was first discovered by Asians who crossed the narrow Bering Strait to Alaska. 3. Beyond a shadow of a doubt, these early settlers spread out all over the place—across North America and then across South America. 4. Recently, a prof at Peking University asserted that five Chinamen had sailed the Pacific to Mexico in A.D. 459. 5. Another group of possible discoverers center around the Irish. 6. The Irish could of sailed to America after the Norsemen went and drove them out of Iceland about A.D. 870. 7. According to legend, some dude from Wales landed on the shores of Mobile Bay in 1170 and established a colony. 8. This most unique legend has served as the basis for a bunch of novels about the Mandan Indians—reckoned by some to be descended from the Welsh settlers. 9. The Norse discovery of the New World seems to be pretty much documented. 10. As regards to Columbus, he sort of blundered into America while trying to locate the Asian mainland, and thinking that he'd reached India, he dubbed them Indians.

PART 6

Understanding Punctuation and Mechanics

My attitude toward punctuation is that it ought to be as conventional as possible. The game of golf would lose a good deal if croquet mallets and billiard cues were allowed on the putting green. You ought to be able to show that you can do it a good deal better than anyone else with the regular tools before you have a license to bring in your own improvements.

—ERNEST HEMINGWAY

Understanding and using punctuation marks (*commas, semicolons, end marks, apostrophes, quotation marks, parentheses, dashes, colons,* and *hyphens*) and mechanics (*capital letters, abbreviations, italics,* and *numbers*) is essential for you to clearly and effectively communicate your ideas in writing.

Using Commas

The comma (,) is the most often used and misused mark of punctuation. When you were learning to read, your teacher probably told you to slow down for commas and come to a full stop for periods. This is good advice for reading, but it does not always work for writing. To clearly express your ideas you need to know and use the generally accepted principals of comma usage. In this chapter you will learn to use commas to set off

- independent clauses
- items in a series
- nonessential material

- introductory material
- miscellaneous expressions
- everyday material

Setting Off Independent Clauses

Use a comma and one of the FANBOYS (*for, and, nor, but, or, yet, so*) to link two independent clauses that are about the same idea.

CONNECTING WORDS	PURPOSES OF CONNECTIONS
For	Cause (reason, object, aim, or purpose of an action or activity)
And	Addition (together or along with, in addition to, as well as)
Nor	Negation (not the case, not either, or not)
But	Contrast (on the contrary, contrary to expectation, exception)
Or	Choice (an alternative, uncertainty, indefiniteness)
Yet	Difference (emphasize or show difference, despite, nevertheless)
So	Effect (result, consequence, in order that)

In ancient Greece the world was one of mystery and surprise, **and** the Greeks tried to explain natural phenomena through their imagined stories—myths.

They believed that strange and mighty spirits lived in the skies and in secret caves of the earth, **and** they came to think of these spirits as gods who also had human qualities.

Note: You may leave out the comma when the clauses are very short.

Go ahead **and** I'll follow.   Take it **or** leave it.

Note: When the independent clauses are long or complex or contain other punctuation, you may use a semicolon between them instead of a comma.

Robert the Bruce, the greatest of Scotland's kings, was born in 1274 and was probably brought up at the English court of King Edward I and had even fought on the English side(,)**; but** at the age of thirty-two, inspired by the fight that William Wallace, the second greatest hero of Scotland, had waged against England, he decided to assert his right to the Scottish throne and fight the English.

Caution 1   Do not join two independent clauses with a comma alone. If you do, the result is a serious grammatical error called a *comma splice*. The comma must be followed by *for, and, nor, but, or, yet,* or *so.*

No   The ancient Greeks did not know what caused lightning or what made the wind **blow, they** tried to explain these conditions through stories.

Yes   The ancient Greeks did not know what caused lightning or what made the wind **blow, so** they tried to explain these conditions through stories.

Caution 2   Put the comma before the joining word, not after it. This is a common careless mistake.

No   The Greeks were careful observers of events in their world **and,** they tried to explain them.

Yes   The Greeks were careful observers of events in their **world, and** they tried to explain them.

Caution 3   Do not use a comma with a joining word when it joins a compound verb or a compound subject.

No   The dog <u>whined</u> all day, and <u>howled</u> all night. (*compound verb*)

Yes   The dog <u>whined</u> all day and <u>howled</u> all night.

No   The gingham <u>dog</u>, and the calico <u>cat</u> were great friends. (*compound subject*)

Yes   The gingham <u>dog</u> and the calico <u>cat</u> were great friends.

EXERCISE 1

Use a comma and one of the FANBOYS to link the paired independent clauses.

1. The Greeks tried to make sense of their world. People have been trying to do this ever since.

2. They saw that the splendors of nature were often linked with danger.

   They believed disasters occurred because the gods were punishing people for their evil deeds.

3. They tried to appease the gods when they experienced floods, earthquakes, and storms.

   They believed that these conditions were weapons used by Jupiter and Neptune to punish them.

4. Jupiter was the supreme Greek god. Neptune was the Greek god of the sea.

5. Greek sailors would return home after being gone for several months. Sometimes they never returned.

6. Often the returning sailors told tales of monsters who tried to devour them. They tried to devour their ship.

   They wanted to tell about their experiences. They were trying to explain the relationship of the cause and effect of these experiences.

7. Some of the most feared sea monsters were called harpies—a loathsome combination of a woman and a fierce bird. They were always hungry.

8. Today, a predatory person may be called a harpy. A shrewish woman may be called a harpy.

9. Sometimes, ships never returned to Greece. To explain the disappearances, the Greeks created fanciful stories.

10. According to one story, the sailors landed on the shores of the African coast. They ate lotus blossoms that destroyed their desire to return home.

Setting Off Items in a Series

▶ **Words, Phrases, or Clauses** Use commas to separate three or more words, phrases, or clauses in a series.

Words	The people offered gifts of food to the gods of the sky, earth, and water.

Phrases   The Greeks believed the gods controlled everything including the rising of the sun, the setting of the sun, the crash of thunder, the flash of lightening, and the growth of plants.

Usually, independent clauses in a series are separated by a semicolon; however, short independent clauses may be separated by commas.

Clauses   She dieted, she starved, she worked out, she ran, and she lost only five pounds.

Note: When the items in the series already contain commas, use semicolons instead of commas between the major divisions.

Did Indiana Jones visit Athens, Greece; Rome, Italy; and Istanbul, Turkey?

Ancient sailors claimed to have encountered the following dangerous female monsters: Circe (**SUR**-see), the enchantress who turned men into **pigs;** Scylla (**SIL**-uh), a sea monster who devoured **sailors;** and Charybdis (kuh-**RIB**-dis), who could drink up whole gulfs.

Caution 1   Do not put a comma before the first or after the last item in a series.

No   Irish stew **contains,** lamb, potatoes, onions, parsley, thyme, water, salt, and pepper.

Yes   Irish stew **contains** lamb, potatoes, onions, parsley, thyme, water, salt, and pepper.

No   Scotch broth contains stewing beef, barley, and **vegetables,** and is simmered slowly.

Yes   Scotch broth contains stewing beef, barley, and **vegetables** and is simmered slowly.

Caution 2   Add the comma before the connecting word that signals the end of the list. Journalists often leave this comma out because they consider it unnecessary, but sometimes leaving this comma out can change the meaning of the sentence.

He wanted his estate to be divided equally among his <u>brothers</u>, <u>sisters</u>, <u>nieces and nephews</u>.

(The estate will be divided *three* ways.)

He wanted his estate to be divided equally among his <u>brothers</u>, <u>sisters</u>, <u>nieces</u>, and <u>nephews</u>.

(The estate will be divided *four* ways.)

Caution 3   Do not put commas between items in a series if *and* or *or* is used between them.

> **No**   The highly colorful house was painted pink, **and** green, **and** yellow, **and** blue.

> **Yes**   The highly colorful house was painted pink **and** green **and** yellow **and** blue.

EXERCISE 2

Add commas as needed to separate items in a series.

1. One of the gods gave wild creatures courage swiftness and strength.

2. This generous god gave some animals wings some fins some sharp claws and some fangs.

3. Prometheus (pruh-**MEE**-thee-uhs) wanted to give fire to the people. With fire, they could fight off wild beasts make their food more palatable and live more comfortably in cold weather.

4. Since Jupiter did not want people to have fire, Prometheus stole it for them. He went to the home of the gods lighted a torch at their hearth shielded the flame in a hollow stalk and delivered it to the people.

5. Jupiter punished Prometheus by stripping him naked hanging him on the side of a mountain and leaving him there for years.

6. Because Jupiter was angry at the people for accepting the forbidden fire, he punished them by giving them diseases such as mumps measles and smallpox.

7. He also gave them disagreeable traits such as jealousy anger selfishness envy and hatred.

8. According to myth, the gods created a woman. They gave her beauty gentleness kindness and dignity.

9. They taught her to speak softly to use winning words and to sing sweet songs.

10. They named her Pandora (pan-**DOR**-uh) gave her a beautiful box told her to never open it and sent her to earth.

▶ **Adjectives**   In most cases use commas to separate two or more adjectives that modify a noun or pronoun.

He is a handsome, well mannered, happy teenager.

The cool, clear water flowed from the pump.

Caution 1 Do not put a comma after the last adjective.

No A tall, slender, graceful, girl suddenly appeared.

Yes A tall, slender, graceful girl suddenly appeared.

Caution 2 When the adjective next to the noun seems to be a part of the noun, do not put a comma after it.

No It was a beautiful, bright, sunshiny, June morning.

Yes It was a beautiful, bright, sunshiny June morning.

June morning is thought of as one unit. The adjectives modify *June morning,* not *morning.*

Caution 3 When one of the adjectives in a series modifies another word in the series, do not put a comma between them.

No She was driving a bright, red Porsche.

Yes She was driving a bright red Porsche.

The adjective *bright* modifies the word *red,* not *Porsche.*

When you are not sure whether to separate adjectives with commas, read the sentence and insert *and* between them or reverse the order of the adjectives. If a sentence reads well when *and* is inserted or when the order of the adjectives is reversed, separate the adjectives with a comma.

No She was driving a bright **and** red Porsche. (Inserted *and* does not work.)

No She was driving a red bright Porsche. (Reversed order does not work.)

Yes The tall **and** blonde **and** beautiful woman drove away in the Porsche. (Inserted *and* works.)

Yes The beautiful, tall, blonde woman drove away in the Porsche. (Reversed order works.)

Caution 4 Do not use commas between adjectives if they are connected by *and* or *or.*

No The ten black**, and** white puppies frolicked around their mother.

Yes The ten black **and** white puppies frolicked around their mother.

EXERCISE 3

Add commas as needed between adjectives. Mark correct sentences with a C.

1. The beautiful all-gifted Pandora was happy on earth, but she often looked at the lovely ornate box that the gods had given her and wondered what it contained.

2. One day she decided that one little quick peek into the box would not cause any problems.

3. It was a thrilling exciting moment.

4. She forced open the intricate little catch and lifted the lid, and all the evils of the world flew out.

5. The lovely happy Pandora became a sad unhappy woman.

6. The inquisitive young woman had brought grief, suffering, and disease to the world.

7. The lovely little box was now empty except for one spirit—hope.

8. Although Jupiter wanted to punish people for accepting the gift of fire, he felt sorry for them and included one good important spirit in the box.

9. Because he pitied them, he gave them the marvelous ever-enduring spirit of hope.

10. The ancient Greeks invented the story of Pandora and her box to explain the enduring abiding hopeful spirit people have in the face of adversity. To paraphrase the poet Wallace Rice, "Hope is a good effective patent medicine for disease, disaster, and sin."

Practice Exercises

Combine paired independent clauses with a comma and one of the FANBOYS (*for, and, nor, but, or, yet,* or *so*). Add necessary commas between items in a series and between adjectives. Mark correct sentences with a C.

EXERCISE 4

1. In Greek mythology the Amazons came from Asia Minor. They were strong fierce and brave.

2. These women governed the tribe. They fought while the men did domestic chores.

3. Theseus, the famous adventurer and Athenian hero, waged war against the Amazons. Later, he abducted their queen.

4. In retaliation the Amazons attacked Athens. After a bloody hard-fought battle, they were defeated.

5. The strong courageous popular Greek hero, Hercules had problems with the Amazons. He is more famous for performing the Twelve Labors of Hercules.

6. He killed a lion a nine-headed water serpent captured a deer and performed nine other great feats.

7. The lion was no ordinary lion. No sword was sharp enough to pierce its skin.

8. After he strangled the lion, he always wore its skin. It protected him from injury.

9. Next, Hercules had to kill a Hydra (**HIE**-druh). He had to do it in its native swampy lair.

10. The Hydra had nine heads. When one head was cut off, two others grew in its place.

EXERCISE 5

1. Neptune, god of the sea, had given a great bull to a king. This bull was wreaking havoc. 2. Hercules caught the bull bound it and ended its destructive rampage. 3. His eighth task took him to the stables again. This time he had to clean out the animals—not their stables. 4. A cruel savage king owned equally savage horses. Their favorite food was human flesh. 5. Hercules killed the king. Then he fed his body to the horses. 6. The ninth task took him into the land of the mighty warlike Amazons. He had been given the task of getting the queen's jeweled girdle. 7. The queen was going to give him the girdle as a gift. She heard a rumor that he really had not come to get the girdle but had come to capture her. 8. The queen called her well-armed trusty guards to defend her. Hercules won the battle and escaped with the girdle. 9. For his tenth task, Hercules had to steal a highly prized red oxen from a monster Spanish king. 10. Hercules went to Spain stole the oxen used a golden bowl as a boat and his lion skin for a sail and escaped unharmed. 11. Hercules could not accomplish his eleventh task alone. He was required to gather golden apples from a garden that only Atlas could find. 12. Atlas could not look for the garden. He was busy holding the heavens on his shoulders. 13. Hercules offered to hold up the heavens for him if he would collect the apples. Atlas happily set off to get the apples. 14. Strong as he was, Hercules found the weight of the heavens to be almost unbearable. He was happy when Atlas returned with the apples. 15. Atlas, however, had enjoyed his vacation. He was not anxious to return to his burdensome task of holding up the heavens. 16. He told Hercules that he would deliver the apples for him. Hercules said that he would be glad to continue holding up the heavens while Atlas delivered the apples. He would like for him to hold the heavens for a minute so that he could rest his back. 17. Atlas took the heavens; and Hercules smiled grabbed the apples ran away and thus completed his eleventh task. 18. For his final task, Hercules had to go to Hades. He had to capture a savage three-headed dog and return to earth. 19. The monster dog went mad when he saw daylight and spit poisonous foam upon the earth. The spots where the foam landed became the birthplaces of all poisonous plants. 20. After all his labors were completed, Jupiter granted his son Hercules immortality transported him to the heavens and gave him a beautiful wife.

Setting Off Nonessential Material

Often sentences contain material that explains or qualifies the main meaning of the sentence. Sometimes it is essential, and sometimes it is not. Nonessential material adds interesting or useful information but does not affect the central meaning of the sentence. To determine whether material is essential or nonessential, leave it out. If the main meaning of the sentence remains unchanged, the word or group of words is not essential and should be set off with commas. If the main meaning of the sentence changes, or the sentence does not make sense when you leave out the material, it is essential and should not be set off with commas.

▶ **Nonessential Clauses**   A *nonessential clause* is a dependent clause that is not essential to the meaning of the sentence. Look for clauses that begin with *who, which, that, whom, whose, when,* or *where* and decide whether the clause is essential or not. If a clause is not essential to the meaning of the sentence, set it off with commas.

Nonessential	Hetty Green, ~~who was probably the world's most miserly woman,~~ left an estate of $95 million.
Essential	Hetty Green was the only millionaire *who ate her food cold rather than spend money for fuel to heat it.*
Essential	The story *which best exemplifies her miserliness* is the one about her son.
Nonessential	Hetty, ~~who tried to get free medical treatment,~~ delayed getting treatment for her son's badly injured leg until it was too late to save his leg.
Essential	A leg *that could have been saved* was amputated.

Note: *That* is used to introduce only essential clauses. *Which* can be used to introduce both essential and nonessential clauses. Many writers prefer to use *which* only for nonessential clauses.

Essential	The longest recorded fight *that was fought with boxers wearing gloves* lasted 110 rounds, 7 hours, and 19 minutes.
Nonessential	The shortest prizefight on record, ~~which occurred in a Golden Gloves Tournament in Minneapolis,~~ lasted four seconds.

▶ **Nonessential Phrases**   A *nonessential phrase,* like a nonessential clause, is set off by commas because it is not necessary to the meaning of the sentence.

-*ing* Words   Look for phrases beginning with an *-ing* word—*walking, saving, feeling, beating,* and so on—or beginning with an *-ed, -t,* or *-en* word—*walked, saved, felt, beaten,* and so on.

Nonessential   Jackie Fields, ~~winning the Olympic boxing championship at the age of sixteen,~~ holds the record for being the youngest Olympic boxing champion.

Essential   Rocky Marciano *retired in 1956* as an undefeated champion.

Nonessential   Rocky Marciano, ~~retired in 1956,~~ is the only heavyweight champion who never lost a professional bout.

Prepositions   Look for groups of words beginning with a preposition.

Nonessential   The trick or treaters, ~~with bags full of candy,~~ scampered home.

Essential   The man *with the bag of candy* seems to think he is Santa Claus.

Appositives   Look for nouns—often with modifiers—put beside another noun to explain or identify it.

Essential   Glenn Campbell's song "*Gentle on My Mind*" became a best-seller.

Nonessential   Scott Gordon, ~~my best friend in college,~~ is a fan of Muhammed Ali.

Nonessential   Muhammed Ali, ~~originally Cassius Marcellus Clay,~~ defeated Sonny Liston, George Foreman, and Leon Spinks.

EXERCISE 6

Use commas to set off nonessential clauses and phrases. Mark correct sentences with a C.

1. In Greek mythology, Pygmalion (pig-**MAYL**-yuhn) a young sculptor was blessed by Venus.

2. He carved an ivory statue of a woman so beautiful that he fell in love with her.

3. He prayed that she would come to life.

4. Venus the goddess of love answered his prayers, and on the day of the festival of Venus, the beautiful statue came to life.

5. Venus helped Hippomenes (hi-**POM**-uh-neez) another lovesick young man win his wife.

6. He was in love with Atalanta the girl who was famed for her speed and hunting ability.

7. Atalanta who had fought and killed a wild boar by herself refused to marry anyone who could not outrun her.

8. Suitors racing with Atalanta and losing were put to death.

9. In the race with Atalanta, Hippomenes carried three golden apples ones that Venus had given to him.

10. Hippomenes with Venus' advice in mind dropped the apples one at a time while they were racing.

11. Atalanta who could not resist stopping to pick up the apples lost the race.

12. Juno the goddess of marriage also took an interest in the love lives of human beings.

13. Alcyone (al-**SEE**-uh-nee) throwing herself into the sea upon learning of her husband's death was changed into a kingfisher.

14. Juno taking pity on Alcyone returned her husband to her in the form of a kingfisher mate.

15. The kingfisher a fabled bird was supposed to calm the wind and the waves of the sea.

16. Our word *halcyon* (**HAL**-see-uhn) meaning "kingfisher" refers to calmness or peacefulness.

17. The word *tantalize* which also has a mythological connection comes from a story about Tantalus.

18. Tantalus Jupiter's son who tattled on the gods was sent to the worst part of Hades to be punished.

19. He had to stand in water that receded when he tried to drink it.

20. The fruit that was hanging above his head receded when he reached for it.

Setting Off Introductory Material

Use a comma after introductory material to make the sentence easier to read and to understand.

▶ **Introductory Words**   Use commas after *yes* and *no* and mild interjections such as *well* and *why*. An *interjection* is an independent word, usually expressing emotion, that can be used as an exclamation.

> *Well,* I thought you would never call.   *Yes,* I did my homework completely.

Note: Generally, use exclamation points, not commas, to set off stronger interjections.

> *Wow!* That was quite a game.

Caution   If the introductory word cannot be left out without changing the meaning of the sentence, do not set it off with a comma.

No man is an island unto himself.   *Why* were you late?

Use a comma after words such as *however* and *consequently (conjunctive adverbs)* and after transitional expressions.

Nevertheless, I will respect your views on the subject.

Of course, I know that you will respect my views.

Note: *See* Part 2: Commonly Used Transitions, the Relationships They Express, and Their Meanings (p. 26).

▶ **Introductory Phrases**   Generally, use a comma after an introductory phrase. An introductory phrase may begin with one or more prepositions, a *verb + -ing* (present time) a *verb + -ed, -d, -t, -en,* or *-n* (past time), or with a *to + a verb* word.

Prepositions	*On* a *sunny afternoon in August,* Barbie invited Ken to ride in her new Ferrari.
Verb + -ing word	*Thinking* that Barbie was not a good driver, Ken kept telling her how to drive.
To + a verb	*To show* her displeasure with his back-seat driving, she told him she was sorry that she invited him to ride in her new car.
Verb + -ed word	*Convinced* that she was truly displeased with his attitude, he stopped giving her instructions.

Caution   Do not confuse a phrase beginning with the *verb + -ing* or *to + a verb* words used as the subject of a sentence with one that is not used as the subject of a sentence. A *verb + -ing* word phrase or a *to + a verb* phrase that serves as the subject of a sentence is not separated from the rest of the sentence with a comma.

Verb + -ing subject	*Drinking and driving* is a lethal combination.
To + a verb subject	*To mix these two activities* is pure foolishness.

Note: A single introductory prepositional phrase need not be followed by a comma unless it is parenthetical (*by the way, on the other hand,* and so on) or unless it is needed to prevent confusion.

Not necessary	*In the morning* he usually takes a brisk walk.
Parenthetical	*By the way,* I cannot walk with you today.
Clarity	*For the physically fit,* exercise is a way of life.

Frequently Used Introductory Words

anyway	also	yes
certainly	besides	no
finally	consequently	well
incidentally	furthermore	why
indeed	however	oh
instead	moreover	(verb +-ed words) angered, frustrated, annoyed
likewise	nevertheless	(verb + -ing words) weeping, smiling, laughing
meanwhile	otherwise	(to + verb words) to love, to succeed, to hate
namely	then	in fact
next	there	of course
now	thus	really
similarly	still	in addition
undoubtedly		

EXERCISE 7

Add commas as needed to set off introductory words and phrases. Mark correct sentences with a C.

1. Supposedly North Dakota has the largest number of game and bird preserves of any state.

2. Incidentally North Dakota is governed under the constitution of 1889.

3. Furthermore few changes have been made in that constitution since it was written.

4. Begun in 1927 and completed in 1941 Mount Rushmore has become one of the nation's most beloved national memorials.

5. Located near Keystone in the Black Hills of South Dakota it is visible for sixty miles.

6. Incidentally when Gutzon Borglum, the mountain's sculptor, announced his plans to carve a massive national monument from a mountain, many South Dakotans did not like the idea.

7. Saying statuary in the Black Hills was incongruous and ridiculous columnists compared it to keeping a cow in the rotunda of the Capitol.

8. Much to the critics' amazement the colossal faces of Presidents Washington, Jefferson, Roosevelt, and Lincoln proved to be neither incongruous nor ridiculous.

9. Indeed this memorial is awesome and impressive.

10. Towering 5,500 feet above sea level with each head as tall as a six-story building it has become one of this country's inspiring symbols of democracy.

▶ **Introductory Dependent Clauses**   Use a comma after an introductory dependent clause. A *clause* is a group of related words that contains a subject and a verb. An *independent clause* makes sense by itself. A *dependent clause* does not make sense by itself. A dependent clause begins with a dependent word such as *after, although, as, because, unless,* and *while. See* Part 2: Dependent Words and the Relationships They Express (p. 28).

> ***Although*** *I like to play in the snow,* I do not like to drive in it.

> ***Whenever*** *I have to drive in snow,* I am extremely careful.

Caution   A dependent clause at the end of a sentence is not usually set off with a comma.

> Jamie could not buy his textbooks ***because*** *he left his money at home.*

EXERCISE 8

Add commas as needed to set off introductory dependent clauses.

1. When Sitting Bull was young he was a thoughtful and careful boy.

2. Because he was quiet and methodical he was named Slow.

3. Although he was only fourteen years old Slow was invited to participate in a war party.

4. When the warriors encountered the other tribe Slow was the first to score a *coup* (kooh)—touch an enemy warrior's body without causing injury.

5. Although any *coup* was important the first *coup* of a battle was the most important one.

6. Since scoring the first *coup* was the greatest honor a Plains Indian could earn in warfare Slow's father changed his son's name from Slow to Sitting Bull.

7. When Sitting Bull was twenty-five years old he killed a Crow chief in a one-on-one battle.

8. After he killed the Crow chief he was elected chief of the Midnight Strong Hearts—the bravest warriors of the Hunkpapa.

9. Although Sitting Bull had contact with white men it was limited until the 1860s.

10. When he met with them it was for the purpose of exchanging buffalo hides for guns and ammunition.

EXERCISE 9

Add commas as needed to set off introductory words and phrases and dependent clauses. Mark correct sentences with a C.

1. For over 20,000 years Native North Americans had lived on the plains and deserts of the West. 2. Through the years the patterns of their lives were fairly constant. 3. For example they farmed the land, hunted game, and fished the rivers and streams as their ancestors did. 4. Then one day in 1519 something happened on the coast of what is now Mexico that changed their lives forever. 5. On that day eleven stallions and five mares were unloaded from a Spanish ship. 6. Before the arrival of this Spanish herd there had been no horses in either North or South America since prehistoric times. 7. Although the modern horse evolved in North America it later became extinct. 8. When the Aztecs first saw men on horseback they thought that the strange animal had the head and torso of a man but had the body of a four-footed animal. 9. After the Spanish introduced the first modern horses into the New World horses spread across the continent. 10. Although horses were bought, sold, and bartered many were stolen.

Setting Off Miscellaneous Expressions

Use commas to set off *interrupters, transitional expressions, contrasting phrases, direct address,* and *tag questions.*

▶ **Interrupters and Transitional Expressions**   Use commas to set off interrupters—words that interrupt or digress—such as *I am sure, on the other hand, on the contrary, after all, by the way,* and so on that qualify other statements and expressions such as *however, therefore, furthermore,* and so on that show a connection between parts of a sentence. *See* Part 2: Commas and Connecting Words (p. 23).

The instructor will, *I am sure,* give us additional time for the assignment.

She may, *however,* change her mind.

▶ **Alternative or Contrasting Phrases**   Use commas to set off alternative or contrasting phrases. In an alternative phrase, a situation presents a choice between two mutually exclusive possibilities.

Do your grocery shopping after you have eaten, *never when you are hungry.*

In an alternative phrase, two conditions are set in opposition in order to show or emphasize differences.

Riding Citation, Eddie Arcaro, *not Willie Shoemaker,* won the Triple Crown in 1948.

▶ **Direct Address**   Use commas to set off the names of people spoken to directly. The direct address may be at the beginning, middle, or end of the sentence. Use one comma to set off a direct address at the beginning or end of a sentence, and use two to set off a direct address in the middle.

Dale, did you go fishing yesterday?   Yes, I went fishing yesterday, *John.*

I'm sure, *my friend,* that you caught and released them.

▶ **Tag Questions**   Use commas to set off tag questions. A tag question is a helping verb plus a pronoun attached to a statement. Use one comma to set off a tag question at the end of a sentence, and use two to set off a tag question in the middle.

You're going to the party, *aren't you?* It doesn't seem possible, *does it,* that the cat is gone.

Practice Exercises

Use commas as needed to set off transitional words and phrases, contrasting elements, direct addresses, and tag questions.

EXERCISE 10

1. You have read about the Battle of Troy haven't you?

2. As you probably know, it had its beginning at a wedding to which all the gods and goddesses were invited except one.

3. Since the goddess Discord was not invited of course she was frustrated, and she threw a golden apple among the guests.

4. Do you know what was inscribed on the apple students?

5. Mr. Johnson I believe it bore the following inscription: "For the fairest."

6. Adam you are correct. You knew you were didn't you?

7. Juno, Minerva, and Venus needless to say claimed the apple.

8. Jupiter not Neptune was asked to proclaim who was the fairest goddess at the wedding.

9. Jupiter however refused to make the decision.

10. He sent the three goddesses to Mt. Ida to get a ruling thereby evading his responsibility.

EXERCISE 11

1. At Mt. Ida, Paris, the Prince of Troy who was tending his sheep, made the decision did he not?

2. Yes, Paris not Neptune was forced to decide which was the fairest of the three goddesses.

3. Juno promised him power and riches didn't she?

4. She did without a doubt and Minerva promised him glory and fame in war.

5. Venus however offered him the fairest of all women for his wife.

6. The young shepherd prince subsequently forgot all about his lovely wife and decided in favor of Venus.

7. Of course, the other goddesses were royally annoyed weren't they?

8. You are absolutely right Suzy. Paris without a doubt had made two dangerous enemies.

9. Paris sailed for Greece did he not?

10. When he reached Greece, he was hospitably received by Menelaus and his wife Helen was he not?

Setting Off Everyday Material

Use commas in dates and addresses, in openings and closings of letters, in long numbers, and between names and titles.

▶ **Dates and Addresses**   Commas are used to separate items in dates and addresses.

John and Mary Smith live at 26030 Dilkon Court, Oakland, California. Their first baby was born Tuesday, October 11, 2001.

Note: Dates may be written without a comma—11 October 2001. Commas are not used to separate the day from the month or the month from the year when the day is left out (September 2001). Commas are not used to separate the street number from the street or the state from the ZIP code.

▶ **Openings and Closings of Letters**   Commas are used after the salutation of a friendly letter and after the closing of any letter.

Dear John,   Sincerely yours,   Cordially,   Love,

▶ **Long Numbers**   Commas are used before every third digit—counting from the right—for a number of four digits or more.

1,500   10,000   135,000   1,365,000

Note: Commas are not used in addresses, telephone numbers, ZIP codes, four-digit year numbers, or page and line numbers.

▶ **Names and Titles or Degrees**   Commas are used after a person's name when it is followed by the abbreviation *Jr.* or *Sr.,* or by the abbreviation of an academic degree.

D. Darrel Ross, **DDS**   Rose Smith, **RN**   Philip Bruce, **Ph.D.**

If the name and title are at the beginning or in the middle of a sentence, use a comma after the title.

Martin Luther King, **Jr.,** was a great orator.

Note: Commas are not used between a name and *I, II, III,* and so on.

EXERCISE 12

Add commas where necessary to set off dates, addresses, openings and closings of letters, long numbers, and titles or degrees. Mark correct sentences with a C.

1. In 1550 many of the estates of St. Peter's Westminster England were appropriated to pay for the repairs of St. Paul's Cathedral.

2. In the United States nearly 5000 people were lynched between 1882 and 1962.

3. During the American Revolution, Charles Lynch, a public-spirited justice of the peace, presided over an unofficial court in Bedford County Virginia.

4. Joseph R. Biden Jr. from Scranton Pennsylvania was born November 20 1942.

5. According to Jack Leary, an American, he hiccuped 160 million times between 1948 and 1956 and tried 60000 remedies.

6. Lee Hartwell Ph.D. president of the Fred Hutchinson Cancer Research Center in Seattle Washington won a Nobel Prize October 2001.

7. A rifle shot fired on the bank of the Missouri River on May 14 1804 signaled the beginning of the Louis and Clark Expedition.

8. On January 18 1803 President Thomas Jefferson asked Congress for money to finance an expedition beyond the Mississippi River, and Congress authorized the spending of $2500.

9. The expedition party reached the Pacific Ocean on November 15 1805 and began the return trip in March 1806.

10. Dear Mom I arrived in California May 2 2002. My new address is 267 Lake Wilderness Drive San Jose California 98088, and I am working as an aide to Michael Moriarty, Ph.D. at the university. Since I will not receive a paycheck until the end of the month, please send $2000 as soon as possible. Your loving son Jim Bob

Caution   The misuse of commas accounts for the following five most common punctuation errors in college writing:

- no comma between two independent clauses joined by *for, and, nor, but, or, yet,* and *so*

- introductory words, phrases, and clauses not set off with commas

- necessary commas left out of items in a series or unnecessary commas added

- nonessential words, phrases, and clauses not set off with commas; or essential words, phrases, and clauses set off with commas

- clauses that begin with *that* set off with commas

Always check your writing for these five errors.

Review Exercises

REVIEW EXERCISE 13

Use commas as needed to set off words and phrases that interrupt, contrasting elements, direct addresses, and tag questions.

1. Helen unknowingly was the prize that Venus had promised to Paris.

2. Helen reputedly was the fairest of all women.

3. She obviously had many suitors before she chose Menelaus as her husband.

4. Before announcing her choice for her husband to be, Odysseus (Oh-**DIS**-eeuhs) not Agamemnon asked all the chieftains of Greece to swear that they would abide by her decision.

5. They agreed furthermore to protect her and avenge any wrong done to her.

6. Helen by the way was devoted to Menelaus prior to Paris' arrival.

7. Helen however soon succumbed to the young Trojan prince's charms, and eventually they became lovers.

8. "Ms. Elkins she did flee to Troy with Paris did she not?" "Yes Tim she did."

9. "Students do you know what Menelaus did as soon as he discovered Helen had fled? He asked all the chieftains of Greece without exception to honor their promise to come to Helen's aid."

10. With only few exceptions, they responded to the call. Odysseus however who did not want to leave his wife and baby son, pretended to be mad and hooked a donkey to a plow and began to sow salt. Aware of Odysseus' duplicity, the messenger put Odysseus' infant son in front of the plow, and of course the father turned the plow aside.

REVIEW EXERCISE 14

Use commas to set off nonessential clauses and phrases. Mark correct sentences with a C.

1. Penelope the epitome of the virtuous woman in Greek mythology was the wife of Odysseus the king of Ithica (**ITH**-uh-kuh). 2. She waited patiently for her husband to return from the Trojan War rejecting all suitors. 3. She kept her suitors at bay for years telling them that she would choose one of them as soon as she finished weaving a garment for her aged father-in-law. 4. Penelope who never finished the garment wove during the day and raveled out the weaving at night. 5. Odysseus who had many adventures finally returned to Ithica. 6. His adventures are recorded in Homer's *Odyssey* one of the greatest works in Western literature. 7. Odysseus disguising himself as an old beggar attended a banquet in his own hall. 8. Telemachus (tuh-**LEM**-uh-kuhs) the son of Penelope and Odysseus gave the banquet and invited all his mother's suitors. 9. It was at this banquet that Penelope was to announce the name of the suitor who would become her husband. 10. Telemachus arranged an archery contest for the banquet which was designed to test the strength and archery ability of the men who wanted to marry Penelope. 11. Telemachus having first removed all the weaponry from the hall brought in the bow that had belonged to his father before he sailed for Troy. 12. None of the suitors could even bend the bow and laughed at the old beggar Odysseus in disguise when he asked to try to bend the bow. 13. Telemachus who had developed the contest with his father assured the suitors that it was customary to let all guests participate in such a contest. 14. Odysseus took the bow expertly nocked the arrow easily drew it and hit the target. 15. He then killed all the suitors the ones who had been sponging off his wife and son for ten years.

Add commas as needed to set off introductory words, phrases, and clauses. Mark correct sentences with a C.

1. At first Native Americans did not know what to make of these strange animals—horses. 2. Although they were not sure whether they should eat them or simply avoid them it did not take them long to learn to tame the horses they caught. 3. Rapidly developing their riding skills soon they became some of the most expert horsemen in the world. 4. Riding bareback they guided their horses with knee pressures and soft whispers. 5. After they acquired horses they could travel farther and faster, and more young men became warriors rather than farmers or hunters. 6. Their equestrian life brought about a change in warfare. 7. Originally warfare was for the purpose of protection or revenge. With the advent of the horse warfare evolved into a glorified game. In this new war game warriors could gain honor and prestige in battle. 8. As with all games the game of war had certain rules and a scoring system. 9. "Counting coup" was part of the scoring system. Touching the enemy with one's hand ranked higher than touching him with a bow or *coup* stick. 10. Killing the enemy was secondary because greater honor could be gained by taking risks and exposing oneself to danger by scoring a *coup*.

Edit the following passage, combining independent clauses and adding appropriate commas.

By capturing an enemy's gun taking a scalp or stealing a horse warriors could attain honor. Stealing horses was an honorable pursuit. There were degrees of honor to be earned by stealing horses. Stealing a horse tied near an enemy's teepee brought more honor than stealing one tied in an open field. If the horse thief succeeded he not only got the horse he also got the acclaim of his tribesmen. When a man had earned four or more *coups* he was considered an "ace." After he became an ace he could then hold positions of honor and leadership. Painting his face and wearing certain feathers he could display the honors he held. Although the Plains Indians considered names to be valuable property they did not pass on names from one generation to the next. When a female was born she was given a name which never changed. Although a male baby was given a name at birth he did not have to keep it. Selling it pawning it giving it away or discarding it were all options. Frequently men changed their names when they got married or scored an important *coup*. Often the names of the Indians lost much in careless or erroneous translations. For example the name of the Dakota Sioux warrior "Young Man Afraid of His Horses" should have been translated to mean "Young Man Whose Very Horses are Feared." When Sitting Bull received his name it meant "The Bull in Possession." The hieroglyph (**HIE**-uhr-uh-**GLIF**) of his Indian name however looked like a seated buffalo.

Using Semicolons

A semicolon (;) combines the symbols of a period and a comma. It is stronger than a comma and weaker than a period. Use semicolons

- between independent clauses

- between independent clauses plus a transitional word

- to separate items in a series that contain commas

Using Semicolons Between Independent Clauses

▶ **Equally Important Ideas**   Use a semicolon between two independent clauses of the same sentence when they are about the same idea, are equally important, and are not joined by *for, and, nor, but, or, yet, so.*

The dog growled and bared his teeth; the would-be burglar left in a hurry.

▶ **Transitional Words**   Use a semicolon between independent clauses of the same sentence when they are about the same idea, are equally important, and are joined by a transitional word such as *nevertheless, however, for example, for instance, accordingly, consequently,* and so on. The transitional word shows the relationship of the two clauses. *See* Part 2: Semicolons and Transitional Expressions (p. 25).

The dress did not **fit; therefore,** Dana returned it.

Note: Some writers leave out the commas after short transitional words such as *then, next,* or *still.*

He registered for the course; then he bought the books.

▶ **Long, Involved Sentences**   You may use a semicolon (instead of a comma) between independent clauses of the same sentence when they are joined by *for, and, nor, but, or, yet, so* if the clauses are long, involved, or contain distracting commas.

Most of the garrison of Roxburgh castle were drinking and carousing, but still they had set watches on the battlements of the castle, in case of any sudden **attack; for** as the Scots had succeeded in so many enterprises of the kind, and as Douglas was known to be in the neighborhood, they conceived themselves obliged to keep a very strict guard.

—Sir Walter Scott, "Taking of Roxburgh Castle"

Using Semicolons Between Items in a Series

Use semicolons between elements arranged in a series when those elements contain commas.

Lloyd has lived in Dayton, **Ohio; Reno, Nevada; Jerome, Idaho; and** Boulder, Colorado.

EXERCISE 17

Add semicolons as needed and replace commas with semicolons when necessary.

1. Hally wanted to be an actress however, she became a waitress.

2. Albert is a great athlete he plays soccer, football, and baseball.

3. Her children are musically gifted. Tim plays the organ, saxophone, and clarinet Suzy plays the piano, drums, and flute and Joe plays the radio, television, and VCR.

4. Jim and Bob left early they were playing in a golf tournament.

5. Please reserve the following tickets: six seats for the soccer game, which is on Friday one ticket for the boat races, which are on Saturday and six tickets for the concert, which is on Sunday.

6. My car needs new tires it needs new brakes, and, yes, you guessed it, it needs a new paint job.

7. Secondary schools have assumed many duties concerning the teaching of children however, many parents feel some of this training should be done in the homes, not in the schools.

8. Patty likes peanut butter and jelly sandwiches, especially when they are made with whole wheat bread, grape jelly, peanut butter, and bananas, but her sister prefers bacon and tomato sandwiches, preferably with sourdough bread, vine-ripened tomatoes, and crisp bacon slices.

9. I liked the movie in fact, I enjoyed it very much.

10. The tornado destroyed the Smith's house however, the house next door to it was not touched.

EXERCISE 18

Write ten sentences illustrating the four uses of the semicolon. Use each rule at least twice.

Add semicolons as needed and replace commas with semicolons when necessary.

1. Gottfried Wilhelm Leibnitz had one of the most amazing minds the world has ever known he was learned in physical sciences, law, history, diplomacy, mathematics, and logic.

2. Leibnitz invented the Calculus, concurrently with but independently of Newton furthermore, manuscripts published in the twentieth century show him to be the founder of symbolic logic.

3. The tragic part of Leibnitz' story is that despite his great genius, he died neglected, poor, and alone, for his work was unrecognized, and he was mourned only by his faithful secretary.

4. Leibnitz' major work, a treatise on John Locke's *Essay Concerning Human Understanding*, was written in 1704, but because of Locke's death, it was not published until 1765.

5. By the time Leibnitz was eight, he had taught himself to read Latin at seventeen he went to the university to study mathematics.

6. At twenty he was ready to take his doctor's degree in law however, the authorities refused to give the degree to such a young person even though they could find no fault with his knowledge of law.

7. Leibnitz and Issac Newton worked separately however, Newton got most of the credit for discovering the law of universal gravitation.

8. His last years were bitter ones people accused him of stealing his discovery from Newton.

9. Leibnitz was an optimist he believed that a divine plan makes this the best of all possible worlds.

10. He argued that all the things that do not seem best to us are really good however, since we do not understand them, we think them evil.

Using End Punctuation

A sentence can end with a period, a question mark, or an exclamation point.

- Use a period (.) to signal the end of a sentence and to mark an abbreviation.

- Use a question mark (?) to signal the end of a direct question.

- Use an exclamation point (!) to show emphasis.

Using Periods

Use a period to mark the end of a sentence and after certain abbreviations.

▶ **Sentences**   Put a period at the end of all sentences (*statements, mild commands, indirect questions,* or *polite requests*), except sentences that ask a direct question or ones that express strong feelings.

Statement	The Beatles' last performance was in San Francisco in 1966.
Mild command	Give it your best shot.
Indirect question	Liz wanted to know if all their singles sold over a million copies.

Note: You may use a period rather than a question mark to end a polite request formed as a question.

    Polite request   Will you please pass the jelly.

▶ **Abbreviations**   Use periods in most abbreviations such as *Mr., Ms., B.A., Ph.D., Dr.,* A.M., A.D., and so on.

Mr. President	Dr. Spock	10 P.M.
Kevin Kizer, D.D.S.	U. S. A.	Paula Webb, R.N.

Caution 1   Do not add another period when an abbreviation comes at the end of a sentence.

    No   We will arrive at l0 P.M..   **Yes**   We will arrive at 10 P.M.

However, if the sentence is a direct question, add a question mark after the period that ends the abbreviation.

    Will you arrive at l0 P.M.?

Caution 2   Use normal punctuation after an abbreviation that falls within a sentence.

    No   If we do not arrive at 10 P.M. I will call you.

    Yes   If we do not arrive at 10 P.M.**,** I will call you.

Generally, do not use periods in **acronyms** (new words made up of the first letters or first few letters of a series of words).

NATO   radar   scuba   FedEx

UPS   OSHA   AIDS

Do not put a period after Postal Service abbreviations for states.

Seattle, WA   Louisville, KY   Piedmont, CA

Dayton, OH   Tempe, AZ   Anchorage, AK

Generally, do not use periods with common abbreviations of corporations, government agencies, or technical expressions.

FBI   CIA   FM   CAT scan   DNA   MGM

Do not use periods with commonly accepted shortened forms of words

gym (gymnasium)   math (mathematics)   lab (laboratory)
deli (delicatessen)

Using Question Marks

Put a question mark after a sentence that asks a direct question.

Are birds often grouped in eight main visual categories?

Using Exclamation Points

Put an exclamation point after exclamatory words—words that express strong, shocking, or surprising feelings.

Strong   Don't leave me!

Shocking   Oh, no!

Surprising   He yelled, "Happy birthday, Betty!"

Caution   Do not try to turn an ordinary statement into an exclamatory one by adding an exclamation point, and do not try to increase emphasis by adding more than one exclamation point.

No We are proud of you!   **Yes** We are proud of you.

No Great job!!!!!   **Yes** Great job!

 Forming Negative Statements and Questions

Form a negative statement by adding the word *not* immediately after the first helping verb of the complete verb.

Statement	John will be here at noon.
Negative Statement	John will *not* be here at noon.

If there is no helping verb, add a form of the verb *do* in front of the word *not*.

Statement	John arrived on time.
Negative Statement	John did *not* arrive on time.

Form a question by putting the helping verb that follows the subject directly in front of the subject.

Statement	John will be here at noon.
Question	Will John be here at noon?

If the verb does not contain a helping verb, add a form of the verb *do* immediately before the subject and use the appropriate verb form.

Statement	John arrived on time.
Question	Did John arrive on time?

EXERCISE 20

Add periods and end marks as needed and cross out unnecessary ones.

1. Did you park your auto. near the wharf and have breakfast at I.H.O.P.

2. Nadine applied for a job at NASA after she earned her MS degree at U.C.L.A

3. I am expecting U.P.S. delivery at 8 AM

4. Fran's father used to be an F.B.I. agent, but now he works for NASA

5. Are you sure you can really trust her to tell the truth??

6. Sandy has a G.E. stove, but her fridge. is a Frigidaire.

7. Did many companies move their plants to Mexico after the signing of the North American Free Trade Agreement (N.A.F.T.A)?

8. Great job!!!!! You are absolutely fantastic!!!!!

9. The radio in our auto. is always set on A.M., not F.M.

10. When you go to the lab., save a seat for me; I'll be there by 10 P.M..

Using Apostrophes

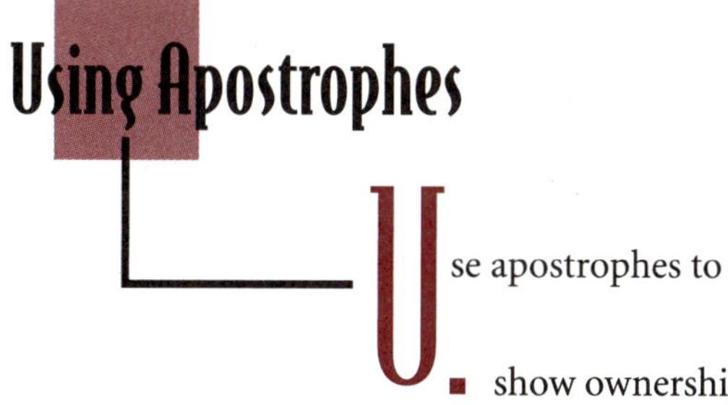

Use apostrophes to

- show ownership

- indicate letters missing in contractions

- form plurals

Forming Possessives

Use an apostrophe to make a noun or a nonspecific (*indefinite*) pronoun show possession.

▶ **Nouns or Nonspecific Pronouns**   Add **'s** to show possession when a noun or non-specific pronoun does not end in *s*. Remember that time nouns may be used to show possession.

Noun	The men**'s** Bible study group will meet at Jim**'s** house.
Nonspecific pronoun	Someone**'s** car is blocking the driveway.
Time	He received one day**'s** pay.

▶ **Singular Nouns That End in s**   Add **'s** to show possession when a singular noun ends in *s*.

Chris**'s** drug prevention program is highly effective.

Note: If the word sounds awkward with the added **'s,** such as in Sophocles**'s** tragedies, drop the *s* after the apostrophe. Either form is acceptable.

▶ **Plural Nouns That End in s**   Use only an apostrophe to show possession when a plural noun ends in *s*.

The **girls'** softball game has been canceled.

My friend's cabin is a three **hours'** drive from my house.

▶ **Compound Words**   Add *'s* to the last word of a compound word or phrase to show possession.

    Word   My **sister-in-law's** cornbread won first prize at the country fair.

    Phrase   **Somebody else's** brownies won first prize.

▶ **Joint or Group Nouns**   Add *'s* to only the last word in joint or group nouns to show possession.

    Joint   Marietta and Millard**'s** horses are well trained.

    Group   Virginia, Elizabeth, and Fern**'s** herb farm grows many exotic plants.

▶ **Individual**   Add *'s* to each noun to show individual possession.
    Marietta**'s** and Millard**'s** horses will be shown this weekend.

Note: Do not add apostrophes to personal pronouns that have specific possessive forms: *his, hers, her, its, our, ours, your, yours, their, theirs, whose.*

Forming Contractions

A *contraction* is a word such as *won't* formed by leaving out or combing some of the sounds of a longer expression. Form contractions by replacing missing sounds with apostrophes.

Commonly Used Contractions

are not = aren't	cannot = can't	could have = could've	did not = didn't	it is = it's
of the clock = o'clock	she is = she's	there is = there's	they are = they're	
was not = wasn't	were not = weren't	you will = you'll		

Forming Plurals

Use an apostrophe plus *s* to form plurals of letters and plurals of words referred to as words.

    Plurals of letters   Some young children have difficulty pronouncing *y's* and *r's.*

    Plurals of words referred to as words   The *what if's* are merely excuses.

MLA Note: "Do not use an apostrophe to form the plural of an abbreviation or a number."

Write **1920s,** not 1920's.   Write **SATs,** not SAT's

EXERCISE 21

Add apostrophes as needed.

1. Isnt the United States of Americas population made up of many ethnic groups?

2. According to legend, Noahs great grandson discovered Armenia.

3. Its believed that Armenia was the original garden of Eden.

4. Early colonists invitations brought Armenians to the New World.

5. Californias gold rush lured hundreds of Basques to California in the 1850s.

6. A Spanish missionary, repulsed by the enslavement of Latin Americas Indians, proposed bringing Africans to the New World to do the white peoples slave labor.

7. The pioneer Chineses history is filled with legal, social, and physical abuse.

8. In the 1850s California passed the Foreign Miners License Tax, which imposed a $3 a month fee on every Chinese miner.

9. Cubans came to the United States in the early 1800s to work in the cigar industry, but large numbers didnt arrive until the late 50s.

10. Czechoslovakia Protestants fled to the United States in the aftermath of Catholic victory in the Thirty Years War.

Using Quotation Marks

Use quotation marks to set off

- a person's exact words

- dialogue

- titles of short works

- definitions

Punctuating Direct Quotations

When you are quoting someone's exact words—whether written or spoken—put quotation marks in front and after the quotation.

> The bus driver waved good-bye to the students and said, "I'll see you in the morning."

> "I'll see you in the morning," the bus driver said as he drove away.

Indirect Quotations   Do not put quotation marks around *indirect quotations.* They are other people's ideas—but not their exact words.

> As he drove away, the bus driver said that he would see us in the morning.

> Fran said that she had left her books on the bus.

Note: A direct quotation is set off from the rest of the sentence by a comma, a question mark, or an exclamation point.

> She said, "I'll cry tomorrow."   "Why did she say that?" I asked.   "Oh no!" She screamed.

Punctuating Quotations Within Quotations

Put single quotation marks around quotations within a quotation.

> I remember the exact words of the professor, "Tomorrow you must be ready to discuss 'The Raven.'"

Punctuating Dialogue

Put quotation marks at the beginning and at the end of a speaker's words, and begin a new paragraph each time the speaker changes so that readers know who is talking.

> "Louise, open the door! I beg; open the door—you will make yourself ill. What are you doing, Louise? For heaven's sake open the door."
> "Go away. I am not making myself ill."
>
> —Kate Chopin, "The Story of an Hour"

Punctuating Titles of Short Works

Put quotation marks around titles of short works such as *magazine* or *newspaper articles, chapters* or *subdivisions of books, poems, short stories, songs,* and *television episodes.*

Article	"Singer's Final Solution"
Chapters	*The Bridges at Toko Ri* contains three chapters: "Sea," "Sky," and "Land."
Poem	"Stopping by Woods on a Snowy Evening"
Short story	"A Rose for Emily"
Song	"Silent Night"

Punctuating Definitions

When you are quoting a dictionary definition of a word, italicize the word and enclose the meaning in quotation marks.

In certain Native American tribes the word *coup* means "a feat of bravery performed in battle."

Using Quotation Marks with Other Punctuation Marks and Capital Letters

Periods and Commas
Periods and commas go inside quotation marks

"There is no artifice as good and desirable as simplicity."

—Frances de Sales

"I will be true to my promise and to you," she softly whispered.

▶ **Colons and Semicolons**   Colons and semicolons go outside quotation marks.

According to the report, "The holdings of Aristotle Onassis were vast and extensive": They included hotels, banks, real estate, an airline, and fleets of tankers and freighters.

Onassis became known as "The Golden Greek"; however, at one time he was a poor foreigner in Buenos Aires who worked for twenty-five cents an hour.

▶ **Exclamation Marks and Question Marks**   Exclamation marks and question marks go inside quotation marks unless the whole sentence is an exclamation or question.

When in the heat of passion, Augustine would fervently pray, "Give me chastity, but not yet!"

"I'm mad as hell, and I'm not going to take it anymore"!

After Calvin Coolidge died, Dorothy Parker asked, "How can they tell?"

"Do you know in which country Panama hats are made"? "Is it Ecuador"?

▶ **Capitalization**   A direct quotation begins with a capital letter.
I heard her say, "**P**ut the car in the garage."

When a quoted sentence is divided into two parts by an interrupting expression—
he said, she asked—the second part begins with a small letter.

"Please, oh please," she begged, "**l**et me borrow your class notes."

If the first part is a complete sentence and the quotation continues, a period goes
after the interrupter and the new sentence begins with a capital letter.

"Hold my hand," she said. "**I** am frightened."

EXERCISE 22

Add quotation marks as needed. Clearly show where the periods and commas, colons and
semicolons, and exclamation points and question marks are located—inside or outside the
quotation marks. Mark correct sentences with a C.

1. "When Christ said, 'I was hungry, and you fed me,' he didn't mean only hunger for food and
   bread; he also meant the hunger to be loved." —Mother Teresa

2. The word *blab* means to reveal secret matters through indiscreet talk.

3. The opening lines of Robert Herrick's poem To the Virgins, to Make Much of Time have often
   been quoted by amorous suitors.

4. The coach said, If a player, except a goalkeeper, closes his hand on the puck, the play will be
   stopped.

5. He also said, A goalkeeper who holds the puck for longer than three seconds will be given a
   minor penalty.

6. Punctuation: what is it, after all, but another way of cutting up time, creating or negating
   relationships, telling words when to take a rest, when to get on with their relentless stories, when
   to catch their breath? —Karen Elizabeth Gordon

7. Spring by Matsuo Basho is a haiku—a three-line poem that traditionally has seventeen
   syllables.

8. In John Updike's short story A & P, Sammy quits his job because he feels some customers have been ill treated.

9. W. R. Espy said that a cow has a calf, but the calf of a mare is a colt, and the colt of a bear is a cub.

10. Mrs. Malaprop in Sheridan's play *The Rivals* says, Sure, if I reprehend anything in this world, it is the use of my oracular tongue.

Review Exercises

Add quotation marks as needed. Clearly show where the periods and commas, colons and semicolons, and exclamation points and question marks are located—inside or outside the quotation marks. Mark correct sentences with a C.

REVIEW EXERCISE 23

1. The speaker in the poem The Man He Killed is a soldier who is relating his wartime experiences.

2. Dudley Randall wrote a poem, Ballad of Birmingham, about the bombing of a church in Birmingham, Alabama.

3. The first paragraph of Eudora Welty's short story Well Worn Path sets the scene for the journey.

4. The theme of John Steinbeck's short story The Chrysanthemums is one of stunted growth and repressed desires.

5. In *The American West,* Dee Brown has many provocative chapter titles such as the following: Dull Knife Marches Home, The Beef Bonanza, and Clack Kettle of the Cheyenne.

6. Supposedly, Stephen Foster wrote the song My Old Kentucky Home at Rowan Manor House near Bardstown, Kentucky.

7. The following songs were at the top of the Billboard national music charts: Goodnight Irene (1950), Theme from a Summer Place (1960), and Bridge over Troubled Water (1970).

8. Easter Wings by George Herbert is a fine example of concrete poetry.

9. Edmund Spenser's poem One Day I Wrote Her Name upon the Strand deals with the transience of the speaker's expressions of love.

10. Was A Problem too Personal an episode in *The Heat of the Night* series?

REVIEW EXERCISE 24

1. Roger asked, Why is a poker hand that contains two aces and two eights called a dead man's hand?

2. My friend said that Wild Bill Hickok was holding these cards in his hand when he was killed.

3. Henry M. Stanley, the journalist who located Dr. Livingstone in Africa, said Wild Bill Hickok is as handsome a specimen of a man as could be found.

4. Monsieur Van Gogh! It's time to wake up!

   Vincent had been waiting for Ursula's voice even while he slept.

   I was awake, Mademoiselle Ursula, he called back.

   "No you weren't, the girl laughed, but you are now." —Irving Stone, *Lust for Life*

5. The coach explained that a golf tee is a peg made of plastic or wood on which the ball is placed for the first stroke of each hole.

6. The word *teed* means to place a golf ball on a tee, and the phrase *tee off* means the act of drivng a golf ball from the tee.

7. T-shirts, or other collarless shirts, and jeans are banned by many golf clubs, he explained.

8. You mean I can't wear a muscle shirt and cutoffs!

9. George, is fourteen the maximum number of clubs that a player is permitted to take on a round of golf?

10. The town of Tombstone became famous because the town boosters overplayed the shoot-out at OK Corral: They invented a town too tough to die, said historian Eugene Hollows.

Using Other Punctuation

Using Parentheses

Use parentheses for *listed numbers* or *letters* and to enclose *nonessential information*.

▶ **Listed Numbers or Letters** Use parentheses to enclose numbers or letters for listed items in a series.

She put the following items in her book bag: (**1**) a pair of scissors, (**2**) a stapler, (**3**) marking pens, (**4**) paper clips, (**5**) white-out, (**6**) and rubber bands.

▶ **Nonessential Information or Minor Digressions**   Use parentheses to set off nonessential information such as minor digressions and afterthoughts.

Jesse James (son of a Baptist minister) is one of America's legendary outlaws.

Supposedly, he was shot in the back for the $10,000 reward (a small fortune in those days).

A Colt .41 (described by Pat Garrett as a "self-cocker") was Billy the Kid's weapon of choice.

Note: Generally, set off most nonessential material with commas; however, when you want to emphasize the material, use dashes; and when you want to de-emphasize the material use parentheses.

Using Dashes

Use dashes to emphasize nonessential material, to clarify nonessential material that contains commas, to introduce a summary, and to mark a sudden interruption.

▶ **Emphasis**   Use dashes to emphasize material that is not essential to the meaning of a sentence such as examples, definitions, appositives, contrasts, and so on.

"I was in a queer mood, thinking myself very old: but now I am a woman again—as I always am when I write." —Virginia Woolf

Despite Napoleon Bonaparte's short stature—or because of it—he exuded power, strength, and ambition.

▶ **Misreading**   Use dashes to prevent misreading nonessential material that contains commas.

For Sam and me, certain junk food is necessary—candy, gum, sodas, and, of course, popcorn—for us to truly enjoy a movie.

▶ **Interruptions**   Use dashes to mark sudden interruptions such as corrections, hesitations, or sudden changes in thoughts.

I would like a cup of coffee with—no make it a cup of tea—cream and sugar.

"But perhaps Miss—Miss—oh, I can't remember her name—she taught English, I think—Miss Milross? She was one of them." —Garrison Keillor

EXERCISES 25

Add parentheses and dashes as needed. Answers may vary because the decision to emphasize or de-emphasize information is sometimes a matter of choice.

1. Julie decided to study the history of four crafts in the following order: 1 bronze, 2 iron, 3 glass, and 4 pottery.

2. Discovering the way to make bronze a landmark in the history of civilization was the second step in the use of metals.

3. Europe was still making and using stone tools first step in the use of metals in 2000 B.C., but bronze was being cast in the Near East.

4. Bronze not a pure metal is an alloy that is a mixture of metals.

5. By 1000 B.C., the Age of Bronze technological period when metals were first used to make tools and weapons was giving way to the Age of Iron the technological period from the first general use of iron to present times.

6. Iron the most sturdy of all metals and steel an alloy of iron and carbon are metals of violence and of industry.

7. Instruments of death and destruction knives and guns are made of iron and steel.

8. Instruments of commerce and industry farming equipment, vehicles, crafts, and buildings are made of iron and steel.

9. According to legend at least this was the story told by the Roman writer Pliny, Phoenician sailors discovered glass when they built a campfire on a beach and lined it with chunks of saltpeter also known as sodium nitrate.

10. Glass is formed when sand one form of the mineral called *silica* fuses with an alkali such as potash or soda.

REVIEW EXERCISE 26

Add parentheses and dashes as needed. Answers may vary because the decision to emphasize or de-emphasize information is sometimes a matter of choice. Mark correct sentences with a C.

1. Julie like many of her fellow classmates became interested in the art of pottery.

2. The art of making pottery anything made of baked clay and hardened by heat is common to most civilizations.

3. Pottery may be divided into two groups earthenware and porcelain.

4. Earthenware is opaque that is it does not allow light to come through.

5. Most earthenware is porous capable of absorbing water.

6. When a glaze a thin coating of clay is applied to pottery and baked in a hot kiln, it becomes nonporous.

7. Porcelain created by the Chinese over two thousand years ago is translucent that is it transmits light but not enough to see distinct images and nonporous.

8. Canton porcelain was produced in the workshops of Canton now Guangzhou.

9. The Chinese refused to reveal the secret ingredient kaolin (**KAY**-uh-lin) a fine clay that they used to make porcelain.

10. True porcelain pottery made with kaolin was not produced in Europe until 1709 when Johann Bottger found a bed of kaolin clay near Meisssen (**MIE**-suhn), Germany, and used it in his pottery.

Using Colons

Use a colon (:) to call attention to the information that follows (*lists, appositives, quotations*), to signal an explanation or a summary, after the opening of a formal letter, and in everyday material.

▶ **Introduce a List**   Use a colon to introduce a list after an independent clause. The clause before a list often includes the words *as follows* or *the following*.

Lacrosse players need the following attributes: strength, perseverance, and courage.

Note: Do not put a comma before a list that follows a verb or preposition.

No   Lacrosse players *need:* strength, perseverance, and courage. (list follows the verb *need*)

Yes   Larry is interested *in* playing lacrosse, football, and soccer. (list follows the preposition *in*)

▶ **Explain, Restate, or Summarize**   Use a colon between two independent clauses when the second clause explains, restates, or summarizes the idea in the first one.

The chef prepared an elegant first course of wild rice and squab: a young, newly hatched pigeon stuffed with truffles and served on a bed of wild rice.

Lacrosse, which traces its roots to the Iroquois, is a full contact sport: Players are armed with crosses and protective gear and physically battle to gain possession of the ball.

▶ **Set Off a Quotation**   Use a colon to set off a quotation introduced by an independent clause.

Agatha Christie said that she did not require a special place to do her writing: "All I needed was a steady table and a typewriter."

▶ **Writing Everyday Material**   Use colons in everyday material (between the hour and the minute, between the minute and the second, between chapter and verse of the Bible, and after the opening of a formal letter).

Hour, minute, and second	The plane arrived at 7:45 P.M. Her record time was 2:32:07.
Biblical chapter and verse	Did you memorize John 3:16 when you were a child?
Formal letter	Dear Mr. Gates:

EXERCISE 27

Add colons as needed.

1. The following men from foreign countries helped the United States gain independence nineteen-year-old Lafayette of France, the brave Jean De Kalb of Germany, Baron von Stubben of Germany, and Polish engineers Thaddeus Kosciusko and Count Pulaski.

2. Of all these great men, Lafayette was in the best position to help the young country He was a brilliant general, fought in several major engagements, and had political influence in France.

3. "The Lord is my shepherd. I shall not want." —Psalm 231

4. Dear Mr. Perot My plane will arrive at 115 P.M.

5. Malcolm X made the following observation "You can't separate peace from freedom because no one can be at peace unless he has his freedom."

6. In *The Nine Bad Shots of Golf and What to Do About Them,* the author says there are only nine bad golf shots "You can hook, you can slice, you can push, pull, sky, top, sclaff, smother, or shank a shot." —Jim Dante and others

7. The most common fault in golf is *slicing* hitting the ball with a club face that is open.

8. In 1555 Nostradamus (NOS-truh-**DAY**-muhs), a French physician and astrologer, wrote *Centuries* a book of rhymed prophecies.

9. Nostradamus predicted the dropping of nuclear bombs on Hiroshima and Nagasaki "Near the harbor and in two cities will be two scourges the like of which have never been seen."

10. Jeane Dixon, American clairvoyant, made the following accurate predictions years before the events occurred the election and assassination of President Kennedy, the death of President Roosevelt, the assassination of Mahatma Gandhi, and that of Martin Luther King, Jr.

Using Hyphens

Use a hyphen (-)

- to break a word at the end of a line

- between some compound words

▶ **Dividing Words**   Use a hyphen to divide a word at the end of a line. Generally, avoid breaking a word at the end of a line, but if you must do so, divide it between syllables. Look the word up in a dictionary and use the main entry as your guide for dividing it.

Note: If you are using a computer, it will probably bring the entire word down to the next line unless you tell it to do otherwise.

▶ **Joining Compound Words**   Use hyphens to join some compound words. Compound words are made up of two or more words. Some are hyphenated; some are written as one word, and others are written as two words. When you are in doubt about when to use a hyphen, look the word up in an up-to-date dictionary.

Hyphenated	twin-size	straight-line	all-star	high-risk hit-or-miss
One word	bulletproof	antisocial	loudspeaker	cornerstone
Two words	brick wall	body bag	hard drive	

Although the hyphenation of words is not uniform and is subject to change, the following suggestions are usually reliable guides to hyphenation.

Compound Adjectives   Use hyphens between compound adjectives in front of nouns, but not after.

Hyphenated	*second-story* room	*door-to-door* sales
	soft-spoken person	*well-run* program

Not hyphenated program was *well run*   person was *soft spoken*

Note: If one of the modifiers is an adverb ending in *-ly,* do not use a hyphen.

Not hyphenated quick**ly** prepared dessert   severe**ly** wrinkled dress

Prefixes and Suffixes Use a hyphen with the prefixes *ex-, self-, all-,* with the suffix *-elect,* and with all prefixes before a specific noun or specific adjective.

*ex-*wife   major-*elect*   *all-*star   *un-*American   *Pan-*American

Compound Numbers Use hyphens with compound numbers from *twenty-one* to *ninety-nine* and with fractions used as adjectives.

Aging baby boomers have been defined as people who are *forty-five* to *sixty-five* years old. Only *one-fifth* of Americans who need a hearing aid actually wear one.

Confusion or Awkwardness Use hyphens to separate letters to prevent confusing one word with another or to prevent awkwardness.

Confusion We have a fine *recreation* program. I enjoyed the *re-creation* of the story.

Awkward identical sounds Is this material *water-r*epellent? He is an *anti-i*ntellectual.

EXERCISE 28

Add hyphens to compounds as needed. Mark correct sentences with a C.

1. Dalton Trumbo, an American screenwriter, was blacklisted and imprisoned for his refusal to participate in the *anti Communist* investigations of the House *Un American* Activities Committee.

2. *Snowbirds* are any of several birds that are common to snowy regions. Is this *snow white snowsuit* on sale?

3. The young sailor refused to *re enlist.*

4. A *caregiver* should be *well trained* before he or she takes care of *semi invalid* patients.

5. The *governor elect* once sold encyclopedias *door to door.*

6. "*Anti Catholicism* is the *anti Semitism* of the intellectual." —Patrick Buchanan

7. The little *five year old* girl won the contest by a *two thirds* majority.

8. "When I was as you are now, towering in the confidence of *twenty one,* little did I suspect that I should be at *forty nine,* what I now am." —Samuel Johnson

9. The project was *well run;* it proceeded like *clock work.*

10. He signed a *one year* contract but was not expected to work three hundred and *sixty five* days.

REVIEW EXERCISE 29

Add the necessary colons and hyphens. Join words that should not be hyphenated. Mark correct sentences with a C.

1. High ranking Incas were polygamous. Multiplicity of wives was a privilege suitable to the great.

2. Among the lowly Incas, monogamy was universal. Spinsters and bachelors were uncommon.

3. At given intervals the village chief would assemble all would be married men and women, arranging men in one row and women in another. He then married each couple in turn as they came to him. This cold blooded arrangement for the about to be wed people probably resulted in some fast footed jockeying for positions.

4. The Incas made a highly potent beer by chewing a grain and spitting it into a pot of brackish water, and this un-appetizing brew was the drink of choice.

5. Emperor Pachacutec, founder of the Inca dynasty in 1438, was a great man. A noble philosopher and a charitable ruler.

6. "Drunkenness, anger, and madness go together. The first two are voluntary and to be removed; whereas, the last is perpetual." —Pachacutec

7. The great chiefs lived in beautiful buildings made of sun baked clay.

8. They used knotted string records for long distance communication.

9. The bare foot express sped news to the far reaching areas of the kingdom. The runners covered more than 1,000 miles in about one week.

10. Each re lay runner ran his relay over a three mile section of the paved route.

Using Capitals

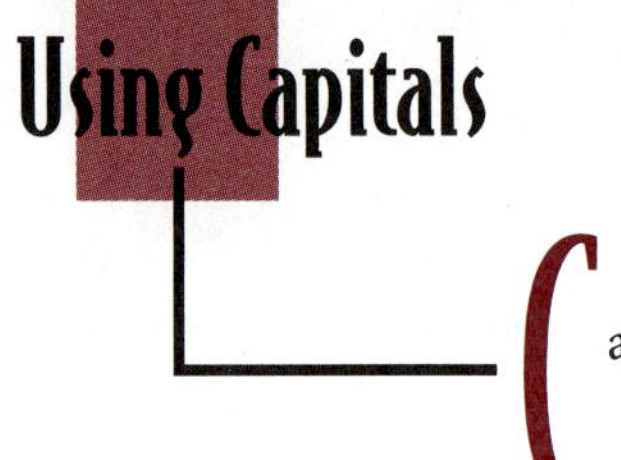

Capitalize

- the pronoun *I*

- the first word in any sentence

- people's titles

- the important words in titles of works

- specific nouns

Capitalizing the Pronoun *I* and the First Word in a Sentence

▶ **The Pronoun I**   Capitalize the pronoun *I*.

Generally, **I** prefer to use the word *detailed* instead of the expression *in-depth*.

▶ **First Word of a Sentence**   Capitalize the first word of a sentence.

The word *indicator* means "a guide" or "an estimate."

▶ **First Word of a Quoted Sentence**   Capitalize the first word of a quoted sentence, but not a quoted phrase.

"**B**ullfighting is the only art in which the artist is in danger of death."
—Ernest Hemingway
William Wadsworth decried the game of golf as being "**a** round of strenuous idleness."

Note: When a quoted sentence is interrupted by explanatory words, do not capitalize the first word after the interruption.

"**I** love you," he softly whispered, "**a**nd will miss you."

Note: You may or may not capitalize the first word after a colon if it begins a complete sentence. Whichever form you use, just remember to be consistent and use the same form in a piece of writing.

"Football combines the two worst things about America: it [or It] is violence punctuated by committee meetings." —George F. Well

Note: Do not capitalize the first word following a colon if it does not begin a complete sentence.

I made a list of things to take: sunglasses, sunscreen, beach towel, and a good book.

Capitalizing Specific Nouns

Capitalize all specific (*proper*) nouns, but not general (*common*) nouns.

▶ **Specific People**   Capitalize the names of specific people, but not general names.

Specific Marilyn Monroe   **General** a woman

Note: Capitalize the specific names of animals, but not general ones except those derived from specific nouns.

The little kitten is a calico cat. Tim's dog Mac is an English setter. Tony's dog Lassie is a collie.

▶ **Geographical Names**   Capitalize specific geographical names, but not general ones.

GEOGRAPHICAL NAMES	SPECIFIC	GENERAL
cities, townships, counties, states	California	a state
states, countries, continent	North America	a continent
islands, peninsulas, straits	Sea Island	an island
beaches	Long Beach	a beach
bodies of water: lakes, rivers, oceans	Red River	a river
mountains	Pikes Peak	a mountain
streets, avenues, roads	Main Street	a street
parks, forests, canyons, dams	Yosemite National Park	a park
heavenly bodies	Saturn	a planet

Note: Capitalize *east, west, north,* and *south* when they denote particular geographical regions, but not when they indicate directions.

The two President Johnsons were from the South. Turn south on the old dirt road.

Caution   Do not try to emphasize general nouns by capitalizing them.

No   The College needs to modernize the Library and hire more Instructors.

Yes   The college needs to modernize the library and hire more instructors.

▶ **Specific Groups of People**   Capitalize specific names of groups of people, but not general ones.

GROUPS OF PEOPLE	SPECIFIC	GENERAL
organizations, business firms	League of Women Voters	an organization
institutions, government bodies	University of California	an institution
nationalities, races	Australian	a nationality

▶ **Specific Events and Calendar Items**   Capitalize specific events and calendar items, but not general ones.

EVENTS AND CALENDAR ITEMS	SPECIFIC	GENERAL
historical events, special events	World War II	a war
days, weeks, months	January	a month
holidays, special periods	Christmas	a holiday

Note: Do not capitalize the seasons (*spring, summer, fall, autumn, winter*) unless they are personified.

"Poor dear, silly Spring, preparing her annual surprise." —Wallace Stevens

We may have an early spring this year.

▶ **Specific Things, Derived Words, and Brand Names**   Capitalize specific things, words derived from specific nouns, and specific brand names, but not the general nouns.

THINGS	SPECIFIC	GENERAL
ships, planes, monuments	*Enterprise*	a ship
awards, other specific things	Lincoln Memorial	a monument

SPECIFIC NOUN	DERIVED WORDS
England	the English people or the English language
Freud	Freudian slip

BRAND NAMES	PRODUCTS
Vaseline	petroleum jelly
Kleenex	tissue

Note: Do not capitalize the names of school subjects except language courses and courses followed by a number. Usually, capitalize rooms and other nouns followed by a numeral or letter.

English   history   History II   Room 8   District 4

Practice Exercises

Add capital letters as needed and cross out unnecessary ones. Mark correct sentences with a C.

EXERCISE 30

1. The Greek philosopher Plato described a vast, beautiful, powerful lost Island that he called Atlantis and placed it beyond the "pillars of hercules"—today's Strait of Gibraltar.

2. Gibraltar is located at the northwest end of the rock of Gibraltar, a Peninsula on the South-central coast of Spain in the Strait of Gibraltar, connecting the Mediterranean Sea and the Atlantic Ocean between Spain and northern Africa.

3. Continents—the principal land masses of the earth—are africa, antarctica, Asia, Australia, Europe, north America, and south America.

4. There are nine known Planets—large celestial bodies that revolve around the Sun: Mercury, Venus, Earth, Mars, Jupiter, Saturn, Uranus, Neptune, and Pluto.

5. In different countries, different colors are associated with death. Mourners in the west generally wear black. In China, white is the accepted color for mourners; gypsies generally wear red.

6. Moslems believe that the soul takes the form of a white bird. During the middle ages this idea spread to Europe, and English mourners wore white for Centuries before black became popular.

7. Phillip Morris owns the following products: Miller Beer, Log Cabin syrup, Minute Rice, Velveeta Cheese, and Maxwell House Coffee.

8. Christmas and Easter originated in pagan celebrations, as did halloween even though its name comes from the Christian Festival of All Hallows' or All Saints' Eve.

9. Linda was accepted at the University of California in Berkeley, California, and has registered for the following courses: First-year Composition 101, Advanced Algebra, American History, and Intermediate Spanish.

10. She rented an apartment on a quiet street south of Shattuck Avenue and will take her toy fox terrier, Peanut, and her Siamese cat, Penelope, with her; but she will leave her Labrador retriever, Muggsy, at home.

EXERCISE 31

1. Henry David Thoreau said, "I went to the woods because I wished to live deliberately, to front only the Essential Facts of Life, and see if I could not learn what it had to teach, and not, when I came to die, discover that I had not lived." [Note: Punctuation errors were not part of the original text.]

2. "The sad truth is," said Shana Alexander, "that excellence makes people nervous."

3. In a letter to George Washington, president Thomas Jefferson wrote, "no government ought to be without censors; and when the Press is free no one ever will." [Note: Punctuation errors were not part of the original text.]

4. "Charity begins at Home" says Tigg in Charles Dickens' *Martin Chuzzlewit* "and justice begins next door." [Note: Punctuation errors were not part of the original text.]

5. In 1233 England mined coal at Newcastle for the first time. The Town became so famous for its coal that the phrase "Carrying Coal to Newcastle" came to mean "superfluous," "overabundance," or "excess."

6. Timothy Dexter of Newburyport, Massachusetts, was born too late to sell Frigidaire Refrigerators to eskimos, but he did sell warming pans and mittens to people in the tropics and coal to people in Newcastle.

7. At the end of the war of independence, he bought a large amount of continental currency very inexpensively; it was almost valueless in America because little trading was done during the War.

8. After the continental money regained its prewar value, Dexter bought ships and began the improbable business of selling Warming Pans (long-handled covered pans that held hot liquid or coals and used to warm beds on cold nights) and Mittens to people of the west Indies.

9. The Islanders bought the Warming Pans and used them for cooking and for ladling syrup in the Molasses Industry and exported the Mittens to russia.

10. When a friend jokingly told Dexter that Newcastle had a great need for coal, he promptly sent several ships full of Virginia coal to England. The shipments arrived during a Newcastle coal strike, and the English bought the entire shipment.

Capitalizing Titles

Capitalize *titles of persons* and *titles of works* such as books, articles, magazine, songs, and so on.

▶ **Titles of Persons**   Capitalize titles of persons when used as part of a proper name, but generally not when used alone.

> **G**eneral Dwight David Eisenhower was an aide to **G**eneral Douglas MacArthur.

> He was promoted to the rank of **b**rigadier **g**eneral in 1941.

Note: Generally, do not capitalize titles that follow a name unless the person is an extremely high official, such as the title *president* when it is used to refer to the President of the United States.

> Bobby Kash, **p**resident of the **s**enior **c**lass

> George Washington, **P**resident of the **U**nited **S**tates

Note: Generally, capitalize titles that are used in place of a person's name.

> Good morning, **C**oach. What is your e-mail address, **C**aptain?

▶ **Family Members**   Capitalize words showing family relationships when used with the person's name or in place of the person's name, but *not* when preceded by a possessive (unless it is part of the name).

> I asked *my* **A**unt Hazel for her recipe for fudge.   (possessive/title part of the name)

> I asked *my* **a**unt for her recipe for fudge.   (possessive/title not part of the name)

> I told **F**ather I would call **M**other tomorrow.   (in place of the person's name)

▶ **Titles of Creative Works**   Capitalize the first, last, and all other words—except prepositions and the words *a, an, the, for, and, nor, but, or, yet,* and *so*—of titles of books, periodicals, poems, stories, documents, movies, paintings and other works of art, and so on.

Books *A Tale of Two Cities*	**Periodicals** *Newsweek*
Poems "Siesta of a Hungarian Snake"	**Stories** "The Jilting of Granny Weatherall"
Articles "Resolving an Internal War"	**Documents** The Declaration of Independence

Movies *Porgy and Bess*	**Paintings** *Arrangement in Gray and Black*
Plays *Oedipus the King*	**Newspapers** *New York Times*
Songs "Gentle on My Mind"	

Note: Capitalize the words *a, an, the* written before a title only when they are part of the title. Do not capitalize these words before the names of magazines and newspapers.

The Dictionary of Diseased English   the *Reader's Digest*

▶ **Religious References**   Capitalize words that refer to the Deity, religions, religious followers, and sacred books.

God, the **A**lmighty **R**oman **C**atholic **B**aptist the **B**ible the **T**orah the **K**oran

Note: Do not capitalize the word *god* when used to refer to the gods of ancient mythology.

The name of the **g**oddess of tension and strife is Discord.

▶ **Initials**   Capitalize acronyms and other names formed with initials such as call letters of radio and television stations.

AIDS   SIDS   NASA   FBI   NBC   WKRP

EXERCISE 32

Add capital letters as needed and cross out unnecessary ones. Mark correct sentences with a C.

1. The divinity of the three great monotheistic Religions (Judaism, Christianity, and Islam) is God. In the old Testament, various names for God are used. Most Christians believe god lived on the earth as Jesus Christ.

2. Eldridge Cleaver once said, "All the gods are dead except the god of war." Mars is the name of the Roman God of War, and Ares is the Greek God of War.

3. America's first regular Newspaper, the *News-Letter,* was published in Boston in 1704.

4. The Gilbert and Sullivan opera *the Mikado* or *the town of Titipu,* inspired by Commodore Perry's opening of Japan in 1853, was an instant success in London.

5. One of the greatest Civil War generals, General William Tecumseh Sherman, who was born in Lancaster, Ohio, said, "War is hell." Supposedly, General Sherman was named after another famous general from Ohio—Chief Tecumseh of the Shawnees, a noted military leader who organized a confederacy of tribes to resist U. S. encroachment.

6. The first U. S. parochial school was founded in 1805 in Baltimore by saint Elizabeth Ann Seton, also called mother Seton.

7. "Good afternoon, Aunt Betty, have you heard from mother or father? They said they would call you or my Sister as soon as they arrived."

8. Herman Melville's *Moby Dick* is only superficially about whaling, and many people think it is possibly the greatest novel in all American Literature. A famous line from this novel is spoken by captain Ahab, "Let me look into a human eye; it is better than to gaze into sea or sky, better than to gaze on god." [Note: Punctuation errors were not part of the original text.]

9. General Electric station wgy in New York broadcast the first regularly scheduled television program beginning May 11, l928.

10. In 1906 the International radio telegraph convention at Berlin adopted the distress call SOS to replace the CQD (Stop Sending and Listen) call. An sos in Morse code—three dots, three dashes, three dots—was adopted in 1912 as a universal distress signal.

Review Exercises

Add capital letters as needed and cross out unnecessary ones. Mark correct sentences with a C.

REVIEW EXERCISE 33

1. John Paul Jones, American Naval hero known as the Father of the U. S. Navy, was born in a small scottish fishing village in 1747 and was apprenticed to a Shipmaster in Virginia when he was twelve years old.

2. Jones said he and the American Flag were twins because the Continental Congress gave him command of his ship the *Ranger* and adopted the stars and stripes at the same time.

3. During the American Revolution he raided british ships off the coast of great britain.

4. Jones captured the British Warship *Drake* and later took his badly damaged *Ranger* into a French Port. Although Congress promised him a new ship, it did not appear. Finally, Benjamin Frankin,

American Public Official, Writer, Scientist, and author of *Poor Richard's Almanac,* found an old French merchant ship for him.

5. Jones named the vessel the *Bonhomme Richard* in honor of Franklin. On September 23, 1778, Captain Jones met Britain's Baltic trading fleet, protected by the British warships *Serapis* and the *Countess of Scarborough.*

6. At sundown one of the most famous sea fights in history began. The small French Ships were of little help, and the British trading Vessels scuttled away. As the moon rose, the battle was between the *Bonhomme Richard* and the mighty British Warship *Serapis.*

7. Heavily outmanned and outgunned, Captain Jones continued to fight. Fires had broken out on both ships. Thinking Captain Jones was going to surrender, the Captain of the Serapis called out, "Have you struck?"

8. Although the *Richard* was full of holes, had four feet of water in the hold, and many of the crew members were dead or wounded, Jones boldly replied, "I have not yet begun to fight!"

9. Jones then moved in close, lashed his sinking ship to the *Serapis,* and the men fought hand-to-hand for over three hours. When the Battle was over, Captain John Paul Jones was the Winner. The *Bonhomme Richard* sank, and he and his crew sailed to France aboard the captured *Serapis.* As a result of the battle, congress heaped him with honors and awarded him a Gold Medal.

10. Later he went to Russia at the request of Catherine the Great, put new life into her Navy, and won many battles. He was only forty-five when he died in Paris. Almost a Century later his beloved adopted Country brought his body back to the United States and laid it to rest in the naval academy at Annapolis, which he had urged Congress to establish.

REVIEW EXERCISE 34

1. The Government of the United States is often personified by Uncle Sam—a tall, thin, white-haired man wearing Red and White Striped Pants, a Swallow-tailed Coat, and a Top hat. The origin of the term *Uncle Sam* is not clear.

2. The Term first appeared in the Troy, New York, *Post,* September 7, 1813, with the following explanation: "The letters U. S. on the government wagons are supposed to have given rise to it."

3. A more colorful explanation involves Samuel Wilson. When the United States declared War on Britain in 1812, Samuel and Ebenezer Wilson, owners of a Meat Packing Plant in New York, won a contract to supply the U. S. Troops with barrels of meat.

4. Samuel Wilson, a friendly outgoing man who wore a high-top hat over his flowing white hair, was affectionately called Uncle Sam by his employees. During the war (the War of 1812), he welcomed visitors to the plant and showed them the barrels of meat he was shipping to the troops.

5. All the barrels were stamped with the initials E. A.—U. S. (Elbert Anderson, the government contractor, and the United States). One curious visitor asked a Plant Employee what the letters meant. "I don't know," said the meat packer, "Unless it means Elbert Anderson and Uncle Sam."

6. If you took United States History 103, you probably learned about the Green Mountain Boys. The Green Mountain Boys was the name of armed bands led by Ethan Allen, one of the founders of what is now the state of Vermont.

7. The colony of New York claimed the whole Region, and Ethan Allen and his Green Mountain Boys used threats, intimidation, and violence to prevent the New Hampshire Grants (now Vermont) from becoming part of new york state.

8. When the War with England came, Allen called up his Band of Fighters and set out through the mountains on what many thought was a hair-brained scheme—take fort Ticonderoga.

9. Under the cover of darkness, they rowed across the lake and stole upon the fort just before daybreak. Allan stationed his troops on the parade ground of the fort. When the signal was given, the men burst out with a rousing cheer.

10. At the same time, Allen plunged into the bedroom of the sleeping British Commander and demanded that he surrender the fort. "By whose authority?" responded the sleepy and startled captain. The famous response was "In the name of the great jehovah and the continental congress!" [Note: Punctuation errors were not part of the original text.]

REVIEW EXERCISE 35

1. No man, except Thomas Jefferson, did more to shape the way Americans think today than Alexander Hamilton. He grew up in the west Indies, and his Aunts sent him to the United States where he entered King's college, now Columbia University. 2. Hamilton was an advocate of a strong single Government. "Without government," he said, "There is no liberty." He, James Madison, and John Jay wrote the "Federalist Papers." Without these papers, the constitution would probably never have been adopted. 3. The "Federalist Papers" first appeared in the *New York independent journal* in October, 1787, and ran for seven months. 4. Hamilton became the first U. S. Secretary of treasury and established the National Bank and Public Credit System. 5. In 1792, Secretary of Treasury Alexander Hamilton averted a U. S. Economic Depression by supporting the Government's 6 percent bonds at par value.

6. Perhaps no Duel is more famous than the one between Hamilton and Aaron Burr, chief rivals in New York State. 7. Aaron Burr became vice president under Thomas Jefferson after a deadlock in the Electoral College was broken by the House of Representatives. During this contentious time, Hamilton threw his influence in favor of Jefferson, and when Burr ran for governor of New York in 1804, Hamilton campaigned against him. 8. On the basis of gossip he had heard about what Hamilton had said, Burr challenged him to a Duel. Hamilton did not approve of dueling and had lost his Son only a few years earlier in a Duel. 9. He accepted the challenge because he felt that if he did not, he would disgrace his family and lose his influence in Public Affairs. When the signal was given, Hamilton fired into the air; Burr shot to kill, and he did. 10. Burr later fled South where he tried to help establish an Independent Nation in Mexico and the southwest. He was tried for Treason but was acquitted for lack of evidence.

Using Abbreviations

Do not use abbreviations in compositions except in situations where abbreviations are usually used.

No I walked across the **st** this A.M. & called to my friend **Chas.,** who is the **bnk. pres.**

Yes I walked across the **street** this **morning and** spoke to my friend **Charles,** who is the **bank president.**

Abbreviate certain titles before and after names, with specific dates, times, numbers, amounts, and certain familiar abbreviations—often written without periods.

Titles before names Ms. Mr. Mrs. Dr. Rev.

Titles and college degrees after names Jr. Sr. B.A. M.A. Ph.D. M.D

Specific times, dates, and amounts 7 A.M. (or a.m.) 12 B.C. No.10 $13.50

Familiar abbreviations NATO FBI AFL-CIO

Write the full name when you are using an unfamiliar name and put the abbreviation after it in parentheses when you first use the term. Thereafter you may use the abbreviation in the piece of writing.

English as a Second Language (ESL)

Note: Do not use the symbol *&* for *and*.

Using Italics (Underlining)

Italicizing Names of Publications

Italicize the names of whole publications.

Books	*American Folklore and Legend* *The American Heritage Dictionary*
Magazines	*People* *U.S. News and World Report*
Newspapers	the *New York Times* the *San Francisco Chronicle*
Long poems	*Paradise Lost* *Evangeline*

Italicizing Titles of Creative Works

Italicize works of art, music, and entertainment.

Plays	*Death of a Salesman* *The Glass Menagerie*
Movies	*Cleopatra* *Gone with the Wind*
Television shows	*Sesame Street* *60 Minutes*
Radio programs	*All Things Considered* *The Hit Parade*
Musicals	*Nutcracker Suite* *My Fair Lady*
Long musical compositions	*The Ninth Symphony* *Das Lied von der Erde*
Paintings	*Mona Lisa* *Guernica*
Sculptures	*David* *The Thinker*
Operas	*Madam Butterfly* *The Legend of the Flying Dutchman*
Comic strips	*The Far Side* *Garfield*

Italicizing Names of Crafts and Vessels

Italicize the names of trains, ships, aircraft, and spacecraft.

Ships	*USS Abraham Lincoln* *The Titanic*
Trains	*Cannonball Express* *Orient Express*
Aircraft	*The Spirit of St. Louis* *Flyer I*
Spacecraft	*Sputnik* *Voyager I*

Italicizing Foreign Words and Words Used as Words

Italicize foreign words and words referred to as such.

| **Foreign words** | Does *carpe diem* mean "seize the day"? |
| **Words as words** | The word *tone* is often combined with other words to create expressions such as *color tone, half tone, tone poem, high-toned,* and so forth. |

Using Numbers

Numbers can be expressed in words or in figures. Usually, the form you use will be determined by the type of writing you are doing. Writers involved in science, technical, or business fields tend to use figures. Writers in other fields tend to use words.

Spelling Out Numbers

▶ **Few Numbers**   If the work you are doing involves only a few numbers, follow the recommendations of the Modern Language Association (MLA) style manual and spell out any number that can be expressed in one or two words.

ONE OR TWO WORDS	MORE THAN TWO WORDS
three	3½
one hundred	101
two thousand	2,001
three million	3,481,591

▶ **Beginning of a Sentence**   Do not begin a sentence with a figure. Write out the number or rephrase the sentence so that the figure is not the first word.

No   150 people attended the party.

Yes   *One hundred fifty* people attended the party.

Yes   They had 150 guests at the party.

▶ **Percentages and Amounts**   You may use words for percentages or amounts of money if you can express them in no more than three words.

   ten dollars   forty-three percent   seventy-five cents

▶ **Twenty-One to Ninety-Nine**   Use hyphens to write out numbers from *twenty-one* to *ninety-nine.*

   Do you know that *twenty-four* students made As on their midterm examination?

Using Figures in Technical or Business Writing

If the work you are doing involves frequent use of numbers, you may want to follow the suggestions in the *Publication Manual of the American Psychological Association* (APA) and use figures for most numbers above ten—except when a sentence begins with a number.

Using Figures According to Widely Accepted Standards

Generally, use figures in the following instances:

Abbreviations or symbols	5:30 P.M. 2% $5 120 B.C.
Dates	July 4, 1776 or 4 July 1776
Addresses	101 Magnolia Avenue, East 33rd Avenue, Suite 8
Percentages	Sales were up 12 percent.
Decimal fractions	3.51
Identification numbers	serial number 23457891
Sections of books	page 9

▶ **Time of Day**   Use the abbreviations A.M. and P.M. only when they are accompanied by a number. When you use a word to express time, use *o'clock* and the part of the day, not A.M. or P.M.

Yes   He arrived at 2 P.M.   **No**   He arrived at two P.M.

Yes   He arrived at two *o'clock* this afternoon.

▶ **Dates**   Do not use an ordinal form in dates.

No   September 4th, 1961

Yes   September 4, 1961

▶ **Consistency**   Avoid shifting between words and figures. If you need figures to express some numbers within the same context, be consistent and use figures throughout the sentence, for numbers that are in the same category. Numbers within the same context that are in a different category may be expressed differently.

No   In the *before* picture, she weighed 250 pounds and wore a size twenty-two dress. In the *after* picture, which was taken three years later, she weighed 125 pounds and wore a size ten dress.

Yes   In the *before* picture, she weighed 250 pounds and wore a size 22 dress. In the *after* picture, which was taken three years later, she weighed 125 pounds and wore a size 10 dress.

Combining Words and Figures

When two numbers are next to each other, use words for one and figures for the other.

5 thousand   103 billion   5 eighteen-wheelers   thirty 5-person tag teams

Practice Exercises

Make the necessary corrections in *abbreviations, italics,* and *numbers.* Mark correct sentences with a C.

EXERCISE 36

1. Ms magazine was first published in July 1972 with former Look editor Ms Patricia Carbine as publisher and Ms Gloria Steinem as editor.

2. Arthur M. Schlesinger, Jr., born in Columbus, Ohio, won a Pulitzer Prize in 1945 for his brilliant Age of Jackson. He also wrote a 3 volume analysis of the New Deal Period: The Age of Roosevelt. Based on his experience as an aide to President Kennedy, he wrote a study of Kennedy's White House years, A Thousand Days, and received a Pulitzer Prize for it in 1965.

3. Jonathan Swift introduced the word yahoo in Gulliver's Travels.

4. The word blurb was coined by American humorist Gelett Burgess, which he defined as "sounding like a publisher."

5. The first American airplane was flown by its inventors, the Wright Brothers, December 17th, 1903, near Kitty Hawk, North Carolina, where Wilbur Wright, thirty-six, and Orville Wright, thirtytwo flew their Flyer I with a chain-drive 12-horsepower motorcycle engine; and on their 4th effort, they achieved a 59-second flight of 852 feet at a 15-foot altitude.

6. The skeleton of the oldest known horse is estimated to be forty-five million years old.

7. Jack Dempsey's eight-to-ten-inch punches traveled at an estimated 135 miles an hour.

8. Elizabeth Kubler-Ross, M. D. was graduated from the University of Zurich in 1957. Her best-selling book On Death and Dying describes the 5 psychological stages experienced by the dying.

9. At the beginning of 1940, the U. S. Army was tiny (one hundred seventy-five thousand people) and had little equipment. 5 years later the number was increased to 8 million and was the best-equipped army in the world.

10. Russia has 12 neighbors—the most of any country—on its borders. Can you name them?

EXERCISE 37

1. "Listen my children, and you shall hear/ Of the midnight ride of Paul Revere,/ On the 18th of April, in seventy-five; /Hardly a man is now alive/Who remembers that famous day and year." — Henry Wadsworth Longfellow [Note: Punctuation errors were not part of the original text.]

2. When Longfellow wrote the 1st of 14 stanzas of the poem he entitled "Paul Revere's Ride," he was one of the men alive who failed to remember "that famous day and year."

3. Dr. Joseph Warren, the commander of the colonial forces, chose 2 experienced couriers—Paul Revere and William Dawes as his messengers.

4. On April 15th, the Saturday before Easter, Dr. Warren received word that the British troops were moving. He sent Paul Revere to Lexington to warn Sam Adams.

5. Paul Revere, on his way back from Lexington, stopped in Charleston and told the minutemen there that the Redcoats would be coming their way. He pointed to the steeple of Christ's Church and said, "2 lanterns if they really come across the river . . . 1 lantern means they're marching overland through Cambridge."

6. The American army was to meet at Concord on the 19th of April to receive equipment and supplies, which included 10 hogsheads of rum.

7. On Tuesday, April 18th, 1775, Warren, through one of his spies, learned that the British were going to move on Concord.

8. Since the man-of-war Somerset was moving down the river, Dr. Warren surmised that the British army would take the water route, and he sent Billy Dawes along the land route to spread the news. When 1 of two guards became suspicious of Billy, the 2nd guard vouched for Billy, saying he was just a harmless country bumpkin with whom he often shared an ale or 2.

9. Late that evening Dr. Warren sent Paul Revere along the water route, and with the help of the sexton at Christ's Church, 2 lights briefly beamed from the steeple. He then borrowed a horse and rode to Lexington.

10. In fact, on that fateful day in April of '75, 2 young men were riding horses between Boston and Lexington and shouting, "The British are coming." Contrary to Longfellow's poem, it was Dawes who rode 1st, rode longest, and did the job right. Revere was sidetracked and was eventually captured by six British soldiers.

EXERCISE 38

Make the necessary corrections in abbreviations, italics, and numbers. Mark correct sentences with a C.

1. When Oliver Hazard Perry, a capt. at the age of 28, entered the Battle of Lake Erie, he was aboard his flagship, the Lawrence, which he had named after Commander James Lawrence, whose dying words were, "Don't give up the ship!"

2. The Lawrence was riddled with holes and ready to sink, but Captain Perry had no intention of giving up. As soon as another ship—the Niagara—came close, he jumped into an open rowboat and under a hail of British fire rowed toward it.

3. The British forces were soon overwhelmed, and Captain Perry sent the following famous message to the gen. on shore who was in command of the battle: "We have met the enemy, and they are ours."

4. The battle took place at Put-in Bay, a bay of Western Lake Erie on an island of Ohio.

5. Captain Perry lived only a few years after his great victory. 6 years later he contracted yellow fever in the West Indies and died there August 23rd, 1819.

6. 15-year-old Sam Houston ran away from home and lived with the Cherokees for 3 years. When the War of 1812 broke out, he enlisted in 1813, and although he was only 20 years old, he soon had a commission under Andrew Jackson.

7. After the war, Jackson was influential in getting Houston to study law. Within one year he became the district attorney for the Nashville District. In eighteen twenty-three he was elected to Congress, and in eighteen twenty-seven he was elected governor of Tennessee.

8. On March 2nd, 1836, Texas declared independence from Mexico and became an independent republic.

9. After getting two small cannons, he led his 783 men against Santa Anna, the Mexican General who soundly defeated the Texan troops at the Battle of the Alamo. Santa Anna had 1,300 to 1,400 men. Houston surprised Santa Anna and his troops, who were camped near the San Jacinto River, and within 15 minutes killed or captured the entire Mexican force.

10. In eighteen thirty-six, Houston became the president of the Texan Republic. When Texas was admitted to the Union, he was one of the 1st senators to be sent to Washington, and in 1859, he was elected governor of Texas.

Reading, Thinking, and Writing Critically

There are very many people who read simply to prevent themselves from thinking.

—G. C. LICHTENBURG
Aphorisms, "Notebook"

Critical thinking is essential to everyone's life. It is the kind of thinking that people do every day to solve problems. You are thinking critically when you approach a problem or situation with healthy skepticism. Peter Elbow calls this approach the "believing and doubting game." The critical thinking that you do in college differs from the everyday type of critical thinking that you do. In college, you have to read material—often complex and abstract—and then respond to it. To write effective responses you need to master strategies for approaching reading material because the more effective your critical reading is, the more effective your responses will be.

Reading Critically

In his *Essays* "Of Studies," Sir Francis Bacon offers sound advice to people who want to read critically: "Read not to contradict and confuse; nor to believe and take for granted; nor to find talk and discourse; but to weigh and consider." Take nothing at face value. Examine new ideas or situations and compare those with what you already know and what you are learning, and then you can arrive at an interpretation or make a judgment. Critical reading involves asking questions and trying to find answers to them. What is the meaning of the piece of writing? How does it compare with what I already know? Do I need to learn more about it from another source?

Developing Strategies for Critical Reading

Before you begin reading, think about your purpose. Why are you reading? Are you reading for entertainment? Are you reading to gain information? Are you reading to gain an appreciation and understanding of literature? Are you reading to review lecture notes or reading notes? Your reason for reading will affect the way you approach the reading and the amount of time you devote to it. The extent of what you already know about a subject will also affect the amount of time you will need to preview, read, summarize, analyze, interpret, synthesize, and evaluate the material.

Previewing

Before you begin to actually read material, preview it. Previewing is an important step in the reading process. Scan the material to discover what it is about, its purpose, and what you already know about the topic.

- **Type** What kind of reading is it? Different types of writings have different purposes: to entertain, to engage in self-expression, to explain or inform, or to persuade.

- **Title** What does it tell you about the topic? Does it give you any clues to content, purpose, or how the author feels about the subject?

- **Author** Are you familiar with the author? If so, what do you know about him or her?

- **First paragraph** Read the first paragraph. Authors often introduce the subject and their idea about the subject in this paragraph.

- **Headings** If the reading contains boldfaced headings, read them because they usually announce the topic for that section.

- **First sentences** Read the first sentence under each heading and the first sentence in each paragraph because these sentences often contain the main idea of the section or paragraph. If the paragraphs are very short, read every third or fourth introductory sentence.

- **Last paragraph** Read the last paragraph because it often summarizes or concludes the reading.

- **Unfamiliar terms** As you skim the material, circle words or expressions that are unfamiliar to you.

Reading Actively

Read the material at least twice. After previewing the text, you will probably have a fairly good understanding of the literal (exact or primary) meaning of it.

- **First reading** Read through it quickly, trying to get more information about the subject and the author's ideas about it. If a sentence or passage suggests an inference (conjecture) or evaluation (value judgment) to you, or if you notice more unfamiliar words, just circle these items, and come back to them later. Do not take notes.

- **Second reading** Read it slowly and carefully, digesting literal meanings, and make inferences and evaluations.

- **Unfamiliar terms** Look up unfamiliar terms: Keep a dictionary with you while you read, or use your computer's reference material and look up the unfamiliar words you circled during the previewing and any other words that are unfamiliar. Sometimes the dictionary definition will suffice, but other times you may need to do a quick encyclopedia check.

- **Notes** Take notes. Underline or highlight important passages. Interact with the author by taking separate notes or writing in the margin of the text. Paraphrase (put in your own words) confusing or difficult passages to help you understand what the writer is trying to say. Talk back to the writer and talk to yourself with your response notes such as the following: "Not logical." "Where is the support?" "Yes!" "Not clear." "How?" "Check this." "Good."

Summarizing

After you finish critically reading the material, write a summary. A *summary* as it is used in this text means a brief restatement of the content of a piece of writing. It should *be written in your own words, emphasize key points,* and *be accurate.* A summary may be short (sometimes called a précis), or it may be a much longer piece. The length of the summary depends on the material you are summarizing and your reason for summarizing it. Summaries serve a variety of purposes. You may write summaries to demonstrate your understanding of a topic or text. You may write summaries to review for exams, and you may write summaries when you write research papers. To write an effective summary, you have to be able re- state the thesis and summarize the main points of the text. When you can do this, you will have a good idea of the subject and the writer's ideas about that subject. See Appendix A7 Restating a Piece of Writing.

Thinking Critically

Analyzing and Interpreting

When you analyze, you examine the elements of the text, and as you analyze, you interpret—try to draw some conclusions about the writer, the subject, and his or her ideas about the subject. After you have written the summary, use the following questions to help you analyze and interpret what you have read:

- **Who is the writer?** Is the writer qualified to write on the subject—either through personal experience or training? Who is the intended audience? Is there more than one audience?

- **What is the thesis?** Is the quality and quantity of the support for the thesis adequate?

- **Do the first sentences of each paragraph contain the main idea of that paragraph?**

- **What is the organizational pattern?** Is it appropriate?

- **What is the writer's tone?** Is the tone appropriate for the subject and the audience?

- **What are some of the assumptions of the writer about the audience?**

- **What are the author's values and beliefs reflected in the work?**

- **Does the writer have biases?**

- **Are your biases, values, or beliefs in conflict with those of the writer?**

- **Do you agree with the writer because his or her ideas confirm your own beliefs, values, or biases?**

- **Has the writer left anything out or tried to cover up something?**

Synthesizing

After you have analyzed and interpreted the material, synthesize it. When you synthesize, you think about the reading and how it relates to what you know, what you are learning, and your own experiences. When you synthesize, use the skills you learned in developing paragraphs. You may develop your synthesis through comparison and/or contrast, cause and/or effect, definitions, examples or illustrations. The type of development you use will depend on the work you are synthesizing and what you want to accomplish. Use the following questions to help you synthesize what you have read.

- **What knowledge do you already have?** Do you have personal experience or reading experience that supports or does not support the ideas in this material?

- **Does the work contain any contradictions?**

- **Does it contain biased language?**

- **Are any of your experiences or knowledge at variance with the ideas presented in the text?**

- **Are these variances real, or are they based on your own biases?**

- **Are these variances major ones, or are they just minor ones?**

- **Are the answers to a complex problem too simple?**

- **What conclusions can you draw?**

Evaluating the Text

Sometimes you will need to judge a text. Use the following questions to help you evaluate the quality, value, or significance of the work.

- **Did you like the text?** Why or why not?

- **Is it unified?** Do all elements contribute to development of the thesis?

- **Is it coherent?** Is it organized according to a definite plan. Is that plan effective? Does one idea follow from the preceding one and flow smoothly into the next one?

- **Has the writer succeeded in accomplishing his or her purpose?**

- **Do you agree or disagree with the writer's ideas?** Can you support your opinions with evidence?

Writing Critically

To write critically about another person's work, employ the skills you learned in developing paragraphs and essays, and develop the material you generated when you were previewing, reading, summarizing, analyzing, interpreting, synthesizing, and evaluating the reading. Begin the introductory paragraph with an appropriate lead-in, supply the necessary background information, state your point in a thesis statement, and give your readers an indication of how you are going to develop the essay. Be sure to include the title of the text and the writer's name. Develop the body paragraphs, and then write the ending paragraph, including a summary of the main points and other appropriate endings such as a prediction and/or recommendation. Be sure to make the last sentence a memorable one.

Reading Selections

The reading selections reflect the thinking of professional writers about current issues that are of interest to many college students. The selections are grouped according to the following themes: *Language and Writing, Everyday World, A Sense of Beauty, History and Culture, Media and Behavior,* and *Men and Women.* Auxiliary material that precedes each selection includes both thematic and rhetorical content, some information about the writer, and a list of related readings. The paragraphs are numbered to make it easier to refer to passages when discussing the work or writing about it. Following each selection are definitions or explanations for words, names, or expressions that may be unfamiliar; vocabulary quizzes drawn from boldfaced words in the text; questions for thinking and discussing the work; and writing suggestions.

Language and Writing

Kurt Vonnegut, "How to Write with Style"

Auxiliary Material

Rhetorical Content   Directional Process Analysis: Explaining How to Do Something

Thematic Content   Writing and Language

Background   from *Palm Sunday,* 1981, Bantam Doubleday Dell Publishing Group, Inc. With wry charm and dark humor, Kurt Vonnegut protests the horrors of the twentieth century. Sometimes the plots resemble science fiction. His novels include *Player Piano, Slaughterhouse Five, Cat's Cradle, Deadeye Dick, Palm Sunday,* and *Hocus Pocus.* In this essay Vonnegut urges beginning writers to use language accurately, clearly, and simply.

Related Readings   Garrison Keillor, "How the Crab Apple Grew," from *Leaving Home.* © 1987. Viking Penguin.

Paul Roberts, "How to Say Nothing in Five Hundred Words," from *Understanding English.* © 1958. Harper Collins Publishers.

Natalie Goldberg, "The Rules of Writing Practice," from *Wild Mind: Living the Writer's Life.* © 1977. Bantam Books.

Tony Earley, "The Quare Gene," *New Yorker,* September 21, 1998.

1   Newspaper reporters and technical writers are trained to reveal almost nothing about themselves in their writings. This makes them freaks in the world of writers, since almost all of the other ink-stained wretches in that world reveal a lot about themselves to readers. We call these revelations, accidental and intentional, elements of literary style.

2   These revelations are fascinating to us as readers. They tell us what sort of person it is with whom we are spending time. Does the writer sound ignorant or informed, crazy or sane, stupid or bright, crooked or honest, humorless or playful—? And on and on.

3   When you yourself put words on paper, remember that the most damning revelation you can make about yourself is that you do not know what is interesting and what is not. Don't you yourself like or dislike writers mainly for what they choose to show you or make you think about? Did you ever admire an empty-headed writer for his or her mastery of the language? No.

4   So your own winning literary style must begin with interesting ideas in your head. Find a subject you care about and which you in your heart feel others should care about. It is this genuine caring, and not your games with language, which will be the most compelling and seductive element in your style.

5   I am not urging you to write a novel, by the way—although I would not be sorry if you wrote one, provided you genuinely cared about something. A petition to the mayor about a pothole in front of your house or a love letter to the girl next door will do.

6   Do not ramble, though.

7   As for your use of language: Remember that two great masters of our language, William Shakespeare and James Joyce, wrote sentences which were almost childlike when their subjects were most profound. "To be or not to be?" asks Shakespeare's Hamlet. The longest word is three letters long. Joyce, when he was frisky, could put together a sentence as intricate and glittering as a necklace for Cleopatra, but my favorite sentence in his short story "Evaline" is this one: "She was tired." At that point of the story, no other words could break the heart of a reader as those words do.

8   Simplicity of language is not only reputable but perhaps even sacred. The Bible opens with a sentence well within the writing skills of a lively fourteen-year-old: "In the beginning God created the heavens and the earth."

9   It may be that you, too, are capable of making necklaces for Cleopatra, so to speak. But your **eloquence** should be the servant of the ideas in your head. Your rule

might be this: If a sentence, no matter how excellent, does not **illuminate** my subject in some new and useful way, scratch it out. Here is the same rule paraphrased to apply to storytelling, to fiction: Never include a sentence which does not either remark on character or advance the action.

10   The writing style which is most natural for you is bound to echo speech you heard as a child. English was the novelist Joseph Conrad's third language, and much that seems **piquant** in his use of English was no doubt colored by his first language, which was Polish. And lucky indeed is the writer who has grown up in Ireland, for the English spoken there is so amusing and musical. I myself grew up in Indianapolis, Indiana, where common speech sounds like a band saw cutting galvanized tin, and employs a vocabulary as unornamental as a monkey wrench.

11   In some of the more remote hollows of Appalachia, children still grow up hearing songs and **locutions** of Elizabethan times. Yes, and many Americans grow up hearing a language other than English, or an English dialect a majority of Americans cannot understand.

12   All these varieties of speech are beautiful. No matter what your first language, you should treasure it all your life. If it happens not to be standard English, and if it shows itself when you write standard English, the result is usually delightful, like a very pretty girl with one eye that is green and one that is blue.

13   I myself find that I trust my own writing most, and others seem to trust it most, too, when I sound most like a person from Indianapolis, which is what I am. What alternatives do I have? The one most **vehemently** recommended by teachers has no doubt been pressed on you, as well: that I write like **cultivated** Englishmen of a century or more ago.

14   I used to be **exasperated** by such teachers, but am no more. I understand now that all those antique essays and stories with which I was to compare my own work were not magnificent for their datedness or foreignness, but for saying precisely what their authors meant them to say. My teachers wished me to write accurately, always selecting the most effective words, and relating the words to one another **unambiguously,** rigidly, like parts of a machine. The teachers did not want to turn me into an Englishman after all. They hoped that I would become understandable— and therefore understood. So you, too, had better avoid Picasso-style or jazz-style writing, if you have something worth saying and wish to be understood.

15   And there went my dream of doing with words what Pablo Picasso did with paint or what any number of jazz idols did with music. If I broke all the rules of punctuation, had words mean whatever I wanted them to mean, and strung them together **higgledy-piggledy,** I would simply not be understood.

16 If it were only teachers who insisted that modern writers stay close to literary styles of the past, we might reasonably ignore them. But readers insist on the very same thing. They want our pages to look very much like pages they have seen before.

17 Why? It is because they themselves have a tough job to do, and they need all the help they can get from us. They have to identify thousands of little marks on paper, and make sense of them immediately. They have to *read*, an art so difficult that most people do not really master it even after having studied it all through grade school and high school—for twelve long years.

18 So this discussion, like all discussions of literary styles, must finally acknowledge that our stylistic options as writers are neither numerous nor glamorous, since our readers are bound to be such imperfect artists. Our audience requires us to be sympathetic and patient teachers, ever willing to simplify and clarify—whereas we would rather soar high above the crowd, singing like nightingales.

19 That is the bad news. The good news is that we Americans are governed under a unique Constitution, which allows us to write whatever we please without fear of punishment. So the meaningful aspect of our styles, which is what we choose to write about, is unlimited.

20 Also: We are members of an **egalitarian** society, so there is no reason for us to write, in case we are not classically educated aristocrats, as though we were classically educated aristocrats.

21 For a discussion of literary style in a narrower sense, in a more technical sense, I commend to your attention *The Elements of Style* by William Strunk, Jr., and E. B. White (Macmillan, 1979). It contains such rules as this: "A participial phrase at the beginning of a sentence must refer to the grammatical subject," and so on. E. B. White is, of course, one of the most admirable literary stylists this country has so far produced.

22 You should realize, too, that no one would care how well or badly Mr. White expressed himself, if he did not have perfectly enchanting things to say.

Understanding Words

▶ **Definitions**

James Joyce (1882–1941) (par. 7) An Irish writer whose literary innovations have had a profound influence on modern fiction. His works include *Ulysses* (1922) and *Finnegans Wake* (1939).

Hamlet (par. 7) The major character in Shakespeare's tragedy of the same name.

Joseph Conrad (1857–1924) (par. 10) A Polish-born British novelist who is a master of atmosphere and narrative techniques. His works include *Lord Jim* (1900) and *Heart of Darkness* (1902).

Pablo Picasso (1881–1973) (par. 15) A Spanish artist who was one of the most prolific and influential artists of the twentieth century. He, along with Georges Braques, launched cubism—a school of painting characterized by fragmentation of natural forms into abstract structures.

▶ **Vocabulary**

Check your understanding of the following words. Read them in context (boldfaced in the text) and fill in the blank with the letter of the word or words that are closest to the meaning of the word in the text.

1. ____**eloquence** expressions that are (a) dramatic (b) powerful and expressive (c) formal

2. ____**illuminate** (a) clarify (b) brighten (c) expose (d) narrow

3. ____**piquant** (a) racy (b) stinging (c) appealing (d) colorful (e) incorrect

4. ____**locutions** (a) styles of speaking (b) archaic expressions (c) vulgarities (d) tales

5. ____**vehemently** (a) insidiously (b) strongly (c) hypocritically (d) likely

6. ____**cultivated** (a) refined (b) agrarian (c) acculturated (d) sophisticated (e) noble

7. ____**exasperated** (a) put down (b) fooled (c) pleased (d) greatly annoyed

8. ____**unambiguously** (a) fluidly (b) clearly (c) carefully (d) eloquently

9. ____**higgledy-piggledy** (a) according to my style (b) topsy-turvy (c) orderly fashion

10. ____**egalitarian** (a) hypocritical (b) equal (c) unequal society (d) aristocratic

Thinking and Discussing

1. In your own words, state Vonnegut's main point in this essay.

2. What is the difference between newspaper reporters and technical writers and other writers?

3. Writing style may be loosely defined as the way words and sentences are used to present the material. Give concrete examples of several ways Vonnegut says that writers can write with style.

4. Do you agree with Vonnegut that teachers often try to get students to write like "dead white men"? Have you ever complained about instructors who want you to write "the way they want you to write—not the way you want to write"? What conclusion does Vonnegut reach about this controversy in writing style?

5. Vonnegut says that "many Americans grow up hearing a language other than English, or an English dialect a majority of Americans cannot understand." Are you familiar with any of the following expressions? From your own experiences, can you add to the list?

"The *booty* is the best part of the pickle." (The *bottom* of a pickle is tastier than the other part.)

"He was driving an old *hoopty*." (He was driving an old, beat-up car.)

"She has *chutzpah*." (She has amazing nerve bordering on arrogance.)

"Aunt Jane is really *quare*." (Aunt Jane is "squirrely"—strange or eccentric.)

"Is everything *copacaetic?*" (Is everything okay or all right?)

6. Paragraphs 7 and 10 contain similes. Find them. Do you find them effective? Why? Study some of your own papers. Have you used similes or metaphors to make your ideas more vivid?

Writing Suggestions

1. Write a paragraph about an experience you have had with another dialect or language—either as the user of the language or the person trying to understand unfamiliar words and expressions. Such experiences can be amusing, embarrassing, touching, or culturally disastrous.

2. Using Vonnegut's essay as a model, write a process analysis essay in which you explain how to achieve a goal, such as

   a. how to get your A out of a class

   b. how to maintain a positive relationship

   c. how to successfully juggle school, work, and a social life

3. Write a short paper in which you discuss your own writing style. What are some of the dominant features? Are there any elements of your style that frequently receive praise? Are there any elements that are often negatively criticized?

Stephanie Ericsson, "The Ways We Lie".

Auxiliary Material

Rhetorical Content Classification: Categorization According to Relationships

Thematic Content Language and Writing—Lying: Truth and Consequences

Background from *Companion into the Dawn: Inner Dialogues on Loving.* Stephanie Ericsson, writer and screenwriter, was born in San Francisco and began writing at the age of fifteen. Her works include *Shamefaced, Women of AA: Recovering Together, Companion through the Darkness: Inner Dialogues on Grief.* "The Ways We Lie" first appeared in *Utne Reader* and is taken from a later work, *Companion into the Dawn: Inner Dialogues on Loving* (1994). In this essay, Ericsson makes a distinction between "telling functional lies and living a lie."

Related Readings Michael W. Cox, "Little Soldiers," from the *New York Times Magazine*, August 6, 1995.

Robert Coles, "I Listen to My Parents and I Wonder What They Believe," from *Redbook* February 1980.

William J. Bennett, "What Really Ails America," from *Reader's Digest*, August 1984.

Stephen L. Carter, "The Culture of Disbelief," from *The Culture of Disbelief.* © 1993. Perscus Books.

Fighting Irish football coach George O'Leary resigns after admitting he lied about his academic and athletic credentials. Subsequently, other athletic notables lost their jobs after their credentials were reviewed. (Notre Dame, South Bend, Indiana, 12/13/01, AP Photo/Joe Raymond)

1   The bank called today, and I told them my deposit was in the mail, even though I hadn't written a check yet. It'd been a rough day. The baby I'm pregnant with decided to do aerobics on my lungs for two hours, our three-year-old daughter painted the living room couch with lipstick, the IRS put me on hold for an hour, and I was late to a business meeting because I was tired.

2   I told my client that the traffic had been bad. When my partner came home, his haggard face told me his day hadn't gone any better than mine, so when he asked, "How was your day?" I said, "Oh, fine," knowing that one more straw might break his back. A friend called and wanted to take me to lunch. I said I was busy. Four lies in the course of a day, none of which I felt the least bit guilty about.

3   We lie. We all do. We exaggerate, we minimize, we avoid confrontation, we spare people's feelings, we conveniently forget, we keep secrets, we justify lying to the big-guy institutions. Like most people, I indulge in small falsehoods and still think of myself as an honest person. Sure I lie, but it doesn't hurt anything. Or does it?

4   I once tried going a whole week without telling a lie, and it was paralyzing. I discovered that telling the truth all the time is nearly impossible. It means living with some serious consequences: The bank charges me $60 in overdraft fees, my partner keels over when I tell him about my **travails,** my client fires me for telling her I didn't feel like being on time, and my friend takes it personally when I say I'm not hungry. There must be some merit to lying.

5   But if I justify lying, what makes me any different from slick politicians or the corporate robbers who raided the S&L industry? Saying it's okay to lie one way and not another is **hedging.** I cannot seem to escape the voice deep inside me that tells me: When someone lies, someone loses.

6   What far-reaching consequences will I, or others, pay as a result of my lie? Will someone's trust be destroyed? Will someone else pay *my* penance because I ducked out? We must consider the *meaning of our actions.* Deception, lies, capital crimes, and misdemeanors all carry meanings. *Webster's* definition of *lie* is specific:

> 1: a false statement or action especially made with the intent to deceive;

> 2: anything that gives or is meant to give a false impression.

7   A definition like this implies that there are many, many ways to tell a lie. Here are just a few.

8   **The White Lie** The white lie assumes that the truth will cause more damage than a simple, harmless untruth. Telling a friend he looks great when he looks like hell can be based on a decision that the friend needs a compliment more than a frank opinion. But, in effect, it is the liar deciding what is best for the lied to. Ultimately, it is a vote of no confidence. It is an act of subtle arrogance for anyone to decide what is best for someone else.

9   Yet not all circumstances are quite so cut and dried. Take, for instance, the sergeant in Vietnam who knew one of his men was killed in action but listed him as missing so that the man's family would receive indefinite compensation instead of the lump-sum **pittance** the military gives widows and children. His intent was honorable. Yet for twenty years this family kept their hopes alive, unable to move on to a new life.

10   **Facades** We all put up **facades** to one degree or another. When I put on a suit to go to see a client, I feel as though I am putting on another face, obeying the expectation that serious business people wear suits rather than sweatpants. But I'm a writer. Normally, I get up, get the kid off to school, and sit at my computer in my pajamas until four in the afternoon. When I answer the phone, the caller thinks I'm wearing a suit (although the UPS man knows better).

11 But facades can be destructive because they are used to seduce others into an illusion. For instance, I recently realized that a former friend was a liar. He presented himself with all the right looks and the right words and offered lots of new consciousness theories, fabulous books to read, and fascinating insights. Then I did some business with him and the time came for him to pay me. He turned out to be all talk and no walk. I heard a **plethora** of reasonable excuses, including in-depth descriptions of the big break around the corner. In six months of work, I saw less than a hundred bucks. When I confronted him, he raised both eyebrows and tried to convince me that I'd heard him wrong, that he'd made no commitment to me. A simple investigation into his past revealed a crowded graveyard of disenchanted former friends.

12 **Ignoring the Plain Facts** In the sixties, the Catholic Church in Massachusetts began hearing complaints that Father James Porter was sexually molesting children. Rather than relieving him of his duties, the ecclesiastical authorities simply moved him from the parish to another between 1960 and 1967, actually providing him with a fresh supply of unsuspecting families and innocent children to abuse. After treatment in 1967 for pedophilia, he went back to work, this time in Minnesota. The new diocese was aware of Father Porter's obsession with children, but they needed priests and recklessly believed treatment had cured him. More children were abused until he was relieved of his duties a year later. By his own admission, Porter may have abused as many as a hundred children.

13 Ignoring the facts may not in and of itself be a form of lying, but consider the context of this situation. If a lie is *a false action done with the intent to deceive,* then the Catholic Church's conscious covering for Porter created irreparable consequences. The church became a co-perpetrator with Porter.

14 **Stereotypes and Clichés** Stereotype and cliché serve a purpose as a form of shorthand. Our need for vast amounts of information in nanoseconds has made the stereotype vital to modern communication. Unfortunately, it often shuts down original thinking, giving those hungry for truth a candy bar of misinformation instead of a balanced meal. The stereotype explains a situation with just enough truth to seem unquestionable.

15 All the *isms*—racism, sexism, ageism, et al.—are founded on and fueled by the stereotype and the cliché, which are lies of exaggeration, omission, and ignorance. They are always dangerous. They take a single tree and make it a landscape. They destroy curiosity. They close minds and separate people. The single mother on welfare is assumed to be cheating. Any black male could tell you how much of his identity is obliterated daily by stereotype. Fat people, ugly people, beautiful people, old people, large-breasted women, short men, the mentally ill, and the home-

less all could tell you how much more they are like us than we want to think. I once admitted to a group of people that I had a mouth like a truck driver. Much to my surprise, a man stood up and said, "I'm a truck driver, and I never cuss." Needless to say, I was humbled.

16 **Out-and-Out Lies** Of all the ways to lie, I like this one the best, probably because I get tired of trying to figure out the real meanings behind things. At least I can trust the bald-faced lie. I once asked my five-year-old nephew, "Who broke the fence?" (I had seen him do it.) He answered, "The murderer." Who could argue?

17 At least when this sort of lie is told it can be easily confronted. As the person who is lied to, I know where I stand. The bald-faced lie doesn't toy with my perceptions— it argues with them. It doesn't try to refashion reality, it tries to **refute** it. Read *my lips.* . . . No sleight of hand. No guessing. If this were the only form of lying, there would be no such thing as floating anxiety or the adult-children of alcoholics movement.

18 These are only a few of the ways we lie. Or are lied to. As I said earlier, it's not easy to entirely eliminate lies from our lives. No matter how **pious** we may try to be, we will still embellish, hedge, and omit to lubricate the daily machinery of living. But there is a world of difference between telling functional lies and living a lie. Martin Buber once said, "The lie is the spirit committing treason against itself." Our acceptance of lies become a cultural cancer that eventually shrouds and reorders reality until moral garbage becomes as invisible to us as water is to a fish.

19 How much do we tolerate before we become sick and tired of being sick and tired? When will we stand up and declare our *right* to trust? When do we stop accepting that the real truth is in the fine print? Whose lips do we read this year when we vote for president? When will we stop being so **reticent** about making judgments? When do we stop turning over our personal power and responsibility to liars?

20 Maybe if I don't tell the bank the check's in the mail I'll be less tolerant of the lies told to me every day. A country song I once heard said it all for me: "You've got to stand for something or you'll fall for anything."

Understanding Words

▶ **Definitions**

pedophilia (par. 12) An adult's sexual attraction to a child or children.

nanosecond (par. 14) One billionth of a second.

▶ **Vocabulary**

Check your understanding of the following words. Study them in context (boldfaced in the text) and fill in the blank with the letter of the word or words that are closest to the meaning of the word in the text.

1. ____**travails** (a) scheduling problems (b) innermost feelings (c) travel plans (d) problems

2. ____**hedging** (a) illogical (b) not making a clear response (c) immoral (d) irresponsible

3. ____**pittance** (a) small amount (b) insurance policy (c) compensation (d) pension

4. ____**facades** (a) deceptive fronts (b) alibis (c) defense mechanisms (d) face-saving devices

5. ____**plethora** (a) few (b) excess (c) several (d) a line

6. ____**refute** (a) substantiate (b) make plausible (c) prove false (d) transcend

7. ____**pious** (a) purposeful (b) morally correct (c) truthful (d) religious

8. ____**reticent** (a) unwilling (b) unable (c) afraid (d) upset

Thinking and Discussing

1. Work in small groups and classify the way members of that group lie. Then compare your group's list with the list of another group. Are there similarities?

2. Ericsson lists five categories of lies. Do you consider all these categories to be lies? If not, which ones are not really lies? What makes the ones in that category different from the ones that are real lies?

3. **Little White Lies** Do you agree with Ericsson that little white lies are damaging because they are "a vote of no confidence" (par. 8)? Would you tell a mother that her newborn baby looks like a miniature Winston Churchill and should be entered in an ugly baby contest? Probably not. If you accepted a dinner invitation to a friend's house and the food was dreadful, would you smile graciously and thank your host for a lovely dinner, or would you tell him or her that you have eaten worse food but just can't remember when? When the truth would serve only to offend and alienate someone, is it not better to tell the little white lies?

4. **Facades** Do you find paragraphs 10 and 11 convincing? Are the two paragraphs sufficiently connected, or do you feel that the author is stretching the point?

5. Often the attempt to cover up a lie leads to more serious consequences than the lie itself: In high places, the Watergate affair (Nixon) and the Oval Office affair (Clinton) are two prime examples. What would have been the outcome of

these two situations if lies had not been used as cover-ups? You may need to do a bit of research before discussing these two cases.

6. Benjamin Disareli said, "There are three kinds of lies: lies, damned lies, and statistics." How would you define these three kinds of lies?

Writing Suggestions

1. Using personal experience, write a paragraph about a situation in which a little white lie was better than the truth.

2. Write a paragraph about the first time you experienced someone deliberately lying for malicious reasons, to save face, or to falsely accuse another person.

3. Keep a "liar's journal" for several days. Record the incidents of your lies—no matter what kind—and the lies of other people. Categorize the kinds of lies. Use Ericsson's essay as a guide and write an essay based on your findings.

4. Choose one of the situations in number 5 in Thinking and Discussing and write an imaginative account of what some segment of history would read like if lies had not been used as cover-ups.

5. "The cruelest lies are often told in silence. A man may have sat in a room for hours and not opened his mouth, and yet come out of that room a disloyal friend or a vile calumniator [slanderer]."—Robert Louis Stevenson Use your own knowledge, personal or otherwise, and write an essay in which you show that silent lies (lies of omission) can be the cruelest lies.

Elizabeth Austin, "A Small Plea to Delete a Ubiquitous Expletive"

Auxiliary Material

Rhetorical Content Argumentation and Persuasion: Attempt to Incite People to Thought or Action
Process Analysis: Explaining

Thematic Content Language and Writing: The "F" Word

Background from *U. S. News and World Report*, April 6, 1998. Austin, who writes for *U. S. News and World Report*, argues that the "F" word is offensive and should be removed from public speech. She wants it eradicated except in extreme cases and among one's intimates and offers suggestions on

(continued)

how to accomplish the eradication. She says that it can be eliminated if "a critical mass of people [are] willing to take up cudgels against it" just as Jesse Jackson engineered the change from "black" to "African-American" and Robin Morgan and other feminist writers changed the nation's words "then commonly used to describe women, both in conversation and in print."

Related Readings

Woody Allen, "Slang Origins," from *Without Feathers.* © 1972–1975.

Tony Earley, "The Quare Gene," *New Yorker,* September 21, 1998.

Inis S. Kadaba, "What's in a Name?" *The Philadelphia Inquirer,* December 7, 1997.

Jesse Wegman, "Six Days: On Learning a New Alphabet," *Atlantic Monthly,* May 1999.

1   Oh, f---.

2   The "F" word, as it's called in more polite circles (including magazines such as this one), is increasingly hard to escape. Those who rarely use it themselves nonetheless hear it frequently—on the street, on the job, at the health club, at the movies—anywhere two or three disgruntled citizens might gather. Most people have uttered the word; everyone can define it. But even those who aren't particularly shocked by it don't want to hear it all the time. The toughest of tough guys cringes inwardly when somebody says it in front of his mother. Becoming a parent induces instant **hypersensitivity** to the word's **ubiquitous** presence in movies, on cable TV, in music, and in the loose talk of childless friends.

3   In its simplest and oldest usage, the "F" word refers to copulation. This usage has a long, frequently jolly, occasionally distinguished history. Shakespeare made glancing puns about it, and Scottish poet Robert Burns included it in his racier verses. More commonly today, though, the "F" word is used to express not desire but **derision,** not heat but hostility. Even when used as a kind of verbal space holder, a rougher, hipper equivalent of "you know" (as in "I f---ing love that f---ing movie," or in the Army patois that has been common for decades), it car-

ries a rude message. It is both a gauge and an engine of our ever plummeting standards of civility. Yet enough people are fed up with it that it's possible to erase the "F" word from public parlance and civil discourse.

4   Last word. A couple of generations back, calling for a public elimination of the "F" word would have been preposterous, since the word was never uttered in polite company (loosely defined as anywhere middle-class women were likely to hear it). In the late '60s, however, the loud, open use of the "F" word became a true shibboleth, dividing the student radicals from the Establishment "pigs" they delighted in tweaking. In Jerry Rubin's words, the "F" word was "the last word left in the English language. America cannot destroy it because she dare not use it."

5   But America took that dare. From the early '70s on, the "F" word started turning up with increasing regularity in movies, literature, and real life, according to Jesse Sheidlower's exhaustive volume, The *F-Word*. Many linguists and social critics celebrated the "F" word's coming out as a healthy abandonment of prudishness; a few still do. But civic virtuecrats today make a stronger case that public use of the word is a prime example of the "broken window" theory of social decay. When we put private frustrations and the right to be foulmouthed ahead of public order and civility, we coarsen society and risk an avalanche of rage and violence. Despite its near universality, the "F" word remains a fighting word.

6   So let's get rid of it. Scholars of social norms say all that's necessary to remove offensive language from public speech is a critical mass of people willing to take up cudgels against it. University of Chicago law Prof. Randal Picker describes such sudden overthrows of social standards as "norms cascades." If society is ripe for change, he contends, a single, powerful **catalyst** can engineer swift, widespread transformation. Picker cites Jesse Jackson, whose call for a switch from "black" to "African-American" changed the nation's nomenclature almost overnight. A more subtle but equally effective norms cascade was engineered by a handful of feminist writers in the early 1970s. Author-activist Robin Morgan remembers furiously listing words then commonly used to describe women, both in conversation and in print. "Produce and animals is what we were," she recalls. "We were 'chicks' and 'lambs' and 'birds' and 'bitches'; and there was always the infamous 'cherry.'" When Morgan and other feminist leaders publicly insisted on being called women, they started a norms cascade that eventually erased not only chick and bitch but girl and lady as well.

7   The "F" word seems like a particularly ripe target for a new generation of linguistic activists from both sides of the ideological divide. Erasing the word from civil discourse is one goal that Phyllis Schlafly could share with Andrea Dworkin. Here are a few modest proposals to help make that happen:

8   Police should start ticketing drivers who use the "F" word (or the correlating hand gesture), thereby boosting civility and calming road rage simultaneously. Although this could raise some First Amendment hackles, keep in mind that "fighting words" are not protected speech. One simple test of the fighting words concept is whether a fight actually ensues. Slapping a $100 ticket on a driver whose uplifted finger sparked a collision should pass any constitutional test.

9   The Motion Picture Association of America movie rating system should be overhauled to give an automatic NC-17 rating to any film that uses the "F" word even once. An NC-17 rating all but guarantees diminished viewership. Writers and directors who considered the word necessary to their artistic expression could still get their movies made; they'd just have to make the decision to trade **lucrative** ticket sales to teenagers for their artistic license.

10   Authors who salt their books with **gratuitous** "F" words should get the same critical treatment as those who sprinkle their prose with casual racial epithets. Certainly, there are times when the "F" word expresses precisely what a writer means to convey. But we need literary critics who understand the distinction between necessary frankness and the adolescent desire to shock.

11   Most important, we must delete the "F" word from our own lives. The most lasting shifts in social standards are those that begin at cocktail parties and around water coolers. We can wipe out the "F" word simply by refusing to use it ourselves and quietly but firmly objecting when others use it within earshot. The next time someone uses the "F" word in casual conversation, Judith Martin, better known as Miss Manners, suggests responding: "I'm not used to that sort of language." (If you can't say that line with a straight face, try: "We don't use that word anymore.")

12   Objecting to the "F" word isn't censorship. You can still use it as a punch line, if you like. You'll just risk the freezing silence and icy glares now reserved for white people who use the "N" word in public. Similarly, you're free to use it among your intimates, as a term of (in Sheidlower's words) "endearment, admiration, [or] derision." The rules of public civility have always included the naked-and-sweaty exemption. How you talk in the locker room or bedroom is up to you.

13   Ultimately, a social norm is nothing more, and nothing less, than the sum of individual decisions. In reconsidering the "F" word, you may prize your right to say it above your neighbor's right not to hear it. But personally, I'm swearing off.

Understanding Words

▶ **Definitions**

parlance (par. 3) A particular way of speaking.

patois (par. 3) Special jargon of a group.

shibboleth (par. 4) A word identified with a particular group.

cudgels (par. 6) Clubs, stout sticks.

nomenclature (par. 6) A system of names; systematic naming in any art or science.

epithets (par. 10) A term used to characterize a person or thing—often abusive or contemptuous.

▶ **Vocabulary**

Check your understanding of the following words. Study them in context (boldfaced in the text) and fill in the blank with the letter of the word or words that are closest to the meaning of the word in the text.

1. ____**hypersensitivity** (a) insensitivity (b) excessively sensitive (c) accustomed to (d) apprehension

2. ____**ubiquitous** (a) vulgar (b) uncensored (c) ever present (d) common

3. ____**derision** (a) vulgarity (b) informality (c) ridicule (d) coolness

4. ____**catalyst** (a) moving force (b) orator (c) plan (d) movement

5. ____**lucrative** (a) nonmalleable (b) ineffectual (c) lost leads (d) profitable

6. ____**gratuitous** (a) shock value words (b) deadwood words (c) unearned (d) unnecessary

Thinking and Discussing

1. What is your personal feeling about the "F" Word? Do you use it as different parts of speech—a noun, an adjective, a verb, or an adverb? Is there an appropriate time and place for using this word? Is it always in poor taste, or are there situations in which only that word seems to express a particular idea? If you do not use the word, are you offended by its use by other people?

2. The First Amendment to the Constitution guarantees freedom of religion, speech, and the press. In your opinion, does this amendment guarantee people the right to use whatever words they please and when they please?

3. Austin says that the word is "both a gauge and an engine of our ever plummeting standards of civility." Explain what you think she means. Do you agree with her?

4. Do words (especially the "F" word and the "N" word) have power in and of themselves, or do they get their power from people's perception of them?

5. Austin points out in paragraph 6 that many terms that were once used to identify females have been erased by the efforts of feminist leaders. Are you familiar with current de-meaning names for women? Make a list of them and think about their origin. Are there similar names for men?

Writing Suggestions

1. Austin says the word *lady* has been erased. Is she correct? What about the word *gentleman*? In breaking news stories, it is common to hear commentators refer to suspects—often suspected of some heinous crime—as the *lady* in question or the *gentleman* of interest. (In a recent story, the *gentleman* of interest had just bludgeoned to death his nephew and hacked to death an elderly woman.) Write your response to some such newscast. What do you think commentators are trying to accomplish by using these words instead of *male* and *female?* Does this usage of language strike you as offensive or as ridiculous?

2. Write an essay in which you discuss the differences between the types and number of names that are used for males and females. Depend-ing upon the stance you take, you may develop your essay using comparison and contrast, logic and persuasion, or division and classification. You may want to consider the barnyard names that are frequently associated with people—pig, dog, cat, hen, biddy, chick, cow, heifer, and so on—body parts, clothing, and food stuffs.

3. Draw upon a recent experience you have had—a movie, a book, a comic routine—in which the "F" word is used. Write a paragraph in which you respond to this experience. Is the word necessary for the artistic quality of the work? Does it add to or detract from the overall effectiveness of the work?

4. Write a paragraph in which you define the "F" word. When can it be used, if ever? By whom?

Everyday World

Leon Botstein, "Let Teenagers Try Adulthood"

Auxiliary Material

Rhetorical Content Argumentation and Persuasion: Attempt to Incite People to Thought or Action
Cause and Effect: Connecting Reasons and Results

Thematic Content Everyday World: Education and Schools

Background from *New York Times,* May 17, 1999. Op-Ed. Leon Botstein, president of Bard College and author of *Jefferson's Children: Education and the Promise of American Culture,* makes his point in the first paragraph: "The American high school is obsolete and should be abolished." He gives reasons to support his point and offers an alternative educational system.

Related Readings E. D. Hirsch, "Why America's Universities Are Better Than Its Schools," from *The Schools We Need and Why We Don't Have Them.* © 1995. Doubleday, a division of Bantam Doubleday Dell Publishing.

Mike Rose, "Crossing Boundaries," from *Lives on the Boundary: The Struggles and Achievements of America's Underprepared.* © 1989. The Free Press, a division of Simon & Schuster.

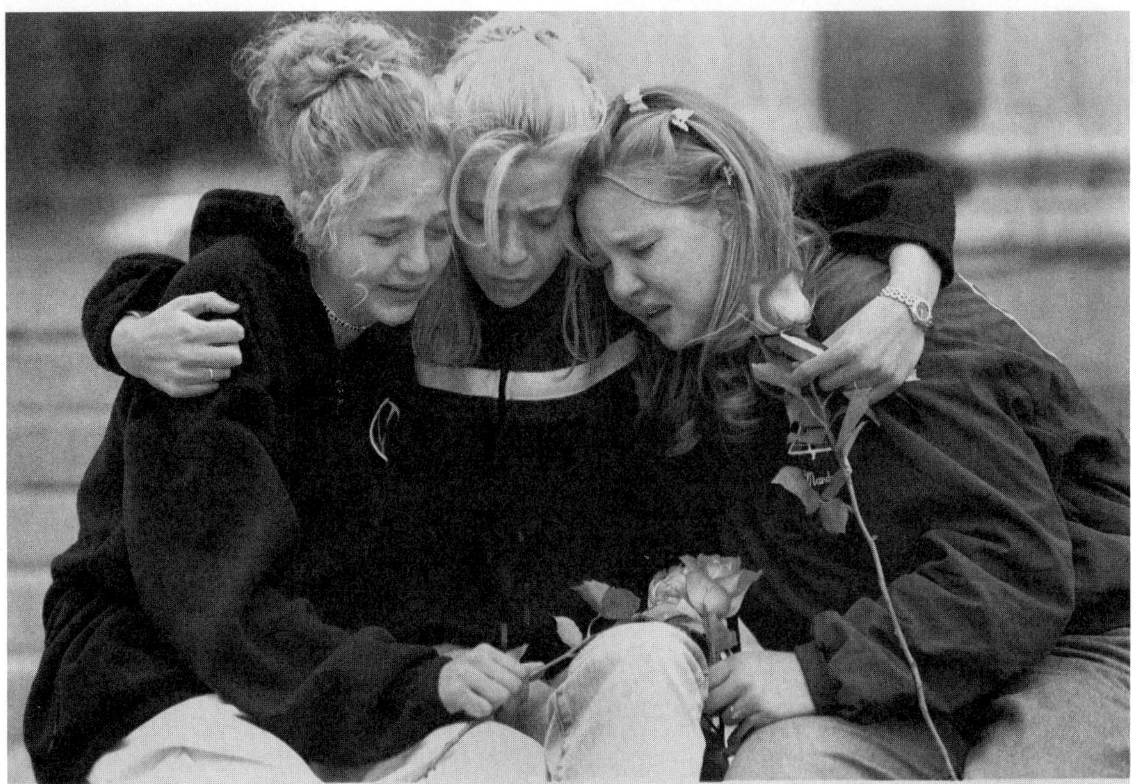

Grieving students at a vigil honoring the victims of the Columbine High School shooting rampage Tuesday, April 20, 1999, in Littleton, Colorado. (Denver, Colorado, 04/21/99, AP Photo/Laura Rauch)

1   The national outpouring after the Littleton shootings has forced us to confront something we have suspected for a long time: the American high school is **obsolete** and should be abolished. In the last month, high school students present and past have come forward with stories about cliques and the artificial intensity of a world defined by insiders and outsiders, in which the insiders hold sway because of superficial definitions of good looks and attractiveness, popularity and sports prowess.

2   The team sports of high school dominate more than student culture. A community's loyalty to the high school system is often based on the extent to which varsity teams succeed. High school administrators and faculty members are often former coaches, and the coaches themselves are placed in a separate, untouchable category. The result is that the culture of the inside elite is not contested by the adults in the school. Individuality and **dissent** are discouraged.

3   But the rules of high school turn out not to be the rules of life. Often the high school outsider becomes the more successful and admired adult. The definitions of masculinity and femininity go through sufficient **transformation** to make the game of popularity in high school an embarrassment. No other group of adults young or old is confined to an age-segregated environment, much like a gang in which individuals of the same age group define each other's world. In no workplace, not even in colleges or universities, is there such a narrow **segmentation** by chronology.

4   Given the poor quality of recruitment and training for high school teachers, it is no wonder that the curriculum and the enterprise of learning hold so little sway over young people. When puberty meets education and learning in modern America, the victory of puberty masquerading as popular culture and the **tyranny** of peer groups based on ludicrous values meet little resistance.

5   By the time those who graduate from high school go on to college and realize what really is at stake in becoming an adult, too many opportunities have been lost and too much time has been wasted. Most thoughtful young people suffer the high school environment in silence and in their junior and senior years mark time waiting for college to begin. The Littleton killers, above and beyond the psychological demons that drove them to violence, felt trapped in the artificiality of the high school world and believed it to be real. They engineered their moment of undivided attention and importance in the absence of any confidence that life after high school could have a different meaning.

6   Adults should face the fact that they don't like adolescents and that they have used high school to isolate the pubescent and hormonally active adolescent away from both the picture-book idealized innocence of childhood and the more accountable world of adulthood. But the primary reason high school doesn't work anymore, if it ever did, is that young people mature substantially earlier in the late 20th century [late 1900s] than they did when the high school was invented. For example, the age of first menstruation has dropped at least two years since the beginning of this century [1900s], and not surprisingly, the onset of sexual activity has dropped in proportion. An institution intended for children in transition now holds young adults back well beyond the developmental point for which high school was originally designed.

7   Furthermore, whatever constraints to the presumption of adulthood among young people may have existed decades ago have now fallen away. Information and images, as well as the real and virtual freedom of movement we associate with adulthood, are now accessible to every 15- and 16-year-old.

8 Secondary education must be rethought. Elementary school should begin at age 4 or 5 and end with the sixth grade. We should entirely abandon the concept of the middle school and junior high school. Beginning with the seventh grade, there should be four years of secondary education that we may call high school. Young people should graduate at 16 rather than 18.

9 They could then enter the real world, the world of work or national service, in which they would take a place of responsibility alongside older adults in mixed company. They could stay at home and attend junior college, or they could go away to college. For all the faults of college, at least the adults who dominate the world of colleges, the faculty, were selected precisely because they were exceptional and different, not because they were popular. Despite the often **cavalier** attitude toward teaching in college, at least physicists know their physics, mathematicians know and love their mathematics, and music is taught by musicians, not by graduates of education schools, where the disciplines are **subordinated** to the study of classroom management.

10 For those 16-year-olds who do not want to do any of the above, we might construct new kinds of institutions, each dedicated to one activity, from science to dance, to which adolescents could devote their energies while working together with professionals in those fields.

11 At 16, young Americans are prepared to be taken seriously and to develop the motivations and interests that will serve them well in adult life. They need to enter a world where they are not in a lunchroom with only their peers, **estranged** from other age groups and cut off from the game of life as it is really played. There is nothing **utopian** about this idea; it is immensely practical and efficient, and its implementation is long overdue. We need to face biological and cultural facts and not prolong the life of a flawed institution that is out of date.

Understanding Words

▶ **Definitions**

Littleton shootings (par. 1) Two high school students killed fellow students and a teacher in Littleton, Colorado.

▶ **Vocabulary**
Check your understanding of the following words. Read them in context (boldfaced in the text) and fill in the blank with the letter of the word or words that are closest to the meaning of the word in the text.

1. ____**obsolete** (a) no longer in use
   (b) unqualified (c) alloyed
   (d) unstructured (e) frustrating

2. ____**dissent** (a) nonconformity
   (b) difference of opinion
   (c) opposition (d) free thought

3. ____**transformation** (a) change in
   appearance (b) internalization
   (c) reorganization (d) disguise

4. ____**segmentation** (a) reduction
   (b) contradiction (c) individualization
   (d) division

5 ____**tyranny** (a) absolute power
   (b) dictatorship (c) control
   (d) leadership

6. ____**cavalier** (a) respectful (b) off-hand
   disregard (c) unrealistic
   (d) professional

7. ____**subordinated** (a) compared (b) made
   inferior (c) elevated (d) contrasted

8. ____**estranged** (a) made strange
   (b) separated (c) omitted
   (d) eradicated

9. ____**utopian** (a) unethical (b) idealistic
   (c) unusual (d) new

Thinking and Discussing

1. Why do you think Botstein used the Littleton shootings as a lead-in?

2. Do you agree with him that the rules of high school are not the rules of life?

3. Would your life have been different had you had a high school experience similar to the one Botstein proposes? Explain.

4. Should high schools have two tracks: one for college-bound students and one for work-bound students?

Writing Suggestions

1. Write a paragraph in which you relate a personal experience with high school cliques.

2. Use your own experiences and write an argumentative essay in which you agree or disagree with Botstein's analysis of the part team sports play in high schools (par. 2).

3. Write a paper in which you explain how well high school prepared you for higher education or for life.

4. Write a paper in which you create a utopian high school and compare and contrast it with today's high schools.

Russell Baker, "The Plot against People"

Auxiliary Material

Rhetorical Content   Classification: Classification According to Relationships

Thematic Content   Everyday World: Inanimate Objects

Background   from the *New York Times,* June 8, 1968. Russell Baker, a humorist and political writer, has been published regularly in the *Washington Post* and the *New York Times.* In 1979 he received a Pulitzer Prize for commentary, and in 1983 he received a second Pulitzer Prize for his autobiography, *Growing Up.* In this essay, he humorously explores stress caused by everyday objects.

Related Readings   Ted Gup, "The End of Serendipity," from *The Chronicle of Higher Education,* December 21, 1997.

James Windolf, "A Nation of Nuts," from *The Wall Street Journal,* October 22, 1997.

John Fiske, "Shopping for Pleasure: Malls, Power, and Resistance," from *Reading Popular.* 1989.

Amy Wu, "Young Cyber Addicts," from *Minutes of the Lead Pencil Club.* 1996 collection.

Christoper Porterfield, "Right before Our Eyes," from *Time 100* special issue, June 8, 1998.

1   **Inanimate** objects are classified scientifically into three major categories—those that don't work, those that break down, and those that get lost.

2   The goal of all inanimate objects is to resist man and ultimately to defeat him, and the three major classifications are based on the method each object uses to achieve

its purpose. As a general rule, any object capable of breaking down at the moment when it is most needed will do so. The automobile is typical of the category.

3   With the **cunning** typical of its breed, the automobile never breaks down when entering a filling station with a large staff of idle mechanics. It waits until it reaches a downtown intersection in the middle of the rush hour, or until it is fully loaded with family and luggage on the Ohio turnpike.

4   Thus it creates maximum misery, inconvenience, frustration, and irritability among its human cargo, thereby reducing its owner's life span.

5   Washing machines, garbage disposals, lawn mowers, light bulbs, automatic laundry dryers, water pipes, furnaces, electrical fuses, television tubes, hose nozzles, tape recorders, slide projectors—all are in league with the automobile to take their turn at breaking down whenever life threatens to flow smoothly for their human enemies.

6   Many inanimate objects, of course, find it extremely difficult to break down. Pliers, for example, and gloves and keys are almost totally incapable of breaking down. Therefore, they have had to evolve a different technique for resisting man.

7   They get lost. Science has still not solved the mystery of how they do it, and no man has ever caught one of them in the act of getting lost. The most **plausible** theory is that they have developed a secret method of locomotion which they are able to conceal the instant a human eye falls upon them.

8   It is not uncommon for a pair of pliers to climb all the way from the cellar to the attic in its single-minded determination to raise its owner's blood pressure. Keys have been known to burrow three feet under mattresses. Women's purses, despite their great weight, frequently travel through six or seven rooms to find a hiding space under a couch.

9   Scientists have been struck by the fact that things that break down virtually never get lost, while things that get lost hardly ever break down.

10   A furnace, for example, will invariably break down at the depth of the first winter cold wave, but it will never get lost. A woman's purse, which after all does have some inherent capacity for breaking down, hardly ever does; it almost invariably chooses to get lost.

11   Some persons believe this **constitutes** evidence that inanimate objects are not entirely hostile to man, and that a negotiated peace is possible. After all, they point out, a furnace could infuriate a man even more thoroughly by getting lost than by breaking down, just as a glove could upset him far more by breaking down than by getting lost.

12   Not everyone agrees, however, that this indicates a **conciliatory** attitude among inanimate objects. Many say it merely proves that furnaces, gloves, and pliers are incredibly stupid.

13   The third class of objects—those that don't work—is the most curious of all. These include such objects as barometers, car clocks, cigarette lighters, flashlights, and toy-train locomotives. It is inaccurate, of course, to say that they never work. They work once, usually for the first few hours after being brought home, and then quit. Thereafter, they never work again.

14   In fact, it is widely assumed that they are built for the purpose of not working. Some people have reached advanced ages without ever seeing some of these objects—barometers, for example—in working order.

15   Science is utterly **baffled** by the entire category. There are many theories about it. The most interesting holds that the things that don't work have attained the highest state possible for an inanimate object, the state to which things that break down and things that get lost can still only **aspire.**

16   They have truly defeated man by conditioning him never to expect anything of them, and in return, they have given man the only peace he receives from inanimate society. He does not expect his barometer to work, his electric locomotive to run, his cigarette lighter to light, or his flashlight to illuminate, and when they don't, it does not raise his blood pressure.

17   He cannot attain that peace with furnaces and keys, and cars and women's purses as long as he demands that they work for their keep.

Understanding Words

▶ **Definitions**

barometer (par. 13) An instrument for measuring atmospheric pressure.

illuminate (par. 16) To provide or brighten with light.

▶ **Vocabulary**

Check your understanding of the following words. Read them in context (boldfaced in the text) and fill in the blank with the letter of the word or words that are closest to the meaning in the text.

1. _____ **inanimate** (a) not living (b) complex (c) everyday appliances (d) capable of being classified

2. _____ **cunning** (a) astuteness (b) shrewdness (c) weirdness (d) obstinacy

3. ____**plausible** (a) far out (b) unreal
   (c) unreasonable (d) believable

4. ____**constitutes** (a) equates
   (b) substantiates (c) validates (d) makes up

5. ____**conciliatory** (a) vindictive
   (b) conspiratorial (c) negative (d) peace
   making

6. ____**baffled** (a) amazed (b) put off
   (c) bewildered (d) awed

7. ____**aspire** (a) strive for (b) wonder about
   (c) try to achieve (d) expect

Thinking and Discussing

1. Although common to you, many aspects of modern technology may present real problems to many people of an older generation. Interview three or four people of your grandparents' generation. Ask them to tell you about their experiences with such things as the Internet, programmed phone services, using a VCR, using computers at the library, and so on. Discuss your findings with your peers. What conclusion can you draw from your findings and those of your peers?

2. Can you think of another category that Baker could have used to classify more inanimate objects?

3. **Tone** What is the writer's attitude toward the subject? What is his attitude toward his audience? Who is his audience?

Writing Suggestions

1. Write a short summary (three or four sentences) of this essay.

2. Write an essay about an experience you have had with an inanimate object—a vending machine that refused to "vend," a pay telephone that "paid off," an appliance that only worked for certain people, and so on.

3. Write a paragraph in which you discuss your pet peeve involving an inanimate object such as computer programs that try to outsmart you, pencil sharpeners that eat—not sharpen—pencils, perforated pages that do not tear evenly, and so on.

4. Use Baker's essay as a model and write an essay about systems that do not work such as the registration process at your college, scheduling or getting the classes you need, getting job experience.

5. Using Baker's essay as a model write an essay about a group of people such as drivers, teachers, parents, friends, dates, and so on.

Clive Wynne, "Do Animals Think?"

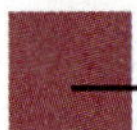 **Auxiliary Material**

Rhetorical Content	Argumentation and Persuasion: Attempt to Incite People to Thought or Action
Thematic Content	Everyday World: Animal Rights
Background	from *Psychology Today,* November, 1999. Full Text: © 1999 Sussex Publishers, Inc. Gale Group. All rights reserved. (Gale Group is a Thompson Corporation Company.)
	In this article, Clive Wynne, Ph.D., senior lecturer at the University of Western Australia in Perth, Australia, takes a close look at some of the research involving the animal mind.
Related Readings	Donald Griffin, "How Human is Enough?" A Response by Donald Griffin, Ph.D., Professor Emeritus.
	The Rockefeller University, associate of the Museum of Comparative Zoology at Harvard University, author of *Animal Minds* (University of Chicago Press, 1992).
	Jon Ferry, "New Calls Made for Changes in Research on Animals." *(News)* (Statistical Data Included) *The Lancet,* December 4, 1999 v. 354 i. 9194 p. 1978).
	Richard Selzer, "How to Build a Slaughterhouse," from *Taking the World in for Repairs* by Richard Selzer. © 1986 by Richard Selzer.
	Vicki Hearne, "What's Wrong with Animal Rights?" from *Harper's Magazine,* September 1992.
	Patricia Curtis, "The Argument against Animal Experimentation," from the *New York Times,* December 31, 1978. © by the New York Times Company.

A gorilla from the Little Rock Zoo examines a cardboard box used to "hide" his lunch. The zoo has created the Primate Enrichment Program in which students at the University of Arkansas develop opportunities for the gorillas to learn and have fun. (Little Rock, Arkansas, 04/15/99, AP Photo/Jim Yates)

1   I was 13 when Benji came into our lives. With his deep brown eyes, floppy ears and cheerful disposition, he was my constant companion throughout my teen-age years. We would play together in the garden and take long walks over the hills behind the house and on the beach. Benji would hang on my every word with his head tilted to one side. Despite being a dog, he seemed to have a sympathy for my problems that went deeper than words could express. He was my best friend.

2   Benji left us about 15 years ago for that great kennel in the sky. But recently I've been thinking about him a lot. Was he really conscious? Could any animal have consciousness like we do? Does it matter whether animals are conscious or not?

3   Some people feel this connection is strong enough to **warrant** special treatment. An international group called the Great Ape Project is pushing the government of New Zealand to adopt a bill that would give some human rights to chimpanzees, gorillas and the rest of the great apes. The Great Ape Project is lobbying the United Nations to adopt a declaration on the rights of great apes modeled on the UN declaration on the Rights of Man. The group believes that apes are "conscious" and deserve legal protection of their rights to life and freedom from imprisonment and torture.

4   If great apes were shown to have consciousness something like our own, I would consider it among the scientific discoveries of the century. I would then agree with the Australian philosopher and founder of the animal rights movement, Peter Singer, that performing medical experiments on chimps would be like experimenting on orphan children. That's a pretty chilling thought, and no amount of human suffering saved could justify such an action. But before we close down the laboratories and stop searching for a vaccine against AIDS, we had better take a long hard look at the evidence for ape consciousness.

What Is Consciousness?

5   The definition of consciousness has eluded us for over a century, but many psychologists as well as supporters of the Great Ape Project agree on three classes of evidence: language, self-awareness, and "theory of mind."

6   LANGUAGE: The mutual possession of language is surely one of the strongest indications that the being you are talking to is conscious like you. Through their work teaching language to chimpanzees, many researchers have found glimmers of "conscious" light in animals' ability to communicate.

7   Washoe, a chimpanzee, had been taught to use American Sign Language. Today, she is enjoying a boat ride on a lake with her trainers when a swan comes into view.

Washoe has never seen a swan before and had no sign in her vocabulary for such a thing. "Waterbird," she signs excitedly to her human companions.

8   Kanzi, a pygmy chimpanzee, first learned to communicate with symbols by watching his mother's lessons. His trainer, Sue Savage-Rumbauch, is testing him for his comprehension of sentences. "Would you please carry the straw?" she asks him. Kanzi picks up a straw. "Give the trash to Jeanine"—Kanzi picks up the trash and brings it to the other trainer.

9   Koko, a gorilla, has been learning American Sign Language from her trainer, Francine Patterson, for over 20 years. In April 1998, Koko was the first nonhuman to go live on the Internet. She answered questions about her life and hopes, her desire for a baby and her dreams of freedom.

10   SELF-AWARENESS: Self-awareness is another key ability of conscious beings. To be conscious is, firstly, to be conscious of one's self—to be aware that "I am a being separate from others and the world around me."

11   Megan, a chimpanzee, is in training with Daniel Povinelli. She has had a mirror in her quarters for several months. Today, Povinelli is testing her self-awareness with a method developed by Gordon Gallup. This morning, Megan was anesthetized. While unconscious, a spot of bright red nontoxic ink was daubed on her forehead. Now it is afternoon and she is fully recovered from the anesthetic. Sure enough, the chimp looks in the mirror and then scratches at the spot on her forehead. To some, this proves that Megan has recognized herself and is consciously self-aware.

12   THEORY of MIND: Theory of mind is an awareness that others have minds as well: "I am not the only conscious being. Others are conscious and I take this into account in my dealings with them."

13   Sheba is another chimpanzee being trained by Daniel Povinelli, but in quite a different experiment. Sheba has been watching one trainer put food into one of four cups. She can't see which cup because they are hidden from her view—but she can clearly see that this trainer (we'll call him the "knower") had some food and put it in a cup. Now the knower comes back into the room together with another trainer (the "guesser"). If Sheba has a theory of mind—an awareness that the trainers have a conscious awareness of their own—she should know that the guesser did not see where the knower put the food.

14   The two trainers are in the room. The knower points to a cup; the guesser points to a cup. The knower points to the cup into which he had placed food earlier; the guesser—well, he just guesses. What does Sheba do? She chooses the cup to which the knower points.

Aping Language

15 Herb Terrace of Columbia University in New York is one of the original researchers on languages in apes and now a critic of such attempts. During the 1970s, he co-ordinated a project teaching American Sign Language to Nim Chimpsky, a young chimpanzee named in humorous honor of the famous linguist Noam Chomsky. Whereas Terrace had hoped that Nim would pick up sign language just by living among a community of people using it, he was disappointed to find that it was only possible to get Nim to learn by bribing him with treats.

16 When funding for the project ran out, Terrace had time to consider his data, and he began to notice certain things: He realized that often Nim was using signs in his response that the trainers had used in their question—in effect just echoing what had been said. He also noted Nim's spontaneous signs were almost always demands for something. He rarely asked questions or commented on the world around him, the way even young children do. And Nim's vocabulary remained small—only about 125 signs after three year's training.

17 Finally, Nim's **utterances** were typically very short—only one or two signs—and completely ungrammatical. The chimp's longest recorded utterance was "Give orange me give eat orange me eat orange give me eat orange give me orange give me you." Easy to understand, but without respect for basic grammar, which even the youngest and least educated humans comprehend.

18 The other ape language researchers pounced on Terrace, claiming that his work contained critical flaws. They pointed to the "creative" use of words, like Washoe's "waterbird" to describe a swan—surely this showed a deeper understanding of language than Nim had demonstrated. How do we know that Washoe was referring to the swan? She could have been naming two things she saw, water and a bird.

19 Sue Savage-Rumbaugh has drawn attention to the fact that Kanzi appeared to pick up symbolic language simply by observing her mother's training. This is an interesting observation, but it does not consider the fact that Kanzi is being rewarded for her use of symbols—she is usually given the thing that she names.

20 Savage-Rumbauch identifies Kanzi's success in obeying commands such as "would you please carry the straw?" as evidence of a grammatical understanding. But was any other interpretation possible? When Kanzi correctly carries out this instruction, does this mean that she understands the structure of the sentence—that she should carry the straw, and not that the straw would carry her. Although different interpretations may be grammatically possible, in reality, only one interpretation was practicable under the circumstances.

Not All Smoke and Mirrors

21   What of Megan, the chimp who wiped the ink off her forehead? Is she showing evidence of advanced consciousness? Gordon Gallup argues that for an animal to recognize itself in a mirror, it must have self-awareness in a form not so different from our own. He is impressed by the observation that great apes are the only mammals to show self-recognition in a mirror. (Although in the 1980s, Robert Epstein, Robert Lanza and B. F. Skinner demonstrated that, with training, even pigeons can pass Gallup's mirror test, which means it may not be so tough.)

22   The problem with Gallup's interpretation is that there are people who cannot recognize themselves in mirrors, and yet nobody doubts they are fully self-aware. Blind people cannot recognize themselves in mirrors but we have plenty of other indications that they are self-aware. People brought up in communities that do not have mirrors do not instantly recognize themselves when they are first shown their own reflection. There is also a form of brain damage called prosopagnosia, which leads to inability to recognize faces. In extreme forms of prosopagnosia, the patient may not even recognize his own reflection.

23   In light of these revelations, it does not make sense to treat mirror recognition in chimps as a measure of self-awareness.

No Monkey Business

24   Provinelli's "guesser-knower" experiment was partially modeled on a theory of mind tests in children: A child or chimp who has an awareness that others have minds, can readily see that one trainer knows something that the other doesn't.

25   If you or I were put in the guesser-knower experiment, we would almost immediately choose the cup the knower points to because we have a theory of mind that guides our behavior. Sheba, the chimp, however, required hundreds of training sessions before she began consistently choosing the cup pointed to by the knower, and even then she was successful only 75% of the time. This suggests she was gradually learning an association between a stimulus (the "knower") and a reward, and not treating them as people with minds.

Human Minds in Ape Bodies?

26   Much has been made of the fact that chimps are our closest living relatives. But DNA doesn't tell us anything about what traits and abilities two species have in common. In making claims for the intelligence of dolphins, no one feels inhibited by the fact that dolphins' closest living relatives out of the ocean are cows and sheep.

27   Chimpanzees and other apes are wonderful animals, fully worthy of ethical treatment and protection. But they are not human beings. They are not 98% human; they are not even half human. They are 100 percent animals on their own terms.

28   I am not disappointed that the attempts to find human-like consciousness in apes have failed. On the contrary, I find it profoundly exciting and liberating. We are surrounded on this planet not by things-like-people dressed in fur and feathers, but by **myriad** beings, each with its own unique psychology. As an animal psychologist, I can't think of any challenge more exciting than trying to understand animals in their own right and not just as dumber versions of ourselves.

Understanding Words

▶ **Definitions**

spontaneous (par. 16) Arising from a natural inclination or impulse.

▶ **Vocabulary**
Check your understanding of the following words. Study them in context (boldfaced in the text) and fill in the blank with the letter of the word or words that are closest in meaning to the word in the text.

1. ____**warrant** (a) scientific (b) legal (c) deserve (d) make necessary

2. ____**utterances** (a) statements (b) nonverbal sounds (c) readily understandable (d) articulations

Thinking and Discussing

1. What comes to your mind when you hear the expression "animal experimentation"?

2. Does the phrase have negative connotations for you? If so, what are they? When did you first encounter the phrase?

3. How do you feel about radical groups such as The Animal Liberation Front? What is the difference between their acts and the acts of people who bomb abortion clinics and harass health care providers in these clinics?

4. Are you familiar with any animal rights groups such as PETA, PAWS, or Greenpeace? What do you know about these organizations? Their philosophy? Their purpose? Their activities? Their financial affairs? Compare your knowledge with that of your peers. Is there a diversity of opinions about these groups?

Writing Suggestions

1. Have you had an experience with a pet that convinced you that the animal possessed human intelligence? Write a narrative essay about this experience.

2. Many important medical advances of the twentieth century are the result of animal experimentation. Write an argumentative essay in which you take the stance that (a) animal research is necessary and justifiable for the advancement of human medical research, (b) animal research is cruel and should be abolished, or (c) choose a middle ground between the two and develop rationale for your beliefs.

3. Write a paragraph in which you summarize a recent animal activists' attack on an institution.

4. Have you had personal experience with an animal rights group? If the experience was brief, write a paragraph about it. If it was a more intense experience, write an essay about it. Did you learn anything from the encounter? Did you change your mind about some aspect of the problem?

 A Sense of Beauty

Dave Barry, "The Ugly Truth about Beauty"

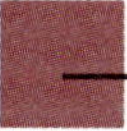 **Auxiliary Material**

Rhetorical Content Cause and Effect: Connecting Reasons and Results

Thematic Content Men and Women: Outward Appearances

Dave Barry, whose humorous observations won him the Pulitzer Prize for commentary in 1988, has written numerous books including *Babies and Other Hazards of Sex: How to Make a Tiny Person in Only Nine Months, with Tools You probably Already Have Around the House* and *Bad Habits: A 100% Fat Free Book*. Barry is based at

(continued)

the *Miami Herald,* and his column is syndicated in over 150 newspapers nationwide. In his witty and humorous discussion about the difference in the way men and women feel about the way they look, he contends that most men think they have average looks, and average is good enough for them. He contends that women are never satisfied with their looks: Their appearance is never good enough for them. He explores the psychological and societal reasons that contribute to women's low self esteem.

Related Readings

Jennifer Silver, "Caught with a Centerfold," *Mademoiselle,* January 1997.

Karen Epstein, "I'm a Barbie Girl," *The Tufts Daily Online,* Tufts University, November 21, 1997.

Karlene J. Robinson, "In Pursuit of the Impossible Body Image," *The Daily Vidette Online,* Illinois State University, February 18, 1998.

Nora Ephron, "Crazy Salad," from *Crazy Salad.* 1975.

Jean Kilbourne, "Beauty . . . And the Beasts of Advertising," from *Media & Values,* Winter 1989.

Patricia McLaughlin, "Venus Envy," *Philadelphia Inquirer Magazine,* November 5, 1995.

Gloria Borger, "Barbie's Newest Values," *U. S. News and World Report,* December 1, 1997

Madonna's corset and Jean Paul Gaultier's evening dress from his "barbes" collection are included in the Metropolitan Museum of Art's exhibition that features extreme alterations of the female body to make it conform to society's concept of beauty. (New York, 12/05/02, AP Photo/Kathy Willens)

1   If you're a man, at some point a woman will ask you how she looks.

2   "How do I look?" she'll ask.

3   You must be careful how you answer this question. The best technique is to form an honest yet sensitive opinion, then collapse on the floor with some kind of fatal seizure. Trust me, this is the easiest way out. Because you will never come up with the right answer.

4   The problem is that women generally do not think of their looks in the same way men do. Most men form an opinion of how they look in seventh grade, and they stick to it for the rest of their lives. Some men form the opinion that they are irresistible stud muffins, and they do not change this opinion even when their faces sag and their noses bloat to the size of eggplants and their eyebrows grow together to form what appears to be a giant forehead-dwelling tropical caterpillar.

5   Most men, I believe, think of themselves as average-looking. Men will think this even if their faces cause heart failure in cattle at a range of 300 yards. Being average does not bother them; average is fine, for men. This is why men never ask anybody how they look. Their primary form of beauty care is to shave themselves, which is essentially the same form of beauty care that they give to their lawns. If, at the end of his four-minute daily beauty **regimen,** a man has managed to wipe most of the shaving cream out of his hair and is not bleeding too badly, he feels that he has done all he can, so he stops thinking about his appearance and devotes his mind to more critical issues, such as the Super Bowl.

6   Women do not look at themselves this way. If I had to express, in three words, what I believe most women think about their appearance, those words would be: "not good enough." No matter how attractive a woman may appear to be to others, when she looks at herself in the mirror, she thinks: woof. She thinks that at any moment a municipal animal-control officer is going to throw a net over her and haul her off to the shelter.

7   Why do women have such low self-esteem? There are many complex psychological and societal reasons, by which I mean Barbie. Girls grow up playing with a doll proportioned such that, if it were a human, it would be seven feet tall and weigh 81 pounds of which 53 pounds would be bosoms. This is a difficult appearance standard to live up to, especially when you contrast it with the standard set for little boys by their dolls . . . excuse me, by their action figures. Most of the action figures that my son played with when he was little were hideous-looking. For example, he was very fond of an action figure (part of the He-Man series) called "Buzz-Off," who was part human, part flying insect. Buzz-Off was not a looker. But he was extremely self-confident. You could not imagine Buzz-Off saying to the other action figures: "Do you think these wings make my hips look big?"

8   But women grow up thinking they need to look like Barbie, which for most women is impossible, although there is a multibillion-dollar beauty industry devoted to convincing women that they must try. I once saw an Oprah show wherein super model Cindy Crawford **dispensed** makeup tips to the studio audience. Cindy had all these middle-aged women applying beauty products to their faces; she stressed how important it was to apply them in a certain way, using the tips of the fingers. All the women dutifully did this, even though it was obvious to any sane observer that, no matter how carefully they applied these products, they would never look remotely like Cindy Crawford, who is some kind of genetic mutation.

9   I'm not saying men are superior. I'm just saying that you're not going to get a group of middle-aged men to sit in a room and apply cosmetics to themselves under the instruction of Brad Pitt, in hopes of looking more like him. Men would realize that

this task was pointless and **demeaning.** They would find some way to **bolster** their self-esteem that did not require looking like Brad Pitt. They would say to Brad: "Oh YEAH? Well what do you know about LAWN CARE, pretty boy?"

10 Of course many women will argue that the reason they become obsessed with trying to look like Cindy Crawford is that men, being as shallow as a drop of spit, WANT women to look that way. To which I have two responses:

11 1. Hey, just because WE'RE idiots, that does not mean YOU have to be; and

12 2. Men don't even notice 97 percent of the beauty efforts you make anyway. Take fingernails. The average woman spends 5,000 hours per year worrying about her fingernails; I have never once, in more than 40 years of listening to men talk about women, heard a man say, "She has a nice set of fingernails!" Many men would not notice if a woman had upward of four hands.

13 Anyway, to get back to my original point: If you're a man, and a woman asks you how she looks, you're in big trouble. Obviously, you can't say she looks bad. But you can't say she looks great, because she'll think you're lying, because she has spent countless hours, with the help of the multibillion-dollar beauty industry, obsessing about the differences between herself and Cindy Crawford. Also, she suspects that you're not qualified to judge anybody's appearance. This is because you have shaving cream in your hair.

Understanding Words

▶ **Definitions**

stud muffins (par. 4) Good looking, virile men

genetic mutation (par. 8) (loosely defined) An organism that has structural changes within a gene or chromosome that is not found in the parental type.

▶ **Vocabulary**

Check your understanding of the following words. Read them in context (boldfaced in the text) and fill in the blank with the letter of the word or words that are closest in meaning to the word in the text.

1. _____**regimen** (a) brief program (b) toilette (c) regulated system (d) treatment

2. _____**dispensed** (a) suggested (b) gave (c) recommended (d) advertised

3. _____**demeaning** (a) unimportant (b) degrading (c) silly (d) mean spirited

4. _____**bolster** (a) prop up (b) aggrandize (c) redefine (d) alter

Thinking and Discussing

Audience is the readership to which writers direct their work. A writer may have more than one audience in mind.

1. On the surface who is Barry's audience? Does he have a wider secondary audience? If so, who are the members of this audience?

Irony is the use of words that suggest the opposite of what is stated.

2. Do you find Barry's reference to super model Cindy Crawford as a *genetic mutation* effective?

Tone is the writer's attitude. Tone may reveal the writer's attitude toward the material or toward the audience.

3. How would you describe Barry's tone? Do you feel that the tone supports or undercuts the serious aspect of this essay?

Writing Suggestions

1. In your own words, summarize Barry's main points.

2. In your own words summarize Barry's opinion of the way men and women see themselves.

3. Men: Write a paragraph explaining how you respond to a woman's question, "How do I look?"

4. Women: Write a paragraph explaining what you really mean when you say to a man, "How do I look?"

5. Write an argumentative essay in which you agree or disagree with Barry's thesis, using your own experiences or observations to support your point.

Grace Suh, "The Eye of the Beholder"

Auxiliary Material

Rhetorical Content	Narration: Telling a Story
	Description: Painting a Mind Picture
Thematic Content	Outward Appearances: Self Image, Cultural Diversity
Background	from *A. Magazine*, 1992. Grace Suh, born in Seoul, Korea, and raised in the United States, works in the publishing industry and is a poetry editor for the *Asian Pacific American Journal*. In this article she relates her Neiman Marcus makeover experience.
Related Readings	Richard Rodriguez, "Complexion," from *Hunger of Memory: The Education of Richard Rodriguez*. 1982.
	Janice Mirikitani, "Recipe" (a poem), from *Shedding Silence*. 1987.
	Lewis Sawaquat (formerly, Lewis Johnson), "For My Indian Daughter," from My Turn column, *Newsweek*, September 5, 1983.
	Carolyn Edgar, "Black and Blue," *Reconstruction*, 1994.

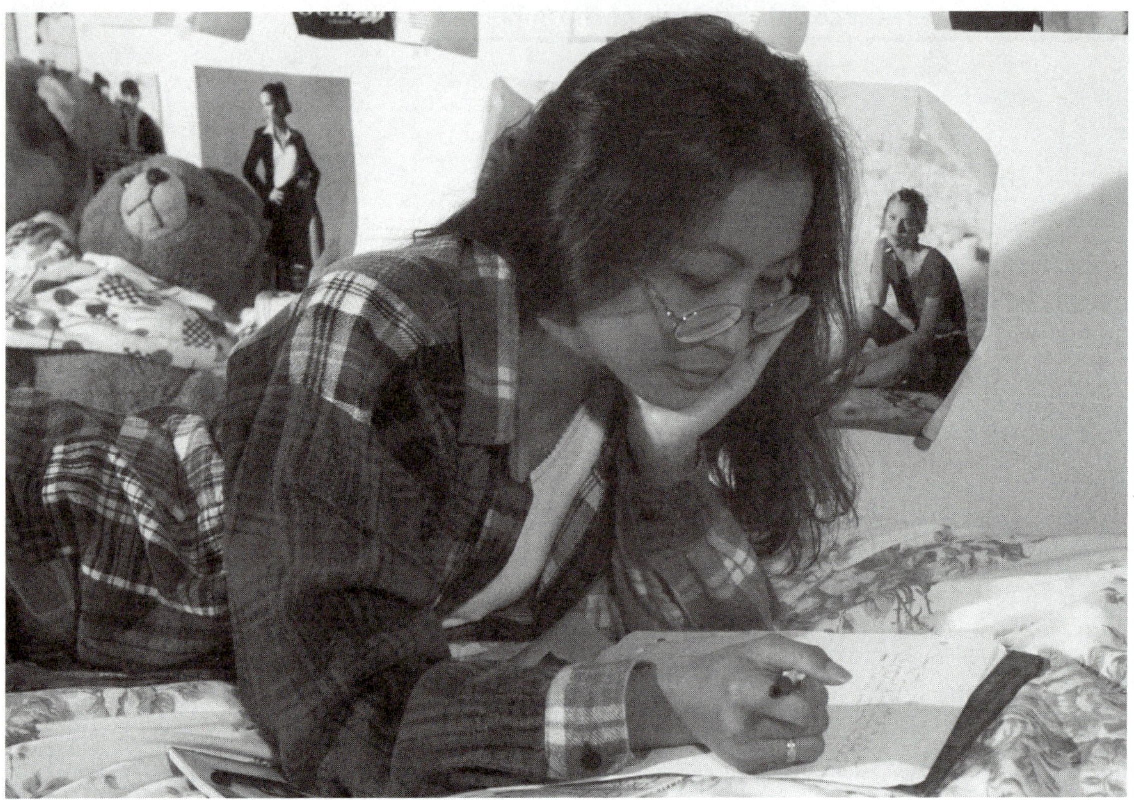

Teenager in her room. (Bill Lai/Index Stock Imagery)

1   Several summers ago, on one of those endless August evenings when the sun hangs suspended just above the horizon, I made up my mind to become beautiful.

2   It happened as I walked by one of those mirrored glass-clad office towers and caught a glimpse of my reflection out of the corner of my eye. The glass on this particular building was green, which might have accounted for the sickly tone of my complexion, but there was no explaining away the limp, ragged hair, the dark circles under my eyes, the facial blemishes, the shapeless, wrinkled clothes. The overall effect—the whole being greater than the sum of its parts—was one of stark ugliness.

3   I'd come home from college having **renounced** bourgeois suburban values, like hygiene and grooming. Now home for the summer, I washed my hair and changed clothes only when I felt like it, and spent most of my time sitting on the lawn eat-

ing mini rice cakes and Snickers and reading dog-eared back issues of *National Geographic.*

4   But that painfully epiphanous day, standing there on the hot sidewalk, I suddenly understood what my mother had been gently hinting these past months: I was no longer just plain, no longer merely unattractive. No, I had broken the Unsightliness Barrier. I was now UGLY, and aggressively so.

5   And so, in an unusual exertion of will, I resolved to fight back against the forces of entropy. I envisioned it as reclamation work, like scything down a lawn that has grown into meadow, or restoring a damaged fresco. For the first time in ages, I felt elated and hopeful. I nearly sprinted into the nearby Neiman Marcus. As I entered the cool, hushed, dimly lit first floor and saw the gleaming counters lined with vials of magical balm, the priestesses of beauty in their sacred smocks, and the glossy photographic icons of the goddesses themselves—Paulina, Linda, Cindy, Vendella—in a wild, reckless burst of inspiration I thought to myself, Heck, why just okay? Why not BEAUTIFUL?

6   At the Estee Lauder counter, I spied a polished, middle-aged woman whom I hoped might be less **imperious** than the aloof amazons at the Chanel counter.

7   "Could I help you?" the woman (I thought of her as "Estee") asked.

8   "Yes," I blurted. "I look terrible. I need a complete makeover—skin, face, everything."

9   After a wordless **scrutiny** of my face, she motioned me to sit down and began. She cleansed my skin with a bright blue mud masque and clear, tingling astringent and then applied a film of moisturizer, working extra amounts into the rough patches. Under the soft pressure of her fingers, I began to relax. From my perch, I happily took in the dizzying, colorful swirl of beautiful women and products all around me. I breathed in the billows of perfume that wafted through the air. I whispered the names of products under my breath like a healing mantra: cooling eye gel, gentle exfoliant, night time neck area reenergizer, moisture recharging intensifier, ultra-hydrating complex, emulsifying immunage. I felt immersed in femininity, intoxicated by beauty.

10   I was flooded with gratitude at the patience and determination with which Estee toiled away at my face, painting on swaths of lip gloss, blush, and foundation. She was not working in vain, I vowed, as I sucked in my cheeks on her command. I would buy all these products. I would use them every day. I studied her gleaming, polished features—her lacquered nails, the glittering mosaic of her eyeshadow, the complex red shimmer of her mouth, her flawless, dewy skin—and tried to imagine myself as impeccably groomed as she.

11   Estee's voice interrupted my **reverie,** telling me to blot my lips. I stuck the tissue into my mouth and clamped down, watching myself in the mirror. My skin was a blankly even shade of pale, my cheeks and lips glaringly bright in contrast. My face had a strange plastic sheen, like a mannequin's. I grimaced as Estee applied the second lipstick coat: Was this right? Didn't I look kind of—fake? But she smiled back at me, clearly pleased with her work. I was ashamed of myself: Well, what did I expect? It wasn't like she had anything to start with.

12   "Now," she announced, "Time for the biggie—Eyes."

13   "Oh. Well, actually, I want to look good and everything, but, I mean, I'm sure you could tell, I'm not really into a complicated beauty routine . . ." My voice faded into a giggle.

14   "So?" Estee snapped.

15   "Sooo . . ." I tried again, "I've never really used eye makeup, except, you know, for a little mascara sometimes, and I don't really feel comfortable—"

16   Estee was firm. "Well, the fact is that the eyes are the windows of the face. They're the focal point. An eye routine doesn't have to be complicated, but it's important to emphasize the eyes with some color, or they'll look washed out."

17   I certainly didn't want that. I leaned back again in my chair and closed my eyes.

18   Estee explained as she went: "I'm covering your lids with this champagne color. It's a real versatile base, 'cause it goes with almost any other color you put on top of it." I felt the velvety pad of the applicator sweep over my lids in a soothing rhythm.

19   "Now, being an Oriental, you don't have a lid fold, so I'm going to draw one with this charcoal shadow. Then, I fill in below the line with a lighter charcoal color with a bit of blue in it—frosted midnight—and then above it, on the outside of your lids, I'm going to apply this plum color. There. Hold on a minute . . . Okay. Open up."

20   I stared at the face in the mirror, at my eyes. The drawn-on fold and dark, heavy shadows distorted and reproportioned my whole face. Not one of the features in the mirror was recognizable, not the waxy white skin or the redrawn crimson or the sharp, deep cheekbones, and especially, not the eyes. I felt **negated;** I had been blotted out and another face drawn in my place. I looked up at Estee, and in that moment I hated her. "I look terrible," I said.

21   Her back stiffened. "What do you mean?" she demanded.

22   "Hideous. I don't even look human. Look at my eyes. You can't even see me!" My voice was hoarse.

23   She looked. After a moment, she straightened up again, "Well, I'll admit, the eyeshadow doesn't look great." She began to put away the pencils and brushes. "But at least now you have an eyelid."

24   I told myself that she was a pathetic, middle-aged woman with a boring job and a meaningless life. I had my whole life before me. All she had was the newest Richard Chamberlain miniseries.

25   But it didn't matter. The fact of the matter was that she was pretty, and I was not. Her blue eyes were recessed in an intricate pattern of folds and hollows. Mine bulged out.

26   I bought the skincare system and the foundation and the blush and the lip liner pencil and the lipstick and the primer and the eyeliner and the eyeshadows—all four colors. The stuff filled a bag the size of a shoebox. It cost a lot. Estee handed me my receipt with a flourish, and I told her, "Thank you."

27   In the mezzanine level washroom, I set my bag on the counter and scrubbed my face with water and slimy pink soap from the dispenser. I splashed my face with cold water until it felt tight, and dried my raw skin with brown paper towels that scratched.

28   As the sun sank into the Chicago skyline, I boarded the Burlington Northern Commuter for home and found a seat in the corner. I set the shopping bag down beside me, and heaped its gilt boxes and frosted glass bottles in my lap. Looking out the window, I saw that night had fallen. Instead of trees and backyard fences I saw my profile—the same reflection, I realized, that I'd seen hours ago in the side of the green office building. I did have eyelids, of course. Just not a fold. I wasn't pretty. But I was familiar and comforting. I was myself.

29   The next stop was mine. I arranged the things carefully back in the rectangular bag, large bottles of toner and moisturizer first, then the short cylinders of masque and scrub and powder, small bottles of foundation and primer, the little logs of pencils and lipstick, then the flat boxed compacts of blush and eye shadow. The packages fit around each other cleverly, like pieces in a puzzle. The conductor called out, "Fairview Avenue," and I stood up. Hurrying down the aisle, I looked back once at the neatly packed bag on the seat behind me, and jumped out just as the doors were closing shut.

Understanding Words

▶ **Definitions**

bourgeois (par. 3) The Middle Class.

ephipanous (par. 4) A sudden revelation.

entropy (par. 5) Inevitable and steady deterioration.

fresco (par. 5) The art of painting on fresh, moist plaster.

mantra (par. 9) A verbal formula repeated in prayer or meditation.

exfoliant (par. 9) A mixture that peels off layers.

emulsifying (par. 9) Combining two liquids that do not mix, such as oil and water.

▶ **Vocabulary**

Check your understanding of the following words. Study the words in context (boldfaced in the text) and fill in the blank with the letter of the word or words that are closest to the meaning of the word in the text.

1. _____**renounced** (a) accepted (b) rejected (c) adopted (d) restated

2. _____**imperious** (a) regal (b) charming (c) arrogant (d) critical

3. _____**scrutiny** (a) criticism (b) rejection (c) appreciative look (d) close look

4. _____**reverie** (a) daydream (b) concentration (c) makeover (d) application

5. _____**negated** (a) wiped out (b) beautified (d) nourished (d) elated

Thinking and Discussing

1. Have you or someone you know had a "makeover"? What kind? If it involved the face, what feature did the makeover artist feel needed the most attention?

2. Who do you think sets the standard of beauty for women in the United States? Is it the cosmetic industry? Is it the media? Are the standards the same irrespective of race or ethnic background? How realistic is it to expect women to look like Barbie or a super model such as Cindy Crawford?

3. The woman at the Estee Lauder counter concentrated on Suh's eyelids: "Now, being an Oriental, you don't have a lid fold, so I'm going to draw one with this charcoal shadow." (par. 19) How do you feel about this statement? Is she trying to be helpful, or is she, not so subtly, saying that by Western standards, Suh's eyes are not beautiful because she does not have lid folds?

4. What is your response to Suh's makeover?

5. Study the dialogue between Suh and Estee. What do you learn about each person from the dialogue?

Writing Suggestions

1. Write a paragraph in which you explain why Suh left the makeup on the bus.

2. Have you ever tried to change the way you look so that you could better fit in with a particular group?

   Write an essay describing the change you attempted to make. Why did you do it? What did you hope to achieve by making the change? Were you satisfied with the result? What lesson did you learn, if any, as the result of the experience?

3. Write a short paper in which you explain what you feel that Suh learned from her makeover at Neiman Marcus.

4. Use Suh's account of the makeover as a model and relate it from the point of view of the Estee Lauder's make-up artist.

John Leo, "The 'Modern Primitives' "

Auxiliary Material

Rhetorical Content   Informational Process Analysis: Explaining

Thematic Content   Outward Appearances: Social Conditions and Trends—Body Modification

Background   from *U. S. News and World Report,* July 31, 1995. John Leo examines body modification—piercing, tattooing, scarring, branding, and stretching—and speculates about the possible motives involved and the messages its practitioners are trying to send. Historically, body modification was generally practiced by extreme groups; however, it is now much more mainstream. Multiple ear piercings are common even among older conservative people, and tongue studs and nose rings seldom rate a second look. Leo considers these motives minor and concentrates on the idea of "new primitivism" as the major motive.

Related Readings   Meg Greenfield, "Kicking Away Your Freedom," *Newsweek,* March 23, 1998.

Henry Han XI Lau, "I Was a Member of the Kung Fu Crew," *New York Times Magazine,* October 1997.

Wendy Chapkis, "Dress As Success: Joolz," from *Beauty Secrets: Women and the Politics of Appearance.* © 1986. South End Press, Boston, MA 02115.

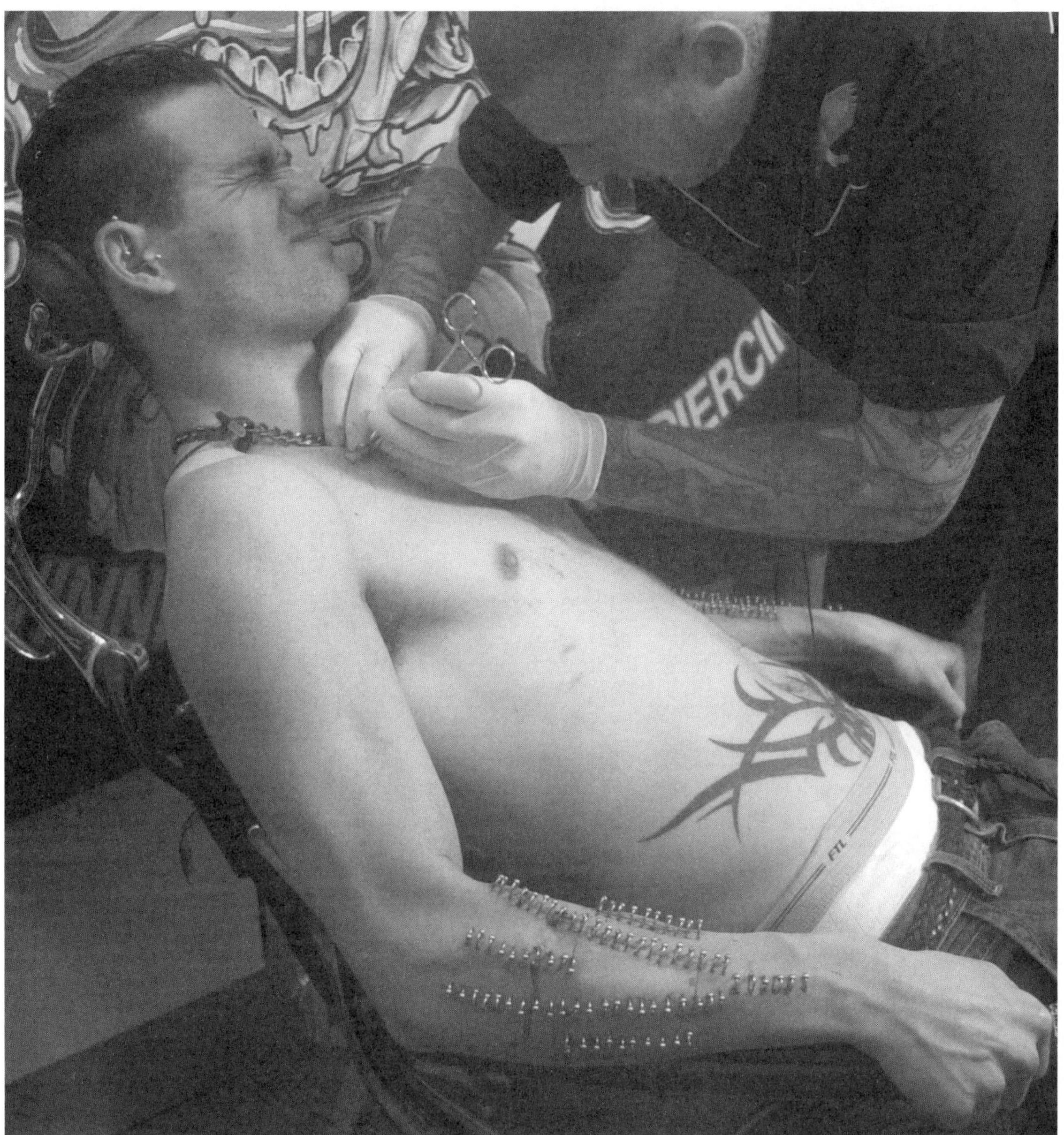

The "Pierce" of Fame. Matt Brown, a 21-year-old college student works on getting into the Guinness Book of World Records by having the most body piercings in one day—171 new piercings. (Omaha, Nebraska, 11/23/01, AP Photo/Dave Weaver)

1   The days when body piercers could draw stares by wearing multiple earrings and a nose stud are long gone. We are now in the late baroque phase of self-penetration. Metal rings and bars hang from eyebrows, noses, nipples, lips, chins, cheeks, navels and (for that **coveted** neo-Frankenstein look) from the side of the neck.

2   "If it sticks out, pierce it" is the motto, and so they do, with special attention to genitals. Some of the same middle-class folks who **decry** genital mutilation in Africa are paying to have needles driven through the scrotum, the labia, the clitoris, or the head or the shaft of the penis. Many genital piercings have their own names, such as the ampallang or the Prince Albert. (Don't ask.)

3   And, in most cases, the body heals without damage, though some women who have had their nipples pierced report damage to the breast's milk ducts, and some men who have been Prince Alberted no longer urinate in quite the same way.

4   What is going on here? Well, the mainstreaming-of-**deviancy** thesis naturally springs to mind. The piercings of nipples and genitals arose in the homosexual sadomasochistic culture of the West Coast. The Gauntlet, founded in Los Angeles in 1975 mostly to do master and slave piercings, now has three shops around the country that are about as controversial as Elizabeth Arden salons. Rumbling through the biker culture and punk, piercing gradually shed its outlaw image and was mass marketed to the impressionable by music videos, rock stars and models.

5   The nasty, aggressive edge of piercing is still there, but now it is coated in happy talk (it's just body decoration, like any other) and a New Age **rationale** (we are becoming more centered, reclaiming our bodies in an antibody culture). Various new pagans, witches and New Agers see piercing as symbolic of unspecified spiritual transformation. One way or another, as Guy Trebay writes in the *Village Voice,* "You will never find anyone on the piercing scene who thinks of what he's doing as **pathological.**"

6   The yearning to irritate parents and shock the middle class seems to rank high as a motive for getting punctured repeatedly. Some ask for dramatic piercings to enhance sexual pleasure, to seem daring or fashionable, to express rage, or to forge a group identity. Some think of it as an ordeal that serves as a rite of passage, like ritual suspension of Indian males from hooks in their chests.

7   Piercing is part of the broader "body modification" movement, which includes tattooing, corsetry, branding and scarring by knife. It's a sign of the times that the more bizarre expressions of this movement keep pushing into the mainstream. The current issue of *Spin* magazine features a hair-raising photo of a woman carving little rivers of blood into another woman's back. "Piercing is like toothbrushing now," one of the cutters told *Spin.* "It's why cutting is becoming popular."

Slicing someone's back is a violent act. But one of the cutters has a **bland** justification: People want to be cut "for adornment, or as a test of endurance, or as a sacrifice toward a transformation." Later on we read that "women are reclaiming their bodies from a culture that has commodified starvation and **faux** sex." One cuttee says: "It creates intimacy. My scars are emotional centers, signs of a life lived."

8   But most of us achieve intimacy, or at least search for it, without a knife in hand. The truth seems to be that the sadomasochistic instinct is being repositioned to look spiritually high-toned. Many people have found that S&M play "is a way of opening up the body-spirit connection," the high priest of the body modification movement, Fakir Musafar, said in one interview.

9   Musafar, who has corseted his waist down to 19 inches and **mortified** his flesh with all kinds of blades, hooks and pins, calls the mostly twentyish people in the body modification movement "the modern primitives." This is another side of the movement: the conscious attempt to **repudiate** Western norms and values by adopting the marks and rings of primitive cultures. In some cases this is expressed by tusks worn in the nose or by stretching and exaggerating holes in the earlobe or nipple.

10   Not everyone who pierces a nipple or wears a tongue stud is buying into this, but something like a new primitivism seems to be emerging in body modification, as in other areas of American life. It plugs into a wider dissatisfaction with traditional Western rationality, logic and sexual norms, as well as anger at the impact of Western technology on the natural environment and anger at the state of American political and social life.

11   Two sympathetic analysts say: "Amidst an almost universal feeling of powerlessness to 'change the world,' individuals are changing what they have power over: their own bodies. . . . By giving visible expression to unknown desires and **latent** obsessions **welling** up from within, individuals can provoke change."

12   Probably not. Cultural crisis can't really be dealt with by letting loose our personal obsessions and marking up our bodies. But the rapid spread of this movement is yet another sign that the crisis is here.

Understanding Words

▶ **Definitions**

Baroque (par. 1) A style in art and architecture developed in Europe about 1500 to 1700, typified by elaborate, ornate scrolls and curves, and other ornamentation.

neo- (par. 1) *prefix* New.

sadomasochistic (par. 4) Deriving sexual pleasure from simultaneous sadism and masochism. (**sadism** Deriving sexual pleasure from inflicting pain on others. **masochism** Deriving sexual pleasure from being physically or emotionally abused.)

Elizabeth Arden (par. 4) Popular brand of cosmetics.

commodified (par. 7) From the word *commodity.* Something that has become common enough to have a standard commercial or cultural position in society.

S & M (par. 8) Sadomasochistic.

▶ **Vocabulary**

Check your understanding of the following words. Study the words in context (boldfaced in the text) and fill in the blank with the letter of the word or words that are closest to the meaning of the word in the text.

1. _____ **coveted** (a) hideous (b) desired (c) frightening (d) classy

2. _____ **decry** (a) condemn (b) are embarrassed by (c) approve of (d) respect

3. _____ **deviancy** (a) difference (b) divine (c) artistic (d) viability

4. _____ **rationale** (a) reason (b) rule (c) concept (d) trend

5. _____ **pathological** (a) half-way-logical (b) compulsive behavior (c) crazy (d) stupid

6. _____ **bland** (a) popular (b) casual (c) critical (d) unreasonable

7. _____ **faux** (a) exciting (b) unusual (c) clandestine (d) false

8. _____ **mortified** (a) shamed (b) disciplined (c) humiliated (d) wounded

9. _____ **repudiate** (a) put in perspective (b) reject (c) classify (d) reorganize

10. _____ **latent** (a) weird (b) unwelcome (c) primitive (d) hidden

11. _____ **welling** (a) pooling (b) rising (c) building (d) festering

Thinking and Discussing

1. What was your first experience with body modification? What were your reactions? Have you changed your opinions about it or some types of it?

2. Do you or any of your friends have one or more piercings or tattos? What was the rationale behind them? Why did you or they do it? What are people's reactions to you or to your friends who have body modifications? Can you group the reactions according to age groups?

3. What is the difference between the commonplace piercing of ears for earrings and piercing of other body parts? Does society as a whole view the piercings in the same light? If not, what might be some explanations for the different perceptions?

Writing Suggestions

1. Write a paragraph explaining a particular type of body modification. If possible write about one with which you have had personal experience. You may write about how the process is done, how it should be maintained, how to deal with responses, or the feelings that the subject experiences during or after the procedure. Remember, a paragraph must have a topic sentence that contains the subject and a controlling idea (your idea about the subject).

2. Write an essay in which you explain the historical—either recent or ancient—procedures and attitudes toward body modification, also called body art in some situations. You may need to support your own information with research. There is a wealth of information—both prose and pictures—readily available. You may want to write a process analysis of a period, or you may want to discuss two periods and compare and contrast them. The comparisons and contrasts may include rationales, procedures, and social attitudes.

3. Choose some topic of body modification that you know something about and write a brief paper explaining some aspect of it.

History and Culture

Bennie M. Currie, "The N-word and How to Use It"

Auxiliary Material

Rhetorical Content	Definition: Expanding the Meaning of a Word or Term
	Example: Illustrating a Point
	Narration: Telling a Story
Thematic Content	History and Culture: History of a Word
Background	from *the Chicago Reader,* December 19, 1997. Bennie M. Currie, a freelance journalist based in Chicago, has worked in public and media relations, done investigative reporting and travel

(continued)

writing. His work has appeared in *American Visions,* the *Chicago Reader,* and *Emerge* magazine. In this essay Currie explores the many-faceted meanings of the n-word and explains how "blacks took the loaded term *nigger* and disarmed it by making it a household word" that is the exclusive property of the black community.

Related Readings   Alex Kotlowitz, "Colorblind," *New York Times Magazine,* January 11, 1998.

Lani Guinier, "Find a Space for Real Conversations on Race," *The Radcliffe Quarterly,* Radclifffe College, Fall–Winter, 1997.

Sandra Cisneros, "An Offering to the Power of Language," the *Los Angeles Times,* October 26, 1997.

Nathan McCall, "The World of White Folks," from *Makes Me Wanna Holler: A Young Black Man in America.* Random House, Inc. © 1994.

1   N-I-G-G-E-R. I'll never forget the first time I accidentally used that word in mixed company. It was twenty years ago at the University of Missouri, and I was engaged in lighthearted chitchat with Kent, my white roommate, when I casually called him a *nigger.*

2   For a second I'd forgotten that I was not among my black friends in my old neighborhood of Saint Louis, where calling a buddy *nigger* was synonymous with calling him *brother* or *man.* It was just another way to talk cool, using a word that had become part of our vocabulary long before we were aware of all its varied meanings and usages.

3   I was barely conscious of my accidental utterance, but their was nothing casual about Kent's reaction. His eyes widened, and his body flinched as though he'd just absorbed a boxer's jab. Then he snapped to an upright position on the edge of his bed, narrowed his eyes, and pointed an index finger at me. "*I'm* not a nigger," he said, his tone implying that he thought *I* was a nigger. He never actually called me a nigger, but the mere suggestion was enough to put me in a fighting mood.

4   "Do I look like a nigger to you?" I shouted.

5   "But *you* just called *me* a nigger," he replied.

6   "Well, that's different. *You* can't call me that. Not ever."

7   Fortunately, our dorm mates stopped this exchange before I could throw a punch at Kent, who probably thought I was nuts. Actually I was simply too angry to realize that I was the one at fault.

8   By calling Kent a nigger, I'd exposed him to what my old neighborhood friends called a "black thing" he didn't understand. The "thing" is the love/hate relationship many black people have with *nigger,* one of the most complex, **perplexing,** and emotionally incendiary words in the American **lexicon.** And to be truthful, black people are hardly unified in their understanding or usage of this piece of slang.

9   There have been times in my life when I've felt very comfortable using the word, but I've also struggled with its usage. And now that I'm a parent I cringe at the notion that my two children will someday have to try to understand what those six letters mean to them, their friends and foes, and the larger society. While my wife and I are readying ourselves for questions like "Where do babies come from?" I know that none will be more **vexing** than the first innocent **query** about the N-word.

10   I could take the easy way out and tell our kids that *nigger* is a bad word that good boys and girls should never use. Or maybe I could recite the old "sticks and stones" **adage** and tell them it's a name that can never hurt them. But neither tactic is likely to work, especially the second, since I don't believe it myself.

11   If my kids are destined to be introduced to a word born of racial hatred, then their parents should be the ones to do it. But television, the Internet, the school playground, and other competitors for our kids' attention may get to them first. Or a dictionary.

12   Last February Kathryn Williams, curator of the museum of African American History in Flint, Michigan, was asked by a little boy, "Am I a nigger because I'm black?" She told the naturally curious child that a nigger was any ignorant person, then advised him to look up the word in the dictionary for reassurance. The kid paged through the venerable *Merriam-Webster's Collegiate Dictionary,* where he found that *nigger* is a term for "a black person—usu. taken to be offensive." With only minor revisions, this definition has existed for nearly half a century.

13   This was a shocking revelation for Williams, who started a petition drive to pressure Merriam-Webster to revise the definition. Her campaign gained momentum last September, when *Emerge* magazine ran a brief article about it. Since then, scores of people have joined her, many of them contending that the current definition inaccurately explains the meaning of the word. Some of them also believe the racial epithet is undeserving of inclusion in a dictionary and want it deleted altogether.

14   I know why Williams and others like her are upset. Being called *nigger* by a white person or a white-run institution is a slap in the face for many blacks. It evokes thoughts of the sorry legacy of slavery and the racism that haunts the nation. And it hurts. When I checked out the definition in my own copy of the Collegiate edition I felt stung—particularly since I knew that dictionaries are almost as ubiquitous as Gideon Bibles.

15   I don't believe the publishers of the Collegiate edition meant to offend anyone. Most likely, they were simply reflecting the confusion that stems from the **paradoxical** usage of the word among Americans of all hues, cultures, and generations.

16   Since my dorm-room experience, several whites have told me of their own struggles to understand the term—and to understand why a word that was used for centuries by white people to **disparage** and dehumanize their black slaves and today is a chief element of hate-speak (witness the Nigger Joke Center on the World Wide Web) is cool for blacks to use but taboo for them. They ask, How can any self-respecting black person stand to use it? Why do black kids call each other "my nigga" in such endearing tones, privately as well as publicly? Is this a "self hatred thing"?

17   I say no. It's what blacks have always done since we hit America's shores 400 years ago. We take what's given to us or thrown at us, and we can find a way to make it our own. Blacks melded African rhythms and European music to create jazz, this country's only original musical art form. We took the parts of livestock whites didn't care to eat—intestines, tongues, ears, and feet—mixed them with our native African dishes and conjured up soul food.

18   In the same manner, blacks took the loaded term *nigger* and disarmed it by making it a household word. In fact, we went on to embrace it by using it to spice up poetry, rap lyrics, and many a comedy stand-up routine. A case in point is Paul Mooney, a comedian and writer (*Saturday Night Live, Good Times* and *In Living Color*). He doesn't just use *nigger* to accent his stand-up act. It's often the focal point of his jokes. In one bit he complains about the flak he catches from whites who sometimes object more **vociferously** to his liberal use of the word than do many blacks. "Make that nigger stop saying *nigger*. He's giving me a nigger headache," he jokes. "Well white folks, you shouldn't have ever made up the word. You fucked up, I say nigger 100 times every morning. It makes my teeth white."

19   Chris Rock, who currently hosts a weekly HBO talk show, is another funny man at peace with his use of *nigger*. While my grandmother has never heard of him, she and Rock assign a similar meaning to the term. The hot comic told B.E.T. *Weekend* magazine he uses it to describe "a certain *kind* of black person who wallows in ignorance and likes being ignorant." During a recent HBO special, Rock expressed this point of view with these one-liners: "Niggers react to books the way vampires react to sunlight." "Niggers always want credit for something they should be doing. 'I take care of my kids.' You're *supposed* to take care of your kids!" "Black people don't give a damn about welfare reform. Niggers are shaking in their boots."

20   Rock, who used to lampoon CBS anchor Bryant Gumbel for "talking white," recently apologized publicly for using such a label. But he doesn't plan to cut *nigger* out of his act anytime soon. "I'll stop when niggas stop," he said. "Niggas robbed my house, robbed my mother's house. Black people didn't do that." He adds, "I would love to have no reason to use the word. I'd love for it to be obsolete."

21   Richard Pryor, one of Rock's role models, was at the height of his legendary career in 1982, when he vowed never again to use the word to refer to another black person. He said he had an epiphany during a visit to Africa. He didn't see any "niggers" in the motherland and realized that blacks there had no need for the word. Pryor shared his pledge with the audience during a stand-up routine that was later released as a feature film, *Richard Pryor Live on the Sunset Strip*. The statement inspired lots of blacks to make the same vow.

22   I haven't made that pledge, but before I saw Pryor's film I never thought twice about why I used *nigger*. I'm less comfortable using it now, but because of my lifelong cultural association with the word, I can't foresee total avoidance. Because my kids have a different culture, I've never used it around them, and I don't intend to.

23   Since my kids aren't going to grow up hearing *nigger* under our roof, the question still remains: How should I explain this word to them? There's only one way to do it—**candidly** and carefully. I'll tell them that the word is a national shame and at times a painful reminder of their ancestors' struggle for freedom. And I'll explain that the term has a history just as relevant as Jim Crow, the Revolutionary War, lynching, or Watergate, which is why forcing a dictionary to delete it would be a mistake, would be censorship.

24   Meanwhile the people at Merriam-Webster are busy **mulling** a revision of their definition of *nigger,* according to spokesman Steve Perrault. He wrote me via e-mail that it's too early to pinpoint when or if a change will be made, but he assured me the issue will be resolved before the dictionary's next scheduled major update, in 2003. "The problem for us is that it's not simply a matter of changing one entry," Perrault said. "If we revise our treatment of the offensive word, we also have to revise our treatment of the many other offensive words in the dictionary. That makes it a fairly major undertaking, and our feeling is that we want to be sure we are getting it right."

25   Sounds like a good idea. But does this really require much deliberation? I don't think so. The third edition of the *American Heritage Dictionary of the English Language* already has it figured out. Its definition of *nigger* begins with the words "offensive *slang* . . . used as a disparaging term for a black person." As an illustration, a quote from James Baldwin: "You can only be destroyed by believing that you really are what the white world calls a Negro."

26   This interpretation seems fair and accurate to me. It's even suitable for the eyes of a child. And it may even enlighten a confused college kid or two.

Understanding Words

▶ **Definitions**

incendiary (par. 8) Capable of causing fire.

curator (par. 12) One who manages or oversees a museum collection or a library collection.

epithet (par. 13) A term characterizing a person or thing, an abusive or contemptuous term.

ubiquitous (par. 14) Being or seeming to be everywhere at the same time.

Gideon Bibles (par. 14) Bibles placed in hotel rooms by members of Gideons, an interdenominational, international Christian society.

conjure (par. 17) To bring forth as if by magic.

soul food (par. 17) Food such as ham hocks and collard greens traditionally eaten by southern American Black people.

lampoon (par. 20) A satirical piece that uses ridicule to attack a person or a group of people.

epiphany (par. 21) A sudden revelation of the essence or meaning of something.

▶ **Vocabulary**

Check your understanding of the following words. Read them in context (boldfaced in the text) and fill in the blank with the letter of the word or words that are closest in meaning to the word in the text.

1. ____**perplexing** (a) misused (b) derogatory (c) unpleasant (d) confusing

2. ____**lexicon** (a) vocabulary (b) slang (c) language (d) dialect

3. ____**vexing** (a) difficult (b) embarrassing (c) irritating (d) distressing

4. ____**query** (a) assumption (b) question (c) retort (d) comment

5. ____**adage** (a) riddle (b) saying (c) game (d) ruse

6. ____**paradoxical** (a) twisted (b) inaccurate (c) self-contradictory (d) convoluted

7. ____**disparage** (a) belittle (b) disgrace (c) embarrass (d) negate

8. ____**vociferously** (a) violently (b) quietly (c) nosily and insistently (d) blatantly

9. ____**candidly** (a) openly (b) without rancor (c) without malice (d) fairly

10. ____**mulling** (a) deciding on (b) working on (c) thinking about (d) trying to avoid

Thinking and Discussing

1. Does the first sentence grab your attention? If so, why? What type of lead-in is it? What do people usually mean when they talk about using a word or expression "in mixed company"?

2. The title suggests that this piece will be a "how to" essay. Does the essay live up to the suggestion, or is the writer using the title to call your attention to the many uses of the word?

3. In paragraph 19, Carrie says that Chris Rock and his grandmother "assign a similar mean-ing to the term." In your own words, explain the similar meaning that they share.

4. If a child has heard the n-word for the first time and asks you what it means, how would you explain it? Would the context in which it was used affect your explanation?

5. Check several dictionaries—older editions as well as up-to-date editions—and compare and contrast the definitions of the n-word. Have there been shifts in definitions or in labels? What are they? When did they occur?

Writing Suggestions

1. Write a paragraph in which you tell how you feel about the n-word.

2. Write an extended definition of the n-word.

3. Write an essay from the point of view that the n-word is only a word and has no power in it-self and casual use of it will rob it of its per-ceived negative power.

4. Write an essay from the point of view that the n-word is so fraught with negativity that it should never be used under any circum-stances.

5. Write an essay from the point of view that only African Americans have the right to use this word. Give examples of the positive ways, as well as negatives ones, that it can be used.

6. In the O. J. Simpson criminal trial, the n-word was pivotal in the case. If you are familiar with the case, write a paper expressing your reasoned

opinions as to why and how the word was pivotal. If you are not familiar with the case, interview someone who is and write a paper expressing his or her opinions about the importance of the word in this trial.

7. Connotation/denotation are terms that specify the way a word has meaning. Connotation refers to an idea or meaning suggested by or associated with a word—shades of meaning. Denotation refers to the exact meaning of a word. The n-word has many "shades of meaning," and often Black stand-up comedians use the n-word as a fundamental part of their routine. Listen to one or more of these routines and write an essay in which you analyze the "shades of meaning" of this word. Can you reach any conclusion about the purpose of the usage? Is it simply to entertain, or is there a more serious message hiding behind the comic mask?

Luis J. Rodriguez, "Stop the Lies"

Auxiliary Material

Rhetorical Content   Argumentation and Persuasion: Attempt to Incite People to Thought or Action

Thematic Content   History and Culture: Race and Truth

Background   from *Hungry Mind Review,* Spring 1998. Luis J. Rodriguez, a poet and journalist and editor of *Tia Chucha Press* in Chicago, is the author of three books of poetry—*Poems Across the Pavement, The Concrete River,* and *Trochemoche.* He won the Carl Sandburg award in 1993 for his memoir, *Always Running: La Vida Loca, Gang Days in L. A.* In "Stop the Lies," Rodriguez contends that race cannot be seriously discussed in America as long as whites continue to perpetrate lies about history.

Related Readings   Gary Soto, "The Concert," from *Small Faces* by Gary Soto © 1986.

Robert Ramierez, "The Barrio," from an anthology entitled *Pain and Promise: The Chicano Today,* 1972. First entitled "The Woolen Serape."

Richard Rodriguez, "The Fear of Losing a Culture," *Time*, July 11, 1988.

Alex Kotloqitz, "Colorblind," *New York Times Magazine*, January 11, 1988.

Lani Guinier, "Finding a Space for Real Conversations on Race," *The Radcliffe Quarterly*, Radcliffe College, Fall–Winter, 1997.

Massachusetts Violence Prevention Fest. (Eric Fowke/Index Stock Imagery)

1 In 1997 President Bill Clinton dared to open up the race debate with a number of so-called town hall meetings. In my view, many of these meetings were **farcical** and insulting. The basic lies were not challenged. I believe because of this the lies were thus perpetuated. Apologies and meaningless gestures of **retribution** are even more insulting. They only give the lies more **adherence** in our conscience.

2   You want to talk about race in America? Then stop the lies.

3   Stop the lie that Aryans were white and superior. According to J. M. Roberts in *A Short History of the World* (Oxford University Press, 1993), they were central Asian warriors and nomads who settled into India, Iran (which means "Land of the Aryans"), and eastern Europe some 2,000 years before Christ. And although they contributed much (including the horse-drawn chariot, the Indo-European family of languages, and the *Vedas*), they also held back certain aspects of culture and development in the areas they conquered.

4   "The Aryans had no culture so advanced as what they found," says Roberts. "Writing disappears with their arrival, not emerging again until the middle of the first millennium B.C.; cities, too, had to be reinvented, and when they appear again lack the elaboration and order of their Indus Valley predecessors."

5   Stop the lie that Jesus Christ was white. He was an Aramaic-speaking brown man who never set foot in Europe. The first Christians were from the Semitic regions of the Mediterranean, including Northern Africa, where many of the original Christians, including the Coptic Church of Egypt and Ethiopia, still exist. The teachings of Jesus Christ are no less profound. He doesn't have to be white!

6   Stop the lie that Europe civilized the world. A case can be made that it was the other way around. For example, the shaping forces of the European **renaissance** of the fourteenth to seventeenth centuries include the opening of trade with China, the Moors' 800-year rule of Spain, and the first circumnavigation of the world by Ferdinand Magellan, the conquest of the Americas (including the looting of gold and silver that fueled the engines of Europe's **incipient** capitalist economy), and the slave trade in Africa. Gypsies, Huns, Arabs, Tartars, Jews, and others have all contributed to "civilization" in Europe.

7   Stop the lie that humans can be **delineated** by race. There are no anthropological, spiritual, or biological grounds for such a concept. The American notion of race is a relatively recent construct predicated on the oppression and exploitation of one people over others.

8   "The traffic grew with the profits—the shuttle service importing human **chattel** to America in overcrowded ships," writes Earl Conrad in his 1967 book *The Invention of the Negro* (Paul S. Eriksson Publishers). "It was on these ships that we find the beginnings—the first **crystallizations**—of the curious doctrine which was to be called 'white supremacy.' . . . Among the first men to develop attitudes of supremacy were the slaveship crew."

9   This doctrine was later supported by pseudo-scientific papers that declared Africans, Amerindians, and Asians as inferior to Europeans, including from the mighty pens of such scholars as Kant and freedom defenders as Thomas Jefferson! *Enlightenment* according to Emmanuel Chukwudi Eze in *Race and the Enlightment* (Blackwell Press, 1997), Kant stated in his master work, *Physical Geography,* that "humanity is at its greatest perfection in the race of the whites." And Jefferson had this to say in "Laws," from *Notes on the State of Virginia:* "Unfortunate difference of color, and perhaps of **faculty,** is a powerful obstacle to the emancipation of [black] people."

10   Stop the lie that we live in a **monolithic** culture. What we call America was forged with the ideas, blood, sweat, labor, laws, and cultural contributions of the **indigenous** peoples of the land as well as Africans, Eastern Europeans, Italians, Spanish, French, British, Irish, Chinese, Japanese, mixed-bloods—and on and on. Things we take for granted, such as cowboys, jazz, karate, chocolate, corn, tobacco, paper, surfing, gunpowder, pasta, rock-n-roll, and our system of government, have roots in non-European cultures.

11   Once a white acquaintance came with me to catch a *Quebradita* dance in Chicago of mostly Mexican and Chicano youth. The young people sported cowboy hats, and leather belts and boots. He looked at me and said, "These kids have no originality— they are trying to be American cowboys!"

12   You can imagine my response, since those cowboy hats and leather styles originated with the Mexican *vaquero* (a combination of Moorish-Spanish and Mexican-U.S. Indian influences) and was later appropriated by Americans conquering the West. In fact, the first cowboys were Indians recruited by the Spanish landowners of California and the Southwest!

13   We also don't properly acknowledge how Native Americans influenced our system of government. In *Indian Givers: How the Indians of the Americas Transformed the World* (Fawcett Columbine Books, 1988), Jack Weatherford credits the Iroquois Confederacy with providing many of the ideas American Revolutionists used to frame a new government. "The Americans followed the model of the Iroquois League not only in broad outline but also in many of the specific provisions," writes Weatherford.

14   James W. Loewen, author of *Lies My Teacher Told Me* (The New Press, 1995), points out that the symbol of the United States, the eagle clutching a bundle of arrows, was a symbol of the Iroquois League.

15   The problem is you can't get rid of racism just by attacking racism. Its strongest foundation as an ideology and practice has been a growing industrial economy. In such growth, industry maintains a brutal competition between the most exploitable workers for the least possible pay. Color privilege is the key to this competition.

16   However, this foundation is eroding. We are entering an era characterized by the "end of work." The technological advances in production, downsizing, and globalization are changing racial politics as we know it. As the nature of work changes—there is simply no longer a need in this country for a large unskilled, and labor intensive workforce—so do the concepts, ideologies, and divisions that arose under the previous circumstances.

17   I have been to the coal counties of the Appalachias, the rust belt of the Great Lakes region, and in towns along rural acres of untended farmland, where unemployment has reached over 50 percent, youth are on the corners with nothing to do, and rates of alcoholism, homicide, gang violence, and broken families are at epidemic levels—among whites.

18   The real social division governing how we live and think is that of *class*. Today class interests are forcing us to look deeper at any so-called unity based on race. But how often have we been told that class issues do not really exist in America?

19   Stop the lies. Stop the lies. Stop the lies.

20   Then let's talk.

Understanding Words

▶ Definitions

Veda (par. 3) The oldest scriptures of Hinduism.

Indus Valley civilization (par. 4) An ancient civilization that flourished along the Indus River in present day Pakistan.

Aramaic-speaking (par. 5) Aram: An ancient country of southwest Asia—present day Syria.

Semitic regions (par. 5) Regions of the near East and northern Africa (Arabs, Arameans, Babylonians, Carthaginians, Ethiopians, Hebrews, and Phoenicians).

Coptic Church (par. 5) The Christian church of Egypt that adheres to the Monophysite doctrine that in the person of Jesus there is but a single, divine nature.

white supremacy (par. 8) The belief that the white race is inherently superior and therefore entitled to rule over all other races.

Appalachias (par. 17) Appalachian Mountains: North American mountain system that runs from Canada's Quebec Province to Alabama.

class (par. 18) Upper class: The highest socioeconomic class in a society. Middle class: The members of society occupying a position between those of the lower working class and the wealthy—professional, salaried, and white collar workers. Lower class: The class of those lower than the middle rank—(working class) those who work for wages, especially manual or industrial laborers.

▶ **Vocabulary**

Check your understanding of the following words. Read the words in context (boldfaced in the text) and fill in the blank with the letter of the word or words that are closest to the meaning of the word in the text.

1. ____**farcical** (a) biased (b) unfair (c) absurd (d) perverse

2. ____**retribution** (a) atonement (b) contrition (c) repayment (d) punishment

3. ____**adherence** (a) sticking to (b) at odds (c) foreign (d) attachment

4. ____**renaissance** (a) new concept (b) beginning (c) trading (d) rebirth

5. ____**incipient** (a) roughish (b) monopoly (c) exclusive (d) beginning

6. ____**delineated** (a) portrayed (b) lined up (c) denigrated (d) divided

7. ____**chattel** (a) real property (b) slaves (c) movable personal property (d) cargo

8. ____**crystallization** (a) dissolution (b) discrimination (c) solid form (d) catalyst

9. ____**faculty** (a) teachers (b) colorblindness (c) education (d) inherent power

10. ____**monolithic** (a) single (b) divisive (c) European (d) many-faceted

11. ____**indigenous** (a) newcomers (b) of European descent (c) culturally deprived (d) native

Thinking and Discussing

1. Among the many lies that Rodriguez tries to expose, which of his arguments are most convincing? The least convincing?

2. In paragraph 8, Rodriguez uses a quotation from Earl Conrad's *The Invention of the Negro* (1967): "Among the first men to develop attitudes of [white] supremacy were the slaveship crew." Why do you think that the crews of the slave ships adopted this stance? Had you been a crew member of a slave ship, would you have needed a rationale for your actions?

3. In paragraph 9, Rodriguez says that the doctrine of white supremacy "was later supported by pseudo-scientific papers." Look up the word *pseudo*. Is his use of this word effective? If so, what makes it effective?

Writing Suggestions

1. Write an essay in which you agree or disagree with one or more of Rodriguez' points about the lies being perpetuated by whites.

2. In *Race Traitor* (1996), the editors—Noel Ignatiev and John Garvey—say "Treason to whiteness is loyalty to humanity." Write a paragraph in which you explain what you think they mean by this statement.

3. Historically, have your people been fairly or unfairly treated? Write an essay explaining your position.

4. If you have ever experienced discrimination because of your race, ethnicity, or sex, write a paragraph describing your reaction to one particular incident.

5. Have you read any of the works Rodriguez mentions in paragraph 9? William Shockley and others produced the first transistor and won the 1956 Nobel Prize in physics. Later, Shockley aroused controversy with his theory of intelligence related to race. Do a bit of research on Shockley's theory and then write a response to some aspect of it.

Av Westin, "You've Got to Be Carefully Taught"

Auxiliary Material

Rhetorical Content   Informative Process Analysis: Explaining

Argumentation and Persuasion: Attempt to Incite People to Thought or Action.

Thematic Content   History and Culture: Television News Biases

Background   *Nieman Reports,* Cambridge, Spring 2001.
© Harvard University, Spring 2001.

Av Westin is a former Freedom Forum Fellow. During five decades of work in broadcast news, Westin held high-ranking positions at ABC, CBS, Time Warner, and King World, winning six Emmys, four Peabodies, three Alfred L. DuPont-Columbia University awards, and two George Polk awards.

While Westin was preparing the handbook, *Best Practices for Television Journalists,* he uncovered race factors that determine which stories were covered and in what way they were aired. Black and Hispanic stories are often ignored, and when they are covered, often different criteria are used for presenting the story.

Related Readings

John Merrill, "Freedom of the Press Must Be Limited," from *The World & I*, a publication of the Washington Times Corporation. © 1977.

Mario Cuomo, "Preserving Freedom of the Press Must Be Unlimited," from *USA Today*, January 1988.

Nathan McCall, "The World of White Folks," from *Makes Me Wanna Holler: A Young Black Man in America*. Random House, Inc. © 1994.

Countee Cullen, "Incident" (poem).

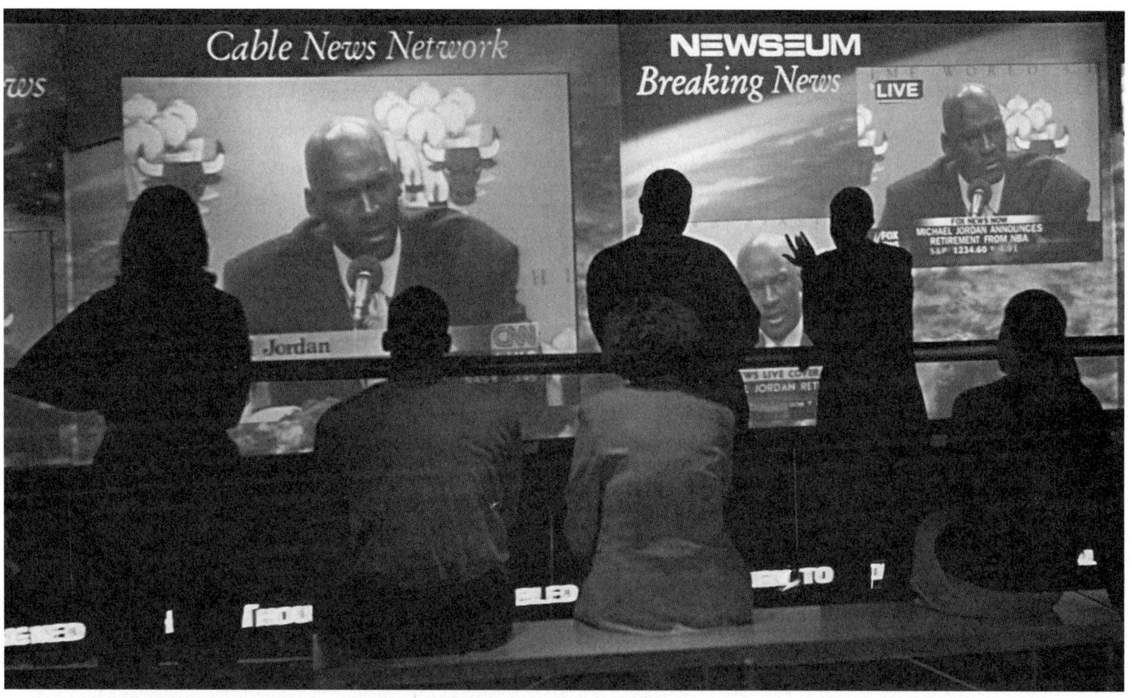

Michael Jordan, NBA's leading scorer for 7 straight years (1987–93), holder of the career record for scoring average (32.3 points per game), NBA's most valuable player for 3 years ('88, '91, '92), retires after 13 seasons and 6 world championships. (Arlington, Virginia, 01/13/99, AP Photo/Doug Mills)

1   There's a song in the Rogers and Hammerstein musical "South Pacific" that **laments** prejudice against minorities. The message of the lyrics is that prejudice is learned, something that is "carefully taught" by parents to their children who

otherwise might remain unaffected by bias. In a sense, that is what has happened in TV newsrooms throughout the country as a variety of forces—many of them related to business concerns—combined to bring racial bias into decision-making about news.

2   It is safe to say that **blatant** bigotry and intolerance do not exist in these newsrooms. Without exception, executive producers and senior producers of network news **fervently** deny that race places a part in their decision-making. But in more than 120 interviews with their staffs, conducted while preparing a handbook, "Best Practices for Television Journalists," we discovered that people who work for those executives have a sharply different impression. (None of the interviewees are named in the handbook because of an interest in promoting honest dialogue about a very difficult subject. We promised **anonymity** in exchange for **candor,** and we got lots of candor. The Freedom Forum published this handbook in 2000, as part of its Free Press/Fair Press Project.)

3   In these interviews, men and women responsible for the hands-on development and production of news insisted again and again that race and ethnicity do have an effect on all **components** of a story. The interviews reveal a clear sense among the rank-and-file that news management's attitudes about race play a role in story selection and content, editorial point of view, and the skin color of the person who will provide the "expert" sound bite. At the network level, producers are "carefully taught" by the conventional wisdom of executive producers and their senior staffs that white viewers (whom advertisers regard as having greater purchasing power) will tune out if blacks or Latinos are the principal characters in segments on their shows.

4   Here are a few of the typical observations we heard.

5   "My bosses have essentially made it clear. 'We do not feature black people.' Period. I mean, it's said. Actually, they whisper it, like cancer. [Whispering] 'Is she white?'"

6   "I love the people I work with, they're nice people, and I don't know where they're getting their information from, but I have been told that when people live in a trailer, people watching at home do not give a crap. And if they're black, no one cares."

7   A producer who worked at NBC and ABC provided some perspective:

8   "It's a subtle thing. A story involving blacks takes longer to get approved. And if it is approved, chances are that it will sit on the shelf a long time before it gets on the air. No one ever says anything. The message gets through."

9   Race as a factor extends to the local station level where news directors and assignment editors consistently fail to cover stories in the black or Hispanic parts of town

while swarming over similar stories in white or **affluent** sections. The former president of a network news division spoke about this pattern of coverage:

10 "I went to Chicago as a news director at one point and there was some horrendous crime committed that seemed worthy of a story. I remember sitting in our morning news meeting thinking 'Wow, this is terrific!' And the producer of the show said, 'Oh, it's a domestic.' I had never heard the term before. I asked, what does that mean? He said, 'Well, it's a domestic; it's a husband and wife in the ghetto who had a fight and they killed each other and their kids.' So he deemed it unworthy of coverage."

11 One television station group executive confirmed this news bias.

12 "There tends to be a belief that crime in the ghetto is less worthy of coverage than a better demo[graphic]. The same is true for stories about welfare, because most viewers who aren't involved in the welfare system don't care about it."

13 "A better demo . . ." Why should it matter? As background, consider this: In the past decade, business considerations—the bottom line—have trumped journalism. First, reducing budgets for news gathering has resulted in smaller staffs, closing bureaus, and hiring less experienced personnel at lower salaries. That means that ethical standards, enterprise reporting, and double-checking sources and facts are no longer standard procedures in many newsrooms. Second, paying attention to the bottom line has meant going "down-market" for ratings resulting in higher advertising revenue. And third, as a **corollary** of that drive for ratings at any price, demographics and minute-by-minute analysis of the Nielsens have influenced story selection.

14 Every business has its code words whose function is to disguise true meaning. TV news is no exception. It is conventional wisdom that, as one former executive told us, "Blacks don't give good demos!" Television ratings measure viewers' demographics (what insiders call "demos") indicating the age range and ethnic and racial composition of the audience. With advanced electronic capability, Nielsen can now provide minute-by-minute results, enabling a producer to actually see what viewers are responding to during each minute of the program. When viewers turn off a program, producers conclude that whatever was being shown at that moment was not appealing. Decisions about what to include in future programs are strongly influenced by the minute-by-minute surveys. "They are bad demos" or "It's not good television" are euphemisms for "Avoid stories about African Americans."

15 There is another pattern, particularly at local stations, that has racial overtones, reinforcing the view that unwed teenage mothers, welfare recipients, and criminals are predominately black. Whenever coverage of surveys involving social problems

is broadcast, file footage from news libraries is trotted out to provide background video for the latest statistics. A few years ago most of the blacks at CNN gathered in a group to lodge a protest about the material being used as "wallpaper" behind the numbers. They complained that every time CNN did a story on poverty, the "b-roll" [thus] illustrative footage showed poor blacks, and every time CNN did a story on crime, the "broll" [thus] focused on black criminals. As a result of the complaints, management went back to look at the file tape and, in fact, it was all black. What CNN's management subsequently did serves to provide an answer to the question: "Can anything be done?"

16 At CNN, Bob Furnad, formerly president of *Headline News,* cleaned out all the racially offensive video in the library and shot new pictures incorporating a more balanced approach to the real world. Furnad also had minority members of his staff produce a remarkable video entitled "Through the Lens." It addresses stereotypical attitudes of whites by illustrating just how pervasive and insidious racially based criteria can be. All employees at CNN were required to view the tape as part of an effective sensitivity training program.

17 Often, all it takes is one individual who is proactive and determined to make sure that the staff knows that there are to be no racial criteria when stories are assigned or people are "cast" to appear in them as experts. An African-American associate producer summed it up this way: "Management has to deliberately set some standards as a best practice or break away from some of the ones that are in place because we don't see other faces. Black faces, Asian faces."

18 In those newsrooms where racial confusion is at a minimum, managers as a general practice seem to hold regular staff meetings sometimes as often as twice a day. One manager described an important dynamic of these meetings. "One of our [senior staff] is a black woman who constantly asks, 'Why was the interview with the black guy conducted standing outside his house while the interview with the white guy was in his living room with a picture of his family and his dog behind him?' It's a small thing but small things can make a difference in shaping a newsroom's attitude. Viewers get the message, too."

19 This direct communication makes a difference by reinforcing the message of sensitivity. Someone who heads up a TV newsroom said that "you generally have to create an atmosphere where people are not afraid to come forward and say I didn't think that was the right thing to do. It's a non-threatening kind of atmosphere where people know they're not going to be punished for disagreeing on something."

20 But being constantly proactive is not easy. Doing so takes its toll on anyone who takes on this role. As one TV news director explained, "We don't like discussing race in our newsrooms because it can make us uncomfortable, and if we're un-

comfortable, how can we have a team? We want everyone to be working together. Newsrooms themselves first have to be prepared to deal with issues of race before covering issues of race. We discuss race. We discuss culture. We explore issues and then know how to transfer them over to the coverage of our news stories."

21   Without singling out any organization for not being aggressive, the best practices in place at NBC News for consciousness raising are worthy of special mention. NBC News has a unique panel—the Diversity Council consisting of nearly one dozen news employees of all ranks. It is assembled when stories or story elements are particularly touchy. One NBC news senior staff member described what happened with one particular story that the council examined. "We had a story on the whole subject of the hate crimes. Someone used some language in a sound bite that was clearly offensive. Interestingly, the council said that in order for people to understand the kind of hatred that's out there, you really need to use this bite; you shouldn't fail to use it. So that's what we did."

22   Once again, the challenge is met by one individual in a key position who adopts a proactive approach. In this case, it was David Doss, then the executive producer of the "NBC Nightly News." As Doss said, "The question that we ask all the time is about bias. Case in point. If we are doing a story about welfare. Should every welfare mother be black? Well the answer, of course, is no. If we are doing a story about unwed mothers. Should every unwed mother be black? No. The fact, of course, is that more unwed mothers are white than are black. If we're doing a story about Wall Street, does it necessarily have to be a white male that we interview as an expert? It shouldn't be. That takes a very proactive effort, and we do it every day."

23   David Doss is now executive producer of the ABC News newsmagazine, *Prime Time Live.* As one of his first acts in his new job he held a staff meeting to make it clear that he wanted stories and their "casts" to reflect the diversity that exists in America. Clearly, the need to be proactive is high on Doss's agenda.

24   WNBC-TV News in New York maintains what some call a "rainbow Rolodex" designed to achieve a variety of opinions from experts who represent the same level of diversity that exists in society. It was the brainchild of the then-news director, an African-American woman, Paula Madison. She believes managers have to "go the extra mile." She instructed her staff to collect business cards—in particular, those from minority populations—at any professional or social function they attended as part of their assignments. The result, she said, was "separate lists of Asian-American contacts, African-American contacts, and Muslim contacts. We just put them in our general contacts sheet."

25   ABC News has a similar resource in the form of a notebook. But, as a cautionary note, even though these materials exist there is no guarantee that they are being

used. At ABC News, the notebook has not been updated in several years and, as one staff member admitted, it has become "a coffee cup coaster." Paul Friedman, executive vice president of ABC News, acknowledges the book might have "fallen into . . . disrepair" but insists that producers are using their own contact lists which management has "every reason to believe are influenced by the news division's concerns about minority representation." Friedman believes ABC News broadcasts today include many more minority experts than in previous eras "partly because the world has changed and partly because [ABC News] has made a conscious effort."

26   In my view, the future of broadcast journalism is, at best, cloudy. There is a generational change of command underway in TV newsrooms across the country. New managers have grown up with different standards than their predecessors. They have been "carefully taught" under regimes that were concerned with ratings rather than journalism. And if, as we've discovered and documented, there is a belief that viewers won't watch stories involving African Americans and other minorities, the lessons learned will continue to perpetuate closet racism as the "dirty little secret" of television news.

Understanding Words

▶ **Definitions**

rank and file (par. 3) The ordinary members of a group, excluding leaders and officers.

euphemism (par. 14) The substitution of a mild, indirect, or vague term for one thought to be more harsh, blunt, or offensive: She *lost her husband.* Her *husband died.*

▶ **Vocabulary**

Check your understanding of the following words. Read them in context (boldfaced in the text) and fill in the blank with the letter of the word or words that are closest to the meaning of the word in the text.

1. _____**laments** (a) celebrates (b) paints a vivid picture (c) deplores (d) mourns

2. _____**blatant** (a) obtrusive (b) loudly (c) secretly (d) some form

3. _____**fervently** (a) vigorously (b) weakly (c) seldom (d) occasionally

4. _____**anonymity** (a) bribes (b) amnesty (c) promotions (d) quality of being unknown

5. _____**candor** (a) quotable material (b) publicity (c) openness (d) a forum

6. ____**components** (a) newsworthy elements (b) types (c) key elements (d) parts

7. ____**affluent** (a) non-segregated (b) prosperous (c) predominantly upper class (d) working class

8. ____**corollary** (a) downside (b) condition (c) aspect (d) result

Thinking and Discussing

1. "I have been told that when people live in a trailer, people watching at home do not give a crap. And if they're black, no one cares." When you are watching the news, does the place where people live or their ethnicity affect your interest or concern in the story?

2. "There tends to be a belief that crime in the ghetto is less worthy of coverage than a better demo[graphic]." Why would ghetto crimes be considered less newsworthy than crimes in an affluent neighborhood?

3. According to Westin, television ratings take precedence over full and fair news reporting. Is this responsible journalism? Is it ethical?

4. From your own television watching experience, do you feel that the shows reinforce the idea that the predominant number of unwed teenage mothers, welfare recipients, and criminals are Black?

Writing Suggestions

1. Watch several news broadcasts involving people of different ethnicity. Are the stories handled differently? Write a summary of your observations.

2. As you watch television news, watch for some of the prejudices that Westin identifies and write a paper describing the situations. If possible, reach conclusions about these incidents.

3. Police officers in several cities have been charged with racial profiling because a disproportionate number of ethnic minorities—especially Black men—are issued citations. Write an essay in which you defend or attack the idea that these people are being discriminated against based on their ethnicity.

4. Astin says, "and if as we've discovered and documented, there is a belief that viewers won't watch stories involving African Americans and other minorities, the lessons learned will continue to perpetuate closet racism as the 'dirty little secret' of television news." Pretend you are an executive producer of a popular news show. Write a paper explaining how you would debunk the belief that viewers are not interested in stories about African Americans and other minorities and establish a proactive stance for your program.

Susan Brady Konig, "They've Got to Be Carefully Taught"

Auxiliary Material

Rhetorical Content   Narration: Telling a story

Thematic Content   History and Culture: Cultural Diversity

Background   from *National Review,* September 15, 1997. Susan Brady Konig, born in Paris, France, and educated in the United States, has written articles for *Us, Travel & Leisure, Ladies' Home Journal,* and the *National Review.* She was an editor for *Seventeen* magazine and has written for the *Washington Post* and the *New York Post.* In this essay she relates her experiences during Cultural Diversity Month at her daughter's preschool. This delightful narrative explores the possibility that emphasis on cultural diversity at this age is often confusing and may be more harmful that helpful.

Related Readings   Meg Greenfield, "Kicking Away Your Freedom," *Newsweek,* March 23, 1998.

Henry Han Xi Lau, "I was a Member of the Kung Fu Crew," *New York Times Magazine,* October 19, 1997.

Richard Rodriguez, "Complexion," from *Hunger of Memory: The Education of Richard Rodriguez.* 1982.

Carolyn Edgar, "Black and Blue," *Reconstruction,* 1994 (vol. 2, no. 3.) (a scholarly publication that deals with race issues).

Grace Suh, "The Eye of the Beholder," *A. Magazine,* 1992.

Lewis Sawaquat, "For My Indian Daughter," first appeared under the author's former name, Lewis Johnson, My Turn column, *Newsweek*, September 5, 1983.

Max Frankel, "Let's Be Chromatically Correct," in Word and Image section, *The New York Times Magazine*, December 6, 1998.

Ishmael Reed, "America: The Multinational Society," from *Writin' Is Fightin'*. © by Ishmael Reed, 1994.

1   At my daughter's pre-school it's time for all the children to learn that they are different from one another. Even though these kids are at that remarkable age when they are thoroughly color-blind, their teachers are spending a month emphasizing race, color, and background. The little tots are being taught in no uncertain terms that their hair is different, their skin is different, and their parents come from different places. It's Cultural Diversity Month.

2   I hadn't really given much thought to the ethnic and national backgrounds of Sarah's classmates. I can guarantee that Sarah, being two and a half, gave the subject absolutely no thought. Her teachers, however, had apparently given it quite a lot of thought. They sent a letter asking each parent to contribute to the cultural-awareness effort by "providing any information and/or material regarding your family's cultural background. For example: favorite recipe or song." All well and good, unless your culture isn't diverse enough.

3   The next day I take Sarah to school and her teacher, Miss Laura, anxious to get this Cultural Diversity show on the road, begins the interrogation.

4   "Where are you and your husband from?" she cheerily demands.

5   "We're Americans," I reply—less, I must confess, out of patriotism than from sheer lack of coffee. It was barely 9:00 A.M.

6   "Yes, of course, but where are you from?" I'm beginning to feel like a nightclub patron being **badgered** by a no-talent stand-up comic.

7 "We're native New Yorkers."

8 "But where are your people from?"

9 "Well," I dive in with a sigh, "my family is originally Irish on both sides. My husband's father was from Czechoslovakia and his mother is from the Bronx, but her grandparents were from the Ukraine."

10 "Can you cook Irish?"

11 "I could bring in potatoes and beer for the whole class."

12 Miss Laura doesn't get it.

13 "Look," I say, "we're Americans. Our kids are Americans. We tell them about American history and George Washington and apple pie and all that stuff. If you want me to do something American, I can do that."

14 She is **decidedly** unexcited.

15 A few days later, she tells me that she was trying to explain to Sarah that her dad is from Ireland.

16 "Wrong," I say, "but go on."

17 "He's not from Ireland?"

18 No, I sigh. He's from Queens. I'm from Ireland. I mean I'm Irish—that is, my great-grandparents were. Don't get me wrong, I'm proud of my heritage but that's entirely beside the point. I told you we tell Sarah she's American.

19 "Well, anyway," she smiles, "Sarah thinks her Daddy's from *Iceland!* Isn't that cute?"

20 Later in the month, Miss Laura admits that her class is not quite getting the whole skin-color thing. "I tried to show them how we all have different skin," she chuckled. Apparently, little Henry is the only one who successfully grasped the concept. He now runs around the classroom announcing to anyone who'll listen, "I'm white!" Miss Laura asked the children what color her own skin was. (She is a light-skinned Hispanic, which would make her skin color . . . what? Caramel? Mochaccino?) The kids opted for purple or orange. "They looked at me like I was crazy!" Miss Laura said. I just smile.

21 The **culmination** of Cultural Diversity Month, the day when the parents come into class and join their children in a glorious celebration of multicultural **disparity,** has arrived. As I arrive I see a large collage on the wall **depicting** the earth, with all the children's names placed next to the country they are from. Next to my daughter's name it says "Ireland." I politely remind Miss Laura that Sarah is, in fact, from

America and suggest that, by insisting otherwise, she is confusing my daughter. She reluctantly changes Sarah's affiliation to USA. It will be the only one of its kind on the wall.

22   The mom from Brazil brings in a bunch of great music, and the whole class is doing the samba and running around in a conga line. It's very cute. Then I get up to teach the children an **indigenous** folk tune from the culture of Sarah's people, passed down through the generations from her grandparents to her parents and now to Sarah—a song called "Take Me Out to the Ballgame." First I explain to the kids that Sarah was born right here in New York—and that's in what country, Sarah? Sarah looks at me and says, "France." I look at Miss Laura, who just shrugs.

23   I stand there in my baseball cap and sing my song. The teacher tries to rush me off. I say, "Don't you want them to learn it?" They took long enough learning to samba! I am granted permission to sing it one more time. The kids join in on the "root, root, root" and the "1, 2, 3 strikes you're out," but they can see their teacher isn't enthusiastic.

24   So now these sweet, innocent babies who thought they were all the same are becoming culturally aware. Two little girls are touching each other's hair and saying, "Your hair is blonde, just like mine." Off to one side a little dark-haired girl stands alone, excluded. She looks confused as to what to do next. She knows she's not blonde. Sure, all children notice these things eventually, but, thanks to the **concerted** efforts of their teachers, these two- and three-year-olds are talking about things that separate rather than connect.

25   And Sarah only knows what she has been taught: Little Henry is white, her daddy's from Iceland, and New York's in France.

Understanding Words

▶ **Definitions**

ethnic (par. 2) The word *ethnic* has been assigned different meanings throughout history. It has been used to mean "gentile," "national," and "foreign." Today it is used to mean a sizable group of people sharing a common and distinctive racial, national, religious, linguistic, or cultural heritage. The word used in this sense was first recorded in 1945.

samba (par. 22) A Brazilian dance of African origin.

conga line (par. 22) A dance of Latin America origin in which dancers from a long, winding line.

▶ **Vocabulary**

Check your understanding of the following words. Read them in context (boldfaced in the text) and fill in the blank with the letter of the word or words that are closest to the meaning of the word in the text.

1. ____**badgered** (a) entertained (b) pestered (c) questioned (d) embarrassed

2. ____**decidedly** (a) definitely (b) clearly (c) unexplainably (d) frustratingly

3. ____**culmination** (a) ceremony (b) joint program (c) completion (d) extension

4. ____**disparity** (a) difference (b) equality (c) similarity (d) parity

5. ____**depicting** (a) describing (b) picturing (c) manifesting (d) representing

6. ____**indigenous** (a) native (b) multicultural (c) popular (d) old

7. ____**concerted** (a) accomplished (b) planned (c) thoughtful (d) divisive

Thinking and Discussing

1. When Konig says (par. 1) that the preschoolers are "thoroughly color-blind," she means that they are not subject to racial prejudice. Near the end of the narrative (par. 24), she points out that "these sweet, innocent babies who thought they were all the same are becoming culturally aware." At what age did you become "culturally aware"? When was the first time you became aware that you were different from your friends? Were you a member of a majority group or a minority group? What were your reactions? Has the experience had an effect on your life or on your relationship with other people?

2. Konig used the present tense throughout the story. How effective is this? Had she used the past tense, would the story have been as compelling?

3. The definition of the word *ethnic,* includes the term *cultural heritage.* What are some of the elements of your cultural heritage?

4. Food plays an important part in Cultural Diversity Month in this story. When the teacher asks Konig if she can cook Irish (par. 10), Konig says "I could bring in potatoes and beer for the whole class." What does she mean, and why does Miss Laura not "get it"? For many people, food is an important part of their cultural heritage. Is food part of your cultural heritage?

5. Konig uses dialogue to get her point across. How effective is it? Do you learn more about the characters than you would if she had not used dialogue?

6. **Tone** is the writer's attitude toward the material and toward the audience. How would you describe Konig's tone? Does it add to or take away from the seriousness of her subject?

Writing Suggestions

Food is an important part of many people's cultural heritage. Following are the names of a few dishes that are culturally important: *lutefish, pirozhki, ham hocks and collard greens, tamales, paella, gumbo, gnocchi, gefilte fish, miso, bagna cauda, baccala, hoko pot.* Do you recognize any of these dishes?

1. Write a paragraph in which you relate your experience with an ethnic dish. What did you learn from the experience?

2. Write a narrative essay based on a dish or foods that are important to your family. Explain the role these dishes play, when they are served, who makes them, and why they are an important part of your culture.

3. Use Konig's essay as a model, and write about your experiences during a planned Cultural Awareness event.

4. Use Konig's essay as a model and rewrite the essay from Miss Laura's point of view.

Chief Seattle, from "This Sacred Soil"

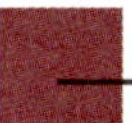

Auxiliary Material

Rhetorical Content   Comparison and Contrast: Exploring Similarities and Differences

Thematic Content   History and Culture: The Environment and Cultural Differences

Background   from *Northwest Gateway:* The Story of the Port of Seattle, 1899. Portland: Benfords & Mort, 1941.

The following excerpt is from the speech of the chief of the Duwamish, Suquamish, and allied Indian tribes of the Northwest when he relinquished millions of acres of lands to the white settlers. His speech contains a warning that was later echoed by President Franklin D. Roosevelt—"the nation that destroys its soil destroys itself." The echo still reverberates.

(continued)

Related Readings

Letter, 1854, to President Franklin Pierce (published in *Brother Eagle, Sister Sky: a Message from Chief Seattle,* 1990). The letter, in which Seattle pleaded that his name should die with the ceding of the Washington State territories, was shown in 1992 to have been largely a forgery, devised by television scriptwriter Ted Perry for a historical epic in 1971.

Richard Rodriguez, "The Fear of Losing a Culture," *Time* magazine, July 11, 1988.

Jane Tompkins, "Indians" Textualism, Morality, and the Problem Industry," *Critical Inquiry* 13:1, 1986, pp. 101–119. © The University of Chicago Press.

Rush Limbaugh, "The Environmental Mindset," from *The Way Things Ought to Be.* © 1992. Pocket Books, a division of Simon & Schuster, Inc.

Arthur B. Robinson and Zachary W. Robinson, "Science Has Spoken: Global Warming is a Myth," from the *The Wall Street Journal,* December 4, 1997.

Gale E. Christianson, "Naysayers, Thriving in the Heat," from the *New York Times,* July 8, 1999.

N. Scott Momaday, "The Way to Rainy Mountain," first published in *The Reporter,* January 26, 1969.

Rachel Carson, "The Obligation to Endure," from *Silent Spring.* © 1962. Renewed 1990 by Roger Christie. Houghton-Mifflin Co.

Joyce Carol Oates, "Against Nature," originally published in *Ontario Review,* 1986.

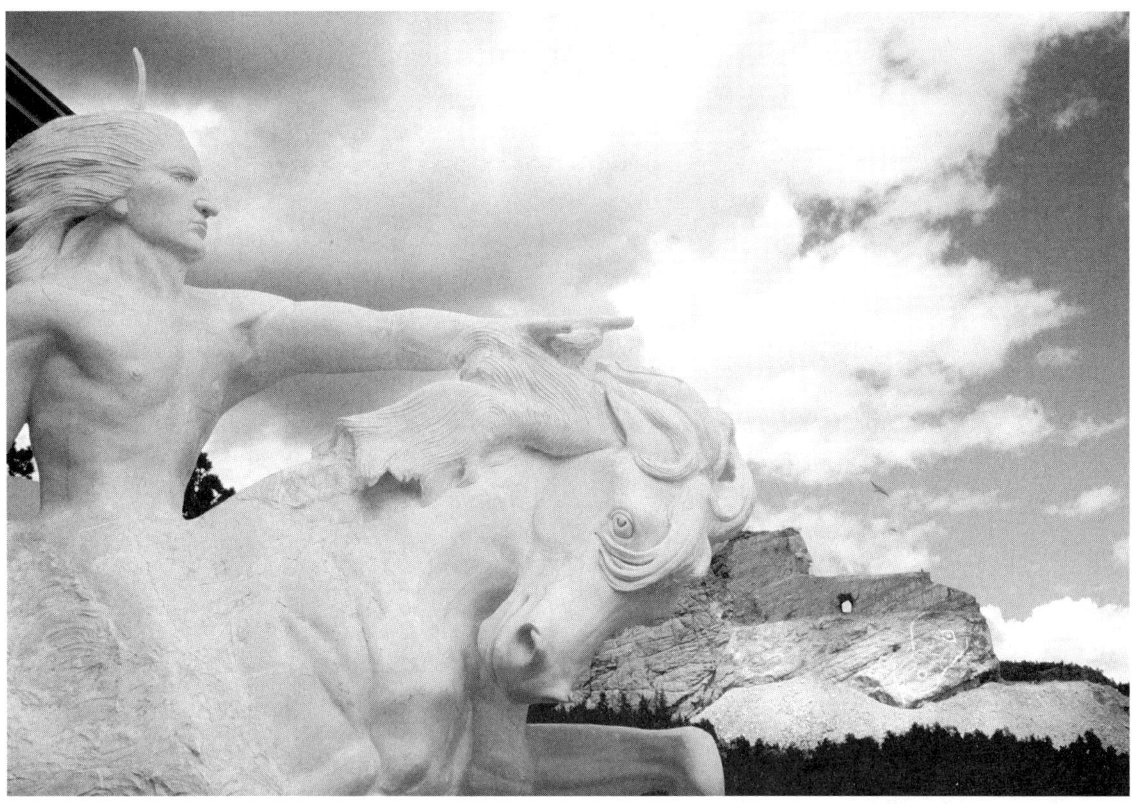

Crazy Horse Memorial at Thunderhead Mountain in the Black Hills of South Dakota is a memorial to the revered chief of the Oglala Sioux who helped defeat Custer at Little Bighorn and to all Native Americans. (Phyllis Picardi/Index Stock Imagery)

"The earth does not belong to us, we belong to the earth." Chief Seattle, 1854

1   Yonder sky that has wept tears of compassion upon my people for centuries untold, and which to us appears changeless and eternal, may change. Today is fair. Tomorrow it may be overcast with clouds. My words are like the stars that never change. Whatever Seattle says the great chief at Washington can rely upon with as much certainty as he can upon the return of the sun or the seasons. The White Chief says that Big Chief at Washington sends us greetings of friendship and goodwill. That is kind of him for we know he has little need of our friendship in return. His people are many. They are like the grass that covers vast prairies. My people are few. They resemble the scattering trees of a storm-swept plain. The great, and I presume—good, White Chief sends us word that he wishes to buy our lands but is willing to allow us enough to live comfortably. . . . I will not dwell on, nor mourn over, our untimely decay, nor reproach our paleface brothers with hastening it, as we too may have been somewhat to blame. . . .

2   Your God is not our God. Your God loves your people and hates mine. He folds his strong and protecting arms lovingly around the paleface and leads him by the hand as a father leads his infant son—but He has forsaken His red children—if they really are his. Our God, the Great Spirit, seems also to have forsaken us. Your God makes your people wax strong every day. Soon they will fill the land. Our people are **ebbing** away like a receding tide that will never return. The white man's God cannot love our people or He would protect them. They seem to be orphans who can look nowhere for help. How then can we be brothers? How can your God become our God and renew our prosperity and awaken in us dreams of returning greatness? If we have a common heavenly father, He must be **partial**—for He came to his paleface children. We never saw Him. He gave you laws but He had no word for his red children whose **teeming** multitudes once filled this vast continent as stars fill the firmament. No, we are two distinct races with separate origins and separate **destinies.** There is little in common between us.

3   To us the ashes of our ancestors are sacred and their resting place is **hallowed** ground. You wander far from the graves of your ancestors and seemingly without regret. Your religion was written upon tables of stone by the iron finger of your God so that you could not forget. The Red Man could never comprehend nor remember it. Our religion is the traditions of our ancestors—the dreams of our old men, given them in solemn hours of night by the Great Spirit; and the visions of our sachems; and it is written in the hearts of our people.

4   Your dead cease to love you and the land of their nativity as soon as they pass the portals of the tomb and wander way beyond the stars. They are soon forgotten and never return. Our dead never forget the beautiful world that gave them being.

5   Day and night cannot dwell together. The Red Man has ever fled the approach of the White Man, as the morning mist flees before the morning sun. However, your proposition seems fair and I think that my people will accept it and will retire to the reservation you offer them. Then we will dwell apart in peace. . . . It matters little where we pass the **remnant** of our days. They will not be many. A few more moons; a few more winters—and not one of the descendants of the mighty hosts that once moved over this broad land or lived in happy homes, protected by the Great Spirit, will remain to mourn over the graves of a people once more powerful and hopeful than yours. But why should I mourn the untimely fate of my people? Tribe follows tribe, and nation follows nation, like the waves of the sea. It is the order of nature, and regret is useless. Your time of decay may be distant, but it will surely come, for even the White Man whose God walked and talked with him as friend with friend cannot be exempt from the common destiny. We may be brothers after all. We will see.

6   We will **ponder** your proposition, and when we decide we will let you know. But should we accept it, I here and now make this condition that we will not be denied the privilege without molestation of visiting at any time the tombs of our ancestors, friends and children. Every part of this soil is sacred in the estimation of my people. Every hillside, every valley, every plain and grove, has been hallowed by some sad or happy event in days long vanished. . . . The very dust upon which you now stand responds more lovingly to their footsteps than to yours, because it is rich with the blood of our ancestors and our bare feet are conscious of the sympathetic touch. . . . Even the little children who lived here and rejoiced here for a brief season will love these somber solitudes and at eventide they greet shadowy returning spirits. And when the last Red Man shall have perished, and the memory of my tribe shall have become a myth among the White Men, these shores will swarm with the invisible dead of my tribe, and when your children's children think themselves alone in the field, the store, the shop, upon the highway, or in the silence of the pathless woods, they will not be alone. . . . At night when the streets of your cities and villages are silent and you think them deserted, they will throng with the returning hosts that once filled and still love this beautiful land. The White Man will never be alone. Let him be just and deal kindly with my people, for the dead are not powerless. Dead, did I say? There is no death, only a change of worlds.

Note: When Captain George Vancouver anchored his ship *Discovery* off an island which he named "Blake Island," it signaled the end of the world as Chief Seattle's people knew it. From the beginning, Seattle saw the futility of opposing the newcomers. He befriended them, and although he had no illusions about them, he was unwavering in his cooperation and nonresistance. When he was offered money for the land, he agreed to sell the land and move to reservations. The governor of Washington territory and his people and Chief Seattle and his people met in a clearing in front of Dr. David Maynard's log cabin which served as a drugstore and real estate office. Governor Isaac Stevens made a speech in which he stated the president of the United States loved the tribes of the Northwest and would take care of them by giving them money and providing fine reservations with schools and various shops. After the governor spoke, Chief Seattle placed his hand on the top of the little governor's head and addressed the crowd. The speech was in Duwamish, but one of the settlers knew the language and wrote it down and later translated it into English. When the treaty was made January 22, 1855, at Point Elliot, Chief Seattle's people sold 2 million acres of land for $150,000. The money was not paid in a lump sum; it was paid over a period of twenty years—not in cash, but in "useful articles."

The city of Seattle, Washington, bears the name of this Native American leader.

Understanding Words

▶ **Definitions**

wax (par. 2) To increase gradually in size, number, strength, or intensity.

sachems (par. 3) A chief of a Native American tribe or confederation.

portal (par. 4) A doorway, or entrance, or a gate, especially one that is large and impressive.

exempt (par. 5) To be free from an obligation, a duty, or a liability to which others are subject.

eventide (par. 6) Evening.

hosts (par. 6) A great number of people.

▶ **Vocabulary**

Check your understanding of the following words. Study them in context (boldfaced in the text) and fill in the blank with the letter of the meaning of the word or words that are closest to the meaning of the word in the text.

1. _____**ebbing** (a) declining (b) dying (c) disappearing (d) struggling

2. _____**partial** (a) have a fondness for (b) unfair (c) unresponsive (d) prejudiced

3. _____**teeming** (a) uncivilized (b) warlike (c) tribal (d) flourishing

4. _____**destinies** (a) deities (b) fates (c) religions (d) beliefs

5. _____**hallowed** (a) holy (b) important (c) not to be disturbed (d) common to all

6. _____**remnant** (a) bits and pieces (b) scraps (c) remainder (d) final

7. _____**ponder** (a) peruse (b) consider (c) take a vote (d) reach consensus

Thinking and Discussing

1. A **figure of speech** is an expression used in a nonliteral way to achieve an effect beyond the range of ordinary language. Chief Seattle's speech is rich in similes, metaphors, and personification.

   ▪ **simile,** a comparison between two dissimilar things that uses the words *as* or *like*

   ▪ **metaphor,** a comparison between two dissimilar things that does not use the words *as* or *like*

   ▪ **personification,** giving human characteristics to animals, ideas, or inanimate objects

   Find several examples of these figures of speech. Are they effective? If so, what makes them effective?

2. According to Chief Seattle, what are some of the differences between white men's and red men's relationship with nature?

3. Do you agree with Chief Seattle's statements in paragraph 4? If you have had experience with a culture different from your own, how does that culture regard their dead—their ancestors? How does it differ from your culture?

Writing Suggestions

1. Write an essay in which you support the idea in President Roosevelt's comment about the environment: "The nation that destroys its soil destroys itself." Support your point with specific evidence.

2. Write a paragraph in which you explain what you think Seattle means in the last part of paragraph 5. "Your time of decay may be distant, but it will surely come, for even the White Man whose God walked and talked with him as friend with friend cannot be exempt from the common destiny."

3. Write an essay about your relationship with nature. What brought you to this understanding of it?

4. **Connotation** and **denotation** are ways of describing the meaning of words. *Connotation* refers to the "shades of meaning" that are attached to a word, while *denotation* is the literal definition of a word—the definition in a dictionary. Write an extended definition essay in which you discuss the denotation and connotation of *nature*.

5. Drawing on your knowledge of Native American history, write a brief paper in which you agree or disagree with the following statement made by Chief Joseph, Nez Perce leader, *North American Review*, Cedar Falls, Iowa, April 1879. "If you tie a horse to a stake, do you expect he will grow fat? If you pen an Indian up on a small spot of earth, and compel him to stay there, he will not be contented, nor will he grow and prosper."

Media and Behavior

Ellen Willis, "Bring in the Noise"

Auxiliary Material

Rhetorical Content   Informational Process Analysis: Explaining

Thematic Content   Media and Behavior: Daytime Talk Shows

(continued)

Background

from *The Nation*, April 1, 1996. In this article, Ellen Willis, commentary writer for *The Nation*, neither argues for nor against issues involved in daytime talk shows. Instead, she analyzes the issues from a different perspective. She suggests that television talk shows enable certain segments of the society to have a voice.

Related Readings

Holman W. Jenkins, Jr., "Porn Again? An Industry Fantasizes about Respect," from *The Wall Street Journal*, April 1, 1998.

William Bennett, "Announcing a Public Campaign Against Select Day-Time Television Talk Shows," from "Contaminating Culture" from *Coming After Oprah* by Vicki Abt and Leonard Mustazza. © 1977 by Bowling Green State University Popular Press.

Donna Gaines, "How Jenny Jones Saved My Life: Why William Bennett Is Wrong About Trash TV," from *Village Voice*, November 21, 1995.

Christopher John Farley, "Songs in the Key of Lauryn Hill," from *Rolling Stone's* cover story, February 18, 1999.

Sally Jessy Raphael talks to high school students. (New York, 04/27/99, AP Photo/Richard Drew)

1   Whenever the right and the left agree on some proposition about culture, I know it's time to grab my raincoat; and so it is with the **incessant** demonizing of popular culture and media. Everywhere they look—tabloid television, MTV, *Married . . . With Children, Pulp Fiction,* gangsta rap, saturation coverage of O.J. Simpson/ the Bobbitts/Amy Fisher—politicians and high-minded journalists see nothing but sleaze and moral **degradation.**

2   The latest target is daytime TV talk shows. Rumblings began last year when Jonathan Schmitz murdered Scott Amedure, a gay man, after Amedure identified Schmitz as his "secret crush" on *Jenny Jones* [see] Jonathan Taylor, "To Die For," [*The Nation,* April 3, 1995]. Since then, William Bennett and Democratic Senator Joe Lieberman of Connecticut have called on talk-show advertisers to withdraw their support. N. E. A. **nemesis** Donald Wildmon's American Family Association has joined the cause with a full-page ad in *The New York Times* and Phil Donahue's

retirement has touched off a round of head-shaking at the contrast between the now-respectable pioneer of the talk show and his **degenerate** successors. Commentators reveal the stop-the-presses news that the talk-show audience prefers sex and violence to analyses of health care and foreign policy. Beyond this indisputable fact the legions of outraged moralists have little enlightenment to offer, since they rarely bother to pay much attention to the **reviled** genre, let alone try to understand what's going on in the imagination of people who do.

3　The popularity of popular culture is a problem for its **detractors:** It would be a **breach** of American democratic etiquette, not to mention an **implicit** rebuke to free-market **platitudes** about supply and demand, for journalists or (especially) politicians simply to claim that their own cultural tastes are superior to those of the barbarian hordes (though they come close to doing this when the subject is black music). The solution is to rely heavily on the assumption that the media are a species of additive drugs, pushed on a **vulnerable** populace by corporations out to make a buck and/or infiltrated by a **perverse** New York and Hollywood cultural elite. The audience is often referred to as "our children," even when the medium in question is aimed at adults. Lieberman indignantly cites a report that claims "children aged 2 to 11 comprise six percent" of talk-show viewers nationally. The other 94 percent? Don't ask!

4　In the case of talk shows, the critic-audience gap is even wider than usual. I doubt that Lieberman and his fellow attack dogs got the idea for their crusade by actually watching Ricki Lake or Richard Bey or Sally Jesse Raphael. But what's more interesting is the **paucity** of sympathetic popcult critics who are talk-show fans: Donna Gaines, with her *Village Voice* testimonial that Jenny Jones saved her life, is the conspicuous exception. Like McDonald's, these shows are genuinely lowbrow; unlike, Quentin Tarantino or Snoop Doggy Dogg, they can't be said to appeal to the so-called cultural elite. They resist hip readings—its hard to watch a talk show ironically, even when you're sure it's as fake as a wrestling match. Anyway, the shows come on at the wrong time for the critical classes, right in the middle of the sacred working day.

5　I first saw the Ricki Lake show because my daughter had mentioned it, and I thought I should check it out. We watched a show together; the subject, as I recall, was women whose boyfriends had impregnated other women. There were moments that made me squirm, but not because I was worried that, as Lieberman would later put it "the constant confrontations and emotional violence" would teach my 11-year-old "a perverse way to solve personal problems" or give her the impression "that is the way normal adults behave." Leaving aside the absurdity of the idea that "normal adults" don't have nasty fights, it took little in the way of probing discussion to confirm that my daughter could tell the difference between real life and stage-managed psychodrama. Anyway, from my own childhood encounters with horror comics, soap operas, graphic sex manuals and other crypto-pornography of the fifties, I know kids have more complicated filters than adults tend to give them credit for. The danger, it seemed to me, was exactly opposite: that my child was seeing Ricki's guests, working-class people willing to spill the beans on TV, as alien and unreal. Or maybe I was afraid that's what I was doing.

6   Like other forms of popular culture, talk shows reflect the peculiar contradictions of today's social and political climate. While conservatives dominate the political system and control the terms of debate on economic issues, their desire to roll back the cultural changes of the sixties and seventies has had much more ambiguous results. The most telling success of the cultural right and in that category I include social conservatives who are political liberals or leftists has been the discrediting of the idea of a pro-freedom, pro-pleasure revolution in everyday life in favor of nostalgia for an idealized past: These days it's even harder to get a serious public hearing for a radical critique of the family than for a radical critique of capitalism. This representation of the utopian impulse has combined with economic insecurity to brew a **protean** anger that leaks out in various forms of sadism—physical, verbal, moral and vicarious. On the other hand, social conservatives have been notably unsuccessful at stemming the democratization of culture, the breakdown of those class, sex and race-bound conventions that once reliably separated high from low, "news" from "gossip," public from unspeakable private, respectable from deviant.

7   Talk shows are a product of this democratization; they let people who have been largely excluded from the public conversation appear on national TV and talk about their sex lives, their family fights, sometimes their literal dirty laundry. What's more taboo than the subject matter itself is the way it's presented—as personal revelation rather than social comment, and as spectacle mostly devoid of pretensions to redeeming social value: "In these shows," William Bennett complains, "indecent exposure is celebrated as virtue. . . . There was once a time when personal or marital failure . . . and perverse taste were accompanied by guilt or embarrassment." Talk shows are meant to entertain, to excite the nerve ends. This in itself is **anathema** to social conservatives, for whom the only legitimate function of popular culture is instructing the masses in the moral values of their betters.

8   It's not that morality is absent from talk shows. True, some guests flaunt "deviant" behavior without being condemned for it; but others indignantly defend conventional moral standards against wayward lovers or children. Talk-show hosts often lecture guests, especially teenagers—Sally Jessy has perfected a stern school-principal style, Ricki a more maternal-therapeutic approach—while members of the audience or other guests (the parents, wronged girlfriends and

so on) may subject the (usually defiant) **miscreant** to verbal stoning. The catch is that their very complicity in public free-for-all undermines their moral authority. And though therapists may be called on to give "expert" commentary or do a bit of ad hoc family counseling, they are about as relevant to the action as those trailers that used to introduce porn movies with homilies on the need for sex education. At the dramatic center of talk shows are mostly black, Latino and low-rent white guests who, by their very willingness to expose intimate, "shameful" matters and yell and scream at each other on the air, assert their lack of deference to middle-class norms.

9   I mean "dramatic" literally; talk shows are theater. Like most kinds of popular entertainment, especially on television, they rely on formula. There's the trial scenario—an accusation ("My ex-husband's wife abuses my kid"), a rebuttal ("I hit her because she's disrespectful, but I don't abuse her") and a parade of witnesses: the alleged victim ("I don't have to obey you, you're not my mother and you threw me downstairs!"), the nervous father who hasn't seen anything and is totally out of it, the "expert" who lectures that it's abusive to hit a kid, even your own. The judge/host presides, asking questions and being fair to all sides. The jury/audience gets into the act, berating the stepmother for overstepping her bounds, the kid for being disrespectful, the father for being out of it. What's missing is a unanimous verdict or any semblance of courtroom decorum.

10   Then there's the increasingly popular "surprise" show, where a guest is tricked into appearing. This ploy makes explicit the basic appeal of talk-show formulas: However often repeated, they're never totally predictable, but offer the exciting possibility that a situation will get out of control. An argument can lead to an outburst of violence; the woman who is proposed to can say no. The talk show is a dangerous ritual like boxing or bullfighting, an improvisatory performance that seems to blur the boundary between actors and audience, yet leave the larger audience safe behind the barrier of the screen. And since talk shows traffic in subjects that have universal resonance—from infidelity, incest and juvenile rebellion to clothes ("My mom dresses like a tramp!")—I suspect that few people are entirely **impervious** to their crude power.

11   As a distant graduate of youth culture and mother of a soon-to-be-teenager, I'm riveted by shows that feature generational collisions. On a recent *Sally Jessy Raphael,* episode, "I'm Ready to Divorce My Children," kids of 12 (has sex and steals) and 13 (throws ashtrays), hiding behind their bad-seed fright masks to ward off who knew what terrors, sullenly confronted their desperate, baffled mother. There was Dantesque torment in that encounter; it stayed with me for days. I'm sure a lot of guests invent or exaggerate their torments, with or without the connivance of producers. But in this case, I could swear the emotions were real. If not, the acting was surely marvelous.

12   I don't mean to romanticize talk shows. If they reflect a democratizing impulse, they're also a symptom of today's anti-utopian and anti-political mood. While great popular art tends to bring disparate groups together—the way the Beatles reached teeny-boppers and intellectuals, or Duke Ellington whites and blacks—talk shows are more likely to reinforce class and racial fragmentation [see Jill Nelson, "Talk is Cheap," *The Nation,* June 5, 1995]: Though viewers from the same social milieus as the guests may identify with them and their problems, my hunch is that for many middle-class talk-show fans, the kick is feeling superior (or as my daughter put it when I posed the question, "lucky").

13   As for the guests themselves, in the absence of any other way to have an impact on history—which is to say, the absence of effective social movements—the opportunity to sound off on national television offers visibility, and therefore validation, to teenagers and people of color and working-class whites; in effect it's the culture's acknowledgment that they exist. But existence proved this way is existence on someone else's terms. Often guests are so vivid or funny, or sure of their right to be who they are that they outflank the manipulative condescension of their producers and hosts. But often they don't, especially when the audience gangs up on them, or when they're set up to be surprised. The Schmitz murder is a disturbing commentary on talk-show tactics, not because "Jenny made him do it"—homophobia made him do it—but because the whole rationale of talk shows is bound up with risking such events. If a show becomes a flash point for the culture's free-floating sadism, or a conduit for politics by other means, is it truly an accident?

14   Finally, though, our problem is not the excesses of talk shows but the brutality and emptiness of our political culture. Popbashing is the humanism of fools: In the name of defending people's dignity it attacks their pleasures and their meager store of power. On talk shows, whatever their drawbacks, the proles get to talk. The rest of the time they're told in a thousand ways to shut up. By any honest reckoning we need more noise, not less.

Understanding Words

▶ **Definitions**

tabloid (par. 1) A newspaper that gives news—generally sensational—in brief form.

genre (par. 2) A type or class of artistic composition.

barbarians (par. 3) A group of people considered by another group to have a primitive civilization.

utopian (par. 6) An impractical, idealistic scheme for reform.

taboo (par. 7) The prohibition of an act or the use of a word or thing.

ad hoc (par. 8) For a specific purpose and for no other.

homily (par. 8) A tedious moralizing lecture.

Dantesque (par. 11) A reference to Dante's *Divine Comedy* in which he details his visionary progress though Hell, Purgatory, and Heaven.

proles (par. 14) A proletarian—a worker. "If there is hope . . . it lies in the proles."— George Orwell

▶ **Vocabulary**

Check your understanding of the following words. Read them in context (boldfaced in the text), and fill in the blank with the letter of the word or words that are closest to the meaning of the word in the text.

1. ____**incessant** (a) never ending (b) unworthy (c) vulgar (d) recent

2. ____**degradation** (a) declining condition (b) filth (c) dilemma (d) decay

3. ____**nemesis** (a) protector (b) advocate (c) detractor (d) avenger

4. ____**degenerate** (a) imitator (b) copycat (c) undesirable (d) formidable

5. ____**reviled** (a) respected (b) abused (c) modern (d) hopeless

6. ____**detractors** (a) debtors (b) advocates (c) proponents (d) faultfinders

7. ____**breach** (a) rift (b) bulwark (c) safety net (d) icon

8. ____**implicit** (a) negligible (b) clear (c) understood (d) understated

9. ____**platitude** (a) trite remark (b) praiseworthy idea (c) unofficial statement (d) attitudes

10. ____**vulnerable** (a) inept (b) naïve (c) defenseless (d) street-wise

11. ____ **perverse** (a) stubborn (b) peevish (c) wicked (d) self-righteous

12. ____**paucity** (a) richness (b) scarcity (c) fullness (d) plethora

13. ____**protean** (a) weak (b) shifting (c) unchangeable (d) deep-seated

14. ____**anathema** (a) equally important (b) unimportant (c) threatening (d) clear

15. ____**miscreant** (a) defendant (b) evildoer (c) misfit (d) malcontent

16. ____**impervious** (a) undaunted (b) unaware of (c) unconcerned (d) unaffected

Thinking and Discussing

1. What is Willis' main concern about daytime television talk shows? How does it differ from your opinion of them?

2. In your opinion, does daytime talk television present an accurate picture of ordinary Americans?

3. If you enjoy watching daytime television talk shows, what makes them enjoyable? If you dislike them, what makes them not likable?

4. As a producer of the segment of one of the daytime television talk shows, what subject would you choose to boost your ratings? With which talk show would your program be competitive?

5. If you had an opportunity to appear on one of these talk shows, would you? Why or why not?

6. Carl Jung, Swiss psychiatrist, founder of analytical psychology said that the *collective subconscious* (acts and mental patterns shared by members of a culture or universally by all human beings) often appears as themes in fairy tales. Think of some of the fairy tales with which you are familiar such as "Beauty and the Beast," "Cinderella," "Snow White and the Seven Dwarfs," and so on. Do you see any themes in these tales that are similar to some of the themes in daytime talk shows? What are they? Do you think talk shows are delving into sleaze just for the sake of "peek through-the-keyhole" entertainment, or could they possibly be dealing with themes of the collective subconscious?

Writing Suggestions

1. Willis says that "the opportunity to sound off on national television offers visibility, and therefore validation, to teenagers and people of color and working-class whites; in effect it's the culture's acknowledgment that they exist." Write an essay in which you agree or disagree with this point of view. You may use your own experiences, or you may use examples from current daytime talk shows to support your ideas.

2. Watch a daytime talk show and write a summary of one of the segments, giving examples of Willis' four-point trial scenario format: (1) accusation, (2) rebuttal, (3) witnesses, (4) the judge (host), and (5) the jury (audience).

3. Do a quick survey of three popular talk shows that deal with Willis' subject. Based on your findings write a paragraph agreeing or disagreeing with her that "the dramatic center of talk shows are mostly black, Latino and low-rent white guests . . ."

4. Choose a topic that has been covered on one of these talk shows—promiscuous twelve-year olds, obese children, underdressed overly sexually active young girls, children who abuse their mothers, out-of-control teenagers, and so on—and write an essay in which you demonstrate the manner in which these people are debased and demeaned.

5. Choose a segment of a talk show in which a guest is set up to be surprised. Write a fictitious account of the aftermath of the episode. Was the guest a victim? How was his or her life changed? Did the intervention of the program in the person's life bring about unalterable changes?

Marilyn Duff, "Meanwhile on MTV, They're Shooting Up Classrooms"

 **Auxiliary Material**

Rhetorical Content	Informational Process Analysis: Explaining
	Definition: Expanding the Meaning of a Word or Term
Thematic Content	Media and Behavior: Kids' Music
Background	from the *Philadelphia Inquirer,* July 25, 1993. Marilyn Duff, contributing editor for *Dispatches*—a newspaper that examines the relation of society and the media—criticizes MTV's casual portrayal of violence that reflects rock or rap concepts. Although this article was written in 1993, it is still relevant.
Related Readings	Nancy Carlsson-Paige and Diane Levin, "The Profiteering That Kills Kids," *The Boston Globe,* April 2, 1998.
	Wendy Kaminer, "A Civic Duty to Annoy," *The Atlantic Monthly,* September 1997.
	Carl Cannon, "Honey, I Warped the Kids," from *Mother Jones.* © 1993.
	John Leonard, "Why Blame TV?" from *The Nation,* December 27, 1993.

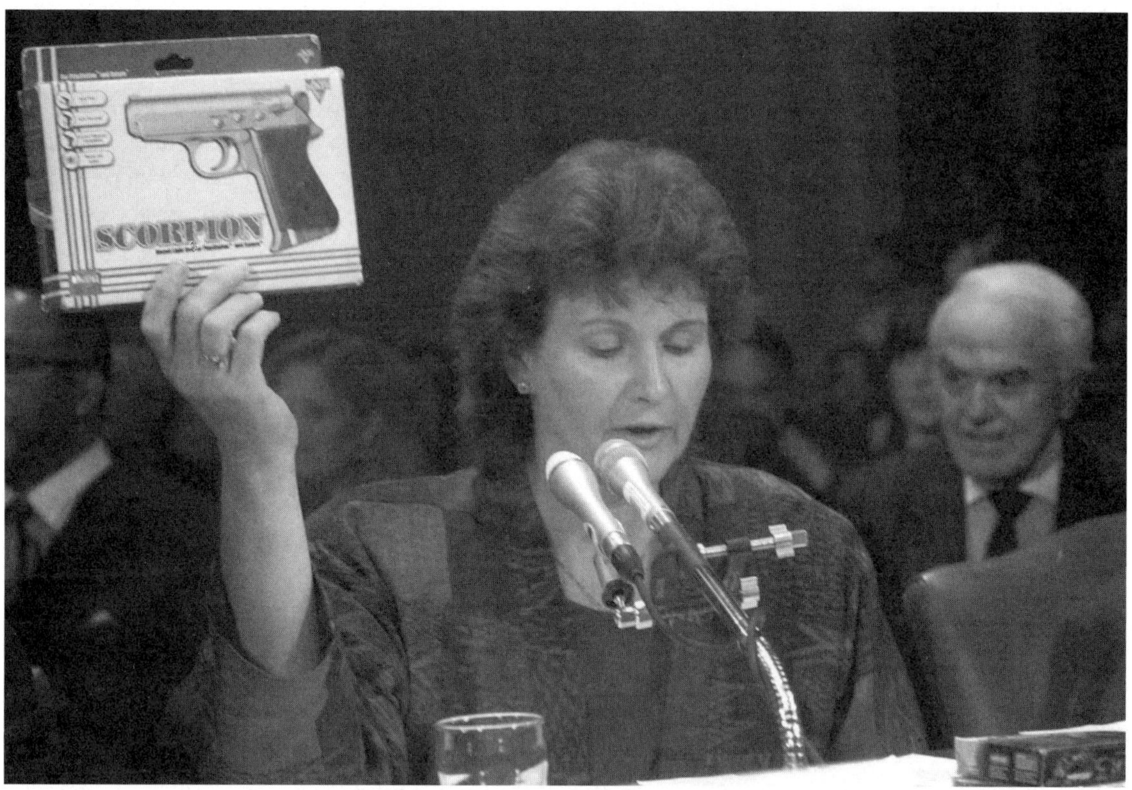

A video game gun, looking as real as a Saturday-Night-Special, is presented at a hearing that focused on the effectiveness of rating systems used to indicate levels of sex and violence in entertainment. (Washington, D. C., 7/25/01, AP Photo/Kenneth Lambert)

1   Boy enters classroom, turns to face classmates, begins to raise hand slowly. Kids sitting in rows cower and shield faces. Soundtrack and pulsing strobe suggest automatic weapon fire. Blood spatters kids' foreheads, hands, shirt-fronts. Heavy metal soundtrack grinds to silence and the TV screen goes black—followed by a commercial for McDonald's Big Mac.

2   A violent TV episode? By any measure. Will it be labeled as such when the networks' new policy goes into effect this fall? No. Why? Because this is a rock video on cable channel MTV and it does not meet the qualifications for labeling. It's not a network prime time show or a drama. It's "kids' music."

3   Yet kids are showing up at school in alarming numbers with guns packed next to their bologna sandwiches. From September to May, every single week, a child somewhere in the United States fired a gun in a classroom or schoolyard—often killing somebody else's child. (Texas has the most incidents, California is a close second.)

4   Why then, when violent television's relationship to violent behavior is such a hot topic, do we only hear about labeling prime time network films and dramas? Rock-video violence is more deadly because it is fashioned by youth for the appetites of youth. It taps the most advanced visual and audio techniques to grab the teenager's eye and weaves in sex, **morbidity,** self-pity, anger and explicit rebellion against schools, parents and police. And MTV, the number one exhibitor of rock videos now reaches 57.3 million homes in the United States (231 million worldwide) seven days a week, around the clock.

5   I first saw Pearl Jam's "Jeremy"—the video described above—on MTV at 10 A.M. on a July morning in 1992 when millions of kids were home on summer vacation and their parents were probably at work. It continued to play on MTV around the clock all summer and into the fall, repeating as recently as Monday July 5 of this year in prime time on "The Top 30 of MTV's Top 200 Hits Ever."

6   And "Jeremy" is by no means an isolated example of violent videos aimed at the channel's youthful audience. References to guns, threatening gun gestures, and violence are recurring **motifs** in the choreography of such MTV videos as Dr. Dre's current rap hit "Dre Day" (which is supposed to be a "joke" about a real-life feud going on between Dre and rapper Easy E).

7   In Naughty by Nature's "Everything's Gonna Be Alright," a kid takes a crowbar to a car window. In Aerosmith's "Living on the Edge (You Can't Help Yourself)" uniformed school girls on roller skates bash parked cars with hockey sticks; two boys break a windshield and steal a car for a joyride; and a boy reaches into his school bag where a gun is clearly visible, chooses a burrito instead. He aims it playfully at his friend.

8   Why, then, can't parents just take responsibility and monitor their kid's music?

9   First, because the whole process is incredibly time-consuming and frustrating. Not all videos are offensive, and the high-tech graphics and special effects are often brilliant. But the subtlety with which violence is **interspersed** makes it necessary to do a great deal of legwork and watch MTV in large blocks of time, something adults may not have.

10   In some cases, it's the lyrics which shock. Record makers at one time agreed to display lyrics so that parents could easily access them. But the industry has made a mockery of the process by packaging the lyrics on folded inserts inside cellophane wrapped cassettes or CDs where they're inaccessible until the album is safely purchased. Even then they're often printed so small, or, as in the case of Pearl Jam's "Ten" album that contains "Jeremy," in such bizarre, "arty" or grafitti-like scrawls, that they're unreadable without magnification.

11 In other cases, lyrics may be **innocuous,** but the accompanying visuals are violent. The current recording of the old standard "I Can't Help Falling In Love With You," by UB40, is lovely. But the video uses outtakes from the film "Sliver," with graphic scenes of seminude Sharon Stone being menaced by a stalker.

12 Second, parents can switch the channel, await the technology to block it or cancel cable entirely. But so ubiquitous is MTV that their kid can still see it next door or down the street, and he may still catch a bullet fired in the classroom by a kid whose parents didn't care what he watched.

13 Third, MTV, in anticipation of eventual outrage from parents and civic groups, has built pre-emptive defenses into its young viewers. Ever since the U.S. Senate hearings of 1985 (requested by Tipper Gore's Parents Music Resource Center) MTV's youthful audience has been bombarded with warnings, contained in some videos and special service announcements, that parents and watchdog groups may seek controls. "I want my MTV!" Is the rallying cry, and many a parent has already experienced their teenager's outrage at any discussion or questioning of MTV's content.

14 Thus MTV is seemingly **impervious** to criticism, able to stand outside of any debate on TV violence, while its profit margin is **buttressed** by an ever-expanding audience and ad revenues from corporate giants like McDonald's, Time-Warner and Coca Cola.

15 The **naïve** senators and parents who grasped eagerly at the solution of labeling "violent TV" should spend a weekend immersed in this most provocative channel. Then, the next time they hear "you can't take kids' music away from them," they'll at least be able to define the term "kids' music."

Understanding Words

▶ **Definitions**

strobe (par. 1) A brilliant light—high-intensity, short duration light pulses.

ubiquitous (par. 12) Seeming to be everywhere at the same time.

pre-emptive (par. 13) An action taken to deter or stop an anticipated situation or occurrence.

watchdog groups (par. 13) Groups who serve as guardians or protectors against waste, loss, or illegal practices.

▶ **Vocabulary**

Check your understanding of the following words. Read the words in context (boldfaced in the text), and fill in the blank with the letter of the word or words that are closest to the meaning of the word in the text.

1. _____**morbidity** (a) psychologically unhealthy (b) immorality (c) stupidity (d) irrationality

2. _____**motifs** (a) models (b) movements (c) shots (d) recurrent themes

3. _____**interspersed** (a) presented (b) epitomized (c) mixed in (d) allowed

4. _____**innocuous** (a) ever-present (b) childlike (c) harmless (d) appropriate

5. _____**impervious** (a) attune (b) unaware of (c) above reproach (d) incapable of being affected

6. _____**buttressed** (a) reinforced (b) carefully thought out (c) protected (d) enhanced

7. _____**naïve** (a) overprotective (b) gullible (c) watchdog (d) overly aware

Thinking and Discussing

1. In paragraph 4, Duff says, "Rock-video violence is more deadly" than prime time network films and dramas. Do you agree or disagree with Duff? Why?

2. What are your opinions about the violence of MTV videos?

3. Should this material be censored?

4. Is labeling an effective way of regulating what children see or hear?

Writing Suggestions

1. Write a paragraph explaining how motifs unite music videos in a popular type of music such as country western or folk.

2. If you are familiar with several kinds of music, write an essay in which you compare and contrast the motifs that are used to unite music videos in two or three different kinds of music.

3. If you agree with Duff's point of view, write a process analysis in which you attempt to solve the problems that she raises.

4. If you disagree with Duff's point of view, write and essay in which you point out the weaknesses of her arguments. You may use your own experiences to refute her thesis.

 Men and Women

Matt Ridley, "Why Should Males Exist?"

 **Auxiliary Material**

Rhetorical Content Cause and Effect: Connecting Reasons and Result

Thematic Content Men and Women: Mate Selection

Background from *U. S. News and World Report,* August 18/August 25, 1997. Matt Ridley, a British author and journalist, has had articles published in several periodicals, including *Smithsonian* and *Atlantic.* His books include *The Red Queen: Sex and the Evolution of Human Nature.* In this article, Ridley contends that male and female roles are the result of thousands of years of males and females choosing mates who possess certain qualities.

Related Readings Judy Brady, "Why I Want a Wife," originally published in *Ms Magazine* in 1971. © 1971 by Judy Brady.

Katha Pollitt, "Feminism at the Crossroads," from *Dissent.* 1994.

Deborah Tannen, "Listening to Men, Then and Now," *New York Times Magazine,* May 16, 1999.

Reggie White, "Women in the Locker Room," *The Wall Street Journal,* April 8, 1999.

The lady is a champ. Margaret McGregor is declared the winner by a unanimous decision in her fight against Loi Chow. It was the first sanctioned man versus woman boxing match. (Seattle, Washington, 10/09/99, AP Photo/Elaine Thompson)

1   You do not need to be a feminist to recognize that men are at the root of a lot of the world's troubles.

2   Compared with women, they are more likely to drive fast, commit murders, desert their spouses, abuse children, develop autism or hemophilia, get into fights, become alcoholics, fail at school, find modern service-sector employment uncongenial, get cancer, and die young. Now that Dolly the cloned sheep has shown us that female mammals can be produced directly from the cells of other females, the human race might well ask whether it's necessary to put up with these troubles anymore. Dolly aside, there are already many species that happily or occasionally indulge in parthenogenesis (Greek for virgin birth): Turkeys can develop (with difficulty) in unfertilized eggs. Whiptail lizards are an all-female species. Various fish, crustaceans, insects, and worms can reproduce without the male sex. Some

microscopic animals, such as *bdelloid* rotifers, appear to have gone without sex for at least 40 million years. Many common plants such as dandelions are wholly asexual. These species stand as living proof that sex is unnecessary.

3   And not just unnecessary but downright wasteful: Sex means giving away 50 percent of the shares in your own offspring. Asexual reproduction means holding on to all the **equity.** Companies that give away 50 percent of their equity every few years have to grow twice as fast as companies that do not, or the market will bury them. This biological paradox is so puzzling that some biologists have been tempted to chalk up sex to an accident of history. It's useless, but species like ours can't get rid of it.

4   If sex were truly useless, though, a species that did manage to get rid of it ought to say good riddance and return to the happy state of the rotifer. But consider the greenfly: It is perfectly able to reproduce asexually, but it reverts to sexual reproduction after only a few generations. It simply would not do so if sex did not carry some evolutionary advantage.

5   Many ideas have been advanced to explain the purpose of sex; the only one that is definitely wrong is the one still given in most textbooks—that sex is good for the species because it helps it to evolve. That would be rather like one company arguing that it's willing to take a 50 percent loss because it's helping the evolution of all other companies in the same business in the process. Few shareholders would be impressed.

6   The search for other explanations for sex starts with the observation of where sex happens and where it does not. Almost all animals and plants living in tropical rain forests and coral reefs are sexual. Many animals and plants living in temporary or unstable habitats—freshwater ponds, **ephemeral** forest clearings, arctic tundras, **alpine** meadows—do without males. This counts against several theories: First to go is the idea that sex is there to repair **mutations.** Animals and plants that live at high altitudes, drenched with mutation-causing ultraviolet light, are among the most likely to be asexual.

7   Second to go are a bunch of theories that explain sex as a sort of reshuffling of the genetic pack to adapt to changing environments. Yet it is precisely in stable environments like rain forests that sex seems most indispensable.

8   In accordance with Sherlock Holmes's famous **dictum**—eliminate the impossible, and whatever remains, however improbable, is the truth—many biologists now lean toward a bizarre but intriguing explanation: Sex is for combating parasites. In warm, rich, stable environments, living creatures are under continuous assault from microscopic parasites, which are constantly evolving new abilities to undermine their hosts' defenses. The hosts need to change their genes regularly if they are to stay one step ahead. Only small, rapidly reproducing creatures living **nomadically** in cold or fast-changing environments can keep ahead of parasites without having sex. This idea, **championed** by Oxford University's William Hamilton, is known as the "Red Queen" theory, after the character in *Through the Looking Glass* who must keep running just to stay in the same place.

9   Having invented males, this theory goes, our ancestors only subsequently found other ways to put them to good use. Most birds and many fish employ males as assistant parents, sharing the duties of building nests, incubating eggs, and feeding babies. But this was not so much the purpose of sex as a byproduct of it—an attempt by females to turn the given fact of sexual reproduction to their advantage by selecting as mates males that were not total freeloaders.

10   Even seemingly destructive male behavior may be explained by this genetic war between the sexes. Male elephant seals and peacocks, for example, are the ultimate boors of the animal world. The male takes no part in child rearing after a brief insemination of the female. Indeed, such is the male elephant seal's aggressiveness that he sometimes tramples babies under foot. Except as a sperm provider, he is a liability.

11   Or is he? Think of it this way: When the female elephant seal hauls her body onto the best part of the breeding beach, she finds that she has unwittingly become the property of the biggest, strongest, healthiest, and most agile of the males. He has fought long and hard to monopolize exactly that spot. Genetically speaking, he is not a bad father at all: He is equipped with superb **innate** abilities, excellent disease resistance, a good brain, a well-put-together body. The long and bloody battles he has fought, the enormous muscles he has grown—females are responsible for these. It is their fault, because they have been choosing to allow the victors of battles to win their hearts for thousands of generations. Seen from this **eugenic** perspective, males are a sort of genetic test bed, a sieve through which the genes of the species are passed in every generation, with only the best being selected.

12   So, far from **railing** against the fact that men fight, take risks, die young, and treat women as property, women should apologize for it. The reason men are that way is most likely that women have bred them that way, gradually and **imperceptibly** over many generations, by choosing macho men as fathers for their sons.

13   Human males stand somewhere in the middle of the boorishness spectrum. They share many of the aggressive tendencies of their fellow male primates, but they also are intimately involved in child rearing in a way that male chimpanzees and gorillas are not. A more accurate description, however, may be to say that human males combine both extremes. Again, that is the fault of females. Many seemingly

monogamous birds, for example, try to have their beefcake and eat it too. The Danish biologist Anders Moller, using DNA fingerprinting to establish the paternity of nestlings, found that female barn swallows select the most nurturing male they can get as a social husband, to build the nest and rear the chicks—then often sneak around the back of the barn and cuckold him by getting sperm from a genetically superior male (as indicated in this species by his long tail).

14   This is uncomfortably close to home. Like swallows, human females have clearly been trying an evolutionary mixed strategy. They have been choosing good and faithful husbands keen on child rearing, but they also have been rewarding macho showoffs with a disproportionate share in the next generation.

15   However, men have their revenge. In most species, female behavior is little influenced by male selection, because males are sexually indiscriminate (which in turn is because sperm is cheap and quick to produce compared with eggs). Sexual selection is one-way traffic, which is why peacocks [males] look ridiculous and peahens [females] look normal.

16   But in humans, almost uniquely, males play the same game: They are quite selective in their choice of a mate, as much as females or even more. Their selectivity, over thousands of generations, has landed female human beings with sexually selected features—swollen breasts, narrow waists, wide hips that have no higher evolutionary purpose than to produce a next generation of females who also will be sexually attractive to men. Women would not have these features if men had not been picking on them for such a long time. Pamela Anderson Lee was made by men, just as Mike Tyson was by women.

Understanding Words

▶ **Definitions**

autism (par. 2) A severe childhood disorder characterized by acceptance of fantasy rather than reality.

hemophilia (par. 2) A hereditary condition in which the blood fails to clot normally.

rotifer (par. 2) Minute multicellular aquatic organisms.

paradox (par. 3) A seemingly contradictory statement that may nonetheless be true.

habitat (par. 6) The place where a person or thing is most likely to be found.

tundras (par. 6) Areas of Arctic regions having a permanently frozen subsoil and supporting low-growing vegetation.

▶ **Vocabulary**

Check your understanding of the following words. Read them in context (boldfaced in the text) and fill in the blank with the letter of the word or words that are closest in meaning to the word in the text.

1. ____**equity** (a) fair (b) just (c) preferred stock (d) impartial

2. ____**ephemeral** (a) aesthetic (b) old growth (c) virgin (d) short lived

3. ____**alpine** (a) relating to high mountains (b) lush (c) verdant (d) related to marshy areas

4. ____**mutations** (a) freaks (b) different from parental strain (c) inferior (d) maladjusted

5. ____**dictum** (a) popular saying (b) dictate (c) philosophy (d) an authoritative statement

6. ____**nomadically** (a) hopelessly (b) in a wandering manner (c) aimlessly (d) hand-to-mouth

7. ____**championed** (a) denied (b) questioned (c) originated (d) supported

8. ____**innate** (a) inborn (b) recognizable (c) profound (d) latent

9. ____**eugenic** (a) illogical (b) hereditary improvement (c) bizarre (d) reasonable

10. ____**railing** (a) talking bitterly (b) fighting (c) taking a stand (d) being ambivalent

11. ____**imperceptibly** (a) surely (b) not noticeable (c) knowingly (d) surreptitiously

Thinking and Discussing

1. In your own words, state the point of this essay.

2. A **rhetorical question** is a question asked only to emphasize a point or provoke ideas, but not to be answered. Is the title of this essay a real question, or is it a rhetorical question?

3. Do you agree or disagree with Ridley's point that men are the way they are because women, through their selection of mates, breed them that way?

4. Do you agree or disagree that the generally accepted concepts of an attractive woman—according to Ridley's ideas—are developed through male selection, and not through commercial manipulation of what is the ideal—Barbie and company?

5. In your own words, explain what Ridley means when he refers to a *biological paradox* (par. 3).

6. An **analogy** is a comparison of two things that are similar in some respects but are otherwise dissimilar, often comparing the familiar with the unfamiliar to better explain the unfamiliar. Do you find the comparison of reproduction and a company's holdings to be an effective analogy?

Writing Suggestions

1. Using Ridley's essay as a model, write an essay entitled "Why Should Females Exist?"

2. Write an essay in which you argue for or against human cloning.

3. Write an essay agreeing or disagreeing with Ridley's point that women are the way they are because that's the way men want them or that men are the way they are because that is the way women want them.

4. Write a paragraph describing the ideal mate for procreation. Write another paragraph describing the ideal husband or wife. Compare the two paragraphs and write a paragraph explaining the differences, if any, between the two.

5. Make a checklist—one for men and one for women—in which you list the attributes Ridley says make men and women attractive as reproduction partners: women (large breasts, narrow waists, and full hips) and men (big, strong, healthy, and agile). Have members of one or more classes rate these characteristics of attraction on a scale of 1–5, with 5 being the most desirable. Write a summary of your findings. Draw conclusions and inferences from your collected data.

Deborah Tannen, "Listening to Men, Then and Now"

Auxiliary Material

Rhetorical Content	Example: Illustrating Ideas
	Comparison and Contrast: Exploring Similarities and Differences
Thematic Content	Men and Women: Historic and Contemporary Similarities and Differences
Background	from *New York Times Magazine*, May 16, 1999. Deborah Tannen, a linguist who earned her Ph.D. from the University of California at Berkeley, is a professor at Georgetown University. She is the author of *Conversational Style: Analyzing Talks among Friends* and *That's Not What I Meant! How Conversational Style Makes or Breaks Your Relations with Others.* Her latest book is *The Argument Culture,* recently

(continued)

published by Ballantine. In this essay, Tannen explores the historical and contemporary similarities and differences in the relations of men and women and the role communication plays in the relations.

Related Readings   Deborah Tannen, "Sex, Lies, and Conversation: Why Is It So Hard for Men and Women to Talk to Each Other?" *Washington Post*, 1990.

Elizabeth Cady Stanton, "Declaration of Sentiments," 1848 speech at the first women's convention, Seneca Falls, New York.

Scott Russell Sanders, "Looking at Women," from *Secrets of the Universe.* © 1991. Scott Russell Sanders.

1   A woman and a man meet at the end of the day. He asks how her day was, and she replies with a long report of what she did, whom she met, what they said and what that made her think and feel. Then she eagerly turns to him:

2   She: How was your day?

3   He: Same old rat race.

4   She: Didn't anything happen?

5   He: Nah, nothing much.

6   Her disappointment is deepened when that evening they go out to dinner with friends and suddenly he **regales** the group with an amusing account of something that happened at work. She is cut to the quick, **crestfallen** at hearing this story as part of an audience of strangers. "How could he have said nothing happened?" she wonders. "Why didn't he tell me this before? What am I? Chopped liver?"

7   The key to this frustration is that women and men typically have different ideas about what makes people friends. For many women, as for girls, talk is the glue of close relationships; your best friend is the one you tell your secrets to, the one you discuss your troubles with. For many men, as for boys, activities are central; your best friend is the one you do everything with (and the one who will stick up for you if there is a fight).

8   As the **millennium** approaches and commentators examine how our lives have changed in the last thousand years, I find myself wondering about the change in re-

lations between the sexes. Clearly there has been a transformation. In the past, the woman was **deferential,** subordinate. Now we are not trying to be partners in a societal arrangement with a clearly defined separation of labor, but rather hoping to be each other's best friends. Yet at least two aspects of women's and men's relations have endured—our differing expectations about the importance of talk in intimacy, and the tendency of women to take the role of listener in conversation with men.

9   In the absence of tape recordings from earlier times, we can look to conversations in literature. For a glimpse of how a 16th-century couple might have talked to each other, I turned to Shakespeare—and my earliest memory of his plays. When I was at Ditmas Junior High in Brooklyn, my classmates were all atitter: our teacher had us reading "Julius Caesar" aloud, and, having read ahead, we knew that the next day some poor girl would have to stand and read a passage in which Brutus's wife uses the word "harlot." Susan Ehrlich had the bad luck to be chosen, and I can still see her, tall and brown-haired, reading, "Portia is Brutus's harlot, not his wife."

10   Revisiting those lines today, what strikes me is how similar the sentiment is to what I hear from contemporary women. Portia wants to be Brutus's best friend—and her idea of what this means is very similar to ours. Waking up to discover that her husband has left their bed, she finds him pacing, and implores him to say what is worrying him. Like the modern woman who feels that best friends tell each other secrets, Portia pleads:

11   Within the bond of marriage, tell me,
           Brutus,
       Is it expected I should know no secrets
       That appertain to you?
           Am I yourself
       But, as it were, in sort or
           limitation,
       To keep with you at meals,
           comfort your bed,
       And talk to you
           sometimes? Dwell I but
           in the suburbs
       Of your good pleasure? If
           it be no more,
       Portia is Brutus's harlot,
           not his wife.

12   A similar sentiment emerges in an even more distant conversation—in the Arabian romance of the Bedouin hero Antar, believed to have been written between

1080 and 1400. In one episode, a character named al-Minhal, escaping a king he has wronged, comes upon a ruined castle inhabited by a female demon named Dahiya. She gives him shelter, feeds him, falls in love with him and wins his love by her attentions, which include her conversation. Sounding rather like Portia, Dahiya says: "I want you to be my companion and to be my lord, and I will be your wife. Disclose to me what is in your heart. Do not believe that I will ever let you go. Open your mind to me for I have need to know your thoughts." They are married on the spot, and, we are told, "Long was their companionship, and they loved each other dearly."

13   I am not suggesting that relationships between women and men were the same then as now. But it's intriguing to think that what women regard as intimacy, talking about what's on your mind, has been a common thread right through the millennium. There's another, related pattern that seems to have endured. It, too, is evident in the case of the husband who can't think of anything to tell his wife but comes up with an amusing story to entertain a dinner gathering. To her, it's a failure of intimacy: If we're truly close, I should hear everything first. To him, I think, the situation of being home with someone he feels close to does not call for a story performance. This creates a paradox. Many women were drawn to the men they fell in love with because the men told captivating stories. After marriage, the women expect that the closer they get, the more the men will open up and tell. Instead, to their deep disappointment, after marriage the men clam up.

14   Once again, looking at how boys and girls are socialized provides a key. Boys' groups are hierarchical; low-status boys are pushed around. One way boys earn and keep status is to hold center stage by verbal performance—boasting, telling jokes or recounting **mesmerizing** stories. And this seems to work well in winning maidens as well.

15   This aspect of storytelling can be seen as far back as "Beowulf," that Anglo-Saxon saga, usually dated to the eighth century. The hero, a member of a Swedish tribe known as the Geats, wins the attention of Wealhtheow, Queen of Hrothgar, who is serving beer to a gathering of men:

16   Beowulf spoke, the son of Ecgtheow: "I resolved, when I set out on the sea, sat down in the sea-boat with my band of men, that I should altogether fulfill the will of your people or else fall in slaughter, fast in the foe's grasp. I shall achieve a deed of manly courage or else have lived to see in the mead-hall my ending day." These words were well-pleasing to the woman, the boast of the Geat. Gold-adorned, the noble folk-queen went to sit by her lord.

17   Boasting, my colleague Catherine Ball tells me, was a customary male activity in the Anglo-Saxon mead-hall, so it is not surprising that Wealhtheow was well

pleased, even though the exploits Beowulf boasts of have not yet taken place. (In fact, he sounds a little like Cassius Clay [Muhammad Ali] predicting what he will do to Sonny Liston.)

18 This scenario—a woman wooed by a man's boasts of exploits in battle—brings us back to Shakespearean icons: Desdemona and Othello. As Othello tells "how I did thrive in this fair lady's love," he explains that she became entranced when she heard him telling "the story of my life":

19 Wherein I spoke of most
    disastrous chances:
Of moving accidents by
    flood and field,
Of hair-breadth scapes
    I' th' imminent deadly
    breach;
Of being taken by the
    insolent foe. . . .
And so on, until:

20 My story being done,
She gave me for my pains
    a world of kisses. . . .
And bade me, if I had a
    friend that lov'd her,
I should but teach him
    how to tell my story,
And that would woo her.

21 As we know, he wooed her himself with his own story.

22 In our era, the tactic of wooing by verbal performance takes a funny turn. Etiquette books of the 50's instructed young women to be good listeners if they wanted to win their men, and you need only look around a restaurant to see many women attentively listening to talking men. In place of battle yarns, what I hear, over and over, is that a woman fell in love because "he makes me laugh." That's why Michelle Pfeiffer said in 1992 she picked a particular boyfriend, and why Joanne Woodward fell for Paul Newman. I don't hear the same explanation from men as to why they fall in love. What I hear is the corresponding one, as for example when Woody Allen said of his relationship with Soon-Yi Previn: "She's a marvel. And she laughs at all my jokes."

23 We seem to have a situation of *plus ca change* [(pluh-sah-**SHAWNJ**)—reference to "the more things change; the more they stay the same"]. Even as relationships

between men and women have changed, our contrasting expectations about the meaning of closeness still cause confusion and disappointment. And though the performance has shifted from heroic tales to amusing entertainment, more often than not the apportionment of roles has stayed the same: Women are the audience and men are the show.

Understanding Words

▶ **Definitions**

Literary reference notes are not needed because the author skillfully weaves in the background information for them.

What am I? Chopped liver? (par. 6) An expression meaning "Am I unimportant?"

paradox (par. 13) A seemingly contradictory statement that may nevertheless be true.

▶ **Vocabulary**

Check your understanding of the following words. Read them in context (boldfaced in the text) and fill in the blank with the letter of the word or words that are closest to the meaning of the word in the text.

1. _____ **regales** (a) overpowers (b) impresses (c) inspires (d) entertains

2. _____ **crestfallen** (a) baffled (b) disappointed (c) dispirited (d) frustrated

3. _____ **millennium** a span of (a) two thousand years (b) one thousand years (c) fifty years (d) ten years

4. _____ **deferential** (a) respectfully reverent (b) readily submissive (c) humble (d) courteous yielding

5. _____ **mesmerizing** (a) off-color (b) spellbinding (c) dull (d) funny

Thinking and Discussing

1. Does the title get your attention and arouse your curiosity? If so, why do you think it does so?

2. Based on your own experiences, are you a talker or a listener when you are conversing (1) with a person of the opposite sex, (2) with a person of the same sex?

3. Do the circumstances alter your role? Give examples.

4. Do you agree with the idea that women tend to be the listeners rather than the talkers in most relationships?

5. Would you agree with the statement that lack of communication or miscommunication

plays a major role in the breakup of many relationships? Explain.

6. In paragraph 7 Tannen says that for many females "talk is the glue of close relationships." Do you agree?

Writing Suggestions

1. Write a brief summary of this essay.

2. Observe a conversation between (1) a man and a woman, (2) a man and a man, and (3) a woman and a woman. In the introductory paragraph, lay out your plan and speculate about what you expect to find out. Write a body paragraph describing each conversation—including body language. In the fifth paragraph, draw your conclusions based on your observations. Do your findings coincide with Tannen's theories? Were your expectations supported or not supported by your findings?

3. Interview a couple of a previous generation (your parents or your grandparents' generation). How do their ideas about conversation between women and men differ from your ideas? Write a comparison and contrast paper showing the similarities and differences of the two generations.

Appendix A

Vantage Points

Using the Pronunciation Key

Pronouncing words correctly is important. To move words from your reading or understanding vocabulary to your speaking vocabulary, you must be able to pronounce them correctly. Sometimes the meaning of a word will change when it is pronounced differently, and careless pronunciation often results in misspelled words. The following key will help you pronounce words that may not be familiar to you. These guides use familiar sounds of individual letters or combinations of letters. These letters or letter combinations are listed in the Pronunciation Key followed by traditional letters and symbols and examples of pronunciation. Hyphens separate the syllables. If a syllable is shown in capital boldfaced letters, say that syllable the loudest. The boldfaced capitalized syllables are traditionally marked with a primary stress mark (ˊ).

parentheses (puh-**REN**-thi-seez)

hyphen (**HIE**-fuhn)

syllable (**SIL**-uh-buhl)

If a syllable is shown in capital, non-boldfaced letters, say that syllable the second loudest. The non-boldfaced capitalized syllables are traditionally marked with a secondary stress mark (ˊ).

pronunciation (pruh-NUN-see-**AY**-shuhn)

combination (KOM-buh-**NAY**-shuhn)

individual (IN-duh-**VIJ**-ooh-uhl)

Pronunciation Key

TWP SYMBOLS	TRADITIONAL SYMBOLS	EXAMPLES	TWP SYMBOLS	TRADITIONAL SYMBOLS	EXAMPLES
a	ă	pat	o	ŏ	pot
ay	ā	pay	o	o	paw, caught
air	â	hair, care	oh	ō	toe
ah	ä	father, are	oo	ŏŏ	book
b	b	bid	ooh	o͞o	boot
ch	ch	church	or	ô	for, horse
d	d	deed	ou	ou	out
e	ĕ	set, bet, berry	oy	oi	boy, noise
e	ē	bee, each	p	p	pop
f	f	fit, fife, phase, rough	r	r	rat
g	g	gag, ghost	s	s	sauce
h	h	hat	sh	sh	ship, dish
hw	hw	which	t	t	tight
i	ĭ	pit, bit	th	th	thin
ie	ī	pie, by, bite	thh	*th*	this
ier	î	pier, clear	u	u	cut
j	j	jam, judge, gem	uh	ə	about, item
k	k	kick, cat, pique, chaos	ur	ûr	urge, term
kw	kw	quart, choir	v	v	valve
l	l	lid, lull	w	w	with
m	m	mom, mum, column	y	y	yes
n	n	no, sudden	z	z	zebra
ng	ng	wing	zh	zh	vision, garage

Pronunciation Key from *Just Plain English,* Harcourt Brace, 1999.

Revising Sentences, Paragraphs, and Essays

The page numbers following words, phrases, or clauses refer to pages in this text. Use these references to help you revise your compositions.

▶ **Checklist: Revising a Single Paragraph**

1. Is the paragraph focused? (pp. 3, 34)

   Is the topic and your idea about it appropriate for a paragraph?

2. Is your purpose clear? (pp. 4, 34)

3. Is your tone appropriate for the topic sentence and the audience? (pp. 4–6)

   Is your tone consistent throughout the paragraph?

   Have you used language that is familiar to your audience?

4. Does the paragraph carry out the purpose and central idea of the topic? (p. 34)

   If it does not, what is the problem?

   Is the topic sentence not clear?

   Have you strayed from the controlling idea in the topic sentence?

5. Is the paragraph unified? (p. 34)

   Is the topic sentence viable? It is not viable if it is too narrow, too broad, makes an announcement, or contains more than one idea.

   Does the paragraph contain a clearly and specifically stated topic sentence?

   Does each sentence in the paragraph support the topic sentence?

   Does the paragraph contain irrelevant or redundant material?

6. Is the paragraph coherent? (pp. 34–41)

   Are the supporting details in the paragraph arranged according to a definite pattern?

   Does the paragraph contain linking words and transitional expressions between sentences that help your readers move smoothly from one idea to the next?

7. Do your readers need more information? (p. 61)

   Do you need to define or explain any terms that may not be familiar to your audience? (p. 61)

   Does the paragraph contain enough appropriate details to be convincing?

8. Is the title provocative? (p. 61)

   Does the title hint at the content—not simply restate the topic, the idea, or both?

▶ **Checklist: Revising the Whole Essay**

1. Is the essay focused? (pp. 3, 34)

   Are the topic and your idea about it appropriate for an essay?

2. Is your reason for writing the essay clear in both the thesis and the body? (pp. 4, 41)

3. Is your tone appropriate for the thesis statement and the audience? (p. 6)

   Is your tone consistent throughout the essay?

   Have you used language that is familiar to your audience?

4. Does the body carry out the purpose and central idea of the thesis sentence? (pp. 62–66)

   If it does not, what causes the problem? Is your thesis not clear or not focused, or when you developed the body paragraphs, did you stray from your thesis and plan of development? Do the body paragraphs follow the same order as they are given in the plan of development?

5. Is the essay unified? (pp. 41, 66)

   Is the thesis viable? It is not viable if it is too narrow, too broad, makes an announcement, or contains more than one idea.

   Does each unified, coherent body paragraph support the thesis?

   Does the essay contain irrelevant or repetitive material?

6. Is the essay coherent? (p. 66)

   Are the paragraphs arranged in a definite pattern?

   Have you used linking words and transitional expressions and sentences between paragraphs to help your readers move smoothly from one idea to the next?

7. Do your readers need more information? (p. 61)

Do you need to define or explain terms that may be unfamiliar to your readers?

Have you given adequate details, examples, reasons, or evidence to support each idea?

8. Does the title hint at the content—not simply restate the topic or the thesis statement? (p. 61)

▶ **Checklist: Revising Paragraphs in an Essay**

1. Is the introductory paragraph engaging and complete? (p. 62)

Does it contain a provocative lead-in?

Does it contain sufficient background information?

Does it contain a clearly stated thesis statement and a plan of development?

Does it contain an implied thesis statement?

2. Is each body paragraph unified? (p. 66)

Does each body paragraph contain a topic sentence that is logically related to the thesis?

Does each sentence in the paragraph support the topic sentence in that paragraph?

Does the paragraph contain irrelevant or redundant material?

3. Is each body paragraph coherent? (p. 66)

Are the details in the paragraph arranged according to a definite plan?

Does each paragraph contain linking words and transitional expressions that help readers move smoothly from one idea to the next?

4. Is each body paragraph sufficiently developed to support the idea in the topic sentence? (p. 67)

5. Did you supply more details than needed in one body paragraph and then skimp on the details in the other paragraphs? (p. 66)

6. Is the ending paragraph consistent with the beginning paragraph? (p. 66)

7. Does the ending paragraph provide a sense of completion? (p. 66) See note on p. 68.

▶ **Checklist: Revising Sentences**

1. Have you used complex sentences as well as simple and compound sentences? (pp. 22–30)

2. Are there any

   sentence fragments (pp. 133–144)

   run-together sentences (pp. 148–152)

   this, that, which, it; they, it, you; repeated subject; who, which, that errors? (p. 164)

   point of view errors—*I, we, you, he she, it, they* (p. 171)

   non-standard verbs (p. 179)

   subject and verb or pronoun and antecedent disagreements (pp. 187–196)

   misused adjectives or adverbs (pp. 204–210)

3. Have you

   put modifiers where they belong (p. 216)

   used parallel structures (pp. 220–221)

   avoided distracting shifts in *tense, number, person, mood, voice,* and from *direct to indirect quotations* (p. 226)

   avoided mixed constructions or illogical connections (p. 234)

   used concrete adjectives (p. 241)

   used strong, active verbs (p. 241)

   used verb + -ing words as nouns (p. 242)

   emphasized main ideas (p. 243)

   used the active voice most of the time (p. 244)

   avoided using meaningless words: filler words, roundabout expressions, or needless repetition (p. 246)

   avoided using pretentious words (p. 248)

   varied sentence lengths and openings (p. 252)

   avoided writing stringy sentences (p. 256)

► **Checklist: Correcting Punctuation, Mechanics, Usage, and Spelling**

1. Have you used commas correctly? (pp. 312–328) Have you used them to set off

   - independent clauses

   - items in a series

   - nonessential material

   - introductory material

   - miscellaneous expressions

   - everyday material

2. Have you used semicolons correctly? (p. 333) Have you used them between

   - independent clauses not joined by *for, and, nor, but, or, yet,* or *so*

   - independent clauses joined by transitional words and expressions such as *for example, nevertheless, consequently,* and so on

   - items in a series when the items contain commas

   - independent clauses when the clauses contain distracting commas

3. Have you put periods or question marks at the ends of statements and questions? (pp. 336–337)

   If you have written a sentence that ends with an exclamation mark or question mark, have you used only one mark?

4. Have you added apostrophes to show ownership—but not incorrectly to words that already show possession? (pp. 339–340)

   Have you avoided confusing the apostrophe that shows ownership with the one that marks the omission of letters to form a contraction?

5. Have you used quotation marks correctly? (p. 341)

   Have you

   - enclosed direct quotations with quotation marks—but not indirect ones

   - placed commas and periods inside quotation marks

   - placed semicolons and colons outside quotation marks

   - placed question marks and marks of exclamation inside quotation marks when they are part of the quotation and outside when they are not part of the quotation

6. Have you used other marks of punctuation correctly? (p. 346) Have you used

   - parentheses to de-emphasize nonessential material

   - dashes to emphasize nonessential information or to show an abrupt change in thought

   - a colon before a list, before a long quotation, and between two independent clauses when the second clause restates or explains the first one

   - a hyphen to break a word at the end of a line and between some compound words

7. Have you used capital letters correctly? (p. 354) Have you capitalized

   - specific nouns, but not general ones

   - the names of nationalities, religions, races, countries, cities, months, days of the week, documents, organizations, and holidays

   - streets, buildings, organizations, historical events, titles, and family relationships when they are used as part of a specific noun

   - geographic locations

   - academic subjects only when they refer to a specific numbered course or are derived from the name of a country (*English, German*)

8. Have you written titles correctly? (p. 359) Have you

   - capitalized all words in the title except prepositions, coordinating conjunctions FANBOYS: (*for, and, nor, but, or, yet, so*), and the words *the, an,* and *a*

   - italicized (underlined) the titles of long works—books, magazines, movies, and so on

   - put quotation marks around short works—short stories, poems, articles, and so on

9. Have you only used abbreviations according to standard practice? (p. 364)

10. Have you italicized (underlined) names of crafts and vessels, foreign words, and words used as words? (p. 365)

11. Have you used words and figures for numbers according to standard practice and appropriate for your purpose and audience? (p. 366) Have you

    - spelled out numbers that begin sentences

    - spelled out numbers expressed in one or two words

    - used numerals for numbers expressed in more than two words

    - used numerals in everyday situations such as dates and addresses

12. Have you used the appropriate form of a word that might look or sound like another word that has a different meaning? (Check your personal list.)

13. Have you checked the spelling of words that you frequently misspell? (Check your personal list.)

14. Have you checked for careless errors such as typos and omitted words?

15. Have you used an appropriate format—instructor's preference or Appendix A Formatting College Papers?

Formatting College Papers

A clean, neatly typed, appropriately formatted paper is the mark of a careful, serious writer. Messy, hard-to-read, cluttered papers often will not receive the high marks that the content warrants. Some of your instructors may give you specific instructions for preparing your papers, and when they do, of course, you will follow those instructions; otherwise, use the following guidelines:

Paper	Use only white 8½ by 11-inch high-quality paper.
Ribbon and Type Style	Use a fresh black ribbon or cartridge.
	Use a plain type style.
Identification	Type your name, your instructor's name, the course and number, and date (written out as January 1, 2003 or 1 January 2003—not abbreviated) one inch from the top of the first page—double-spaced—flush with the left-hand margin unless your instructor requires a separate title page.
	If a title page is required, ask your instructor for guidelines.

Title

Center the title.

Do not underline the title or enclose it in quotation marks.

Never put a period after a title, even if it is a sentence.

Capitalize the first, last, and all important words of titles.

Do not capitalize the words *a, an, the, for, and, nor, but, yet, so,* the word *to* in front of a verb, and prepositions unless they are the first or last word of the title.

If a title is longer than one line, double-space and center the second line below the first line.

Page Numbers

Number all pages consecutively—including the first page—in the upper right-hand corner, one-half inch from the top of the page.

Do not put *p* or *pp* or any punctuation mark with the number.

Do put your last name before the page number.

Spacing

Except for page numbers, leave a one-inch margin at the top, at the bottom, and on both sides of the page. Double-space the entire paper.

Double-space between the last line of the title and the first line of the text.

Indent new paragraphs five spaces.

Model

$\updownarrow$ 1/2″
Pearson 1

1″$\updownarrow$

Morgan B. Pearson

Professor Johnson

$\leftrightarrow$1″   English 100

1 January 2003

A Definition of a Word or a Phrase

A definition is a brief explanation stating what is meant by the subject and how it is
distinguished from all others. It helps writers conceive a clear idea of their subject and   1″$\leftrightarrow$
enables them to write a sensible explanation of it.

1″ $\updownarrow$

(The top of the first page of a college paper)

Handwritten Papers   If your instructor accepts handwritten papers, follow
the preceding guidelines* when applicable.

Submit neat, legible papers.

Use only white 8½ by 11-inch paper with standard
ruled lines.

Skip every other ruled line.

Use black or dark blue ink.

Do not submit pages with ragged edges.

Use only one side of the paper.

Shaping a Five-Paragraph Essay

An essay is a relatively short piece of writing (usually between 400 and 600 words)
on a single subject. It contains several paragraphs in which the writer discusses a
topic or tries to persuade the reader to take an action or to accept a point of view. A

*Guidelines are consistent with the ones in *MLA Handbook for Writers of Research Papers,* 4th ed.

good college essay should have three parts: an introductory paragraph in which the writer introduces the main point of the paper; body paragraphs that support the main idea; and a concluding paragraph in which the writer restates the main point, summarizes, or makes observations about the main point. Although there are many different kinds of essays, one of the most often used types in college essays is called a "five-paragraph theme" or "five-paragraph essay" (also called a *one, three, one* essay—one paragraph for the introduction, three for the body, and one for the conclusion). The following chart gives the structure of this standard college essay form.

Title

Paragraph I. Introduction

    A. Lead-in

    B. Background

    C. Thesis Statement

    D. Three-point (Points 1, 2, and 3) Plan of Development

Paragraph II. Body Paragraph 1

    A. Topic Sentence Supporting Point 1

    B. Logical, Adequate Support for Topic Sentence

Paragraph III. Body Paragraph 2

    A. Topic Sentence Supporting Point 2

    B. Logical, Adequate Support for Topic Sentence

Paragraph IV. Body Paragraph 3

    A. Topic Sentence Supporting Point 3

    B. Logical, Adequate Support for Topic Sentence

Paragraph V. Conclusion

Using Response Symbols to Revise and Edit Papers

The following symbols are ones that many instructors use to indicate needed changes in a writing assignment. The references following each editing skill refer to pages of this book.

ab   Fix abbreviation error. (p. 364)

\#   Add space.

ad   Use correct adjective or adverb. (p. 203)

agr	Make subject-verb agree or pronoun-antecedent agree. (p. 187)
art	Use correct article. (p. 268)
awk	Reword awkward construction. (p. 234)
$\wedge$	Caret: Insert word(s) or symbol(s).
cap	Add capital letter. (p. 354)
cl	Do not use cliché's. (p. 306)
close	Close the space.
coh	Make it coherent (stick together). (p. 48)
cord	Make coordinated parts fit together logically. (p. 234)
cs	Fix comma splice sentence. (pp. 148–152)
cut	Delete.
dev	Develop more fully.
discrim	Do not use sexist or discriminatory language. (p. 303)
dm	Put the dangling part next to the word(s) it modifies. (p. 216)
frag	Fix the sentence fragment. (pp. 133–141)
fs	Fix the fused sentence. (pp. 148–152)
gap	Add missing words/details.
gd	Good point, phrase, idea, and so on.
ital	Fix the italics (underlining) error. (pp. 365–366)
lc	Use lower case (small) letter. (pp. 354–359)
log	Make it logical. (p. 90)
mixed	Logically fit complete subject and complete verb together. (p. 234)
mm	Put misplaced part (modifier) next to the word(s) it modifies. (pp. 216–218)
ms	Use standard manuscript form. (p. 499)
num	Fix the number use error. (pp. 366–367)
¶	Begin a new paragraph.

no¶	Do not begin a new paragraph.
//	Make elements parallel. (pp. 220–221)
pl	Fix plural ending error. (p. 287)
prep	Use correct preposition. (pp. 124–125)
pro	Fix the pronoun error. (pp. 157–171)
?	Explain more clearly or write it legibly.
quot	Fix the quotation mark error. (pp. 342–343)
rel	Relocate or transpose (letters, words, phrases, and so on).
rep	Cut repetitious material. (p. 247)
ro	Fix run-on sentence. (pp. 148–152)
rt	Fix run-together sentence. (pp. 148–152)
shift	Correct needless shift. (p. 226)
sl	Do not use slang. (p. 297)
sp	Spell word correctly. (pp. 282–290)
stet	Keep the original form.
sub	Subordinate (put the least important idea in a dependent clause). (p. 152)
trans	Add or improve a transition. (p. 48)
unify	Unify the paragraph by relating all ideas to the main idea. (p. 34)
us	Fix the usage error. (pp. 264–274)
verb	Use the correct verb form. (pp. 174, 187–194)
var	Vary the sentence patterns. (pp. 22, 243)
wordy	Say the same thing in fewer words. (p. 246)

Writing Essay Test Answers

Essay questions contain **signal words** that indicate the types of response that are expected.

SIGNAL WORDS	RESPONSES
1. **Analyze**	Examine, discuss, and interpret the whole subject or divide it into its logical parts and discuss, examine, interpret or explain those parts.
2. **Apply**	Take one concept, idea, or formula and apply it to another situation.
3. **Argue**	Take a position on one side of an arguable topic and use logical, ethical, and/or emotional appeals to support your position.
4. **Compare**	Show the similarities of two or more people, places, things, or ideas.
5. **Contrast**	Show the differences of two or more people, places, things, or ideas.
6. **Clarify**	Make clear by defining key terms and use examples to illustrate it.
7. **Classify/Categorize**	Place in groups that are based on shared characteristics.
8. **Criticize/Evaluate**	Make judgment statements—recognizing both strengths and weaknesses—about the value or worth of the subject.
9. **Define**	Put the subject in its general class, and then differentiate it by showing how it differs from other members of that class.
10. **Describe**	Give a detailed account; use details to support ideas or impressions.
11. **Diagram**	Use a labeled sketch or drawing to show how the subject works.
12. **Discuss**	Examine and consider as many elements of the subject as possible.
13. **Explain**	Make an idea clear and comprehensible; offer reasons and causes.
14. **Identify**	Establish the identity of the subject through origin, nature, or definitive characteristics.

15. **Illustrate**   Explain clearly by using concrete examples and/or comparisons.

16. **Interpret**   Explain the meaning and significance of the subject.

17. **Justify**   Demonstrate through logic or details that the judgment statement is valid, correct, or just.

18. **List**   Give a series of names or points.

19. **Outline**   Give a general description covering the main parts of the subject or list the elements of the subject in headings and subheadings.

20. **Prove**   Support with facts or logical arguments.

21. **Relate**   Show a connection between two or more ideas or events.

22. **Review**   Reexamine and/or reconsider the subject and possibly criticize it.

23. **Show**   Point out something or demonstrate it by reasoning or procedure.

24. **State**   Explain precisely; lay out the main points of the subject.

25. **Summarize**   Give a shortened account of the main points and supporting material and conclusions. Do not include unnecessary details.

26. **Support**   Give details that support one side of an arguable topic.

27. **Trace**   Arrange, in time order, the events or progress of the subject.

Restating a Piece of Writing

One of the best ways to understand a difficult piece of writing is to restate its meaning in your own words. These restatements may take the form of a paraphrase, a summary, or a précis.

Before you begin rewording a text, do the following.

- Read it carefully.

- Use an up-to-date dictionary and check the meaning of unfamiliar words.

- Find the main idea of the text and get it firmly fixed in your mind.

  After you have reworded the text, revise and fix what you have written.
- Eliminate redundant material and minor details.

- Fix any errors in grammar, word choice, punctuation, mechanics, and spelling.

Writing a Paraphrase

A paraphrase is a restatement of a text or passage in another form or in other words. It says in different or simpler words exactly what the passage being paraphrased says. It is not necessarily shorter than the original text.

- Usually paraphrase one sentence at a time.

- Use your own words, not those of the original author.

Writing a Summary

A summary is a brief restatement of the substance of a text. It presents, in other words, a condensation of a body of material. Summaries are either **objective** or **evaluative.** In an objective summary you do not include your own thoughts or opinions. It should be objective, complete, and concise. In an evaluative summary you include your thoughts, opinions, and speculations on the author's line of thinking.

- Determine the purpose of the text (to inform, to explain, to compare, to contrast, to illustrate, to persuade, or to entertain).

- Find the thesis and, in your own words, restate it in one or two sentences.

- In your own words sum up the content of each paragraph in one or two sentences.

- Be sure to include all key ideas along with supporting examples.

- Begin the summary with the author's name, the title of the piece, the author's purpose, and your restatement of the author's thesis.

- Then, add your summaries of each paragraph, in order.

- Do not include repetitious material or minor details.

- Do not include your own opinions about the text in an objective summary.

- Do include your own opinions about the text in an evaluative summary.

- Put quotation marks around any material that you take word for word from the text.

Writing a Précis

A **précis** is a short summary. It is concise—expresses much in a few words clearly and succinctly. It is often used to summarize articles and essays. It may be a twenty-five word summary that does no more than gives the major points. It may be a one-hundred word précis that gives the major points and a few important details, or it may be longer and include examples and illustrations in addition to the major points and important details.

- Find the author's main point and write it in your own words.

- Write the précis entirely in your own words—not in the words of the original passage.

- Do not borrow long phrases or sentences from the original, except for a few key words that you feel are absolutely necessary.

- Write it from the point of view of the author who wrote the original.

- For the more complete précis, generally, keep the length one-third or less the length of the original work.

- Begin as if you were writing about your own work.

- Do not begin with expressions such as "The author says" or "This paragraph or essay means."

- Do not include any of your own opinions in an objective précis.

Appendix B

Essays

Characteristics of Essays—A, B, C, D

▶ **Characteristics of an "A" Superior Essay**

Content and Logic

Thesis present and clear

Perception and insights evident and controlled

Logical support, ample and compelling

Audience awareness highly developed

Clearly appropriate tone for audience and topic

Organization

Introduction interesting and focused

Topic sentences in body paragraphs support thesis

Paragraphs fully developed and flow smoothly

Clear, smooth transitions between paragraphs

Conclusion strong and satisfying and in keeping with the introduction

Style

Appropriate and varied vocabulary

Good command of sentence variety

Precise and imaginative word choice

Language appropriate to the topic, purpose, and audience

Control of literal and figurative language

Few, if any, clichés; passive voice constructions; or overreliance on the *to be* verbs

Almost no repetitiveness, redundancy, or wordiness

Grammar, Usage, and Mechanics

Contains no

- fragments or run-together sentences

- awkward sentences, agreement problems, tense shifts, or oral/aural usage problems

- spelling, punctuation, or capitalization errors

- adjective and adverb usage errors, preposition errors, or idiom errors

- few, if any, misplaced or dangling modifiers, errors in parallelism, or errors in coordination or subordination

▶ **Characteristics of a "B" Above Average Essay**

Content and Logic

Thesis present and clear

Thought process evident

Logical support

Adequate support

Adequate awareness of audience

Generally, appropriate tone

Organization

Introduction interesting and focused

Body paragraphs contain topic sentences related to the thesis but may not clearly show the relationship

Paragraph structures adequate

Some transitions between paragraphs missing, forced, or inappropriate

Conclusion adequate

Style

Some sentence variety

Vocabulary adequate

Generally, word choice good but some words misused

Generally, language appropriate to the topic, purpose, and audience

Some, but not many clichés, passive voice constructions or overreliance on *to be* verbs

Little repetitiveness, redundancy, or wordiness

Grammar, Usage, and Mechanics

Few, if any, fundamental errors: fragments, run-together sentences, awkward sentences, agreement problems, tense shifts, or oral/aural usage problems

A few, but not many, less fundamental errors: spelling, punctuation, capitalization, adjective and adverb usage, prepositions, and idioms

A few errors related to increased sentence complexity: dangling or misplaced modifiers, parallelism, coordination, and subordination

▶ Characteristics of a "C" Average Essay

Content and Logic

Thesis present and relatively clear

Thought process evident but not cohesive

Supporting evidence and details present but not sufficient or not well-chosen

Inadequate awareness of audience

Tone possibly not appropriate for audience

Organization

Introduction inadequate or uninteresting

Topic sentences in body paragraph absent or not clearly related to thesis

Some paragraph structure but not adequate

Transitions between paragraphs missing, weak, or erratic

Conclusion weak: merely summarizes points and/or introduces new or irrelevant material

Style

Insufficient sentence variety

Limited vocabulary

Word choice often inappropriate to context

Reliance on clichés, excessive passive voice, and *to be* verbs and other weak verbs

Often repetitive, redundant, or wordy

Grammar, Usage, and Mechanics

Some fundamental errors: fragments, run-together sentences, predication, agreement problems, oral/aural language-related problems

Many less fundamental errors: spelling, punctuation and capitalization, adjective and adverb usage, prepositions, and idioms

▶ **Characteristics of a "D" Below Average Essay**

Content and Logic

Thesis absent or unclear

Thought process unclear or contradictory

Supporting evidence and details lacking

Awareness of audience lacking

Inappropriate tone

Not fully developed

Overreliance or total reliance on narrative presentation

Organization

Introduction inadequate or inappropriate

Body paragraphs missing topic sentences, or sentences not related to thesis

Structure in paragraphs lacking

Transitions between paragraphs lacking

Conclusion absent or inadequate

Style

Almost no sentence variety

Limited vocabulary

Reliance on informal language or language inappropriate to context

Overuse of *to be* verbs and other weak verbs

Repetitive and redundant

Grammar, Usage, and Mechanics

Many fundamental errors: fragments, run-together sentences, predication, agreement problems, shifts in tense, and oral/aural language-related problems.

Many less fundamental errors: spelling, punctuation, capitalization, adjective and adverb usage, prepositions, and idioms.

Evaluating Essays

▶ **Phase 1 Reader and Writer Responsibilities**

Reader, as you read and respond to this piece of writing keep in mind the following:

- The reason for writing is to send a purposeful message to a particular reader or readers.

- This piece of writing represents the writer's first attempt to put his or her message on paper, and it is a message in progress—not a finished product. Revising and editing will be done later.

- Your suggestions need to be concrete and specific. Expressions such as "Nice," "Very good," "Great" are of no value. What makes something "good" or "great"? Is it a good idea, choice of words, sentence structure, and so on?

- You are to help and encourage—not judge.

- All negative criticisms must be honestly and sensitively stated with concrete suggestions for possible improvements or solutions to problems.

Writer, as you read your peer reviews keep in mind the following:

- Remember, most of your peers are uncomfortable in their role as reviewer. Try to put them at ease by letting them know that you value their opinions and observations.

- Keep an open mind. Consider the readers' suggestions. Some may have merit. Some may not.

- Try to accept constructive criticism gracefully (or, at least appear to do so).

- Try to understand what caused readers to see something as they did.

- Do not be too aggressive in defending your work. Remember it is a "work in progress."

- Ask for clarification if you do not understand a comment.

- Remember, this is your work. You decide which suggestions you take and which ones you reject.

> If you are concerned about your usage of English expressions, try to get a friend, preferably a native speaker of the English language, to look over your first draft and give you some suggestions for clearing up misused words and phrases. These informal responses will enable you to get better formal responses when you are doing peer evaluation because your peers can concentrate on your ideas without having to worry about usage problems.

▶ **Phase 1 Reader Response: Commenting on First Draft**

Writer _______________________   First Draft Date _______________________

Reader _______________________   Date _______________________

1. Is the purpose clearly stated? __________ If yes, what is it? _______________

2. Is the central message (thesis) clear? ______ If yes, try to put it in your own words.

    ____

    ____

3. Who are the intended readers (audience)? __________ What does the writer do that gives you a clue as to the potential readers? _______________

    ____

4. Is the writer's attitude (tone) toward the audience and the material clear? __________ If yes, what is it? _______________________________ Is it appropriate? ______ Why, or why not? _______________________________

5. Write a sentence explaining what the introduction promises the reader. _____

____

6. Put a question mark by material that is not clear to you.

7. Put a check mark by passages that you think are clear and strong.

8. Put a minus sign by material that you think needs to be more fully developed.

9. Can you find the thesis in the introductory paragraph and a topic sentence in each body paragraph? If not, what is missing? _____________________

____

10. Write a sentence explaining the strongest point of this paper. _____________

____

11. Write a sentence explaining the weakest point of this paper. _____________

____

12. If the thesis is not appropriate for this assignment, write a sentence explaining why it is not appropriate. _______________________________

▶ **Phase 2 Reader Response: Revising the Essay**

1. Does the focus (idea about the subject) need tightening? _______ If so, what would you suggest?____

____

2. Has the writer strayed from his or her purpose? _____ How? _____________

3. Is the writer still clearly focused on the audience? _______ Has he or she strayed from his or her original tone? _______ Give an example. _________

____

4. Is the paper balanced, or has the writer spent too much time on one part and scrimped on the development of other parts? _______ Which parts are overdeveloped and which ones are underdeveloped? _______________

____

5. Has the writer kept his or her promise that he or she made in the introduction? ____
Briefly explain how this was or was not accomplished. _______________
____

6. Is the content adequate? _________

   a. Has the writer provided sufficient support for his or her point to be convincing? ____

   b. What is the most compelling evidence presented to support the thesis?
   ____

7. What organizational plan did the writer use? _____________________
Did he or she stray from the organizational pattern? ________________
How? ____

8. Does the essay flow, or is it jerky? ___________ If it is jerky what would you recommend that he or she do to make it flow more smoothly—add transitional words, pronouns, or more derived words?________________________
____

9. Do you need more information? ________ What and where? _____________
____

Additional Questions for Argumentation Essays:

10. Has the opposing argument been fairly presented? ______
How did the writer handle the opposing argument? _________________
____

11. Did you find the negation of the opposition convincing? ____________
What made it convincing? ____________________________________
____

▶ **Phase 3 Reader Response: Revising Sentences**

1. Flag any run-together (RT) sentences or sentence fragments (frags).

2. Mark missing words with a caret (^).

3. Are grammatical series in parallel form—especially the plan of development? ____________ If not, mark them.

4. Note any awkward sentence constructions such as misplaced or dangling modifiers.

5. Mark any unnecessary shifts in time, person, or number.

6. If the writer has not varied the sentence patterns, suggest that he or she combine some of them to form compound sentences, and/or combine two simple sentences by subordinating one of them.

7. If the writer has made some weak or incorrect word choices, pencil in a possible alternative word.

8. If the writer relies too heavily on weak verbs (particularly *am, are, is, was, were, be, being, been*), suggest some more active verbs.

9. If the writer tends to be wordy, don't just tell him or her that the work is wordy—mark some wordy passages.

▶ Phase 3 Reader Response: Editing

Circle editing elements that the writer may need to check.

1. Have standard conventions of end marks and capitalization been followed?

2. Have commas been used correctly?

3. Are there any errors involving the semicolon?

4. Are titles of long works italicized?

5. Are titles of short works in quotation marks?

6. Are all words spelled correctly?

7. Has the writer used the appropriate form of words that are often confused with other words or words that look or sound alike but have a different meaning?

8. Is the paper properly formatted?

▶ **Evaluation Form A**

Peer Evaluation Form for a Five-Paragraph Essay (100 points)

	Reader 1	Reader 2	Reader 3	Reader 4	Consensus
Title and Introduction					
Title 0–2 pts.	_____	_____	_____	_____	_____
Lead-in 0–3 pts.	_____	_____	_____	_____	_____
Background 0–3 pts.	_____	_____	_____	_____	_____
Thesis 0–6 pts.	_____	_____	_____	_____	_____
Plan of development 0–5 pts.	_____	_____	_____	_____	_____
Body (3 paragraphs)					
Topic sentence 0–10 pts.	_____	_____	_____	_____	_____
Appropriate support 0–10 pts.	_____	_____	_____	_____	_____
Topic sentence 0–10 pts.	_____	_____	_____	_____	_____
Appropriate support 0–10 pts.	_____	_____	_____	_____	_____
Topic sentence 0–10 pts.	_____	_____	_____	_____	_____
Appropriate support 0–10 pts.	_____	_____	_____	_____	_____
Conclusion					
Complete/satisfying 0–6 pts.	_____	_____	_____	_____	_____
Editing Skills					
Grammar, mechanics, usage 0–15 pts.	_____	_____	_____	_____	_____
Deductibles					
Major error: deduct _____ pts*	(_____)	(_____)	(_____)	(_____)	(_____)
Minor error: deduct _____ pts*	(_____)	(_____)	(_____)	(_____)	(_____)
Unacceptable Essays					
Inappropriate pattern	_____________				
More than 600 words	_____________				

Less than 400 words   ________________

More than ______ editing errors*   ________________

*Instructor's decision

Reader 1: What I liked about your paper ____

____

____

Ways it could be improved ____

____

____

Reader 2: What I liked about your paper ____

____

____

Ways it could be improved ____

____

____

Reader 3: What I liked about your paper ____

____

____

Ways it could be improved ____

____

____

Reader 4: What I liked about your paper ____

____

____

Ways it could be improved ____

____

____

▶ **Evaluation Form B**

Peer Evaluation Form for a Five-Hundred Word Essay (100 Points)

	Reader 1	Reader 2	Reader 3	Reader 4	Consensus
Appropriate Title 0–2 pts.	_____	_____	_____	_____	_____
Introduction 0–18 pts. (about 60–80 words) Lead-in Background Thesis Plan of development	_____	_____	_____	_____	_____
Body Paragraph 1 0–20 pts. (about 130–150 words) Topic sentence and specific, logical, adequate support	_____	_____	_____	_____	_____
Body Paragraph 2 0–20 pts. (about 130–150 words) Topic sentence and specific, logical, adequate support	_____	_____	_____	_____	_____
Body Paragraph 3 0–20 pts. (about 130–150 words) Topic sentence and specific, logical, adequate support	_____	_____	_____	_____	_____
Conclusion 0–10 pts. (about 60–80 words) Summary/other remarks/both	_____	_____	_____	_____	_____
Editing Skills 0–10 pts. Grammar, mechanics, usage	_____	_____	_____	_____	_____
Total Number of Points	_____	_____	_____	_____	_____
Editing Deductibles					
Grammar, mechanics, usage					
Major error: deduct _____ pts.*	(_____)	(_____)	(_____)	(_____)	(_____)
Minor error: deduct _____pts.*	(_____)	(_____)	(_____)	(_____)	(_____)

*Instructor's decision

▶ **Evaluation Form C**

Peer Evaluation Form

1 - Poor	2 - Weak	3 - Average	4 - Good	5 - Excellent

	Reader 1	Reader 2	Reader 3	Reader 4	Consensus
Title Evocative	____	____	____	____	____
Opening					
Creates interest	____	____	____	____	____
Clearly shows purpose	____	____	____	____	____
Tone					
Consistent	____	____	____	____	____
Appropriate	____	____	____	____	____
Audience Identified	____	____	____	____	____
Transitions Sufficient	____	____	____	____	____
Development					
Complete	____	____	____	____	____
Logical	____	____	____	____	____
Style					
Smooth	____	____	____	____	____
Concise sentences	____	____	____	____	____
Word choice	____	____	____	____	____
Conclusion Satisfying	____	____	____	____	____
Editing					
Grammar	____	____	____	____	____
Usage	____	____	____	____	____
Mechanics	____	____	____	____	____
Interest Level	____	____	____	____	____
Overall Grade	____	____	____	____	____

▶ **Evaluation Form D**

Essay Evaluation

1. Has standard format for college papers been observed? _______________________________

2. Does the essay have a lead-in? __________________What type is it? _____________________

3. Is the lead-in appropriate, effective, and/or interesting? ____________________________

4. Does the essay contain background information? _____ Is it adequate and appropriate? _________

5. Is the thesis clearly stated? ____

6. Is the purpose clear? _________________ What is it? _______________________________

7. Is there a clear plan of development? _____ Is it written in parallel form? ______________

8. Does each body paragraph have a topic sentence? _________________________________

9. Is each body paragraph supported with adequate details? ____________________________

10. Are there a sufficient number of transitions between ideas? _____ Between paragraphs? _________

11. Is the sense of audience clear? _____ Who is the audience? __________________________

12. Is the tone clear? _____ Is it appropriate for the audience? _________________________

13. Is writer consistent in the use of _____ time?_____ person? _____voice? __________________

14. If the essay contains terms that may be unfamiliar to the audience, are they defined? __________

15. Does the conclusion summarize main points? _____ Is the last sentence strong? ____________

16. Is the essay fully developed? _____Are more details needed? _____ What kind? _____________

17. Is the essay relatively free of mechanical flaws? _____ grammatical flaws? __________________

18. Does the title create interest? _____ Is it appropriate? _____ Is it a topic, not a title? ____________

19. On a scale of 1–5 (with 5 being the best), what grade would this essay receive at this time? ___________

20. Is the essay satisfying? _____ convincing? _____ interesting? _____ If not, why? ___________________

21. What is the strongest or best part of this essay? ____

22. How can it be improved? ____

Argumentative Essays:

23. Is the thesis arguable? ____

    Is the logic flawed? _____ How? ____

24. Are opposing viewpoints presented? ____

    Are they fairly presented? ____

    Are they acknowledged and/or refuted? ____

25. Are appropriate logical appeals used? ____

26. Are emotional appeals used? _____ Are they effective? Explain. ____

27. Is the argument convincing? ____

Appendix C

Placement of the Topic Sentence

After you become proficient at writing unified paragraphs by writing a viable topic sentence and placing it at the beginning of the paragraph, you may want to experiment with putting the topic sentence elsewhere in the paragraph. It may be near the beginning, in the middle, at the end, or it may be implied. You may find that you are able to write more varied and interesting sentences by varying the position of the topic sentence, and this type of variation will be particularly useful when you develop essays.

Delayed Topic Sentence

Delay the topic sentence when you are writing about a topic that offers a great deal of information; sometimes you may want to write the topic sentence and then limit or clarify it in the next sentence or two.

> *Add one more item to the endangered-delicacies list. Since the l970s . . . snails originally harvested from the Burgundy region of France have been succumbing to the effects of pollution. . . .*—"Disappearing Escargot," *Gourmet*, Dec. 1999

When you want to get the readers' attention in the first sentence or two, then you may make the second or third sentence the topic sentence.

> Having smoking and nonsmoking areas in small restaurants is ridiculous. Because of the smallness of the areas, nonsmokers are forced to breathe second-hand smoke. *Smoking should be banned in restaurants that have fewer than six tables.*

Delayed Topic Sentence

Here's some good news for the estimated 40% of women and 15% of men who crave a daily dose of chocolate. *It [chocolate] may have some redeeming nutritional qualities.* Chocolate contains antioxidants similar to those in red wine that may help lower LDL cholesterol, says Kathy Knight, R.D., Ph.D., associate professor of family and consumer science at the University of Mississippi. Chocolate is also a good source of magnesium and contains no cholesterol—but it's high in saturated fat, so indulging too much may offset any health benefits. —*Cooking Light,* March 1999

Topic Sentence in the Middle of the Paragraph

Putting the topic sentence in the middle of the paragraph is akin to using the first sentence to get your readers' attention. In this instance, present several sentences such as reasons, examples, statistics, or startling statements about the topic, and then write the topic sentence.

Topic Sentence in the Middle

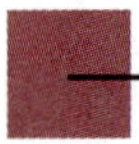

Exclamation points are the most irritating of all [punctuation marks]. Look! they say, look at what I just said! How amazing is my thought! *A sentence that really has something of importance to say, something quite remarkable . . . doesn't need a mark to point it out.* And if it is really after all, a banal sentence needing more zing, the exclamation point simply emphasizes its banality! —Lewis Thomas, "Notes on Punctuation"

Topic Sentence at the End of the Paragraph

Put the topic sentence at the end of the paragraph when you want to present your supporting material to build interest in the main idea.

Topic Sentence at the End

The "gentlemen" of the "upper classes" were firmly of the opinion that the "lower classes" were meant to labor industriously and to obey and support the leisure class. They sincerely believed that it was right for them to pass laws deciding who should vote, who should pay taxes and how much, what the "lower classes" should wear, and even what wages they should receive. *The people of the upper class had a genuine contempt for the people of the lower class.*

Implied Topic Sentence

When you read paragraphs written by professional writers, you may not be able to identify one sentence that is the topic sentence, for experienced writers often imply the topic sentence and do not state it directly. These writers are able to show the readers the main idea without stating it. Do not write paragraphs with implied topic sentences until you have the necessary skills to write them effectively.

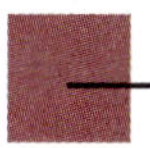

Implied Topic Sentence

Each of the thirteen colonies had a general government that decided all public questions for the entire colony. This general government consisted of a governor and an assembly, the latter being made up of representatives who were elected by the voters and sent as representatives to the towns from the colonies. The colonies had three different ways of choosing the governor. In the democratic colonies—Rhode Island and Connecticut—the governor was elected by the freemen of the colony. In the proprietary colonies—Pennsylvania, Delaware, and Maryland—the governor was appointed by the proprietor to whom the land of the colony had originally been granted by the king. In the royal colonies—Massachusetts, New Hampshire, New York, New Jersey, Virginia, North and South Carolina, and Georgia—the governor was appointed by the King of England. (Implied topic sentence: *The voters of the colonies were not fairly represented because in only two colonies were the powerful governors elected by the voters themselves.*)

Appendix D

English as a Second Language

Prepositions

Prepositions relate a noun or pronoun to some other word in the sentence. They express a number of relationships including *time, place or direction, method, manner, condition, quantity or measure,* and *purpose.* When you read, pay attention to the way prepositions are used in context. Following are some uses of common prepositions.

TIME	PLACE OR DIRECTION	METHOD
It was **about** 10 o'clock	They walked **around** the tree.	He was hit **by** a car.
I will call you **after** dinner.	They were **at** home.	His money comes **from** crime.
I will see you **at** noon.	She strolled **down** the street.	He survived **on** wild plants.
He called **at** last. (finally)	They drove **from** here to there.	He cut his nails **with** clippers.
Be here **by** 1 o'clock. (no later)	They were **in** their truck.	
We talked **for** an hour.	They parked north **of** the river.	**MANNER AND CONDITION**
He worked **from** noon to night.	They swam **in** the river.	He left **by** himself.
Call me **in** the morning.	They played **on** the beach.	He was **in** a bad mood.
It happened **on** Tuesday.	They drove **through** a town.	He looked **like** the devil.
	They went **to** church.	He was **on** drugs.
	They walked **up** hill.	He needs to be **with** friends.
	They went **with** friends.	

MEASUREMENT AND PURPOSE

We bought potatoes **by** the pound.

We asked you **for** your opinion.

We worked **for** three days.

We sold it **for** fifty cents.

Idioms

An idiom is an expression long-established by custom—often peculiar in grammatical construction—whose meaning cannot be understood from the individual meaning of the words such as "by and large," "catch a cold," "head over heels in love," and "stood him in good stead." The use and meaning of prepositions, especially, depend upon the idiom of the language. Using the wrong preposition after certain verbs is a common problem. Study the following list of words and their appropriate prepositions. Add your own problematic idiomatic expressions to this list. Keep the list current, crossing off expressions as you master them.

account *for*

agree *on* something

agree *with* someone

accuse *of* a crime

agree *with* a person

agree *to* a proposal

agree *on* a plan

angry *with*

apologize *to*

apply *for*

approved *of*

argue *with* (someone)

ask *for*

believe *in*

belong *to*

blame someone *for* something

blame something *on* someone

capable *of*

charge *for*

charge *with* a crime

convince someone *of* something

differ *with* a person

differ *from* appearance

differ *about* or *over* a question

disappointed *by* or *in* a person

disappointed *in* or *with* a thing

fond *of*

have respect *for*

impatient *for* an event

impatient *with* a person

independent *of*

inferior *to*

in accordance *with*

independent *of*

listen *for* a sound

listen *to* someone

look *at* someone or something

look *for* (meaning search)

look forward *to* an event

object *to*

plan *on*

recover *from*

remind someone *of*

search *for*

see *about*

substitute *for*

talk *about*

think *about* (meaning consider)

think *of* (meaning remember)

wait *for*

wait *on* (meaning serve)

Common Irregular Verbs

The present participle of a verb is formed by adding *-ing* to the base form of the verb (sleep + ing) and linking it to a helping verb.

Subject + helping verb + present participle

The baby is   sleeping.

The past participle of most verbs is the same as the simple past tense. (present: bend, past: bent, past participle: bent)

Subject + helping verb + past participle

The baby has   slept.

PRESENT	PAST	PAST PARTICIPLE
bend	bent	bent
bleed	bled	bled
bring	brought	brought
build	built	built
buy	bought	bought
catch	caught	caught

cling	clung	clung
creep	crept	crept
deal	dealt	dealt
drag	dragged	dragged
feed	fed	fed
feel	felt	felt
fight	fought	fought
have	had	had
hang (object)	hung	hung
hang (person)	hanged	hanged
hear	heard	heard
hold	held	held
lay (to place)	laid	laid
lead	led	led
leave	left	left
lie	lay	lain
light	lighted, lit	lighted, lit
keep	kept	kept
leave	left	left
lend	lent	lent
meet	met	met
pay	paid	paid
seek	sought	sought
sell	sold	sold
set (to place)	set	set
sit (not stand)	sat	sat
sleep	slept	slept

spend	spent	spent
sling	slung	slung
spin	spun	spun
stick	stuck	stuck
sting	stung	stung
sweep	swept	swept
swing	swung	swung
teach	taught	taught
tell	told	told
think	thought	thought
weep	wept	wept
win	won	won
wring	wrung	wrung

Many frequently used English verbs have irregular past tense and past participle forms.

The past participles of these verbs involve changing internal vowels and endings.

PRESENT	PAST	PAST PARTICIPLE
arise	arose	arisen
am/is/are	was/were	been
bear	bore	born
begin	began	begun
bite	bit	bitten/bit
blow	blew	blown
break	broke	broken
choose	chose	chosen
come	came	come
do	did	done

draw	drew	drawn
dream	dreamed	dreamt
drink	drank	drunk
drive	drove	driven
eat	ate	eaten
fall	fell	fallen
fly	flew	flown
forget	forgot	forgotten
forgive	forgave	forgiven
freeze	froze	frozen
get	got	gotten
give	gave	given
go	went	gone
grow	grew	grown
know	knew	known
lie	lay	lain
ride	rode	ridden
ring	rang	rung
rise	rose	risen
run	ran	run
see	saw	seen
shake	shook	shaken
sing	sang	sung
speak	spoke	spoken
spring	sprang	sprung
steal	stole	stolen
swear	swore	sworn

swim	swam	swum
take	took	taken
tear	tore	torn
throw	threw	thrown
wake	woke	waken
wear	wore	worn

Answer Key

Part 1   Understanding the Writing Process

Planning—Thinking Before Writing (2)

Exercise 1   Answers will vary.

Exercise 2   Answers will vary.

Notes: Vocabulary and tone will probably be quite different depending upon the age of the writer and the age and attitude of the grandmother and the relationship of her and the writer. The sex and the relationship of the two friends will dictate the vocabulary, tone, and purpose of the letter to the high school friend.

Exercise 3   Answers will vary.

The letter to the manufacturer of the product should clearly explain the nature of the problem, include all necessary data, include a possible solution to the problem (the purpose of the letter), and include a time frame for resolving the issue. It must be businesslike and firm, but courteous. The purpose of the letter to the friend may be to amuse by sharing a mutual small disaster, or it may be to ask advice about handling the situation. The purpose and relationship of the friend will determine the tone and level of usage.

Prewriting—Generating Ideas and Information (7)

Exercises 4–11   Answers will vary.

Writing—Composing and Organizing (16)

No exercises.

Revising—Overhauling the Whole Composition (17)

No exercises.

Editing, Formatting, and Proofreading (19)

No exercises.

Part 2   Building Sentences, Paragraphs, and Essays

Building Sentences (22)

Exercise 1   Answers will vary.

Exercise 2

1. holidays, but technically
2. employees, yet most
3. world, and it
4. April 25, but the
5. Germany, and according
6. Rome, so they
7. Trinity, and this
8. Patrick, and he
9. Feast, but in
10. others, for they

Exercise 3   Answers will vary.

1. holiday; indeed, it
2. year; furthermore, they
3. date; moreover, to honor
4. superstitions; accordingly, it
5. celebrations; consequently, bonfires
6. apples; moreover, spirits
7. States; indeed, it commemorates
8. Veterans Day; therefore, it was
9. Christmas tree; however, it was
10. druids; accordingly, they used

Exercise 4   Answers will vary.

Exercise 5   Answers will vary. Your answers may be as good or better than the following ones.

1. When gold was discovered in the Klondike in the late 1890s, it set off . . .
2. When news of the discovery reached the outside world, thousands of people . . .
3. The Klondike was located in the Yukon Territory of Canada, although most people . . .
4. Boomtowns sprang up overnight as over thirty . . .
5. It was one of the greatest gold rushes in history because people . . .
6. Shiploads of people from Vancouver, Seattle, and San Francisco headed for the gold fields, although most of them landed at Skagway.
7. The gold fever reached its peak when gold . . .
8. Over 100 million dollars in gold was mined in about ten years, although many . . .
9. After the gold rush was over, ten thousand . . .
10. Today, people travel through Alaska so that they can see . . .

Exercise 6   Answers will vary.

1. Because William H. Seward, the secretary of state, negotiated Alaska's purchase from Russia, he was allowed to name it, and he chose an Aleut word . . .

2. In 1741 Captain Vitus Bering and his men were exploring the Aleutian Islands when they ventured onto the mainland, and they were . . .

3. When Captain Bering died on the way home, his men returned to Russia across Siberia, and they claimed . . .

4. After the explorers returned to Russia, many traders and trappers went to Alaska, and they . . .

5. Although the Russians claimed much of the land, by the late 1700s English explorers claimed the coast of south Alaska, and the British . . .

6. Although an American trading company had established posts in Alaska by 1788, it eventually merged with a Russian company, and the new company had problems, but the owners signed . . .

7. When a white settlement was established on Kodiak Island, it was a sad day for the indigenous people, for the newcomers oppressed them, and they were no better than slaves.

8. After the settlers on Kodiak Island had depleted the nearby hunting grounds of game, they moved to Sitka, and they resumed their lucrative business.

9. Since the Civil War interfered with the American government's plan to buy Alaska from the Russians, an agreement was not reached until 1867, and it was . . .

10. When U. S. Secretary of State Seward got his treaty through the Senate, the vast territory that had belonged to Russia now belonged to the United States, and "Seward's Folly" . . .

Exercises 7–8 Review Exercises   No answers provided.

Building Paragraphs and Essays (34)

Exercise 9

1. TB   2. TB   3. TS   4. TB   5. TN   6. TN   7. TS   8. TS   9. TN   10. TS

Exercise 10   Answers will vary.

Exercise 11

a. 1   b. 2   c. 2   d. 3   e. 2   f. 3   g. 3   h. 2   i. 3   j. 3   k. 3   l. 2   m. NS

Exercise 12   Answers will vary.

Exercises 13–15 Review Exercises   No answers provided.

Exercise 16

1. TN   2. TB   3. TN   4. THS   5. TB   6. TN   7. THS   8. TN   9. TN   10. THS

Exercise 17

1. THS   2. 2   3. A   4. THS   5. THS   6. 2   7. A   8. THS   9. A   10. 2

Exercise 18   Answers will vary.

Exercises 19–20 Review Exercises   No answers provided.

Exercise 21   Answers will vary.

Exercise 22

2. I   3. Of course, I, civil liberty, although, I, liberty, its   4. I, liberty, civil
5. civil liberty, we, we, it, us   6. I, it, law, of all, law, of all, law   7. these, we, such conditions

Exercise 23

1. The ideas of justice, courage, and ~~practicing~~ self-restraint are concepts.

2. where we are born and ~~the status of~~ *who* our parents *are*

3. had a right to have more than one wife and that ~~it was all right for~~ parents *had a right* to

4. imprisoned, tortured, and ~~being~~ put to death

5. and it is worse to do an act of injustice than ~~being~~ *to be* treated

6. may suffer pain, ~~losing~~ *lose* their property, and ~~being~~ *be* treated unjustly

7. real evil was thinking an unjust or unkind thought or ~~to do~~ *doing* an unjust or unkind act

8. Aristotle was the son of the court physician at King Philip of Macedon's court, was Plato's most brilliant student, and ~~tutored~~ *was the tutor of* the young prince

9. Aristotle returned to Athens, ~~establishing~~ *established* a school there, and ~~teaching~~ *taught* his

10. Socrates wanted to make the world better by leading his students to think truer and higher thoughts, and Plato wanted to do the same by planning a better form of government; however, Aristotle~~'s plan~~ *wanted* to improve the world ~~included~~ *by* widening the sum of knowledge.

Exercise 24   Answers will vary.

Exercise 25   Answers will vary.

Developing Different Kinds of Paragraphs and Essays (68)
No exercises; responses will vary for writing suggestions and questions for thinking and discussing.

Part 3   Understanding Sentences

Understanding Subjects and Verbs (106)

Exercise 1

1.	recounted	6.	taught
2.	enjoyed	7.	related
3.	wrote	8.	brought
4.	published	9.	survived
5.	printed	10.	satirized

Exercise 2

1.	felt	6.	tastes
2.	are	7.	sounds
3.	appears	8.	appears
4.	is	9.	are
5.	became	10.	is

Exercise 3

1.	smell	6.	looked
2.	sounded	7.	felt
3.	tasted	8.	turned
4.	stayed	9.	looked
5.	smelled	10.	grew

Exercise 4   Answers will vary.

1.	were published	6.	have bought
2.	were writing	7.	was published
3.	was included	8.	will open
4.	were enjoying	9.	have bought
5.	did read	10.	have seen

Exercise 5

1. do
2. should have been
3. is
4. must have been
5. have
6. had
7. might have been
8. shall go
9. may be
10. must have done

Exercise 6

1. C are form
2. C are have
3. VP may be called
4. VP is called
5. VP were pushed
6. O is
7. O stretches
8. VP is located
9. VP do run
10. O form

Exercise 7   Answers will vary.

Exercise 8

1. wanted
2. was
3. was
4. offered
5. asked
6. had been helping
7. tried
8. helped
9. would be working
10. kept

Exercise 9   Answers will vary.

Exercise 10

1. Q   2. S   3. S   4. Q   5. S   6. C   7. S   8. C   9. Q   10. S

Exercise 11

1. system/is made
2. planets/circle
3. moon/orbits
4. Jupiter/is named
5. She/was abducted taken
6. It/was sighted
7. Titan/is
8. It/is

9. Titans/were

10. They/were overthrown supplanted

Exercise 12

1. A cloud of comets / is at the outer edge of the solar system.

2. Seven large moons / are in the solar system.

3. Four planets / are closer to the sun than the others: Mercury, Venus, Earth, and Mars.

4. They / are known as the Earthlike planets.

5. The gas giants Jupiter, Saturn, Uranus, and Neptune / lie beyond Mars.

6. A copy of a book about the solar system / is here.

7. A few questions from students / are here.

8. You / can see Saturn through a telescope here.

9. One of the most beautiful things that can be seen through a telescope / is here.

10. A beautiful system of rings / surrounds Saturn.

Exercise 13

1. You / are sugar sensitive.

2. As a child you / did hide candy.

3. As an adult you/ do often eat sweets.

4. You / do eat an entire container of sweets and then hide the container.

5. You / have lied about how much sweet food you eat.

6. You / do hide your sweet treats from others.

7. You / do eat sweets such as sugar, jelly, or honey straight from the container.

8. People / can be addicted to sugar.

9. You / do turn to sweets for solace.

10. You / do often eat sweets as snacks between meals.

Exercise 14

1. (You) / please pass the chocolate.

2. (You) / try to control yourself.

3. (You) / have your credit card ready.

4. You / should spend two hours on homework for every in-class hour.

5. You / can expect a call from my lawyer in a few days.

6. (You) / buy now and pay later.

7. You / can become a good writer.

8. (You) / stop by my office sometime tomorrow.

9. (You) / drop and roll if you are in flames.

10. (You) / be calm during an emergency.

Exercise 15

1. knowledge experiences / guide

2. we / are

3. assumptions beliefs / are

4. Some / are embedded   They / may be

5. assumptions / may include   assumptions / may be

6. assumptions / bias prevent

7. thinkers / will examine

8. assumptions / should be examined

9. thinkers / hold believe

10. evidence / does alter   They / force

Exercise 16

1. Women / make
2. man / should be
3. Women / are
4. Men / are
5. Men / may be
6. men / do cry
7. Children / should be seen heard
8. people / are
9. money / can buy
10. Criminals / should be punished

Exercises 17–24 Review Exercises   No answers provided.

Identifying and Correcting Sentence Fragments (132)

Exercise 25   Answers will vary.

1. "hill dweller," but to others it means "highlanders."

2. The symbol "&" for ampersand means "and" and is one of the few

3. Martin Luther, a Protestant reformer of the sixteenth century ~~being~~ was one of the first persons

4. Cigarettes were invented by

5. They rolled cigarettes, using the paper that they used for firing their guns.

6. Copper was scarce and not enough coins were being minted.

7. Kansas has many nicknames: Central State, Cyclone State, and Grasshopper State.

8. Anthony ~~being~~ was the only candidate.

9. Katie called her mother to let her know she was well and happy.

10. He opened his door to his friends and opened his pocketbook to the poor.

Exercise 26   Answers will vary.

1. George Eastman invented the first Kodak camera in 1888 and chose the name Kodak, which has no meaning. It simply satisfied trademark laws and was easy to spell.

2. Roman soldiers probably invented the military salute, raising their right hand and showing that

3. We have Christmas dinner at home, but we go out for New Year's Eve dinner.

4. Before the development of elementary vocal language, primitive people used a combination

5. Because their vocal language was limited, they used facial

6. For example, today we still use sign language for specific purposes, and we use it in everyday situations—such as waving goodbye or signaling a greeting.

7. Although we may not think about it, sign language is used in many other ways. It is used to give directions to actors and to signal information during the production of radio and television shows.

8. When people want to add emphasis to spoken language, they often use the language of silence.

9. Although many gestures mean about the same thing in many places, others have different meanings in different parts of the world. In most parts of the world, a hand wave says "goodbye," but this is not the meaning in the East.

10. Head movement is another example of sign language. In Mediterranean countries, head shaking means "yes," but elsewhere "yes" is signaled by head nodding.

Exercise 27   Answers will vary.

1. Sign language has a variety of uses, especially, in broadcasting

2. In broadcasting, a finger pointing to the throat means "cut."

3. To identify cheaters at the card table, a dealer will place

4. Sign language, a substitute for speech, is derived from

5. It is used where silence is a rule or to overcome language barriers, as among Trappist monks and

6. American Sign Language, also called *Ameslan,* is a system of communication

7. Sign language for the deaf was systematized in France in the eighteenth century.

8. Sign language is often taught along with other systems, specifically, the manual

9. Melinda is an excellent interpreter—quick, accurate, and clear.

10. Semaphore, a visual system for sending information by means of two flags, uses an alphabetic

Exercise 28   Answers will vary.

Exercises 29–33 Review Exercises   No answers provided

Identifying and Correcting Run-Together Sentences (146)

Exercise 34

1. F   2. CS   3. F   4. F   5. CS   6. CS   7. F   8. F   9. F   10. F

Exercise 35   Answers will vary.

1. Are legendary lands and beasts merely travelers' tales, or are they

2. In the West, dragons represented evil, but in the East

3. Chinese dragons came in different colors: black representing destruction, yellow representing luck, and azure heralding the birth of great men, and, according to legend, two

4. Chinese dragons could change their shapes, and they could

5. Many of them resided at the bottom of the sea, and they lived in pearl palaces.

6. Dragon bones were popular elements of traditional Chinese medicine, but these bones

7. In the West, treasures were often guarded by man-eating dragons, and these dragons

8. They differ in size, color, and attitude, but dragons exist in the legends of many lands.

9. Dinosaurs disappeared from the earth 70 million years ago, but human beings did not appear until a few million years ago, so dragon legends cannot be folk memory of a time when huge animals existed.

10. Possibly, ancient human beings discovered fossilized bones of dinosaurs, and they thought

Exercise 36 Answers will vary.

1. a lion and a dragon; however, after James

2. Ancient writers wrote about the unicorn's abilities; they also wrote

3. The unicorn was so strong that it could impale and carry away three elephants on its horn; however, it was unable to shake

4. During the Renaissance, assassination by poison was a common hazard; cups made of

5. Venomous insects could not cross a line that had been drawn with a unicorn horn; furthermore, poisonous

6. These magic horns were enormously expensive; supposedly, Queen Elizabeth's crown

7. Queen Elizabeth's valuable horn was probably the tusk of a narwhal; this small whale grows

8. According to one writer, there was only one way to tame a unicorn; a virgin had to convince the unicorn to lay its head on her lap. The trusting unicorn placed his head on the maiden's lap and slept; subsequently, the unicorn hunters

9. In 400 B.C. a Greek writer described a unicorn; the description appears to be that of

10. The legend could also have been born when hunters saw the profile of a long-horned antelope with one horn broken off; consequently, they thought it was an animal

Exercise 37 Answers will vary.

1. Well-sealed bottles have been sea-going messengers for many years. They can bob

2. These seemingly fragile objects made of glass are extremely seaworthy and for most practical purposes ~~glass lasts~~ *last* forever.

3. In 1954 bottles were salvaged from a ship sunk 250 years earlier. *Although* the contents of the bottles were unrecognizable, ~~but~~ the bottles themselves were in good shape.

4. Many people have experimented with dropping bottles in the ocean and ~~they~~ have found that it is impossible to predict the direction a bottle will take.

5. Two bottles dropped off the Brazilian coast took two entirely different routes. *One* bobbed east for 130 days and landed on a beach in Africa. *The* other bobbed northwest for 190 days and landed in Nicaragua.

6. The longest recorded bottle voyage was that of a bottle named the Flying Dutchman. *It* was launched in the southern Indian Ocean *and* had a message inside that could be read

7. *When* it was found, it was reported and ~~it~~ was thrown back into the water.

8. Six years after it began its journey, it landed on the west coast of Australia. *During* its journey, it covered 16,000 miles ~~it~~ and averaged six nautical miles a day.

9. *When* Benjamin Franklin was the postmaster general for the American colonies, ~~and~~ he became

10. He wondered why whaler captains were crossing the Atlantic more quickly than the British mail ships and ~~he~~ thought it might have something to do with the currents. *He* dropped bottles into the Gulf Stream and gathered and recorded information about the currents from the bobbing bottles ~~and.~~ *The* information he obtained about the currents has changed very little since his time.

Exercises 38–41 Review Exercises   No answers provided.

Learning More About Pronouns (157)

Exercise 42

1. (a) They like bears better than she likes bears.   (b) They like bears better than they like her.   2. I   3. I   4. (a) George cares more about Linda's sister than she cares about her sister.   (b) George cares more about Linda's sister than he cares about her. 5. he

Exercise 43

1. I   2. me   3. he   4. him   5. she, he   6. he, she   7. him, her   8. me   9. me
10. me, he

Exercise 44

1. I   2. me   3. me   4. she, I myself   5. He, himself   6. She

Exercise 45

1. I   2. me   3. he   4. him   5. she   6. her   7. I   8. me   9. I   10. she, she

Exercise 46

1. His   2. I   3. Their   4. their   5. he   6. Your   7. she   8. I   9. Your   10. His

Exercises 47–49 Review Exercises   No answers provided.

Exercise 50   Answers will vary.

1. Cindy said to Cher, "*You* have taken first place in the talent show."

2. When the dog bit the cat, she hit ~~it~~ *the dog* with a folded newspaper.

3. When Tess put a pie in the oven, ~~it~~ *the oven* burst into flames.

4. The lines were long, and numerous forms had to be completed. ~~This~~ *The loss of time* frustrated the applicant.

5. The Pilgrims landed at Plymouth Rock in 1620, ~~which~~ *and this event* is still celebrated.

6. After taking the skin off the fish, he put ~~it~~ *the fish* in the refrigerator.

7. The skyscrapers seemed to reach the sky; trolley cars rattled down crooked streets; sailboats were gliding over the bay. ~~It~~ *The scene* was impressive.

8. After washing their new cars, Joe and Jack asked their girlfriends to polish ~~them~~ *the vehicles.*

9. Ted's sweater has a hole in *it* and a missing button that needs to be replaced.

10. Hank had many spelling errors and wrong words in his letter of application. ~~That~~ *Those errors* resulted in his not getting an interview.

Exercise 51   Answers will vary.

1. Many people say that when ~~you~~ *women* are pregnant ~~you~~ *they* have a special glow.

2. *An article in* ~~In~~ yesterday's *Chronicle* ~~it~~ said that domestic violence is a major problem here.

3. She is a conscientious, hardworking student, but ~~it~~ *these traits* ~~doesn't~~ do not always result in high marks.

4. My friend Annette ~~she~~ drives a snowplow.

5. In a recent food report ~~it~~ *one writer* says ~~you~~ *people* should eat butter, not margarine.

6. My instructor ~~he~~ never takes attendance.

7. Our college has developed a new plan for solving the parking problem. ~~They~~ *The administration* will give an annual $50 rebate to each student who does not buy a parking permit.

8. The Boy Scout, the one with all the awards, ~~he~~ helped the elderly lady across the street.

9. The *Progressive Grocer* is an annual report of the grocery industry. ~~They say that~~ *According to this report,* Saturday and Thursday are the most popular days to buy groceries.

10. ~~You have students graduating~~ *Students* who cannot fill out a simple job application *are being graduated* from high school.

Exercise 52

1. A Dutch oven, <u>which</u> is one of the most useful outdoor cooking pots, is made

2. A double skillet is a matched pair of skillets—one shallow and one deep— <u>that</u> can be locked

3. An outdoor cook <u>who</u> knows

4. Jerky is meat <u>that</u> is not cooked,

5. Someone once said, "An electric knife sharpener is the best friend of the man <u>who</u> sells knives and the worst enemy of the man <u>who</u> uses them."

6. Rufus, <u>who</u> is an Abyssinian cat, likes asparagus and cantaloupe.

7. The only house cats <u>that</u> have never been fully domesticated are Abyssinians.

8. Joel Chandler Harris is remembered for his charming stories about Uncle Remus and animals <u>that</u> act like men and women.

9. *The Jungle,* <u>which</u> was written by Upton Sinclair about the life of a poor immigrant <u>who</u> is a worker in the Chicago stockyards, led to the passage of the first Pure Food and Drug Act.

10. Willa Cather, <u>who</u> wrote exquisite descriptions of life on the American deserts and plains, is best known for her novel *My Antonia,* <u>which</u> is a story about pioneer farm life.

Exercises 53–55 Review Exercises   No answers provided.

Exercise 56

1. You, you   2. We   3. we, we, we   4. you   5. you   6. ~~you~~ we   7. ~~you~~ I ~~you~~ I
8.–10. Answers will vary.

Learning More about Verbs (174)

Exercise 57

1. affect   2. lasts   3. called, asked   4. told   5. interlocks   6. is   7. paid, became   8. practice   9. completed   10. washes

Exercise 58

1. ~~refer~~ refers   2. ~~close~~ closed   3. ~~enter~~ entered   4. ~~refuse~~ refused   5. ~~derive~~ derived ~~suspend~~ suspended   6. ~~inspire~~ inspired   7. ~~sees~~ see ~~retain~~ retains
8. ~~flood~~ flooded ~~were~~ was ~~seal~~ sealed   9. was ~~were~~   10. ~~close~~ closed ~~open~~ opened

Exercise 59

1. Dennis *has* been

2. ~~want~~ wants to know if I *will* be

3. ~~are~~ is who ~~put~~ puts

4. I ~~ask~~ asked Mildred if she *would*

5. ~~begin~~ begins you *must* be ~~wants~~ want ~~enjoys~~ enjoy

6. We *have* been we *will* be

7. ~~write~~ writes ~~work~~ works

8. ~~ask~~ asked ~~refuse~~ refused ~~suppose~~ supposed

9. ~~get~~ gets ~~try~~ tries

10. ~~gives~~ give ~~do~~ does ~~believe~~ believes ~~make~~ makes

Exercise 60

1. ~~has~~ have   2. ~~do~~ does   3. ~~does~~ do   4. ~~has~~ have   5. ~~do~~ does   6. ~~does~~ do
7. ~~has~~ have   8. ~~does~~ do ~~does~~ do   9. ~~have~~ has   10. ~~do~~ does

Exercise 61

1. ~~be~~ are   2. ~~be~~ is   3. ~~be~~ is and *has* been   4. ~~were~~ was   5. I *have* been   6. ~~is~~ are
7. ~~are~~ is   8. ~~is~~ are they *are* not ~~be~~ getting they ~~is~~ are   9. ~~are~~ is   10. ~~been~~ are ~~be~~ are

Exercise 62

1. ~~have~~ has, ~~do~~ does   2. ~~was~~ were ~~were~~ was   3. ~~were~~ was   4. ~~has~~ have   5. ~~does~~ do not ~~have~~ has   6. ~~was~~ were   7. ~~who~~ that ~~are~~ is   8. He ~~be~~ *has* been   9. cats *have* been   10. ~~were~~ was ~~do~~ does

Exercises 63–65 Review Exercises   No answers provided.

Making Words Agree (187)

Exercise 66

1. <u>people</u> <u>use</u>   6. <u>Rob</u> <u>wants</u>

2. <u>Sandy</u> <u>seeks</u>   7. <u>Health on the Net Foundation</u> <u>has</u>

3. <u>avalanche</u> <u>is</u>   8. <u>code</u> <u>is</u>

4. <u>Sam</u> <u>steers</u>   9. <u>sites</u> <u>follow</u>

5. <u>information</u> <u>is</u>   10. <u>Cancers</u> <u>account</u>

Exercise 67

1. needs   2. is   3. has   4. is   5. are   6. is   7. likes   8. makes   9. enlightens, reverberates   10. was

Exercise 68

1. has   2. has   3. deserves   4. was   5. has   6. eats   7. was   8. was   9. look   10. arrive

Exercise 69

1. were   2. was   3. are   4. were   5. are   6. has   7. are   8. has   9. appears   10. think

Exercise 70

1. is   2. helps   3. sells   4. is   5. is   6. was   7. has   8. causes   9. is   10. tries

Exercises 71–73 Review Exercises   No answers provided.

Exercise 74

1. she, she, her   2. they   3. his or her   4. its   5. its   6. their   7. his or her, he or she   8. his   9. their   10. his or her

Exercise 75

1. his or her   2. its   3. their   4. their   5. it   6. their   7. his or her   8. he or she   9. their   10. his or her

Exercises 76–78 Review Exercises   No answers provided.

Using Modifiers: Adjectives and Adverbs (203)

Exercise 79

1. fast   2. sleepy   3. sleepily   4. elderly   5. slowly   6. properly   7. quickly   8. dangerous   9. poorly   10. slowly

Exercise 80

1. unhealthy   2. innocently   3. calm   4. suspicious   5. coolly   6. sad   7. increasingly   8. content   9. terrible   10. great

Exercise 81

1. well   2. bad   3. well   4. good   5. bad   6. well   7. badly   8. good   9. badly   10. well

Exercise 82

1. ~~best~~ better   2. ~~more~~   3. an ~~a most~~   4. ~~smallest~~ smaller   5. all *other* spices   6. ~~more~~ most   7. ~~most~~   8. ~~more~~ any *other* mushroom   9. ~~better~~ best   10. ~~best~~ better

Exercises 83–86 Review Exercises   No answers provided.

Part 4   Improving Sentences

Putting Modifiers Where They Belong (216)

Exercise 1   Answers will vary.

1. In the store Morgan saw a leather coat that he liked.

2. We saw a little boy with a pacifier in his mouth riding a merry-go-round horse.

3. Marvin's broken leg in the cast began to hurt during the night.

4. Last week I asked my supervisor when I should report for work.

5. In an e-mail Ted invited Laura to go to the movies.

6. The driver said to the passenger, "Fasten your seat belt."

7. With your friend Mandy arrange the flowers and candles on the table.

8. A carton of Double-Dutch Fudge ice cream is melting on the sink.

9. The little girl in the playpen is her baby.

10. Students receive higher marks when they attend class often.

or

10. Students often receive higher marks when they attend class.

Exercise 2   Answers will vary.

1. While the baboons were squatting and grooming themselves, the zoology students studied them.

2. My former boyfriend rang the doorbell when I was cooking a gourmet dinner for my new boyfriend.

3. When I was a child, my grandfather took me to many ball games.

4. Although the old man is bent with age, one can see that he was handsome in his younger days.

5. When I am hurrying to dress for school, the zipper in my pants always sticks.

6. When we played balderdash, the game took over an hour.

7. The time passed quickly when we were absorbed in an interesting experiment.

8. My father taught me to play the stock market when I was only a teenager.

9. Because he is an extrovert, my friend is always comfortable with strangers.

10. The fireworks frightened the puppy when he was left alone on the Fourth of July.

Exercises 3–4 Review Exercises   No answers provided.

Using Parallelism (220)

Exercise 5   Answers will vary.

1. ~~to read~~ reading   2. ~~to visit~~ visiting   3. ~~with a great deal of accuracy~~ accurately
4. ~~with longing~~ longingly   5. ~~the frequent~~ frequently ~~review of~~ reviewing
6. ~~the amount of~~ time   7. ~~about his being~~ that he was   8. ~~felt~~   9. ~~felt~~   10. ~~is a good friend~~ friendly

Exercise 6

1. Neither the students nor the counselors liked the enrollment procedures.

2. Either you do your work, or you will be fired.

3. She changed both her schedule and her major.

4. Dallas collects both blue vases and ceramic frogs.

5. Jon studied both geography and cartography in college.

6. Lenny likes not only golfing but also fishing.

7. Sammy won both first prize in the talent show and first prize in the science fair.

8. The waiter was both efficient and courteous.

9. Both the rain and the mud slide contributed to the hazardous road conditions.

10. You may eat either a hamburger or a hot dog for lunch.

Exercise 7 Answers will vary.

1. He was told to report to the locker room and ~~that he would be issued~~ to request his uniform.

2. When we took the achievement test, we were told that we should bring our own SCANTRON and ~~to have a~~ our own number 2 pencil.

3. Candidates for this program may qualify ~~either~~ by taking *either* an examination or ~~they can take~~ a specific course.

4. My brothers are good students as well as ~~athletic~~ *good athletes*.

5. When Mary chose her new dog, she had to decide whether to buy a purebred puppy or ~~she would~~ to rescue a dog from the pound.

6. He had to decide *whether* to buy a new car or ~~repairing the old one would be too expensive~~ *to repair the old one*.

7. Working crossword puzzles is more fun than *working* jigsaw puzzles.

8. Her physician recommended she wear a leg brace and ~~using~~ *use* crutches.

9. Knowing how to take notes and *how* to budget time are important skills for college students.

10. Betty's bikini is briefer than Ann's *bikini*.

Exercises 8–9 Review Exercises No answers provided.

Revising Awkward or Confusing Sentences (226)

Exercise 10

1. ~~are~~ were ~~develop~~ developed   2. ~~have~~ had ~~are~~ were   3. ~~are~~ were   4. ~~begin~~ began   5. ~~is~~ was   6. ~~increases~~ increased ~~is~~ was   7. ~~lead~~ led ~~had~~ have ~~call~~ called   8. ~~are~~ were   9. ~~annihilate~~ annihilated ~~are~~ were   10. ~~have~~ had ~~is~~ was ~~are~~ were

Exercise 11 Answers will vary.

1. ~~your~~ his or her   2. ~~it~~ they   3. ~~their~~ her   4. ~~he or she~~ they   5. ~~they~~ he or she ~~their~~ his or her   6. ~~they~~ it ~~your~~ her   7. ~~you~~ they   8. ~~you~~ they ~~your~~ their   9. ~~you are~~ he or she is   10. ~~its~~ their

Exercise 12 Answers will vary.

1. ~~your~~ its   2. ~~you~~ he or she   3. ~~one~~ you   4. ~~you study~~ he or she studies
5. ~~one learns~~ you learn   6. ~~one encounters~~ you encounter   7. ~~one~~ you 8. ~~One~~
You   9. ~~one knows~~ you know   10. ~~one~~ you

Exercise 13 Answers will vary.

1. finger ~~, and you should~~ *and* hold

2. seconds ~~, and you should~~ *and* look

3. ceiling ~~, and then you should~~ *and* stretch

4. ~~Your dog's teeth need to be brushed often~~
   Brush your dog's teeth often and use special

5. class, ~~and I should~~ *and* I

6. wall ~~, and you should~~ *and* have

7. ivy ~~,and you should~~ *and* poison oak

8. *To* properly cook~~ing~~ abalone ~~is important, and~~ you should never overcook it.

9. ~~You should know~~ the value of hands and the principles of betting.

10. Organizing your time ~~is important and always remember~~ and remembering
    to schedule your time wisely are important.

Exercise 14 Answers will vary.

1. Psychologists once believed that only bigots used stereotypes, but recent
   studies reveal

2. Many people use stereotypes, but they do it unknowingly.

3. Historically, theories about stereotypes were concerned with unabashed
   racism and sexism, but today psychologists are considering more subtle and
   insidious types of stereotyping.

4. Through the ages both sexes of all races have sought some kind of love
   potion.

5. When people use stereotypes, they take in the gender, the age, the skin color,
   and then their minds process the information and respond to it by sending
   such messages as

6. I do not like classical music as much as I like jazz.

7. Several people robbed the bank, and one of them wrote a book about the
   robbery.

8. When Anne was promoted, she was congratulated by her co-workers.

9. The children carefully examined their Halloween candy, but they found no
   suspicious sweets.

10. Since Jane knew that efficiency was essential in her new job, she took a time management

Exercise 15   Answers will vary.

1. He asked me whether I would take notes for him and if I would drop them off at his house.

2. Sally said that she would call Liz and that she expects me to call Kathy.

3. The shopper asked, "Is the fish fresh, and are the vegetables organically grown?"

4. The student cook asked, "Do I use the stems or the leaves of fresh herbs, and what does the term *sprig of herbs* mean?"

5. The instructor told him that, generally, cooks use only the leaves, but that they use the tender stems of some herbs such as cilantro and parsley.

6. Becky Pate of *Cooking Light* says that ketchup is her favorite condiment and that she truly appreciates how long and how many tomatoes it takes to create this delectable sauce.

7. If you spend a great deal of time at your computer, the American Occupational Therapy Association (AOTA) says, "Position the monitor directly in front of you, eighteen to twenty inches from your forehead, with the top of the screen at eye level."

8. AOTA also says that you should sit up straight with your head, shoulders, and hips in alignment with both feet flat on the floor (or on an angled footrest).

9. The instructor asked the students if they knew that farmers' markets were once a universal element of everyday life in America and if they knew that in 1918 more than half of all American cities with populations of 30,000 or more had public markets.

10. He said, "Clarence Saunders introduced the first self-service grocery store in 1918 at his Piggly Wiggly in Memphis, Tennessee, and this new type of one-stop, self-service grocery store heralded the end of traditional public markets."

Exercise 16   Answers will vary.

1. Some people think that people swear because they have limited vocabularies.

2. Using sunscreen is the best way to prevent sunburn.

3. The campers built a fire so that they could cook their dinner.

4. Working as a cocktail waitress, she earned money to pay her college expenses.

5. A special place is a location where you feel at peace with yourself and the world.

6. The tomato plants died because she did not water them.

7. Elizabeth's playing the piano was the high point of the recital.

8. Because the windows were covered with frost, it was difficult to see the mountains.

9. You may have an anger management problem if you cannot control your temper.

10. People are reasoning fallaciously when they argue that the crime rate is not related to violence on television.

Exercises 17–20 Review Exercises   No answers provided.

Writing Effective Sentences (241)

Exercise 21   Answers will vary.

Exercise 22   Answers will vary.

1. Doc Holiday lived a dangerous life, gambling and fighting, although he was dying of tuberculosis.

2. Gambling and fighting were his chief interests, taking precedence over everything else, including his dentistry.

3. Doc Holiday never appeared drunk, although he was thought of as a drunken killer, often drinking four quarts of whiskey a day.

4. Doc's wife, who was as wild as he, took care of him when he was ill or in danger—nursing him during long bouts of coughing or breaking him out of jail.

5. Their relationship was ended forever when they had a fight in Tombstone and Kate falsely accused Doc of robbing a stagecoach.

6. Doc was always loyal to the Earp brothers and saved Wyatt Earp's life more than once, although the Earps did not particularly like him.

7–8 Answers will vary.

Exercise 23   Answers will vary.

1. C	6. C
2. C	7. C
3. The baseball hit the batter.	8. C
4. In college, students are expected	9. Members of the family enjoyed
5. Megan wrecked the car.	10. professor invited us bottles, which he had arranged

Exercise 24   Answers will vary.

1. My English composition teacher is too picky, and many students think this quality makes her an ineffective teacher.

2. When she finds three or four run-together sentences in essays, she stops reading and stamps "Rewrite" on them and returns them to the students.

3. Many students think that she does not respect them because she insists on their following rules and does not allow them to express their creativity.

4. Other English teachers are not as fussy as Ms. Prim N. Proper—the nickname her students use when she isn't present.

5. Her comments are often offensive.

6. She seems to want to make students feel bad about their writing ability by writing comments such as "not logical," "irrelevant information," "wordy," and "unnecessary shifts."

7. The most interesting instructor in the English Department is Mr. Smith, a former priest, who coaches the swim team at a summer camp.

8. I first met Coach Smith four years ago when I was attending summer camp because my parents thought the experience would be good for me.

9. Often, he would join a group of campers to discuss their hopes, dreams, plans, and aspirations.

10. Since he was a former priest, many of the campers often visited him in his office, and he always gave them good advice.

Exercises 25–28 Review Exercises   No answers provided.

Writing Varied Sentences (252)

Exercise 29   Answers will vary.

1. On August 16, 1896, George Carmack, Dawson Charlie, and Skookum Jim discovered gold.

2. A tributary of the Klondike River, Bonanza Creek, was the site of the discovery.

3. A town, situated at the confluence of the Yukon and Klondike Rivers, Dawson City, is just 144 miles south of the Arctic Circle.

4. Booming and bustling, Dawson City was the center of excitement of one of the world's most famous gold strikes.

5. In the summer of 1897, miners from Dawson City arrived in Seattle and San Francisco with nearly $2 million.

6. Passing through Seattle and Alaska's Chilkoot and White passes, more than sixty thousand men and women were on their way to the Klondike by the next spring.

7. Because it had a large population, telephone service, and running water, Dawson City became known as the "Paris of the North."

8. Numerous exciting and historical attractions are part of Dawson City's current appeal.

9. To transport passengers and vehicles across the Yukon River to the Top of the World Highway, the Canadian government operates a free ferry service.

10. Although Dawson City's economy is based more on tourism than gold mining, mining operations continue in the area.

Exercise 30   Answers will vary.

1. Known as Klondike Kate, Kathleen Eloisa Rockwell, born in 1876 in Junction City, Kansas, symbolized the life and times of the Klondike.

2. As a teenage chorus girl, she joined a vaudeville company and traveled west by train from New York to Spokane, Washington.

3. She disliked her job, which required her to encourage men to buy as many drinks as they could drink, and decided to quit because it was not the kind of job she had expected.

4. Because she had no money and was in debt for her train ticket, she could not leave; so she accepted her fate and eventually learned to like the job.

5. Kate decided to quit the show and go North when she read headlines about the Klondike gold rush, so she and four other entertainers (who turned back midway) began their journey to the Klondike.

6. Kate was determined and continued on her way, earning money by doing her "buck and wing (tap) dancing."

7. Red-haired Kate, the girl who could dance and sing, arrived in Dawson City in 1900 and began working at the Palace Grand where she became very popular, especially with the miners.

8. In Dawson City she worked as a variety entertainer and as a dance hall girl.

9. She had a relationship with Alexander Pantages, the owner of Dawson's Orpheum Theater.

10. After the relationship ended, she sued him for $25,000 for breach of promise and later left Dawson City.

Exercise 31   Answers will vary.

1. Because everything was so different from high school, I had trouble getting used to college, but now that I am accustomed to being on my own I enjoy it.

2. The large campus has many trees and well-marked paths, but I have a poor sense of direction and sometimes get confused at night if the lighting is poor.

3. Being bored with high school courses that were too easy, I got a taste of college life by enrolling in a program designed for high school students.

4. I did not like my first college class because it was different from my high school classes in that the expectations were higher and the instructor gave us a list of his expectations—unrealistic I thought.

5. My college instructor was knowledgeable and friendly but did not accept late work, a policy I felt was unfair because I had other obligations and could not always meet his deadlines.

6. His not accepting late work was a problem for me, but his refusing to give extra credit assignments that could be substituted for missing assignments or used as extra credit work to raise my grade was a real blow.

7. I developed writer's block when I began writing my first college essay because in high school I had never bothered with planning, prewriting, and revising (a waste of time I thought) and always wrote one draft, turned it in, and usually received high marks.

8. I was accustomed to freely expressing my ideas creatively and did not like his rules for writing essays, so I wrote the essay in my usual style; however, he rejected it and asked me to rewrite it because it was a first person narrative—not an expository essay.

9. As a full-time college student, I respect the requirements of instructors, attend class regularly, am seldom late, and complete all assignments on time.

10. Although my first college instructor seemed to be too strict and sometimes unfair, I did learn a few things from him that helped me with my subsequent courses, and when I see him on campus, he remembers me and asks how I am doing in my classes.

Exercises 32–34 Review Exercises   No answers provided.

Part 5   Using the Right Words

Understanding Commonly Confused Words (264)

Exercise 1

1. all right, all right
2. a lot, a lot
3. have, have
4. it's , its, its, its, its, its, its, its
5. may be, maybe, may be
6. their, their, their, there, they're
7. threw, through, through, through, through
8. where, where, where, where, were
9. whose, whose, who's, who's
10. your, your, your, your, your, you're, you're

Exercise 2 Answers will vary.

Exercise 3

11. an, a	16. born, born
12. accept	17. break
13. effects, affects, effect	18. capital, capital
14. aggravates, aggravated	19. past
15. alters	20. too, too, too, to, two, two

Exercise 4 Answers will vary.

Exercise 5

21. choose, chose	26. quit, quits, quite, Quiet
22. latter, later	27. then, then, then, then, then, than, than, than
23. lead, lead, led	28. advise, advice
24. cloths, clothes	29. angle, angels, angle
25. loose, lose	30. breathed, breath, breath, breathes

Exercise 6 Answers will vary.

Exercise 7

31. all ready, already	40. hanged, hung
32. among, among, between	41. here, hear, hear
33. number, amount	42. knew, new
34. altogether, all together	43. principles, principal, principal, principal
35. conscience, conscious	44. some time, sometime, sometimes
36. desert, desert, dessert	45. we, us
37. coarse, course, course, courses	46. weather, whether, whether
38. less, less, Fewer	47. who, who, who, whom, whom
39. well, well, well, well, good	

Exercise 8 Answers will vary.

Exercises 9–12 Review Exercises No answers provided.

Improving Spelling (282)

Exercises 13–19 Practice Exercises

Exercise 20

1. chairs 2. dresses 3. boxes 4. bushes 5. flies 6. ladies 7. salaries
8. monkeys 9. enemies 10. rodeos 11. mosquitoes 12. heroes 13. candies

14. benches   15. matches   16. valleys   17. geniuses   18. videos   19. parties
20. O'Mallys

Exercise 21   Answers will vary.

Exercise 22

1. chiefs   2. wives   3. prognoses   4. welfare states   5. geese   6. two moose
7. oxen   8. cupfuls   9. drive-ins   10. stonewalls

Exercise 23

1. foreign   2. brief   3. fiend   4. leisure   5. belief   6. receipt   7. weird
8. believe   9. seize   10. thief   11. perceive   12. achieve   13. retrieve
14. piece   15. grief   16. relieve   17. conceive   18. ancient   19. caffeine
20. chief

Exercise 24

1. arrangement   2. ninety   3. completion   4. noticeable   5. icy
6. replaceable   7. grading   8. mutation   9. ninth   10. duly

Exercise 25

1. alliance   2. buying   3. justification   4. wryly   5. rosiness   6. pitiful
7. bullying   8. conveyor   9. angrily   10. betrayal

Exercise 26

1. humming   2. reference   3. conference   4. occurrence   5. stirred
6. occurred   7. rotten   8. tipping   9. preferential   10. slipped

Exercise 27

1. acceptable   2. changeable   3. desirable   4. eatable   5. noticeable
6. plausible   7. incredible   8. lovable   9. salable or saleable   10. audible

Exercises 28–33 Review Exercises   No answers provided.

Choosing Appropriate Language (296)

Exercise 34   Answers will vary.

1. ~~As a fact~~ I remember ~~of~~ seeing him.

2. The judge prohibited Melissa ~~to drive~~ *from driving* an automobile for six months.

3. She ~~don't~~ does not like him, and he *had* better get ~~use~~ used to it.

4. I should ~~of~~ have returned my library book today.

5. ~~I've got to~~ *I must* be more punctual, but I lose ~~loose~~ track of time.

6. Henry was ~~suppose~~ supposed to remind me, but he has ~~a lot~~ *many things* on his mind.

7. ~~The reason~~ I ordered a hamburger ~~was~~ because the steak was ~~way~~ too ~~high~~ *expensive.*

8. *In a* ~~A~~ diner ~~is a place where you~~ people can get ~~good~~ food that is different ~~than~~ *from* the food ~~you~~ *they* get in fast-food ~~joints~~ *restaurants.*

9. Jim, who ~~is hip to the happenings in our~~ *keeps track of the* chemistry *class schedule,* told me that the instructor wants ~~for~~ us to finish our ~~lab~~ laboratory experiment tomorrow.

10. Recently, I read ~~where~~ that Groucho Marx said, "Finding a four-leaf-clover is a sign that you have been down on your hands and knees."

Exercise 35 Answers will vary.

1. My *Caucasian* neighbor is a ~~WASP~~ *Protestant.*

2. ~~rednecks or crackers~~ *white rural laborers*

3. ~~Wops~~ *Italians*

4. ~~queer~~ *homosexual* (or is *gay*)

5. ~~JAP~~ *Jewish woman who likes to be well treated*

6. ~~Jew~~ *Jewish*

7. He tried to ~~welsh~~ *renege* on his bet.

8. ~~lesbos and homos~~ *lesbians and gays*

9. ~~a cripple~~ *physically challenged*

10. ~~decrepit old man was deaf~~ *elderly man, weakened by illness and hard work, had difficulty hearing*

Exercise 36 Answers will vary.

1. ~~a chick~~ *an attractive young woman;* ~~an old hen~~ *a fussy elderly woman;* ~~an old biddy~~ *a talkative elderly woman*

2. ~~mailman~~ *mail carrier*

3. ~~boy~~ *person*

4. ~~firemen~~ *firefighters* ~~he~~ *they*

5. ~~child~~ *children* ~~he understands~~ *they understand* ~~him~~ *them*

6. ~~mankind~~ *people*

7. ~~him~~ *him or her* ~~he~~ *he or she*

8. ~~Man~~ *People*

9. ~~chairman~~ *head*

10. ~~congressman~~ *congressional representative*

Exercise 37   Answers will vary.

Exercise 38   Answers will vary.

1. ~~penurious~~ *stingy*
2. ~~perambulated~~ *walked*
3. ~~observed~~ *seen* ~~cemetery~~ *graveyard*
4. ~~ingested~~ *took* ~~alopecia~~ *baldness*
5. ~~bifurcate~~ *separate into two parts*
6. ~~eleemosynary~~ *nonprofit*
7. ~~ancient canine expire~~ *old dog die*
8. ~~besmirched~~ *soiled*
9. ~~disputatious~~ *quarrelsome*
10. ~~vainglorious~~ *boastful*

Exercise 39   Answers will vary.

1. ~~bury the hatchet~~ *make up*
2. ~~few and far between~~ *difficult to find*
3. ~~a diamond in the rough~~ *has great potential*
4. ~~budding genius~~ *exceptionally intelligent* ~~know when to come in out of the rain~~ *have common sense*
5. ~~at death's door~~ *was dying*
6. ~~To make a long story short~~ ~~none the worse for wear~~ *not seriously affected*
7. ~~in no uncertain terms~~ *candidly* ~~to a ripe old age~~ *a long life* ~~last but not least~~
8. ~~good as gold~~ *exceptionally good people* ~~true-blue friends~~ *loyal friends*
9. ~~Beyond the shadow of a doubt~~ *Unquestionably* ~~trials and tribulations~~ *problems*
10. ~~After all is said and done~~ ~~fair and square~~ *honest*

Exercises 40–41 Review Exercises   No answers provided.

Part 6   Understanding Punctuation and Mechanics

Using Commas (312)

Exercise 1

1. world, and people have
2. danger, so they
3. storms, for they
4. god, and Neptune
5. months, but sometimes
6. them, and they described
7. bird, and they were
8. harpy, or a shrewish
9. Greece, so to explain
10. African coast, and they ate

Exercise 2

1. courage, swiftness, and strength
2. wings, some fins, some sharp claws, and some fangs

3. wild beasts, make their food more palatable, and live more comfortably

4. gods, lighted a torch at their hearth, shielded the flame in a hollow stalk, and delivered

5. stripping him naked, hanging him on the side of a mountain, and leaving him

6. mumps, measles, and smallpox

7. jealousy, anger, selfishness, envy, and hatred

8. beauty, gentleness, kindness, and dignity

9. to speak softly, to use winning words, and to sing sweet songs

10. named her Pandora, gave her a beautiful box, told her to never open it, and sent her to earth

Exercise 3

1. beautiful, all-gifted . . . lovely, ornate

2. C

3. thrilling, exciting moment

4. C

5. lovely, happy Pandora . . . sad, unhappy woman

6. C

7. C

8. one good, important spirit

9. the marvelous, ever-enduring spirit

10. enduring, abiding . . . good, effective patent medicine

Exercise 4

1. Asia Minor, and they

2. tribe, and they fought

3. Amazons, and later he abducted

4. Athens, but after

5. strong, courageous, the Amazons, but he

6. lion, serpent, deer, and performed

7. ordinary lion, for no sword

8. wore its skin, for it protected

9. Hydra, and he had

10. nine heads, and when one

Exercise 5

1. bull to a king, and this bull

2. caught the bull, bound it, and ended

3. stables again, but this time

4. cruel, savage king . . . savage horses, for

5. killed the king, and then he fed

6. like Amazons, for he had

7. gift, but she heard

8. defend her, but Hercules

9. C

10. Spain, stole the oxen, . . . sail, and

11. task alone, for he was

12. garden, for he was busy

13. collect the apples, and Atlas

14. almost unbearable, and he was

15. vacation, and he was

16. apples, but he would like

17. smiled, grabbed the apples,
    ran away, and

18. Hades, and he

19. earth, and the spots

20. immortality, transported . . .
    heavens, and gave

Exercise 6

1. Pygmalion, a young sculptor, was

2. C

3. C

4. Venus, the goddess of love,

5. Hippomenes, another lovesick
   young man,

6. Atalanta, the girl

7. Atlanta, who . . . herself,
   refused

8. C

9. apples, ones that

10. Hippomenes, with Venus' advice
    in mind,

11. Atalanta, who . . . apples, lost

12. Juno, the goddess of marriage, also
    took

13. Alcyone, throwing . . . husband's
    death, was

14. Juno, taking pity on Alcyone,
    returned

15. kingfisher, a fabled bird, was
    supposed

16. *halcyon*, meaning "kingfisher," refers

17. *tantalize*, which . . . connection,
    comes

18. Tantalus, Jupiter's . . . gods, was
    sent

19. C

20. C

Exercise 7

1. Supposedly, North Dakota

2. Incidentally, North Dakota

3. Furthermore, few

4. Begun in 1927 and completed in 1941,

5. Located . . . Dakota, it is

6. Incidentally, when Gutzon

7. Saying . . . ridiculous,
   columnists

8. C

9. Indeed, this memorial

10. Towering . . . building, it

Exercise 8

1. When Sitting Bull was young, he was

2. Because he was quiet and methodical, he was

3. Although he was only fourteen years old, Slow

4. When the warriors encountered the other tribe, Slow was

5. Although any *coup* was important, the first *coup*

6. Since scoring . . . warfare, Slow's father

7. When Sitting Bull . . . old, he killed

8. After he killed the Crow chief, he was elected

9. Although Sitting Bull . . . white men, it was limited

10. When he met with them, it was

Exercise 9

1. C

2. C

3. For example, they farmed

4. C or Then, one day

5. C

6. Before the arrival . . . herd, there

7. Although the modern . . . America, it later

8. When the Aztecs . . . horseback, they thought

9. After the Spanish . . . World, horses

10. bartered, many were

Exercise 10

1. Troy, haven't you

2. invited, except one

3. invited, of course, she was frustrated

4. apple, students

5. Mr. Johnson, I believe

6. Adam, you . . . were, didn't you

7. Venus, needless to say, claimed

8. Jupiter, not Neptune, was asked to

9. Jupiter, however, refused to make the decision

10. ruling, thereby

Exercise 11

1. made the decision, did he not

2. Yes, Paris, not Neptune, was

3. riches, didn't she

4. She did, without a doubt, and

5. Venus, however, offered

6. prince, subsequently, forgot

7. annoyed, weren't they

8. right, Suzy. Paris, without a doubt, had

9. Greece, did he not

10. Helen, was he not

Exercise 12

1. Westminster, England, were

2. 5,000 people

3. Bedford County, Virginia

4. Joseph R. Biden, Jr., from Scranton, Pennsylvania, was born November 20, 1942.

   5. 60,000 remedies

   6. Hartwell, Ph.D., president . . . Seattle, Washington,

   7. May 14, 1804, signaled

   8. On January 18, 1803, President . . . spending of $2,500

   9. November 15, 1805,

10. Dear Mom, I arrived in California, May 2, 2002. My new address is 267 Lake Wilderness Drive, San Jose, California 98088. . . . Moriarty, Ph.D., . . . $2,000. . . . . son, Jim Bob

Exercises 13–16 Review Exercises No answers provided.

Using Semicolons (333)

Exercise 17

   1. actress; however, she

   2. athlete; he plays

   3. clarinet; Suzy . . . flute; and Joe

   4. early; they

   5. Friday; one . . . Saturday; and

   6. tires; it needs new brakes; and

   7. children; however,

   8. bananas; but her sister

   9. movie; in fact,

10. house; however,

Exercise 18 Answers will vary.

Exercise 19 Review Exercise No answers provided.

Using End Punctuation (335)

Exercise 20

   1. Did you park your auto near the wharf and have breakfast at IHOP?

   2. Nadine applied for a job at NASA after she earned her M.S. degree at UCLA.

   3. I am expecting an UPS [if used as an acronym] or a UPS [if used as letters] at 8 A.M.

   4. Fran's father used to be an FBI agent, but now he works for NASA.

   5. Are you sure you can really trust her to tell the truth?

   6. Sandy has a G. E. stove, but her fridge is a Frigidaire.

   7. Did many companies move their plants to Mexico after the signing of the North American Free Trade Agreement (NAFTA)?

   8. Great job! You are fantastic!

   9. The radio in our auto is always set on AM, not FM.

10. When you go to the lab, save a seat for me; I'll be there by 10 P.M.

Using Apostrophes (339)

Exercise 21

1. Isn't the United States of America's population
2. According to legend, Noah's great grandson
3. It's believed
4. Early colonists' invitations
5. California's gold rush
6. to do the white people's slave labor
7. The pioneer Chinese's history
8. Foreign Miners' License Tax
9. but large numbers didn't arrive
10. Thirty Years' War

Using Quotation Marks (341)

Exercise 22

1. "When Christ said, 'I was hungry, and you fed me,' he didn't mean only the hunger for food and bread; he also meant the hunger to be loved." —Mother Teresa
2. The word *blab* means "to reveal secret matters through indiscreet talk."
3. The opening lines of Robert Herrick's poem "To the Virgins, to Make Much of Time" have
4. The coach said, "If a player, except a goalkeeper . . . stopped."
5. He also said, "A goalkeeper who holds the puck . . . minor penalty."
6. "Punctuation: what is it, after . . . breath?"
7. "Spring" by Matsuo Basho . . .
8. In John Updike's short story "A & P," Sammy quits his job . . . treated. "Did you say something, Sammy?"
9. C
10. Mrs. Malaprop in Sheridan's play *The Rivals* says, "Sure, if I reprehend anything in this world, it is the use of my oracular tongue."

Exercises 23–24 Review Exercises No answers provided.

Using Other Punctuation (346)

Exercise 25 Answers will vary.

1. (1) bronze, (2) iron, (3) glass, and (4) pottery
2. Discovering the way to make bronze—a landmark in the history of civilization—
3. stone tools—first step in the use of metals—in 2000 B.C.—but

4. Bronze (not a pure metal) is

5. Bronze (technological period when metals were first used to make tools and weapons) was giving way to the Age of Iron (the technological period from the first general use of iron to present times)

6. Iron (the most sturdy of all metals) and steel (an alloy of iron and carbon) are

7. destruction—knives and guns—are

8. industry—farming equipment, vehicles, crafts, and buildings—are

9. legend (at least this was the story told by the Roman writer Pliny), Phoenician sailors . . . saltpeter—also known as

10. sand (one form of the mineral called *silica*) fuses

Exercise 26 Review Exercise   No answers provided.

Exercise 27

1. independence: nineteen
2. country: He was
3. Psalm 23:1
4. Dear Mr. Perot: My plane will arrive at 1:15 P.M.
5. observation: You
6. golf shots: "You can
7. *slicing:* hitting
8. *Centuries:* a book
9. Nagasaki: "Near
10. occurred: the election

Exercise 28

1. *anti-Communist Un-American*
2. *Snowbirds snow-white snowsuit*
3. *re-enlist*
4. *caregiver well trained semi-invalid*
5. *governor-elect . . . door-to-door*
6. *Anti-Catholicism anti-Semitism*
7. *five-year-old girl . . . two-thirds majority*
8. *twenty-one . . . forty-nine*
9. C
10. *one-year . . . sixty-five*

Exercise 29 Review Exercise   No answers provided.

Using Capitals (354)

Exercise 30

1. ~~Island~~ island ~~pillars of hercules~~ Pillars of Hercules

2. ~~rock of Gibraltar~~ Rock of Gibraltar . . . ~~Peninsula~~ peninsula ~~South~~ south-central

3. ~~africa~~ Africa ~~antarctica~~ Antarctica . . . ~~north~~ North America and ~~south~~ South America

4. ~~Planets~~ planets . . . ~~Sun~~ sun

5. ~~west~~ West

6. ~~Centuries~~ centuries

7. ~~Beer~~ beer . . . ~~Rice~~ rice ~~Cheese~~ cheese . . . ~~Coffee~~ coffee

8. ~~halloween~~ Halloween . . . ~~Festival~~ festival of All Saints' Eve

9. ~~Advanced Algebra~~ advanced algebra, American ~~History~~ history, and ~~Intermediate~~ intermediate Spanish

10. C

Exercise 31

1. ~~Essential Facts of Life~~ essential facts of life

2. C

3. "~~no~~ "No government, . . . the ~~Press~~ press

4. "Charity begins at ~~Home~~ home"

5. ~~Town~~ town "~~Carrying Coal~~" "carrying coal to Newcastle"

6. Frigidaire ~~Refrigerators~~ refrigerators to ~~eskimos~~ Eskimos

7. ~~war of independence~~ War of Independence . . . ~~continental~~ Continental during the ~~War~~ war

8. ~~continental~~ Continental . . . ~~Warming Pans~~ warming pans . . . ~~Mittens~~ mittens . . . ~~west~~ West Indies

9. ~~Islanders~~ islanders ~~Warming Pans~~ warming pans ~~Molasses Insustry~~ molasses industry ~~Mittens~~ mittens ~~russia~~ Russia

10. C

Exercise 32

1. ~~Religions~~ religions . . . ~~god~~ God

2. Roman ~~God of War~~ god of war . . . Greek ~~God of War~~ god of war

3. regular ~~Newspaper~~ newspaper

4. ~~the~~ *The Mikado* or ~~the town~~ *The Town of Titipu*

5. C

6. ~~saint~~ Saint Elizabeth Ann Seton . . . ~~mother~~ Mother Seton

7. ~~mother or father~~ Mother or Father ~~Sister~~ sister

8. ~~Literature~~ literature . . . ~~god~~ God

9. ~~wgy~~ WGY

10. ~~radio telegraph~~ Radio Telegraph . . . ~~Stop Sending and Listen~~ stop sending and listen . . . ~~sos~~ SOS

Exercises 33–35 Review Exercises   No answers provided.

Using Abbreviations (364)

Exercise 36

1. Ms. Patricia Carbine . . . Ms. Gloria Steinem

2. He wrote a ~~3~~ three-volume . . . ~~The Age of Roosevelt~~ *The Age of Roosevelt* . . . ~~A Thousand Days~~ *A Thousand Days*

3. ~~yahoo~~ *yahoo* in ~~Gulliver's Travels~~ *Gulliver's Travels*

4. ~~blurb~~ *blurb*

5. December ~~17th~~ . . . 17 ~~thirty-six~~ 36 . . . ~~thirty-two~~ 32 . . . ~~4th~~ fourth

6. ~~forty-five~~ 45 million

7. ~~eight-to-ten-inch~~ 8-to-10-inch

8. ~~On Death and Dying~~ *On Death and Dying* ~~5~~ five psychological

9. ~~one hundred seventy-five thousand~~ 175,000 people . . . ~~5 years later~~ The number was increased to 8 million and 5 years later

10. ~~12~~ twelve neighbors

Exercise 37

1. ~~18th~~ eighteenth

2. ~~1st of 14~~ first of fourteen

3. chose ~~2~~ two

4. April ~~15th~~ 15

5. ~~2~~ Two lanterns . . . ~~1~~ One lantern

6. ~~19th~~ nineteenth ~~10~~ ten hogsheads

7. April ~~18th~~ 18

8. ~~Somerset~~ *Somerset* . . . When ~~1~~ one of two guards . . . the ~~2nd~~ second guard . . . an ale or ~~2~~ two

9. ~~2~~ two lights

10. ~~2~~ two young men . . . Dawes who rode ~~1st~~ first

Exercise 38 Review Exercise   No answers provided.